P9-DUJ-918

DATE DUE

JA 31 02			
JE - 6 89			

BEYOND THE BROKER STATE

BUSINESS, SOCIETY, AND THE STATE

Beyond the Broker State

Federal Policies

toward Small Business,

1936–1961

JONATHAN J. BEAN

The University of North Carolina Press

Chapel Hill and London

The paper in this book meets the guidelines for permanence and
durability of the Committee on Production Guidelines for Book
Longevity of the Council on Library Resources.

Library of Congress Cataloging-in-Publication Data

Bean, Jonathan J.

Beyond the broker state : federal policies toward small business,
1936–1961 / by Jonathan J. Bean.

p. cm. — (Business, society, and the state)

Includes bibliographical references and index.

ISBN 0-8078-2296-5 (cloth: alk. paper)

1. Small business—Government policy—United States—History—
20th century. 2. Small business—Law and legislation—United
States. I. Title. II. Series.

HD2346.U5B343 1996 96-10868

3386'42' 0973—dc20 CIP

00 99 98 97 96 5 4 3 2 1

TO MY LOVING WIFE, ALICE

She kept my eyes on the prize, my nose to the grindstone,
and my feet on the ground.

CONTENTS

ILLUSTRATIONS

ACKNOWLEDGMENTS

My dissertation adviser at Ohio State University, Professor Mansel G. Blackford, provided me with invaluable guidance and encouragement; I could not ask for a better mentor. Professor K. Austin Kerr first suggested the need for this study, and in part, it springs from an essay he wrote on the history of small business in America. Thanks go to Professor William Childs, as well, for his comments and suggestions. I would also like to express my gratitude to my parents for encouraging me in my intellectual endeavors.

Several organizations helped to finance the research and writing of this book, including the University of Illinois Foundation (John E. Rovensky Fellowship), the Franklin D. Roosevelt Library, and the Harry S. Truman Library. The B. F. Goodrich Company made available its corporate records, which aided my study of the federal government's antitrust policy. The archivists at the National Archives and those at the Roosevelt, Truman, Eisenhower, and Lyndon B. Johnson Presidential Libraries helped me find the sources needed to complete this work. In particular, I thank Tab Lewis, Dwight Strandberg, and Dennis Bilger for their diligent efforts on my behalf.

Illustrations were provided through the generosity and assistance of the following institutions: Cleveland State University Press Collection, Rutgers University (New Brunswick), the Lyndon B. Johnson Presidential Library, the Dwight D. Eisenhower Presidential Library, the Library of Congress, the Montana Historical Society, and the Bettmann Archive. A portion of Chapter 5 appeared in volume 6, no. 3 of the *Journal of Policy History* as an article entitled "World War II and the 'Crisis' of Small Business: The Smaller War Plants Corporation, 1942–1946."

ABBREVIATIONS USED IN TEXT

ABA	American Bankers Association
AFTC	American Fair Trade Council
AFTL	American Fair Trade League
AGNC	Attorney General's National Committee to Study the Antitrust Laws
CASBO	Congress of American Small Business Organizations
CCSB	Cabinet Committee on Small Business
DCD	Division of Contract Distribution
DNC	Democratic National Committee
FTC	Federal Trade Commission
NAITD	National Association of Independent Tire Dealers
NAM	National Association of Manufacturers
NARD	National Association of Retail Druggists
NARG	National Association of Retail Grocers
NDAC	National Defense Advisory Council
NFIB	National Federation of Independent Business
NPA	National Production Authority
NRA	National Recovery Administration
NSBMA	National Small Business Men's Association
NTDRA	National Tire Dealers and Retreaders Association
ODM	Office of Defense Mobilization
OPA	Office of Price Administration
OPM	Office of Production Management
RFC	Reconstruction Finance Corporation
RNC	Republican National Committee
RPM	Resale price maintenance ("fair trade")
SBA	Small Business Administration
SBANE	Small Business Association of New England
SBIC	Small Business Investment Company

SDPA   Small Defense Plants Administration
SDPC   Small Defense Plants Corporation
SWPC   Smaller War Plants Corporation
TNEC   Temporary National Economic Committee
USWGA   United States Wholesale Grocers Association
WPB   War Production Board

BEYOND THE BROKER STATE

Small Business as the
Backbone of Democracy

Who is this small or independent businessman—the independent

producer and the independent distributor? Why, he is an American

institution. He is just as much a part of the life of every community as its

church or schoolhouse. He knows when there is sickness in the neigh-

borhood, when there is a wedding, a death, or a birth. . . . He is local

business with a heart, and often too much heart for his own good. . . .

I see this great humane and worthy institution, this bulwark of demo-

cratic Government—the small independent businessman.

Millard E. Tydings, U.S. Senator (1938)

In 1914, President Woodrow Wilson called for antitrust legislation to "make men in a small way of business as free to succeed as men in a big way."[1] Wilson was responding to a widespread concern that the competitive advantages of big businesses might enable them to eliminate the opportunity for Americans to open their own small businesses. This concern had arisen with the emergence of large manufacturers in the late nineteenth and early twentieth centuries. The subsequent rise of chain store retailers in the 1920s and 1930s renewed this concern that big business posed a threat to small business, a concern that continued to pervade discussion of business-government relations well into the twentieth century. Thus, in 1953, four decades after Wilson uttered his speech in behalf of small business, Congress created the Small Business Administration, prompting a *Fortune* writer to note that "the small-business 'problem' has unquestionably become one of the great and continuing themes of American politics."[2]

This book examines the impact of this concern on federal government policy between 1936 and 1961. Although earlier antitrust legislation had as one of its aims the preservation of small business, the so-called small business "movement" began in earnest during the Great Depression of the 1930s, when congressional anxiety over the fate of small business resulted in the passage of anti-chain-store laws, including the Robinson-Patman Act (1936) and the Miller-Tydings "Fair Trade" Act (1937). The congressional champions of small business later achieved the creation of House and Senate Small Business Committees (1940–41) and the establishment of temporary small business agencies during World War II and the Korean War. Finally, during President Dwight D. Eisenhower's second term, Congress made the Small Business Administration a permanent agency. By the end of the 1950s, Congress had institutionalized the interest of small business in a federal bureaucracy and had enacted into law most of the federal government's present-day policies toward small business. Although the enthusiasm of the small business advocates has since become a historical memory, their actions left an indelible mark on the American system of government.

The Political Importance of
Small Business in America

Small business has always had a special place in the mythology of American democracy. In fact, twentieth-century advocates of small business embraced an ideology that had its roots in Jeffersonian republicanism. Like Thomas Jefferson, they believed that a widespread distribution of wealth ensured the survival of democracy. The small business advocates saw economic and political democracy as intertwined: if wealth were concentrated in the hands of a few, democracy would give way to tyranny. In their view, a propertied middle class provided the social basis for democratic capitalism; therefore, they described small business as the "backbone of democracy" and free enterprise.[3]

The small business ideology also built upon the nineteenth-century "myth of the self-made man." In his study of this myth, Irvin Wyllie described how opinion leaders (journalists, ministers, politicians) extolled the virtues of independence and self-reliance. The promoters of the myth distrusted education; instead, they emphasized those inner qualities associated with the Protestant ethic, including hard work, perseverance, sobriety, and frugality. Thus, in the popular stories of Horatio Alger, a poor but ambitious youth could work his way up from "rags to respectability." Although Wyllie may have exaggerated the level of prestige attached to business activities, many self-made business owners did become cultural heroes.[4]

However, in the late nineteenth century, the sudden emergence of large corporations, popularly known as "trusts" (a term reflecting their original form of organization), generated public concern about their impact on small business. Those who believed in the myth of the self-made man assumed that America offered enough opportunity for young people to establish themselves in business with little or no capital, but the rise of big business challenged this belief. In many industries, potential entrepreneurs needed to raise massive amounts of capital and hire college-educated managers to run their enterprises. Critics of big business feared that Jefferson's nation of shopkeepers would soon give way to a nation of wage slaves lacking independence and self-reliance. Even Andrew Carnegie, a self-made man and founder of one of the largest businesses in America, worried that businesses like his own had made it difficult "for a young man without capital to get a start for himself," and he expressed concern that his salaried employees might become little more than "human machines."[5]

At the same time, critics charged that corporate executives subverted democracy by exerting their influence through bribery and other forms of political corruption. The critics also maintained that big businesses achieved their position of dominance in American industry by illegally placing restraints on trade and by intimidating small companies. Although economists attributed the rise of big business to "natural" changes in the structure of the American economy, this understanding had not yet "trickled down" to the common people and their representatives. In reality, corporate executives created economies of scale and speed by eliminating middlemen and incorporating their functions within the confines of a large bureaucratic firm. Thus, the "visible hand" of management replaced the "invisible hand" of the marketplace in organizing production and distribution.[6] But at the time, according to historian Thomas K. McCraw, the "trusts" appeared to be "sinister new political forces," and to many Americans they seemed "*unnatural*, the bastard offsprings of unscrupulous promoters."[7]

Congress responded to the pleas of small business owners by enacting the Sherman Act (1890), the nation's first federal antitrust law, which prohibited price-fixing and other restraints on trade. The Sherman Act failed to stem the growth of big business, however, so the "trust problem" continued to dominate the discussion of business-government relations in the Progressive Era. This debate over big business climaxed in 1914, when a heterogeneous coalition of corporate executives, small business owners, and consumer advocates pressured Congress into passing two new antitrust laws: the Federal Trade Commission Act and the Clayton Antitrust Act. This legislation outlawed certain anti-competitive business practices and created the Federal Trade Commission

(FTC) to eliminate all "unfair methods of competition." In practice, however, these laws did more to legitimate big business than to boost the market position of small firms; thus, it soon became clear to most observers that the large corporation was here to stay.

Nevertheless, the emergence of big business did not shatter the myth of the self-made man. U.S. Supreme Court Justice Louis Brandeis, "the indefatigable champion of small enterprise," used the myth in his continuing crusade against big business. As a lawyer, Brandeis had represented many independent business owners, and as an economic adviser to Woodrow Wilson, he had urged the president to break up large companies in order to preserve opportunity for smaller ones. As an economic thinker, Brandeis believed that the nation's largest businesses exceeded the optimum scale of efficiency and survived only by using their market power to destroy their more efficient rivals and then bilk the consumer. In truth, however, Brandeis cared little for the consumer and a great deal for small business. Economic considerations aside, he believed that bigness per se was a "social menace" because it eliminated small business opportunity and might lead to corporate control of the government.[8]

The rapid growth of chain stores in the 1920s and 1930s, and their intrusion into rural communities, intensified this concern with the fate of small business. Chain store opponents included Brandeis, economist Henry C. Simons, law professor Felix Frankfurter, and Congressmen Wright Patman, Gerald Nye, William Borah, and Joseph Robinson. The critics of the chain store joined with independent merchants in supporting state legislation imposing discriminatory taxes on chain stores. In addition, many states passed "fair trade" laws legalizing retail price-fixing in an unsuccessful attempt to overcome the chain stores' competitive advantage. Congress also sided with small business by passing the Robinson-Patman Act (1936), which limited the discounts available to chain stores, and the Miller-Tydings Act (1937), which exempted fair trade agreements from the antitrust laws.[9]

The small business advocates engaged in Orwellian doubletalk as they argued for this government intervention on behalf of "free enterprise." The historian Ellis Hawley has described their agenda as "an anticompetitive program . . . made possible by the use of competitive symbols." They justified this contradiction by resorting to crisis rhetoric, arguing that small firms would perish at the hands of big business and that, therefore, the government should exert a countervailing influence in order to bolster independent enterprise. The political and ideological appeal of "doing something" for small business, which had become a shibboleth among American politicians, also persuaded members of Congress to support small business legislation.[10]

By the end of the 1930s, with the rise of totalitarian regimes in Europe, the small business ideology had taken on a new meaning, for in the eyes of some Americans, the decline of small business in Europe had contributed to the rise of fascism.[11] Small business advocates believed that if large corporations con-trolled the American economy, the federal government would also be forced to expand its regulatory powers, thus threatening the American democratic sys-tem. Therefore, Americans had to preserve small business if they were to resist the threat of totalitarianism at home. Representative Wright Patman (D.-Tex.), one of the leading small business advocates in Congress, summarized the modernized ideology of small business in this way: "The wide distribution of economic power among many independent proprietors is the foundation of the Nation's economy. Both Franklin and Jefferson feared that industrializa-tion would lead to a labor proletariat without property and without hope. Small-business enterprise is a symbol of a society in which the hired man can become his own boss. . . . History shows that the elimination of the indepen-dent businessman has been the first step in the development of totalitarian-ism." Thus, small business was a "safeguard against concentration of power."[12]

In the years during and after World War II, the heirs of Brandeis continued to champion small business as an institution essential for the survival of de-mocracy. But they had lost much of their faith in the efficacy of antitrust legislation and therefore sought positive aid for small business, including fi-nancial assistance and representation within the federal government. Their efforts resulted in the creation of agencies to represent small manufacturers during World War II and the Korean War and eventually culminated in the establishment of a permanent Small Business Administration, the first agency to represent all of the nation's small business owners.

Small Business and Big Government
in the Twentieth Century

This study of federal government policy toward small business examines one aspect of a larger issue in American history: the growth of government in the twentieth century. Of course, government involvement in the American econ-omy is not a new experience. Historians never tire of reminding Americans of the mythical nature of their laissez-faire past. Since colonial times American governments have regulated everything from the price of bread to the clothes that could be worn on Sunday. For most of the past two hundred years, government at all levels has grown faster than the private sector. As historian Jonathan Hughes puts it, "big" government is "the All American way." Hughes

notes that before the rise of big government at the federal level, state legislatures acted as "trailblazers of the world in the creation of government interference in free markets."[13] Still, "laissez-faire is a comparative thing," and
although the "governmental habit" has roots deep in American history, the
rapid growth of government in the twentieth century is unprecedented; indeed, one can speak of a "takeoff" in the scale and scope of the American
state.[14] Since 1913, the share of the economy taken up by government spending
has increased sevenfold, from less than 6 percent of GNP to 40 percent in
1990.[15] Government regulation has also expanded to cover nearly every aspect
of American life. Whether one considers this a progressive development or a
regressive one placing us on "the road to serfdom," it is important to understand how and why this tremendous growth has taken place.[16]

American historians disagree in their interpretations of government growth
in the twentieth century. Early in the twentieth century, Progressive historians
attributed the expansion of government to the efforts of reformers who sought
to advance the cause of the disenfranchised. In this view, Progressive policymakers represented "the people" and the "have-nots" and promoted the "public interest" by eliminating the abuses of big business and by redistributing
wealth to the poor.[17] However, the Progressive interpretation failed to explain
why corporate executives had so much influence on the formulation and administration of Progressive legislation. Moreover, most government programs
have benefited the middle-class "haves" rather than the poorer "have-nots."[18]

The inadequacies of the Progressive interpretation led scholars to develop a
range of interest-group theories to explain the growth of government. In the
"broker-state" model of American politics, organized interest groups seek
government assistance, while policymakers broker between these competing interests.[19] "Corporate-liberal" historians trace the origins of the broker
state to the "organizational revolution" that produced big business and other
organized groups in the late nineteenth and twentieth centuries. Together
these groups formed the basis of America's "organizational commonwealth."[20]
Scholars differ, however, over the relative balance of forces in the broker state.
Political scientists in the "pluralist" school argue that the existence of many
interests prevents any one group from dominating the policymaking agenda.[21]
"Neo-pluralists," on the other hand, contend that the best-organized interests
often prevail at the expense of unorganized groups.[22] Similarly, "public choice"
theorists stress the ability of special interests to pressure the government for
benefits while dispersing the costs among taxpayers.[23] Neo-Marxists promote a
more radical version of corporate liberalism, maintaining that big business
executives dominate the American political system and legitimate their control

by creating programs that offer the superficial appearance of pluralism and consensus.[24]

The broker-state model of politics explains the piecemeal character of a welfare-regulatory state designed to serve various interests. But interest-group theories ignore the role played by policy entrepreneurs within the government. The very existence of competing interest groups allows government officials to play one interest off against another.[25] Thus, according to one school of thought, bureaucrats enjoy the autonomy needed to follow their own interests in expanding the government. This "bureaucratic imperative" leads them to construct their own little empires, sometimes at the expense of their clientele. However, although there have been cases of government officials motivated by the desire to expand their domain for reasons of personal prestige or simply to promote their organization's mission, it is not clear why most bureaucrats would have a strong incentive to increase their agency's revenue, since their pay is fixed according to their civil service rank. More important, many agencies have not grown in real terms; in fact, since the 1950s the number of government employees has declined as a proportion of the workforce. The growth in government expenditures has flowed to the beneficiaries of entitlement programs rather than to the bureaucrats who run these programs.[26]

Theories based solely on interest-group politics or on a bureaucratic imperative fail to explain adequately the evolution of the federal government's policies toward small business. At times, these elements did affect the outcome of small business legislation, but the federal government's policies can best be understood as the result of three interrelated factors: crisis, ideology, and political entrepreneurship. Several other scholars have emphasized the importance of these elements in explaining the growth of government in America and abroad. Thirty years ago, the British economists Alan T. Peacock and Jack Wiseman developed a "crisis" theory to explain the "periodic jumps" in the size of the British government. Peacock and Wiseman argued that crises (wars and depressions) stimulate public demands for government action and lower the public's resistance to higher levels of taxation. With each succeeding crisis, the British people came to accept greater government intervention in their lives.[27]

In his 1987 book, *Crisis and Leviathan*, the economic historian Robert Higgs applied this crisis theory to the American experience. Higgs, too, found that the federal government experienced much of its growth during times of crisis.[28] During a crisis, Higgs argues, the public demands action and abandons any reservations it may have regarding state intervention in the private sector. Meanwhile, various interest groups find new ways to profit from the expanding public sector by establishing close ties with governmental leaders. Programs created to meet the emergency survive and continue to grow as bureaucrats find new missions for their agencies.

Ideological change looms large in Higgs's approach to the study of government growth. He argues that in the Progressive Era the emergence of statist ideologies among a "new class" of intellectuals and reform-minded politicians set the stage for public acceptance of bigger government, an acceptance that grew with each succeeding crisis.[29] According to Higgs, these "ideological entrepreneurs" appeal to voters' anxieties by espousing crisis rhetoric in the form of political symbols that represent widely held values in the society.[30] Crises also magnify the importance of ideology in politics by polarizing issues. Thus, ideological entrepreneurs describe their cause as a struggle between good and evil, between chaos and the preservation of a way of life.[31]

Higgs's work provides a useful conceptual framework for understanding the federal government's policies toward small business. In the mid-twentieth century, ideological entrepreneurs sought to represent small business owners and secure a place for them within the post–New Deal broker state. These small business activists enjoyed some of their greatest successes during times of crisis, while in more prosperous and peaceful times, their "movement" drifted along without the support of an active pressure group behind them. Eventually, however, after twenty-five years of agitation, they secured the establishment of permanent Small Business Committees and a permanent Small Business Administration. This institutionalization of small business in the federal government paved the way for increased aid to small business in response to future crises in the cities and in the economy at large.

In sum, crisis and ideology were significant factors in determining the federal government's policies toward small business. But interest-group politics, bureaucratic rivalries, and the personal philosophies of American presidents also played important roles in determining the outcome of small business legislation. The interplay of these factors produced a complex chapter in the history of American government in the twentieth century.

The Politics of Small Business:
A Historiographical Review

Until recently, most historians have ignored small business and focused almost exclusively on the history of big business in America. In the area of business history the work of Alfred D. Chandler Jr. defined the labors of a generation of scholars. In his Pulitzer Prize–winning *Visible Hand: The Managerial Revolu-*

tion in American Business (1977), Chandler contrasted the complexities of "modern" (big) business with the simplicity of "traditional" (small) business.[32] Although Chandler conceded that small business still dominates the more labor-intensive sectors of the economy, his single-minded focus on the large corporation has given the impression that small business is an anachronistic throwback to a preindustrial era. Thus, in Chandler's drama, corporate actors play the starring roles, while small business owners remain on the periphery as players of bit parts.

In recent years, however, historians have finally come to recognize the continuing importance of small firms in the American economy. In fact, some historians have always done so. In their studies of small retailers and manufacturers, Lewis Atherton, Martha Taber, Theodore Marburg, and James Soltow pioneered in small business history.[33] Since the 1970s, as the popular appeal of small business has grown, so has academic interest in the subject. Mansel Blackford, John Ingham, and Philip Scranton, among others, have produced works highlighting various aspects of small business history. In 1992, Blackford produced the first general history of small business in America, a sign that this area of historical inquiry is coming of age.[34]

Yet while historians have begun to examine the economic activities of small firms, they have still paid too little attention to the political history of small business. Most historians have viewed the passage of weak antitrust legislation during the Progressive Era as the embodiment of a final accommodation with big business. Thus Robert Wiebe, Samuel Hays, and others noted the influence corporate leaders had on the formulation of antitrust legislation. Gabriel Kolko described the entire era as one in which big business interests triumphed at the expense of farmers, workers, and small business owners. More recently, Martin Sklar has argued that federal antitrust legislation represented the victory of corporate liberalism over an older small business ethic. Sklar concluded that the antitrust legislation passed during the Wilson administration "ended the debate over the legitimacy of the large corporation."[35]

Although public-policy historians have generally overlooked the continued debate over the politics of small business in mid-twentieth-century America, there are a few notable exceptions. In his classic study *The New Deal and the Problem of Monopoly*, published in 1966, Ellis Hawley discussed how the American public's ambivalence toward both big and small business shaped the economic policies of Franklin D. Roosevelt's administration during the Great Depression.[36] Carl Ryant and David Horowitz have described local and regional aspects of the anti-chain-store movement, while Jim Heath has examined the federal government's attempts to aid small manufacturers during the early phase of the World War II mobilization effort. Until now, though, no historian has examined how the government's policies changed over time.[37]

Political scientists have shown a greater interest than historians in studying the federal government's policies toward small business. In his history of the anti-chain-store movement of the 1930s, Joseph C. Palamountain emphasized the important roles played by well-organized trade associations in securing the passage of laws designed to protect small business from chain store competition.[38] Harmon Zeigler's study *The Politics of Small Business* (1961) remains the standard work on the history of public policy toward small business in the 1940s and 1950s. Zeigler noted the divergent positions taken by various small business associations and concluded that "there is no small business interest"; the heterogeneous nature of the small business community simply made it impossible for a single organization to represent the interests of all of the nation's small firms. Consequently, members of the congressional Small Business Committees took it upon themselves to secure the creation of small business agencies.[39]

Several scholars have debated whether a single ideology united the diverse members of the small business community. John Bunzel studied the views of two small business associations and concluded that there was such a "general ideology" of small business. Bunzel believed that although they hypocritically accepted government aid, small business owners still longed for a mythical laissez-faire past. He described them as the last reactionary representatives of an anti-industrial "agrarian spirit." In similar fashion, Richard Hofstadter portrayed the typical small business owner as "a parochial and archaic opponent of liberal ideas, a supporter of vigilante groups and of right-wing cranks."[40] But others challenged this notion of small business conservatism. Harmon Zeigler, who studied some of the associations overlooked by Bunzel, found "no small business ideology" and no political consensus among small business activists. Richard Hamilton cited opinion polls showing that small business owners reflected the divisions within society at large. After conducting interviews with Seattle small business people in the 1970s, Ralph Murphy also found that "their overriding sense of self-sufficient individualism" kept them from viewing themselves as members of a cohesive interest group. Taken together, the works of Zeigler, Hamilton, and Murphy demonstrate convincingly the fallacy of assuming the existence of a small business point of view.[41]

These varied works shed light on the political history of small business, but they suffer from limitations. First, the authors had to rely almost solely on published materials and oral histories. Zeigler, for example, suggests the key role played by individuals in Congress and the executive branch, but he lacked access to the unpublished papers of politicians and the records of small business agencies. Second, these works focus on legislative history and ignore what Samuel P. Hays has called the "politics of administration." Hays recognized that policy history involves more than legislative politics and decision-making; the implementation of legislation is as important as the passage of the law itself.[42] As the enforcers of small business legislation, the Federal Trade Commission and the Small Business Administration have always faced political choices in deciding how to apply the law. By making use of the unpublished papers of politicians and government officials, this book overcomes these limitations and provides insights into the behind-the-scenes decision-making process in Congress and the executive branch, both before and after the passage of small business legislation.

Other scholars have shown that small business owners never united on the basis of ideology. Yet congressional small business advocates—the politicians—did achieve a consensus based on a shared desire to aid small business, and without such an ideology, it is difficult to explain why congressional representatives from opposite ends of the political spectrum reached common ground on issues affecting small business. Still, these small business advocates often disagreed over the means used to preserve the "backbone of democracy," and when one examines their views closely, it becomes clear that they had different conceptions of the small business ideology.

Small Business: Problems of Definition

Once, when asked to define small business, a spokesman for a small business association struggled for an answer, then finally said, "We know a small business when we see one."[43] Those who have tried to define "small" business have found it difficult, for in the end, smallness is in the eye of the beholder. Congressional small business advocates often failed to agree on a definition; thus, in 1942, a Senate Subcommittee on Small Business "tried to define it, but could not do so."[44] Like most Americans, many members of Congress had a "mom-and-pop" operation in mind when they spoke of small business. Others sought to promote competition and check the power of big business by offering government aid to "small" firms with many employees. Representative Wright Patman, for example, considered Zenith Radio a "relatively small corporation" because it challenged larger firms in its industry.[45]

Most scholars who study small business define it by delineating those characteristics that distinguish small firms from larger ones. Mansel Blackford, for example, characterizes a "small" business as one that is locally owned and

operated by a single proprietor or a few partners. These small businesses typically serve a local market rather than the national and international markets.
Also, small firms usually hire workers from the local area, and the owners of
these companies often take an active role in civic matters affecting their community. Defining small business in this way allows economists and historians
to contrast "small" firms with "big," bureaucratic corporations; but because
this is a history of the politics surrounding small business, the term "small
business" will refer to those companies that fit the arbitrary definitions set
forth by government agencies (e.g., "those with fewer than 500 employees").[46]

The Scope of This Study

This book examines the evolution of federal policies toward small business on
two planes. The first half of the book discusses how congressional small business advocates secured the passage of antitrust legislation designed to place
restraints on chain stores. The second half looks at their attempts to secure
positive aid for small businesses during the 1940s and 1950s. Several themes
predominate throughout: 1) the importance of political entrepreneurs in Congress, 2) their use of ideology and crisis rhetoric as a substitute for an organized pressure group of small business owners, 3) the disparity between the
intended and the actual consequences of their legislation, and 4) the persistence of small business despite the shortcomings of the federal government's
small business policies.

   This is a history of the federal government's policies toward small business;
however, many of the initiatives for small business legislation first emerged at
the state level, and thus the following chapters will analyze congressional reac-
tion to the passage of state laws designed to aid small business. Where it is
appropriate, I will also discuss how court decisions influenced the formulation
of the federal government's small business policies; but because the politics of
small business centered in the halls of Congress and in the corridors of the
executive branch of government, I will focus on developments in those areas.

   The years between 1936 and 1961 encompass an important period in the
development of the federal government's policies toward small business. Although the sponsors of earlier antitrust legislation sought to protect small
business from "unfair competition," the 1930s witnessed the first sustained
efforts to pass legislation designed specifically to aid small firms.[47] Indeed, the
small business advocates themselves traced the beginning of their so-called
movement to the passage of the Robinson-Patman Act (1936), often called the

"Magna Charta of small business." Their campaign to secure positive aid for small business climaxed with the creation of a permanent Small Business Administration (SBA) in the Eisenhower years. Later, in the 1960s and 1970s, the character of federal small business legislation changed as the SBA took on new missions to wage war on poverty and aid minorities. That story is left for another volume.

Chapter 1 begins with a discussion of small business and the antitrust tradition. During the late nineteenth and early twentieth centuries, small manufacturers secured federal antitrust legislation, but court interpretations of the law limited its effectiveness. In retailing, campaigns against mail-order companies and department stores failed to generate much political support because these new forms of competition did not threaten the interests of most independent merchants. Chain stores posed a much more serious threat to independent retailers; this type of mass marketing spread rapidly before and during the Great Depression, a time of general crisis for small business. Congressional small business advocates exploited the crisis by obtaining passage of the Robinson-Patman Act, a law that limited the discounts available to chain stores. Yet the sponsors of the Robinson-Patman Act failed to perceive how difficult it would be to reconcile the interests of small business owners and consumers.

Chapter 2 offers a case study of the Robinson-Patman Act's impact on the tire industry. The trade association representing independent tire dealers lobbied for the passage of this act, and during the next quarter century the tire dealers and their congressional allies pressured the Federal Trade Commission to enforce the law. However, the relative prosperity of small tire dealers belied their crisis rhetoric. The tire dealers' influence in Congress was also limited by the ideological differences of small business advocates and the near-unanimous opposition of economists. During the 1970s, presidential and congressional concern with fighting inflation reduced the Robinson-Patman Act to the status of a "dead-letter law."

Chapter 3 examines the history of federal fair trade legislation from the passage of the Miller-Tydings Act (1937) to its repeal in 1975. Small retailers hoped to limit price competition from chain stores by securing legislation allowing manufacturers to fix minimum prices on their brand-name goods. But manufacturers found it difficult to enforce their price agreements, and the development of discount retailing further diminished the appeal of fair trade. Proponents of fair trade also faced opposition from the judicial and executive branches of government. The Miller-Tydings Act, like the Robinson-Patman Act, finally fell victim to the changed economic climate of the 1970s, as legislators took fair trade laws off the books in an attempt to foster greater price competition.

Why did politicians from all ends of the political spectrum champion small business? Chapter 4 explores this question by presenting a collective biography of those congressmen who served on the House and Senate Small Business Committees between 1940 and 1961. This analysis shows that the small business ideology united a diverse group of politicians; but leading small business advocates also had differing conceptions of the ideology, which led them into disagreements over the means used to assist small business.

The remaining chapters examine the small business advocates' efforts to secure positive aid for small firms. Chapter 5 looks at the Smaller War Plants Corporation (SWPC), the first federal agency devoted solely to the interests of small business. Pressured by the crisis rhetoric of a few prominent representatives, Congress created the agency to help small manufacturers secure defense work during World War II. The SWPC's brief and unsuccessful history indicates the problems faced by an agency lacking the support of an organized constituency. The agency suffered from partisan politics and the opposition of rival government agencies. Critics of big business and champions of small business faced added difficulties in the immediate postwar years, a period when the American public admired those who managed the nation's largest corporations.

Chapter 6 examines the operations of the Small Defense Plants Administration (SDPA), an agency created to represent small manufacturers during the Korean War. The SDPA experienced the same difficulties as its World War II predecessor and was no more successful in helping small firms to secure defense contracts. In 1953, Congress abolished the SDPA and established the Small Business Administration, the first peacetime agency to represent all types of small businesses.

Chapter 7 discusses the partisan politics that swirled around the SBA during the Eisenhower years. The budget-conscious administration of President Dwight D. Eisenhower clashed with the congressional Small Business Committees over the recommended level of spending by the SBA. Administration officials tried to limit the activities of the SBA in order to maintain a balanced budget, but congressional pressure eventually resulted in the expansion of the agency's small business programs. Nevertheless, the vast and heterogeneous nature of the small business community limited what the SBA could do for small business.

The concluding chapter places the evolution of the federal government's policy toward small business within the larger context of business-government relations in modern America. The chapter ends with an analysis of the problems that have historically plagued those who sought to aid small business and a discussion of their present-day implications.

1

The Robinson-Patman Act:
The Magna Charta of Small Business

In 1933, Congressman Wright Patman declared, "The time has come in this country when we must get back to local businesses, locally owned and owner operated."[1] Three years later, Patman and other congressional small business advocates achieved their first significant political victory when they secured passage of the Robinson-Patman Act. The sponsors of this "Magna Charta of small business" hoped to preserve the market share of independent retailers by limiting the discounts granted to those mass-marketers who purchased huge quantities of goods from manufacturers. These quantity discounts gave chain stores a price advantage over their smaller rivals. Thus, by passing the Robinson-Patman Act, congressional small business advocates hoped to create a "level playing field" for small business.

The rise of chain store competition in the tire industry played an important role in the passage of this act. A controversial series of contracts between Sears & Roebuck and Goodyear Rubber & Tire Company in the 1920s and 1930s had enabled this large retailer to purchase a high volume of tires at a steep discount. Sears's entry into the tire market sparked a price war that drove many independent dealers out of business. This confrontation involved two American symbols: Sears, "the Great American Company," and the small business owner, "the backbone of democracy." It also represented a conflict between the interests of the consumer and of small business. On the one hand, Sears's agreement with Goodyear allowed the company to mass-market a low-cost product to American consumers. But the sponsors of the Robinson-Patman Act cited this as an example of big business forcing small firms from the field of competition.

As opponents of big business, they worked within the antitrust tradition and believed that additional antitrust legislation might restore an earlier condition of competition, which they defined as the existence of many small firms in a single market. Yet their brainchild, the Robinson-Patman Act, reflected an ambivalent attitude toward competition: it was good if it benefited the consumer, bad if it led to the elimination of small business. It remained to be seen, however, whether the act could promote the interests of the consumer as well as those of the small business owner.

The Road to Robinson-Patman:
Small Business and the Antitrust Tradition

The Robinson-Patman Act emerged out of the antitrust tradition, which dated back to the sudden rise of big business in the 1870s and 1880s. At the time, small business owners responded to increased competition from big business by exerting their political influence to secure legislation restricting the business practices of large firms. Small manufacturers and merchants were prominent leaders in their communities and often held political office at the local and state level. Consequently, state legislatures throughout America responded to the pleas of these business owners by using the power of licensing to protect them from outside competitors. For example, when I. M. Singer & Company, a large manufacturer of sewing machines, tried to bypass local merchants by selling through its own traveling salesmen, state legislatures passed legislation that required the licensing of sewing machine vendors and imposed other restrictions on the peddlers of Singer products.[2]

Small business owners also turned to the federal government for assistance. The rise of big business in meatpacking, the nation's largest industry, initially sparked their demands for federal government action.[3] In the 1880s, small meatpackers in the Midwest, threatened by increased competition from several large national firms (the so-called Beef Trust) led the drive for restrictive legislation.[4] Large meatpackers had developed refrigerated railway cars to distribute meat to the entire nation. This innovative use of technology and transportation enabled these companies to attract business away from the independent meatpacker, thus making this one of the most highly concentrated industries in the country. Yet as they lobbied Congress, the small meatpackers argued that the Beef Trust and other oligopolies had emerged only as a result of price-fixing and other restraints on trade.

These protests from meatpackers and other small business groups contrib-

uted to congressional passage of the Sherman Act of 1890, the nation's first federal antitrust law. The act prohibited "every contract, combination in the form
of trust or otherwise, or conspiracy in restraint of trade or commerce."[5] To
ensure compliance with the law, Congress imposed criminal penalties and
allowed firms to sue for treble damages resulting from any illegal restraint on
trade.

Although small businesses led the lobbying effort in Congress, the congressional debate over the Sherman Act reflected more than simply a concern
with the interests of small business. Many historians have argued that the act
reflected "a bewildering variety of goals."[6] The authors of the Sherman Act
professed several motives, including the protection of small business, the preservation of competition, and the promotion of the consumer welfare. This
mixture of apparent motives has led some scholars to downplay the small
business character of the Sherman Act. Some historians note that Congress
was also responding to public opinion, which was hostile toward monopoly.[7]
Others, including Robert Bork, have maintained that Congress was primarily
concerned with the welfare of the consumer.[8] Recent scholarship suggests,
however, that the proconsumer, procompetitive language of the act's sponsors
was no more than a cover for legislation designed to benefit small business at
the expense of the consumer. In the first place, contemporary economists
believed that big business increased competition and benefited the consumer;
indeed, congressional supporters of the Sherman Act admitted that big business had drastically lowered prices, at least temporarily; therefore, in debates
and hearings, they emphasized the social and political threat of oligopolies
rather than the economic consequences of industrial concentration.[9] There is
also evidence that the Republican majority in Congress characterized the Sherman Act as a piece of consumer legislation in order to defend themselves from
the criticism that would soon result from their upcoming vote for the McKin-
ley Tariff Act, a bill that raised the tariff on imported goods and thus increased
the cost to the consumers buying those products. Consequently, the Republicans "condemned the trusts in self-defense" against charges that they were a
"Party of Monopolists" unconcerned with the welfare of small business and
the consumer.[10]

In short, the Sherman Act should be viewed not as a consumer measure but,
rather, as the first substantial piece of federal small business legislation, motivated by Republican politicians' concern with appeasing public opinion. Historian Jonathan Hughes reflects this understanding when he writes that the
"moving spirits of the Sherman Act knew precisely what they were doing: they

were attempting to rein in the power of large business organizations in the interests of the more numerous, and politically effective, small businesses of the country."[11] In later years, congressional small business advocates would build on this foundation as they attempted to stem the rise of big business.

Although the Sherman Act banned "every" restraint on trade, the law's sponsors maintained that it merely embodied the common law tradition, which applied a "rule of reason" to cases involving restraints on trade. According to common law precedent, businesses could restrict trade among themselves if their agreement did not prevent new firms from entering the market. Initially the courts followed this line of reasoning, but beginning in 1897, the U.S. Supreme Court abandoned the "rule of reason" and struck down nearly all combinations that restrained trade, "whether reasonable or unreasonable."[12] Yet ironically, this tougher approach worked to the detriment of small business, because the antitrust lawyers at the Justice Department found it easier to prove cases of price-fixing cartels involving many small firms. In 1911, the Supreme Court returned to its earlier reliance on the common law "rule of reason," an interpretation of the law that has generally held sway for the remainder of the twentieth century; nonetheless, though, the government continued to prosecute small firms.[13]

Meanwhile, the issue of big business continued to dominate political discourse outside the judicial arena. In the Progressive Era, several groups demanded additional antitrust legislation: consumers concerned with price-fixing, corporate executives seeking the government's advance approval for their mergers and acquisitions, and small business owners looking for measures to restrain their larger rivals.[14] In 1914, Congress responded to pressure from these various interests by passing the Clayton Act and the Federal Trade Commission Act, two measures embodying a compromise among these groups. As an amendment to the Sherman Act, the Clayton Act offered a more detailed definition of "restraint of trade." The act prohibited several specific business practices when they "substantially lessen" competition, including: price discrimination between buyers, "tying contracts" (exclusive agreements that prevented the suppliers of a large firm from dealing with that firm's competitors), mergers and acquisitions, and interlocking directorates between firms in the same industry.[15] The Federal Trade Commission Act, a companion bill to the Clayton Act, declared "unfair methods of competition" illegal and created the Federal Trade Commission (FTC) to determine which business practices constituted "unfair" competition. The FTC could order violators of the law to "cease and desist" from their unlawful activities. If a violator refused to do so, the FTC could bring its case against the company into the courts. In creating the Federal Trade Commission, Congress hoped the agency would finally resolve the debate over the trusts by reconciling the interests of small business, big business, and the consumer.[16]

In practice, this antitrust legislation did little to bolster the competitive advantage of small firms. Throughout the 1910s and 1920s, a lack of strong leadership weakened the Federal Trade Commission, and several adverse court decisions further limited the agency's effectiveness in enforcing the law. For example, in the *Gratz* case of 1920, the U.S. Supreme Court ruled that the courts were to determine what constituted "unfair methods" of competition; and in a case involving the U.S. Steel Corporation, also decided in 1920, the Court reiterated its rule of reason, declaring that "the law does not make mere size an offense."[17] These court rulings, coupled with the FTC's decision to prosecute small firms that violated the Clayton Act, eroded congressional small business advocates' faith in the efficacy of this legislation. In the future, they would again seek new antitrust laws, but they would have to wait until another threat to small business generated public concern with the fate of independent enterprise.

In sum, between 1890 and 1914, Congress passed several important laws designed, in part, to preserve a place for small business in the American economy. But the ambiguous nature of this legislation meant that the courts and the antitrust agencies would ultimately determine the outcome of this legislation. The prevailing judicial philosophy dictated an acceptance of big business, while the FTC's prosecution-minded lawyers earned their reputations by winning scores of "easy" cases involving small firms. Thus, paradoxically, this "antitrust" legislation did more to restore the reputation of big business than to increase the market share of small business.

Mass Marketing Meets Main Street:
Department Stores, Mail Order, and the Chain Store Menace

Early antitrust legislation had resulted from congressional concern with the rapid relative decline of small business in the manufacturing sector of the economy. In the years after 1914, small business advocates called for new antitrust legislation to counter the rise of big business in retailing. This concern with preserving the market share of small retailers had its roots in the late nineteenth century, when merchants faced competition from department stores and mail-order firms. However, a more serious threat to small business emerged in the 1920s and 1930s, with the spread of chain stores. This chain store "menace" sparked a national movement that resulted in the passage of state and federal legislation regulating mass-marketers.

Until the late nineteenth century, small businesses handled nearly all of the nation's retail trade. Markets were small, and merchants frequently enjoyed a local monopoly within their line of trade. This situation changed with the birth of department stores in America's largest cities. Alexander T. Stewart constructed the first large department store in 1846 in New York City. Other department stores—including Marshall Field's, Lazarus, and Macy's—appeared after the Civil War. Urbanization had created large, concentrated markets served by new means of mass transit, including electric trolleys and subways. Department stores took advantage of this mass market by selling a high volume of goods at low prices. These stores also broke with tradition by adopting fixed prices, relying heavily on advertising, carrying a variety of goods, and offering a satisfaction guarantee. Elegant displays turned department stores into "palaces of consumption" that dazzled the American consumer.[18]

Department stores provoked fear and outrage among small merchants and among newspaper editors, who depended on the advertising revenues of small business owners. Apocalyptic articles attacking this "colossus of trade" appeared in big-city newspapers.[19] In 1889, the author of one such article in the *Chicago Tribune* complained that "when each fresh department was added to Marshall Field store it was like a cyclone had gone forth among the smaller houses which were in the same line of business. . . . Against such a power . . . nothing could stand." The *Philadelphia Gazette* provided a forum for another merchant, who attacked the "greedy, grasping and godless spirit" that led department stores to destroy smaller businesses. This merchant traced the origins of the menace to Alexander Stewart, whom he described as "one of the meanest merchants that ever lived."[20]

Small merchants did more than complain. Trade associations representing small druggists and booksellers boycotted manufacturers who sold to department stores, but without much success.[21] In the 1880s and 1890s, small retailers convinced state legislators to introduce bills banning the construction of new department stores and imposing special taxes on existing ones. These bills never became law, in part because small retailers in the largest cities were the only ones concerned with the issue, and they simply lacked the votes needed to secure passage of state legislation discriminating against department stores.

They were no more successful at the federal level. The Industrial Commission, a body created by Congress in 1898 to study the "trust question," investigated the impact of department stores on small retailers and concluded that this new form of retailing benefited consumers. The investigation also revealed that many small retailers had imitated department store methods, leading the commission to conclude that "the growth of the department store must be regarded as being a benefit to the small retailer who has profited by incorporation of many of its techniques." Indeed, a study of retail trade in Boston found that the total number of retail firms increased in eighteen of twenty-five categories between 1874 and 1898. Furthermore, in the early twentieth century, the competitive pressure on independent merchants eased when department stores began specializing in luxury items, leaving the market for other goods to smaller retailers.[22]

Unlike their urban cousins, small-town merchants faced very little direct competition from department stores. Railroads offered excursion trips to big cities, but the inconvenience of having to travel far from home discouraged most residents from making the trip.[23] But small-town merchants did encounter competition from the mail-order firm, another new form of mass marketing. Aaron Montgomery Ward created the first national mail-order firm in 1872, and his firm was soon joined by Sears, Roebuck, and Company. Ward and Sears took advantage of the nation's newly constructed railway net to ship goods to small towns across America. Later, the creation of Rural Free Delivery (1896) and parcel post (1913) enabled these companies to mail goods to the customer's doorstep. By buying in bulk and eliminating the middleman, these mail-order companies undercut small-town merchants. Mail-order firms sold an enormous variety of goods (Sears carried 100,000 items in 1908) and backed them up with a liberal return policy ("Satisfaction Guaranteed or Your Money Back"). The guarantee transformed the way American merchants did business: to remain competitive with department stores and mail-order firms, smaller merchants had to abandon the old philosophy of *caveat emptor* ("buyer beware") in favor of *caveat venditor* ("seller beware"). The notion that "the customer is always right" became part of the new way of doing business. Meanwhile, farmers, who had long resented the high prices and limited selection of goods offered by small merchants, eagerly sent away for the catalogs of Montgomery Ward and Sears, Roebuck. (The latter became known as "the Farmer's Bible.")[24]

Consumers might have benefited, but small merchants felt threatened by mail order. Many merchants refused to call the companies by name; they referred to them as "Shears and Rawbuck" and "Monkey Ward." Southern merchants played on racism by spreading rumors that Sears, Ward, and other mail-order magnates were black.[25] Newspaper editors alleged that mail order was "making commercial graveyards of once prosperous towns," while local chambers of commerce organized "trade at home" campaigns encouraging residents to shop in town rather than through the mail.[26] Occasionally politicians became involved—a mayoral candidate in Warsaw, Iowa, promised to fire city employees who ordered from mail-order catalogs!—but except for an unsuccessful attempt to block the legislation authorizing parcel post, small merchants relied more on moral suasion and demonstrations than on political action. Perhaps the most flamboyant of their protests were the book burnings conducted by chambers of commerce. The books in question were, of course, mail-order catalogs. In his study of the Sears catalog, David L. Cohn writes that the catalogs "were reduced to ashes at the incitement of local merchants and newspaper editors who believed that to destroy the catalogs was to destroy the competition of the mail-order houses."[27] This phenomenon made its way into American fiction: in George Milburn's novel *Catalogue* (1936), the central characters are the mail-order catalogs that arrive in a small Oklahoma town, much to the chagrin of local businesspeople. At the suggestion of the local newspaper editor, the merchants decide to purchase mail-order catalogs from the town's residents and use them to make a bonfire during the "Home Town Industry Jubilee":

> They had the catalogues—a great sprawling mound of them—dumped on one corner of the circus lots. . . . As the flames crackled up, members of the Chamber of Commerce worked hard, dousing the catalogues in coal oil, tossing them on the fire. A few stood by with long poles, poking up the slow-burning blocks of paper. Others held dripping gunny sacks, ready to flout any blazing patch of grass. . . . There were several hundred people there, nearly all town-dwellers, standing along the flaming ditch, their faces showing drawn and ghostly in the firelight. . . . Sometimes, when the goaded flames flared high, small boys would whoop, but only the bustling members of the Chamber of Commerce seemed to be having much fun. Few people seemed happy to see all the mail-order catalogues destroyed.[28]

This dramatic gesture failed to alter the buying habits of the townspeople; the very next day the local post office received an avalanche of postcards and letters requesting new mail-order catalogs.

Why did the anti-mail-order campaigns achieve so little? First, there was, as David Cohn put it, "no patriotism of the purse."[29] Farmers were not the natural allies of small merchants; few agonized over whether to purchase goods from a mail-order house. In fact, the congressional debate over parcel post revealed the divisions between farmers and small business owners: the

Small-town merchants expressed their opposition to mail-order competition by placing these Buster Brown cartoons (circa 1916) in their newspaper advertisements. (From Frank B. Latham, *1872–1972: A Century of Serving Consumers, The Story of Montgomery Ward* [Chicago: Montgomery Ward, 1972])

former testified in favor of parcel post, while the latter lobbied against it.[30] The mail-order firms also adopted measures to shield customers from the criticisms of local merchants. Sears, for example, shipped its goods in plain brown wrapping. In parts of the country where anti-mail-order sentiment was exceptionally strong, the company protected the reputation of its suppliers by refusing to print their names in the catalog (for example, saws were listed as "from a factory in Southeastern Michigan").[31] Sears also instituted a "Good Neighbor Policy" in response to this opposition: the company hired a small army of letter-writers to communicate with customers on topics both business and personal, thus giving Sears the image of a friendly neighbor.[32] The mail-order firms occasionally went on the offensive, attacking the notion that they were "monopolistic." In 1902, Montgomery Ward reprinted a piece entitled "Tyranny of Village," which stated, "We believe the farmers of today are tyrannized over by the country merchants to a far worse extent than they realize. . . . [The] mail-order business has solved the problem for the farmer and released him from serfdom."[33] Richard W. Sears portrayed himself as an opponent of monopoly, declaring, "We are Waging War against Combinations, Associations, Trusts, and High Prices."[34]

The verbal heat generated by the controversy over department stores and mail-order catalogs was out of all proportion to the amount of market share that small retailers lost to these mass-marketers. As late as 1920, department stores and mail-order firms accounted for less than 10 percent of total retail sales. But small merchants soon faced an even greater threat in the form of the

Two Cleveland, Ohio, meat dealers next to their chain-store competitor A&P
(Courtesy of Cleveland State University, The *Cleveland Press* Collection)

chain store, which extended the "visible hand" into retailing and into America's small towns. The chain store's advantage lay in its low operating costs and in the discounts it received for quantity purchases. Chain stores eliminated services offered by traditional merchants, including credit and home delivery, but offered lower prices to attract customers.[35]

This form of mass marketing spread rapidly in the 1920s, as the automobile connected small towns to the larger urban markets. Almost overnight, the rise of the chain store upset the world of the independent merchant, destroying the local monopolies enjoyed by many small business owners. Between 1919 and 1929, the chains increased their share of retail sales from 4 percent to 20 percent, and the nation's first modern chain, The Great Atlantic & Pacific Tea Company (A&P), increased its number of stores from 4,600 to nearly 16,000. The total number of chain-store units in the country rose from 300 in 1900 to over 100,000 in 1930. Chain-store sales continued to increase during the cost-conscious depression years; by 1935, the chains handled 23 percent of all retail sales. The "Chain-Store Age" had dawned on America.[36]

Many small retailers responded to chain-store competition by improving their service and selection of goods. Some merchants imitated chain-store methods by cutting costs and increasing turnover, while others formed voluntary chains to secure quantity discounts. By 1930, independent retailers had formed thirty-three such chains, containing over 40,000 stores. The largest voluntary chains were McKesson & Robbin pharmaceuticals (12,000 members), Red & White groceries (4,500 stores), and Nation Wide (2,500 stores). This buying strategy grew increasingly popular during the Great Depression, and by 1940, over 100,000 independent grocers were members of voluntary chains.[37]

Independent retailers also engaged in public relations efforts aimed at diminishing the appeal of the chain store. For example, local store owners sponsored advertising campaigns encouraging Americans to "trade at home" and joined together to boycott manufacturers who sold to chain stores. Organized merchants promoted "fair trade" by urging the government to amend the antitrust laws to allow manufacturers to fix minimum retail prices in an attempt to overcome the chain stores' competitive advantage. However, these attempts at persuasion failed to change the attitudes of consumers or manufacturers. Most manufacturers continued to sell discount goods, and Americans continued to buy them.[38]

This economic contest soon played itself out in the political arena, as ambitious politicians seized upon anti-chain-store sentiment and used the issue to attract the votes of independent merchants and others critical of big business. Although the United States had been urbanizing for nearly a century, most Americans still lived on farms or in towns with a population of less than 10,000, and many of these small-town Americans viewed the chain store as a menace to their way of life.[39] In 1930, Godfrey Lebhar, editor of *Chain Store Age*, succinctly summed up their criticisms of the chain store:

1. The chains take money out of a community.
2. Chains do not employ local help.
3. Chains pay exceptionally low wages.
4. Chains take no interest in local activities.
5. Chains pay less taxes than local merchants.
6. Chains are of little value to local bankers.
7. Chains tend to make us a nation of clerks and limit the opportunity of American manhood.
8. The growth of the chain store system tends to centralize the business of the country in few hands.[40]

This list did not exhaust the charges hurled at the chain stores in the 1920s and 1930s. The critics claimed that the young men who worked in chain stores could not earn enough to support a family and that "girls are employed at wages so low that the moral status of this country is in danger."[41] Thus, in their view, the chain store threatened the most basic unit of society, the family. The anti-chain-store movement also gained particular momentum in the South and West, where politicians played on the long-standing populist fear of out-side corporations' controlling the local economy.[42] In this area of the country, critics propagated the notion that chain stores were part of a Wall Street conspiracy aimed at making small-town workers and consumers dependent on the absentee owners of large corporations.

Despite all this hubbub, the chain store did have its defenders. Government statistics showed that chain stores paid higher wages and provided better working conditions for their employees than did their smaller competitors. The chains also responded to the torrent of criticism by hiring managers from the local communities and encouraging them to act as civic leaders. Support-ers of the chain stores considered their lower prices a community asset, since the savings remained with local residents. Finally, business writers noted that many small retailers had learned to survive in an economic world inhabited by large chain stores, and they predicted that there would be room enough for both big and small business.[43]

These positive arguments failed to sway those Americans who feared that the rapid rise of the chain store might mean the end of a cherished way of life. This fear first found expression in a Maryland state law, passed in 1927, that prohibited the expansion of chain stores and imposed a progressive tax on the chains based on the number of units they owned. A circuit court judge struck the law down, however, on the grounds that it denied chain stores the equal protection of the laws under the Fourteenth Amendment. Consequently, be-tween 1927 and 1930, few states considered chain tax legislation, because law-yers assumed that the courts would nullify such laws. Then, in 1931, the U.S. Supreme Court upheld the legality of chain taxes imposed in Indiana and North Carolina. The Court ruled that the larger size of chain stores made them qualitatively different from their single-store competitors, and, therefore, that state legislatures could discriminate between the two types of retailers. This decision opened the floodgate to anti-chain-store legislation: other states, desperate for sources of revenue during the depression, passed similar mea-sures, and by 1939, twenty-seven states had enacted some form of chain tax legislation.[44]

These taxes did not impose much of a burden on most chain stores, but they did squeeze grocery chains and filling stations. Operating on exceptionally narrow profit margins, grocery chains could not pass the cost on to the con-

Critics alleged that chain stores lacked civic pride. This cartoon ran in the first issue of *Truth*, one of the many short-lived journals inspired by the anti-chain-store movement of the 1930s. (Courtesy of Rutgers University)

sumer, and they lost market share in the late 1930s. Chain taxes also affected the distribution of gasoline through filling stations, another chain that operated on a thin profit margin. This taxation encouraged petroleum refiners to convert their wholly owned outlets into franchises. Franchising motivated dealers to increase sales and benefited both the oil companies and their franchisees. Thus, this anti-chain-store legislation helped give birth to the "franchise revolution" that would later transform retailing in America.[45]

It is difficult to gauge the level of grassroots support for anti-chain-store legislation. Very few small business owners joined anti-chain-store organizations; indeed, most did not even belong to a single trade association. Moreover, many anti-chain-store organizations simply promoted the careers of their charismatic founders. W. K. Henderson, owner and operator of KWKH (Shreveport, Louisiana), became "the first American radio demagogue of the Depression years" after predicting in 1929 that the growth of the chain stores would result in economic collapse. During the next year, Henderson gathered together an organization of "Minute Men" committed to spreading anti-chain-store propaganda, but his Minute Man Movement fell apart when the Federal Trade Commission revealed that Henderson had siphoned off over $150,000 from membership dues for his own benefit. Henderson was not alone in his attempt to rally support for small business legislation. Throughout the nation, anti-chain-store demagogues used the power of the radio to spread their message. In Oregon, for example, Montaville Flowers and "Fighting" Bob Duncan succeeded in pressuring the Portland City Council into passing the nation's first municipal chain store tax.[46] Yet although they secured the passage of anti-chain laws, these political entrepreneurs left behind no organization to carry on their anti-chain activity after their personal appeal faded.

A number of older trade associations claimed to speak for small business, but most enlisted the support of only a tiny minority of the businesspeople in their trade. For example, the National Association of Retail Grocers (NARG), an organization that lobbied for chain taxes, represented only 10 percent of the nation's grocers.[47] Furthermore, if the views of these trade associations are any indication of the opinions held by those in the small business community, small business people did not agree on the need for a political solution to the problem of chain store competition. While groups representing grocers and druggists lobbied for anti-chain-store legislation, other organizations, including the National Retail Dry Goods Association and the Ohio Retailers Council, worried about the dangerous precedent that might be set by legislation that discriminated against chain stores. The head of the Ohio group opposed chain taxes because "a legislature which taxes chains today will tax all stores tomorrow."[48]

Still, although no group spoke as the "voice" of small business, the nearly universal political appeal of anti-chain-store legislation at the local and state level suggests that this issue struck a chord among voters. Public sentiment for the preservation of the way of life associated with small business did not crystallize in an all-encompassing small business organization, but it was strong enough to produce a flurry of laws designed to preserve this American institution. State and local politicians believed they had little to lose by voting for legislation that discriminated against an outside corporation, while they had something to gain from responding to this public sentiment for the "little guy."

Chain store critics did not confine their efforts to the state level. In 1928, the federal government became involved in the chain store debate when the National Association of Retail Grocers secured a Senate resolution calling for an FTC investigation of chain store practices. Congressional small business advocates hoped the investigation would prove that the chains used their buying power to extract "unfair" discounts from manufacturers (i.e., discounts not justified by the cost savings accruing to the manufacturer). The data from the FTC's six-year investigation, however, revealed that the chain store's competitive advantage resulted primarily from low operating costs. Furthermore, the FTC found that manufacturers' cost savings justified the discounts granted to chain stores. Special discounts and allowances accounted for only 1 percent of the price difference between the chain stores and small retailers. Yet the members of the FTC let political considerations cloud their judgment of the issue, and in its final report the commission contradicted its research findings by singling out quantity discounts as the source of the chain stores' success.[49]

During the Great Depression, disgruntled small business owners also urged the federal government to adopt measures aimed at restricting the buying power of the chain store. Thus, under the National Recovery Administration, independent wholesalers and retailers tried unsuccessfully to limit quantity discounts. At the same time, small business people sought judicial relief from price discrimination by bringing cases under Section 2 of the Clayton Antitrust Act. This law offered inadequate protection, however, because while it prohibited price discrimination, it permitted discounts made because of differences in the quantity or quality of the goods sold (manufacturers did not have to relate the size of their discount to actual cost savings). In their interpretations of the law, the courts ruled that a manufacturer had the right to freely determine discount schedules. This interpretation restricted the scope of FTC action, and the agency hesitated to use the law against chain stores.[50]

The Goodyear-Sears Investigation, 1933–1936

The entry of chain stores into the tire market prompted the FTC to change its policy. In the 1920s, the availability of inexpensive automobiles had led increasing numbers of Americans to move to the cities and suburbs. Sears and Roebuck, the nation's largest mail-order company, exploited this new market by establishing hundreds of retail stores throughout the nation.[51] As a result, Sears became an intruder in the tire market, an area of retailing once dominated by independent dealers. In 1926 Sears signed an exclusive contract with Goodyear for the manufacture of Allstate tires. The contract benefited both parties. Sears agreed to pay Goodyear the cost of manufacturing plus an operating profit of 6 percent. This long-term contract also protected Goodyear from any sudden increase in the cost of rubber. By scheduling its production for Sears over the entire year, Goodyear overcame the seasonal nature of tire sales, thus reducing its idle capacity and lowering its production costs.[52] The agreement allowed Sears to secure a steady supply of low-cost tires, and between 1925 and 1929, the company increased its sales of tires from 700,000 to 4.5 million. Sears's success encouraged its chief rival, Montgomery Ward, to sign similar contracts with U.S. Rubber and B. F. Goodrich, and together, by the early 1930s, Sears and Ward accounted for nearly 20 percent of the retail tire market.[53]

Independent tire dealers also faced increased competition from oil companies and manufacturers' outlets. In 1929 the Standard Oil Companies established Atlas Supply as a tire distributor for their service stations and began to purchase mass quantities of low-cost tires from B. F. Goodrich and U.S. Rubber. Consequently, between 1929 and 1936, the percentage of tires sold by the oil companies increased from less than 1 percent to nearly 10 percent. Meanwhile, the nation's largest tire companies tried to boost their own sales and profits by increasing their ownership of retail outlets. In the early 1930s, the Big Four (Goodyear, B. F. Goodrich, U.S. Rubber, and Firestone) opened more than 1,000 new retail stores, and by the middle of the decade, the sales of these manufacturers amounted to 10 percent of the tire market—a gain that came at the expense of the independent dealer.[54]

The introduction of these new forms of competition led to a steady erosion in the market position of independent tire dealers, and between 1926 and 1937 their share of retail tire sales plummeted from 91 percent to 53 percent. The National Association of Independent Tire Dealers (NAITD) complained that its members could no longer compete because manufacturers sold lower-priced tires to chain stores, oil companies, and manufacturers' outlets.[55] In 1933 the FTC responded to the complaints of the tire dealers by beginning an investigation of the Goodyear-Sears contract. The agency found that Sears paid 26 percent less for its tires than did the average independent dealer. FTC officials believed that Goodyear could not justify this price discrimination, and on March 5, 1936, they ordered the cancellation of the contract. Goodyear claimed, however, that it could justify its contract with Sears, and it appealed the order. Eventually the courts decided that the Sears-Goodyear contract was legal at the time of the FTC decision; but nonetheless, the case fueled anti-chain-store sentiment and played into the hands of those seeking legislation to restrict price discrimination.[56]

The Robinson-Patman Act, 1935–1936

Along with the tire dealers, wholesale grocers led the drive to limit quantity discounts. Like independent retailers, wholesalers had lost market share to the chain stores. Chain stores acted as wholesalers by performing the functions of distribution (shipping, warehousing, etc.), and like wholesalers, they received "functional" discounts from manufacturers. Organized wholesalers sought legislation to eliminate this competition. Thus, in May 1935, a lawyer for the United States Wholesale Grocers' Association (USWGA) drafted a bill to amend Section 2 of the Clayton Act. The proposed amendment protected the functional discounts of wholesalers while requiring manufacturers to cost-justify their discounts to chain stores. The bill offered a narrow definition of allowable cost savings; chain stores would have to pay a share of the manufacturer's total cost even if they did not use all of the services reflected in these costs. The authors of the bill still feared that discounts, even if they were justified, might be so large as to foster monopoly—congressional small business advocates cited the Goodyear-Sears contract as just such a case; therefore, they included a provision allowing the FTC to set a quantity limit on discounts.[57]

The wholesalers brought their bill to the attention of Representative Wright Patman (D.-Tex.), a fiery populist known for his hatred of big business. In April 1935, a Texarkana grocer approached Patman with the USWGA proposal in hand. The grocer told Patman that the wholesale grocers had chosen him to introduce this legislation because he was "an untiring worker and never know[s] defeat." Moreover, as chairman of a special committee investigating the lobbying activities of chain stores, Patman seemed the perfect vehicle for this legislation. Patman relished the opportunity to lead the anti-chain-store fight in Congress, and on 5 June 1935 he introduced the bill in the House.[58]

The measure also attracted the support of Democratic leaders in Congress and the approval of the Roosevelt administration. On June 23, Senate Majority Leader Joseph T. Robinson (D.-Ark.) offered a companion bill in the Senate. Robinson's endorsement reflected the popularity of the issue in the South. During the next year, other prominent southern politicians, including Representatives Millard Tydings (D.-Md.) and John E. Miller (D.-Ark.), helped push the bills through Congress. Popular support for anti-chain-store legislation was reaching its peak in the South, and these congressmen hoped to exploit the political potential of the issue. However, their support did not necessarily run very deep. After the election of 1936, Robinson admitted that his support of the bill was lukewarm at best. Historian Cecil Edward Weller Jr. suggests that President Franklin D. Roosevelt also had "lukewarm" feelings about the act but that he chose not to oppose Robinson because he needed the Senate majority leader's support in passing other New Deal measures. Likewise, other senators supported Robinson because he had the power to appoint them to influential committees.[59]

Although it began as a piece of special-interest legislation, the bill's sponsors offered the Robinson-Patman Act as a panacea for the ills afflicting small business and the nation at large. In the first place, Patman's bill gave expression to anti-chain-store sentiment. Like many of his rural constituents, the Texas congressman saw the chain store as part of a Wall Street conspiracy aimed at controlling the retail trade of the nation. Yet Patman and Robinson insisted that they did not seek the death of the chain store; they claimed that their legislation simply promoted "fairness" by making the same discounts available to all purchasers. Thus Patman stated that his bill would instill "the Golden Rule in business."[60]

The proponents of this legislation also considered the bill a partial substitute for the National Recovery Administration (NRA), which had recently been declared unconstitutional, and believed that by regulating discounts they might be able to finally end the Great Depression.[61] They based this hope on their assumption that the cost savings inherent in mass distribution did not justify chain store discounts. Patman argued that these discounts came out of the wages of workers and that, therefore, by prohibiting "unfair" price discrimination, his bill would increase purchasing power and help to revive the economy. Patman also predicted that the discounts once available to only a few chain stores would become available to all retailers and that as a result, consumers would benefit from lower prices.[62]

This view did not go unchallenged, however. As Robinson and Patman gathered support for their legislation, Representative Emanuel Celler (D.-N.Y.) led the opposition. Celler considered himself an advocate of small business but believed that the blatantly anticompetitive nature of the Patman bill violated the spirit of antitrust legislation. Celler dismissed the threat of a "chain store monopoly," noting that chains accounted for only a quarter of all retail sales. He cited the testimony of economists who predicted that the act would increase prices by preventing manufacturers from passing cost savings on to the consumer. Finally, Celler argued that Patman's bill would hurt small businesses because it would force the largest manufacturers to avoid price discrimination altogether by dealing with a few mass-distributors on a flat-price basis. Celler summarized his arguments by describing Patman's bill as "an antimanufacturers bill . . . an anticonsumer bill . . . an antifarmers bill. . . . It is an anti-almost everything" bill.[63]

Celler had the support of chain stores, manufacturers, consumer advocates, and nearly all economists. Initially, these groups reacted slowly to the threat of the Robinson-Patman Act; but once it became clear that Congress would pass Patman's bill, they quickly organized, and over the course of a year they succeeded in watering down the proposed legislation. Passed in June 1936, the final act allowed manufacturers to grant functional discounts to chain stores as well as wholesalers. Sellers still had to justify their quantity discounts, but Congress broadened the definition of allowable cost savings. The act also included a "good faith" defense to charges of illegal price discrimination (i.e., discounts were legal if made in good faith to meet the price of a competitor). The law prohibited discriminatory brokerage fees and forced sellers to make advertising allowances available to all purchasers. Violations of the act were a criminal offense.[64]

Like earlier antitrust legislation, the Robinson-Patman Act embodied a compromise among competing interests: it promised to preserve small business, enhance consumer welfare, and give due process to large chain stores and manufacturers. The act also applied a "rule of reason" by allowing manufacturers to make "reasonable" (i.e., cost-justified) discounts available to chain stores. The vague and ambiguous wording of the act meant that the Federal Trade Commission and the courts would have to define "reasonableness"; but congressional small business advocates did not intend to remain on the sidelines. In the coming years, they would encourage the FTC to vigorously enforce the law and, when necessary, to take sides with small business.

Assessing the Magna Charta of Small Business

Elements of crisis and ideology played important roles in determining the outcome of the debate over the Robinson-Patman Act. The depression of the 1930s, the greatest economic crisis of the twentieth century, provided a unique opportunity for congressional small business advocates to promote their ideology. By 1936, the federal government's efforts to cartelize the economy (through the National Recovery Administration) had failed to bring an end to the depression, and policymakers searched for new ways to revive the economy; thus, Patman's small business legislation represented one approach to the problem of economic stagnation. At the same time, the sudden appearance of chain stores in thousands of small towns across the nation sparked a movement designed to preserve a way of life. This combination of economic crisis and social unrest enabled the USWGA and its congressional allies to secure passage of the Robinson-Patman Act, the first piece of antitrust legislation that had been enacted into law in nearly a quarter century.

Legal scholars disagree over the congressional intent behind the passage of the Robinson-Patman Act. Robert H. Bork maintains that Congress primarily intended to promote the consumer welfare, but others argue that the sponsors of the act consciously placed the interests of small business above those of the consumer.[65] This chapter has shown, however, that most congressional small business advocates saw no conflict between the interests of small business and those of the consumer. The sponsors of the Robinson-Patman Act believed that by requiring manufacturers to cost-justify their discounts to mass-marketers, the bill would force American companies to stop granting "unfair" discounts to chain stores and start making greater discounts available to small merchants. The "level playing field" that resulted would, they believed, increase price competition and thereby benefit the consumer. But subsequent investigations demonstrated that manufacturers could indeed justify their discounts to mass-marketers; consequently, the interests of the consumer and small business could not be reconciled. Supporters of the Robinson-Patman Act would have to choose between the welfare of small business and that of the consumer.

2

Minnows Cannot Compete with Whales: The Politics of Small Business in the Tire Industry, 1936–1961

With the passage of the Robinson-Patman Act, congressional small business advocates shifted their focus to the politics of administration. This chapter examines their efforts to use the act on behalf of small business owners in the tire trade. The small business advocates remained concerned with the plight of the independent tire dealer, and they continued to champion the tire merchant as "a small-business man of classic caliber."[1] Thus, organized dealers and their allies in Congress pressured the Federal Trade Commission into using the Robinson-Patman Act to challenge the marketing practices of the nation's largest tire companies. In one important case, the FTC placed a ceiling on the discounts allowed for quantity purchases of tires. This case might have revolutionized the pricing structure of American business had the courts not overturned the government's order.

The radical potential of the small business ideology also became evident when President Franklin D. Roosevelt suspended America's antitrust laws during World War II. Small business advocates found themselves temporarily unable to use the Robinson-Patman Act, and they responded by seeking legislation to guarantee independent dealers the entire retail market for tires. Their failure to secure this legislation revealed some of the problems that continued to plague them in their efforts to aid small business. Like small business people in other trades, most tire dealers remained unorganized, politically apathetic, and divided among themselves. Independent dealers prospered without government aid and did not respond to the crisis rhetoric of congressional small business advocates. Conservative small business advocates also refused to support radical legislative measures in peacetime. Politicians on the left and right espoused rhetoric equating small business with "free enterprise," but the two sides differed over how far they would go to preserve small business.

The Business Response to the Robinson-Patman Act

The complex and ambiguous nature of the Robinson-Patman Act befuddled contemporary observers as well as later antitrust scholars, many of whom have criticized the imprecise language of this act. One scholar has described the act as "one of the most tortuous legislative pronouncements ever to go on the statute books" and "a cryptic and sloppy legislative enactment." Another has called it "the misshapen progeny of intolerable draftsmanship coupled to wholly mistaken economic theory."[2] Nonetheless, chain store opponents viewed the passage of the Robinson-Patman Act as a great victory for their cause, and declared it a "Magna Charta for small business," which marked "independence day for the independents."[3] The act caused confusion in the business community as executives struggled to understand a law described by a contemporary observer as "impossible of comprehension even for lawyers."[4] Patman responded to demands for clarification of the law's meaning by compiling a four-hundred-page book addressing the questions of businesspeople. As executives awaited the FTC's interpretation of the act, companies simplified their discount schedules and cut back on their advertising allowances and brokerage fees. A few chain stores tried to evade the act by purchasing raw materials and then handing them over to manufacturers to be processed.[5]

The Robinson-Patman Act had an immediate impact on the tire industry. Goodyear canceled its contract with Sears, and B. F. Goodrich terminated its agreement with Atlas Supply. (U.S. Rubber continued to produce Atlas tires, and several small companies stepped in to supply Sears). Meanwhile, at the request of the National Association of Independent Tire Dealers (NAITD), the FTC held a trade practice conference in June 1936. Tire manufacturers and distributors agreed to incorporate the provisions of the Robinson-Patman Act into a new set of rules governing the industry. Nevertheless, the tire companies still believed they could justify substantial price discriminations and therefore continued to offer quantity discounts of up to 30 percent.[6] Industry observers waited to see if the FTC would challenge these discounts by invoking the Robinson-Patman Act.

FTC Enforcement of Robinson-Patman
in the Late 1930s

Meanwhile, FTC officials hoped the Robinson-Patman Act would revive the flagging fortunes of their agency. During the early 1930s, the commission had lost much of its talent to other more important agencies, such as the National Recovery Administration (NRA). In those years, Washington's "best and brightest" avoided the FTC because they considered it weak and ineffective. The Robinson-Patman Act now strengthened the power of the FTC by restricting court rulings to the facts as determined by the agency. Yet although it had become more powerful on paper, the FTC still lacked the funds it needed to enforce the act aggressively. In its budget requests, the FTC noted that Robinson-Patman cases involved "expensive and time consuming" cost-accounting investigations, but Congress did not appropriate additional funds until May 1937.[7]

Nevertheless, supporters of the Robinson-Patman Act remained optimistic and hoped to take advantage of renewed popular interest in the problem of monopoly. Following the demise of the NRA in 1935, the small business ideology of Louis Brandeis had gained new adherents. The Brandeis camp now claimed the support of key administration officials, populist members of Congress, journalists, and academics. During the late 1930s, these antimonopolists reiterated their belief that price-fixing by big business had caused the depression and had led to the countervailing emergence of big labor, big agriculture, and big government. Thus, in 1937, Secretary of the Interior Harold Ickes warned that the United States would become a "Big Business Fascist America" unless the government renewed its campaign against monopoly.[8]

At the same time, a new breed of trustbuster, led by Thurman Arnold, the head of the Justice Department's Antitrust Division, championed antitrust policy as a powerful macroeconomic tool to stimulate the economy. Arnold drew heavily upon the work of such scholars as Adolf Berle and Gardiner Means, who coauthored The Modern Corporation and Private Property (1932), described by Time magazine as "the economic Bible of the Roosevelt administration." Berle and Means argued that too often corporations could "administer" prices without regard for consumer welfare.[9] Arnold believed that a renewed antitrust campaign would discourage price administering, increase competition, and lower prices—thus providing consumers with the purchasing power needed to lift the economy out of the depression. To achieve these results, Arnold launched a series of industrywide investigations directed at the distribution sector of the economy. His policy became "Hit hard, hit everyone, and hit them all at once."[10]

Much to the relief of corporate executives, the strident rhetoric of the anti-trusters did not translate into an indiscriminate attack on big business. During the late 1930s, the FTC lent a sympathetic ear to industry concern about the effects of the Robinson-Patman Act. In August 1936, FTC officials met with grocery manufacturers to "think out loud" about the agency's interpretation of the act. As it had done with earlier antitrust legislation, the FTC indicated that it would apply a "rule of reason" and accept all good-faith efforts to meet the law's requirements. The heads of America's largest companies welcomed this policy of "business as usual."[11]

Indeed, the FTC's early decisions in Robinson-Patman cases did not threaten the interests of big business. In July 1937, the commission dismissed price-discrimination complaints brought against Montgomery Ward and the Bird Company (a carpet manufacturer). Bird provided the commission with a cost analysis showing that the contract resulted in savings of 28 percent, while Ward's discount amounted to only 15 percent. Ironically, this case demonstrated that the so-called Magna Charta of small business might be a boon to big business. Mass-marketers applauded the decision and hoped that with new cost analyses they might receive discounts even larger than those available before the Robinson-Patman era.[12]

The irony was not confined to discounting; FTC enforcement of the Robinson-Patman Act worked to the detriment of small business in other ways as well. The agency avoided the expense involved in trying large companies for price discrimination and instead focused its attention on firms that were violating the brokerage clause of the act. This clause prohibited all discriminatory brokerage payments, and this made it easy to prosecute companies engaging in the practice. (The commission won all court appeals involving this provision of the law.) In effect, this policy targeted small business, because many small firms acted as brokers between buyers and sellers. The FTC charged these small brokerage firms with discrimination when they tried to attract customers by selectively lowering their fees. FTC enforcement of this clause also prevented cooperative groups of small business owners from achieving purchasing economies by eliminating the brokerage fee.[13]

The NAITD and its allies in Congress forced the FTC to act more vigorously in the tire industry. In 1938, the Senate Committee on Interstate Commerce called for an FTC investigation into the pricing practices of tire manufacturers. As a result of this investigation, the government took legal actions against several leading tire companies. In 1939, the government filed price-fixing charges against B. F. Goodrich and seventeen other companies. Between 1936 and 1938, the federal government received identical bids from these companies and claimed losses as a result of this collusion. For the first time ever, the U.S. government sought triple damages for itself under the Sherman Act. The tire companies set their prices in line with NRA minimums and claimed that they were simply following a pricing policy advocated by the government during the NRA period (ignoring, of course, the demise of that agency). In March 1940, the U.S. District Court for the Southern District of New York threw out the case on the grounds that the government was not a legal "person" due the protection of the Sherman Act. The government appealed, but the higher courts sustained the ruling.[14]

The FTC took several other actions against the tire manufacturers. In 1939, the commission ordered B. F. Goodrich, Goodyear, and Firestone to halt deceptive advertising campaigns. In that same year, the FTC ordered U.S. Rubber to stop making unjustified quantity discounts to large purchasers. But the company could still cost-justify some of its discounts, so the FTC's chief counsel recommended use of the quantity-limit clause of the Robinson-Patman Act to equalize the prices paid by large and small purchasers of tires. However, the tire manufacturers had responded to the FTC ruling in the U.S. Rubber case by narrowing the spread between the prices paid by small and large dealers; consequently, the FTC decided not to establish a quantity-limit rule for the industry.[15]

In the late 1930s, the FTC's administration of the Robinson-Patman Act generally reflected a continuation of earlier trends in its enforcement of antitrust legislation. Thus, much to the dismay of small business advocates, the agency continued to build a statistical track record of legal victories by prosecuting small firms. But when it came to challenging large corporations, the commission acted cautiously and adopted the traditional "rule of reason." The Robinson-Patman Act did, however, force the FTC to break with antitrust tradition in one important respect: by requiring manufacturers to justify their quantity discount schedules, the act encouraged companies to develop more sophisticated cost-accounting techniques. Yet ironically, this cost-accounting analysis demonstrated that manufacturers could justify large discounts to chain stores. Therefore, if small business advocates wished to further narrow the price differences between chain stores and independents, they would have to resort to the quantity-limit clause of the Robinson-Patman Act. The FTC came close to invoking this clause in the tire industry, but instead it adopted a wait-and-see attitude. In later years, small business advocates would reopen this issue and force the commission finally to decide whether to set a cap on the discounts allowed in the tire trade.

Small Business Legislation in the Late 1930s

During the late 1930s, small business advocates had become disappointed with the FTC's sporadic enforcement of the Robinson-Patman Act. At the same time, the congressional champions of small business lost several battles on the legislative front. In 1937, Congress passed the Miller-Tydings "Fair Trade" Act, which allowed manufacturers to fix minimum prices in order to protect small retailers from the price competition of chain stores, but the Roosevelt administration opposed the measure, and the FTC campaigned for its repeal. In 1938, Wright Patman introduced a tax bill designed as a "death sentence" for the chains, and for several years he waged a one-man campaign on its behalf; but Congress never voted on the measure, and President Franklin D. Roosevelt refused to support it. When it became clear that Roosevelt had no interest in taxing chains out of existence, Patman proposed freezing the number of chain store units by imposing a tax on new stores only. Administration officials continued to express their opposition to any federal tax on chain stores, however; and meanwhile, in Congress, Emanuel Celler led the opposition to Patman's bill, denouncing it as a crude attempt to "murder the chain stores."[16]

Other members of Congress, dissatisfied with the antitrust approach to the problems of small business, tried unsuccessfully to secure financial aid for small firms. In 1934, Congress had authorized the Reconstruction Finance Corporation and the Federal Reserve to make loans to businesses, but the conservative lending policies of these agencies limited the amount of funds available to small business. One critic noted that "if the struggling enterprise was strong enough to satisfy the requirements of the Reconstruction Finance Corporation . . . it was ordinarily easier to borrow privately." Similarly, the chairman of the Federal Reserve admitted that the powers granted to him in the area of small business financing were "almost useless." In the late 1930s, Senator James M. Mead (D.-N.Y.) introduced bills to remedy this situation, but his measures elicited a collective yawn from Congress.[17]

Clearly, by 1939 the political climate had changed dramatically since the passage of the Robinson-Patman Act in 1936. Congress had grown more conservative, especially after the 1937 recession and Roosevelt's ill-advised attempt to pack the Supreme Court. The growth of the chain stores had slowed by 1935, and during the latter half of the decade independent retailers increased their market share slightly. With the nation's recovery from the recession, improved economic conditions further dampened the resentment of many small business owners.[18]

The chain stores also acquired new political allies. A&P, the nation's largest

grocery chain, attracted the support of farmers and organized labor by marketing surplus crops and agreeing to unionize its stores. The company also
conducted a massive advertising campaign highlighting the chain store's benefits to the consumer. This campaign improved the image of the chain store,
and by 1939, the public opposed further anti-chain-store legislation. An opinion poll taken in that year showed that only 6 percent of Americans favored
measures designed to put the chains out of business.[19] Congressional small
business advocates could no longer rely on public sentiment to secure passage
of anti-chain-store legislation.

By the end of the decade, the so-called small business movement was losing
steam. Congress had considered hundreds of bills designed to aid small business but had enacted only a handful into law. Moreover, ten years of state and
federal legislation had failed to significantly alter the economic position of
small business. Although they lost some ground to independent retailers in the
later 1930s, over the course of the entire decade the share of retail sales held by
chain stores increased from 20 percent to 21.7 percent. Paradoxically, chain
taxes and other measures aimed at preserving small business encouraged the
chains to create supermarkets and other large retail units. This failure took its
toll on the small business advocates, and *Business Week* noted in the summer of
1939 that they had lost their old "fire eating enthusiasm."[20] It would take
another crisis to rekindle congressional interest in small business.

World War II: Renewed Interest in Small Business

The outbreak of war in Europe in 1939 further weakened the small business
movement by shifting the Roosevelt administration's attention from domestic
affairs to foreign policy. With America's entrance into World War II, President
Roosevelt lost interest in small business, as "Dr. New Deal" became "Dr. Win-
the-War." Roosevelt sought the cooperation of the nation's largest manufacturers because they could meet the demands of the war effort; therefore, in
March 1942, the president ordered his attorney general to suspend all antitrust
suits pending against these corporations. Later that year, Roosevelt wrote,
"This Small Business problem has baffled me . . . for nearly two years. We have
not met it—and I am not sure that it can be met."[21]

While the war led Roosevelt to abandon the cause of small business, it
sparked a renewed congressional concern with the fate of small business. In
1940 and 1941, the Senate and House created special Small Business Committees to respond to the criticism that small business had not received its "fair"
share of military contracts. The chairman of the Senate committee was James

Murray (D.-Mont.), a liberal New Dealer. The leader of the anti-chain-store movement, Wright Patman (D.-Tex.), presided over the House committee. Murray and Patman valued small business as a social institution but had little faith in the ability of small business to compete with big business. Thus, in 1941, Murray's committee concluded that "minnows cannot compete with whales"—that small business could not survive the war without government aid.[22]

The war galvanized small business advocates and led them to change their political strategy. By 1941, many members of the Small Business Committees had lost faith in the antitrust option. They criticized the FTC for not doing enough for small business and lambasted the Supreme Court for its conservative interpretation of antitrust legislation. President Roosevelt's suspension of the antitrust laws removed any remaining hope they may have had for an administrative solution to the problems of small business. The committees therefore focused their attention on securing positive aid for small business. In 1942, for example, they responded to the complaints of small manufacturers by securing the establishment of the Smaller War Plants Corporation (SWPC), the nation's first small business agency.[23]

The Small Business Committees were concerned with the fate of small retailers as well as with the futures of small manufacturers. Small firms predominated in retail trade, a sector of the economy particularly hard-hit by wartime regulations. The military buildup benefited manufacturers, both large and small, but retailers suffered because of the limits placed on civilian production. In 1942, the Small Business Committees introduced bills to provide financial assistance to firms that were dislocated by the war, but the military opposed measures that might detract from the war effort, and Congress enacted only one of these bills into law.[24]

Congressional small business advocates remained especially concerned with the plight of the independent tire dealer. In August 1941, the Senate Small Business Committee published a pessimistic report on the future of small business in the tire trade. The committee warned that the war would subject the industry to strict rationing. The nation's military machine ran on rubber; therefore, as the United States entered the war, the government ordered a cutback of 90 percent in the production of passenger tires. The Office of Price Administration (OPA) froze the market share of company-owned stores to prevent manufacturers from monopolizing the remaining tire trade, but the Small Business Committees demanded more radical measures. They insisted that because chain stores and manufacturers sold a variety of other products, they should hand their tire sales over to independent dealers. Thus, Wright

Patman and Senator Allen Ellender (D.-La.) drafted legislation to guarantee these dealers the entire replacement market for tires. The Ellender-Patman bills also authorized the appointment of a deputy administrator to oversee all government programs related to tires. This administrator could require the periodic inspection of tires through independent dealerships. Ellender and Patman temporarily withheld their bills in the hope that chain stores and manufacturers would voluntarily relinquish their shares of the tire market.[25]

The Senate Small Business Committee held hearings on the tire-selling issue in March 1942. The president of the National Association of Independent Tire Dealers, William M. Hickey, warned that independent dealers could not survive the war without government aid. Hickey also noted that Americans would have to repair their tires more frequently and argued that only independent dealers could provide this service in large and small towns. Thus, Hickey insisted that the Ellender-Patman bill would not only preserve small business but also help to maintain Americans' standard of living during the war.

The NAITD failed, however, to come up with a satisfactory definition of an "independent tire dealer." (Years later, a spokesman for the association would admit that "we are not sure just what constitutes an independent tire dealer.") Small business advocates could usually skirt the problem of defining "small" business, but the issue now caused a split in the ranks of independent tire dealers. The NAITD represented those small business owners who specialized in tire sales, but most dealers sold a diversified line of goods. (There are no available figures for the war years, but in 1953 only 3 percent of all tire dealers relied on tire sales for more than half of their business.) Service station owners, for example, complained that this legislation favored independent tire dealers at the expense of small business people in other fields.[26]

The organized tire dealers failed to attract the support of other small business associations, but they did secure the financial backing of J. P. Seiberling, the president of Seiberling Rubber Company. The Seiberling Company had a long-standing commitment to the independent tire dealer, and Seiberling believed that the small tire companies and small retailers shared a common enemy in big business.[27] Seiberling joined forces with George Burger, president of Burger Tire Consultant Service, and together the two men organized a lobbying effort in support of this legislation. During the first months of 1942, the Seiberling Company spent over $20,000 on this campaign. Seiberling placed advertisements in several trade journals and financed a direct mailing to 70,000 dealers urging them to support the measure. Burger also distributed 100,000 copies of a speech that Representative Walter Ploeser (R.-Mo.) had made in support of the tire bill.[28]

Although the Seiberling Company supported this legislation, the bill met with opposition from other tire manufacturers. Seiberling had hoped that the small tire companies would oppose the growth of chain stores and company-owned outlets, but he remained alone in his support of the tire bill, because many small manufacturers profited from their private-label contracts with chain stores and did not wish to lose this business.[29] Meanwhile, spokesmen for the Big Four united in opposition to this legislation. John L. Collyer, president of B. F. Goodrich, testified that his company was "deeply interested in the welfare of independent tire dealers" because they handled most of the company's tire sales. During the war the nation would need all of its available service facilities; therefore, Collyer argued, this legislation was not in the public interest. The president of Goodyear, Edwin J. Thomas, warned that this legislation would set a dangerous precedent and divide the small business community. He maintained that if Congress enacted this legislation, independent tire dealers would lose business because automobile dealers would demand the exclusive right to repair cars, and service station operators would demand a monopoly on all gasoline sales. Similarly, a Sears spokesman argued that the legislation would hurt those small manufacturers who produced for mass-distributors. A U.S. Rubber representative stated his company's opposition to the measure but recommended that the government purchase its own passenger tires from independent dealers.[30]

In May 1942, the Senate Small Business Committee met with tire manufacturers and dealers in Atlantic City, New Jersey, in a last-ditch effort to reach an agreement on measures to aid the industry's small business owners. When the tire companies still refused to relinquish their share of the tire trade, the committee issued a unanimous report in support of Ellender's bill, and the senator introduced his legislation on 1 June.[31] At this point, congressional small business advocates decided that radical measures were needed to see tire dealers through the end of the war.

The crisis atmosphere of wartime caused conservative small business advocates to abandon their usual opposition to direct government aid for business. The conservatives justified their action on the grounds that the government itself had created a crisis for the independent dealers by curtailing the production of tires. Perhaps the most telling comment came from Senator Alexander Wiley (R.-Wis.), who described himself as "not one of those who think you can cure economic ills by legislation. . . . But I think you can in a great emergency." During the war, liberal and conservative small business advocates found that they shared a common ground. Thus Senator Murray, a liberal Democrat, joined with "Mr. Republican," Robert A. Taft (R.-Ohio), in support of the bill drawn up by their colleague on the Small Business Committee. The politics of small business certainly made for strange bedfellows![32]

Despite this promising start, it soon became clear that the tire dealers were fighting a lost cause. According to Seiberling, President Roosevelt continued to stonewall the issue, and many members of the Small Business Committees "were just fooling around for some front-page publicity" as they campaigned for reelection. In November, the Senate Banking and Currency Committee approved the legislation, but the Democratic leadership postponed further consideration of the bills until after the elections.[33] Thus, although supporters of the tire bill stressed the urgency of the situation, they failed to convince either the president or the Congress to move quickly in resolving it.

The Senate Small Business Committee resumed hearings on the tire bill in the spring of 1943, but by then the sense of crisis had passed. In 1943, the OPA authorized increases in the production of passenger tires, and within one year the industry's output of tires reached approximately half its prewar level. Yet consumer demand for tires still exceeded the supply, and many independent tire dealers found that they could sell tires at or near list price. At the same time, the tire manufacturers wanted to protect their primary channel of distribution, so during the war they offered tire dealers various forms of assistance, including financing and advice on store layout. The tire manufacturers also encouraged dealers to diversify into more profitable lines, including automobile services and electrical appliances. Firestone, for example, allowed its dealers to participate in its mail-order business; the company's wartime catalog listed over three thousand items, including waffle irons, luggage, wallpaper, and sports equipment. This policy of diversification helped boost the wartime profits of independent tire dealers, and by the end of the war they enjoyed a net profit rate double that of the prewar period.[34]

The prosperity of the tire dealers undercut the NAITD's crisis appeals; therefore, the association shifted its attack to the company-owned store by claiming that the tire manufacturers operated these outlets at a loss in order to increase their market share at the expense of the independent dealer. The NAITD also criticized the tire manufacturers for alleged price discriminations favoring their company stores. As Congress heard testimony related to this issue, the association found an unexpected ally in William Jeffers, director of the War Production Board's Rubber Division. Jeffers testified that he was "rather sympathetic with the independent tire dealer" because they had provided invaluable service during the war and that therefore he had "no objection" to the tire bill.[35] Jeffer's endorsement offered a glimmer of hope to the sponsors of this legislation, but they would need even stronger backing in order for their bill to become law.

The tire bill continued to meet with stiff opposition from the tire manufacturers, the chain stores, the oil companies, and the National Association of Manufacturers. Spokesmen for the Big Four emphasized the prosperity of independent tire dealers. A Goodyear representative predicted that his company's dealers could expect a doubling of sales in 1943. He also warned of the dangers inherent in "class legislation" that threatened the interests of the consumer. J. W. Keener, the director of business research for B. F. Goodrich, defended his company's operation of retail outlets. Keener insisted that company stores posed no real threat to the independent dealer because they still accounted for less than a tenth of the tire market. Keener also countered charges of price discrimination by citing evidence that the resale prices of independent dealers were lower than those of the average company store. In fact, Keener argued, Goodrich preferred to distribute through independent dealers and opened retail outlets only when faced with inadequate dealer representation.[36]

In the spring of 1943, opponents of this legislation gained a new ally in Senator Taft. Taft spoke out against this tire bill (S. 1122) because, unlike the legislation introduced in 1942 (S. 2560), the 1943 bill would give independent dealers a *permanent* monopoly of the tire trade. From the beginning, Taft had taken a middle-of-the-road position on the issue; he admitted to B. F. Goodrich president John Collyer that the dealers' "complaints are overstated." Nonetheless, he remained concerned with "unfair and excessive" competition in the tire industry. Taft feared that if the tire companies monopolized the retail trade during the war, the public would clamor for government takeover and regulation of the industry. He also questioned the benefits of company-owned stores, noting that the Big Four had reluctantly entered the retail end of the trade in response to chain store competition in the 1930s. Taft asked the companies voluntarily to agree to "a gradual retirement from the retail business," but meanwhile he worked to help the Big Four defeat the tire bill.[37]

Eventually Seiberling became disillusioned with the constant legislative delays, and he too halted his lobbying efforts in support of the tire legislation. A frustrated Seiberling concluded that the "legislative approach" was "hopeless" because the tire dealers remained politically apathetic and divided among themselves. "The trouble," Seiberling wrote, "is that there are not enough of them and, such as they are, they do not control enough votes."[38] Seiberling had also become disgusted with "two-faced, yellow streak, double talking legislators."[39] He still longed for a return to the "good old days" when independent dealers held the entire tire market, but he had lost all hope in the ability of Congress to act on small business legislation.[40] Seiberling believed that Congress refused to act because other small business owners would demand similar legislation and politicians simply did not want to face pressure from all types of retailers.[41] Senator Murray had also begun to use his Small Business Committee to promote liberal causes, and Seiberling, a conservative Republican, refused to work with the "Left Wing New Dealers" on Murray's staff.[42]

The Banking and Currency Committees continued to hold hearings on the tire legislation through the end of the war, but Congress never voted on the measures. Nonetheless, contrary to the rhetoric of the small business advocates, independent tire dealers prospered without government aid; in fact, between 1941 and 1946 they increased their market share from 48 percent to 52 percent. The opponents of small business legislation pointed to this gap between rhetoric and reality. When the Senate held hearings on yet another tire bill in 1946, B. F. Goodrich attorney John A. Danaher noted that "the independent tire dealers never had three better years . . . than they had in 1943, 1944, 1945." Danaher opposed this legislation and recommended that the government use the Robinson-Patman Act to deal with monopolistic practices.[43] The small business advocates agreed; in the postwar period they renewed their antitrust campaign and deemphasized their efforts to directly aid independent tire dealers.

The tire bills introduced during World War II represented an unsuccessful attempt to restructure a single line of trade to benefit one group of small business owners. The outcome of this legislation demonstrated the limits of a style of politics based solely on crisis rhetoric and the ideological appeal of small business. The prosperity of independent tire dealers belied the crisis rhetoric of George Burger and the NAITD. Their legislation also divided the small business community by pitting service station owners against tire dealers, while large manufacturers and chain stores united in opposition. Furthermore, the debate over this legislation resulted in a split among congressional small business advocates, since the conservatives' conception of the small business ideology led them to oppose any permanent restructuring of the tire trade. Supporters of the tire bill also lost the support of President Roosevelt when he responded to the wartime crisis by seeking the cooperation of big business. In the years after the war, however, organized tire dealers found a more favorable audience with Roosevelt's successor, President Harry S. Truman.

The Postwar Revival of Antitrust

In the immediate postwar period, members of the congressional Small Business Committees called for stricter antitrust enforcement in lieu of legislative measures to aid independent tire dealers. With the wartime crisis over, conservative small business advocates withdrew their support for the tire bill. Senator Taft reiterated his opposition to this legislation, because he "always thought it went too far," and instead he called for vigorous enforcement of the Robinson-Patman Act as a way to regulate the tire trade without sacrificing free market principles.[44]

Liberal small business advocates also urged President Truman to revive the antitrust option. In 1946, Senator Murray vowed that his Small Business Committee would continue its "death struggle" with the evils of big business. At the same time, the House Small Business Committee's Subcommittee on Monopoly, chaired by Estes Kefauver (D.-Tenn.), issued a report that concluded that big business had benefited disproportionately from the wartime boom. Large tire manufacturers, for example, increased their share of the industry's employment from 39 percent to 45 percent. The Kefauver report criticized the performance of the government's antitrust agencies, claiming that the Justice Department and the FTC had ignored "serious areas of concentration" while focusing on minor cases involving small firms. The report also criticized the FTC, the Justice Department, the Commerce Department, and the Reconstruction Finance Corporation for failing to coordinate their activities. The subcommittee stated, "There is probably less real joint action between these four agencies than there is between the four leading producers in a concentrated industry."[45]

Kefauver's subcommittee asked the FTC to conduct economic studies to establish an "Official Index of Concentration." The committee also called for an amendment to the Clayton Act that would allow the government to break up monopolies resulting from the acquisition of corporate assets. (Under current law, the government could only challenge stock acquisitions.) Last, Kefauver asked Congress to give the FTC the power to forbid mergers and acquisitions above a certain size. These measures, Kefauver argued, would prevent any further increases in industrial concentration.[46]

The renewed interest in antitrust policy was not confined to Congress. The trustbusters also enjoyed the support of President Truman, who was himself a former small business owner and an avowed "advocate of small business."[47] Although Truman admired the work of Louis Brandeis, he later explained that his interest in antitrust matters stemmed not from books but from his "own desire to aid small business."[48] As a Missouri senator, Truman had chaired the Special Committee Investigating the National Defense (the "Truman Committee"), which highlighted the wartime problems of small business. During the war, Truman "saw cliques in labor and in capital, each greedy for gain, while small production plants by the hundreds were being pushed aside and kept inactive by big business."[49] Truman carried a concern for small business into the Oval Office. During his first term in office, Truman appointed several small business advocates to the Federal Trade Commission, including James M. Mead, a former New York senator and one-time member of the Small Business Committee. (Mead became chairman of the commission in 1949.) Thus, under Truman the FTC came to consider itself "the servant of the interests of small business."[50]

Truman also scored several victories on the legislative front. Although he met with opposition from a budget-conscious Congress, he succeeded in more than tripling the government's expenditures on antimonopoly cases. This increased funding enabled the administration to respond to the 1949 recession by increasing the number of antitrust suits, in the hope that this renewed campaign might lead to greater competition and lower prices. In his second term, Truman also vetoed bills designed to weaken the Robinson-Patman Act and backed the passage of the Celler-Kefauver Act (1950), an amendment to the Clayton Act that closed the loophole allowing companies to evade the antitrust laws by purchasing the assets of a company. More than any other piece of antitrust legislation, this act discouraged companies from forming horizontal mergers between firms in the same industry. In short, by the end of Truman's term in office, the FTC could report that "the Commission has recovered its wartime losses."[51]

Antitrust Activity in the Tire Industry, 1947–1957

As they waged their postwar campaign against big business, the antitrusters again targeted the tire industry. George Burger and the NAITD criticized the FTC for failing to ensure compliance with its cease-and-desist orders. The NAITD now considered the "tire industry situation" a "Department of Justice case," and in 1946 it convinced the Justice Department's Antitrust Division to begin an investigation of the tire industry. Justice Department officials expressed the hope that this and other investigations of price-fixing by large corporations in the meatpacking, aluminum, oil, and steel industries would help to constrain further price increases and thus reduce the high rate of postwar inflation. The investigation of the tire industry would eventually lead to the most radical attempt yet to use the Robinson-Patman Act on behalf of small business.[52]

After completing its investigation in August 1947, the Justice Department charged the Rubber Manufacturers' Association and six tire companies with price-fixing and price discriminations dating back to the late 1930s. But the results of this case disappointed the NAITD. Both the Justice Department and the tire companies considered it a "stale case" because the alleged violations took place a decade earlier, and for this reason they reached an out-of-court settlement. The government accepted a plea of *nolo contendere* (no contest) from the defendants, dropped the case against individual executives, and imposed nominal fines.[53]

The Justice Department also disappointed NAITD officials by refusing to act on their request for civil action; consequently, in October 1948 the NAITD filed a private antitrust suit seeking an injunction against alleged violations of the Robinson-Patman Act. The NAITD claimed that the tire companies had narrowed the profit margins of independent dealers by agreeing on uniform discounts and sought damages of $4.2 million on behalf of its members. The case dragged on in the courts, however, and in 1952 the NAITD finally settled for an unstated amount of money.[54]

Meanwhile, as the NAITD pressured the Justice Department, the House Small Business Committee urged the FTC to begin an investigation of the tire industry. In May 1947, the chairman of the committee, Walter G. Ploeser (R.-Mo.), requested that the FTC look into allegations of illegal price discrimination. Ploeser hoped the FTC would join with the Justice Department in "eliminating the monopoly problems in the industry." Specifically, he asked the FTC to invoke the quantity-limit clause of the Robinson-Patman Act. The act's author, Wright Patman, had always considered this provision of the law the most powerful weapon against price discrimination because it prevented sellers from offering a cost-justification defense. If the buyers in an industry were objectionably "few," the FTC could set a limit on discounts. Ploeser, Patman, and other members of the Small Business Committee hoped that the establishment of a discount limit in the tire industry would "set a pattern for similar action in other industries." Thus they sought to use the Robinson-Patman Act to restructure the American economy.[55]

Pressure from congressional small business advocates and from a pro–small business president convinced the FTC, which had never invoked this clause, to consider the establishment of a quantity-limit rule for the tire industry, and during the summer of 1947 the commission requested sales information from the nation's tire manufacturers. The intent behind this investigation was clear: the chief counsel for the FTC, W. T. Kelley, noted that the quantity-limit proceedings were "directed generally toward helping the small business man, a problem which is uppermost in the minds of the Congress and the administration."[56]

The FTC's investigation sparked a lengthy debate within the agency about the merits of the quantity-limit rule. In his study of the FTC of the 1970s, Robert Katzmann describes an agency divided between prosecution-minded lawyers and consumer-oriented economists.[57] This same conflict occurred when the FTC considered whether to establish a discount limit. The head of the Bureau of Industrial Economics, Corwin D. Edwards, did not think the FTC's findings warranted such action. Whereas proponents of the rule believed a "bilateral oligopoly" existed between the largest tire manufacturers and distributors, Edwards accepted evidence provided by the Big Four showing that small manufacturers supplied the mass-marketers with tires. On the other hand, the FTC's chief antimonopoly lawyer, Everett MacIntyre, argued for the establishment of a discount limit because "doubts must be resolved in favor of action." (MacIntyre also had a personal interest in the Robinson-Patman Act: in 1935 he had helped Wright Patman draft this legislation, and he continued to favor its vigorous enforcement.)[58]

This time the lawyers won their case. On 28 September 1949, the FTC responded to congressional pressure by announcing that it would hold hearings on a proposed limit on tire discounts.[59] Under the proposed rule, a seller could not grant a higher discount for purchases exceeding a 20,000-pound carload of tires. The tire manufacturers claimed that they would suffer "irreparable injury" and sought a court injunction to halt further action by the FTC, but the court ruled that the tire companies had to exhaust all administrative remedies before appealing for judicial relief.[60]

As the FTC conducted hearings on the issue in January and February 1950, it soon became clear that the proposed rule did not entirely please the tire dealers. The NAITD opposed the single-shipment ceiling on discounts and instead favored the establishment of an annual volume limit because it would conform to present practices in the industry. (The FTC believed that a cumulative volume limit would lessen competition by forcing buyers to purchase from only one seller.)[61] On the other hand, George Burger, spokesman for the National Federation of Independent Business (NFIB), endorsed the FTC's proposed rule because he believed that the government needed to take immediate action to reverse "the increasing mortality" among independent tire dealers.[62]

Organized tire dealers tried once again to promote the notion of a big business threat to their welfare. In the 1930s, they had considered the chain store "the merchandising Frankenstein" of the industry, but during the war the market share of the chains dropped from 20 percent to 14 percent. Thus, in the postwar period, the NAITD found a new bogey in the oil company. Under the "override" system of distribution, manufacturers paid a commission to oil companies that promoted the sale of their tires to service stations. During the war, the oil companies used this sales commission plan to increase their share of the tire market from 15 percent to 23 percent; consequently, the NAITD complained that "the tire manufacturers are turning over their distribution to the oil companies."[63]

Opponents of the rule challenged the crisis rhetoric of George Burger and the NAITD. The FTC emphasized the decline of the independent dealers' market share from 91 percent in 1926 to 51 percent in 1947, but the tire companies challenged the agency's statistics by pointing out that the 1926 definition of an "independent tire dealer" encompassed many types of retail outlets (including grocery stores!). The government's current statistics, on the other hand, excluded many independents. If the FTC included service station operators in the category of independent tire dealers, tire officials argued, the market share of the independents would jump to 77 percent.[64] Dr. Warren W. Leigh, a marketing expert and consultant for the tire companies, also demonstrated that independent dealers enjoyed high profits and a low failure rate. The oil companies had increased their market share, but they did so at the expense of chain stores. Finally, Leigh warned that the ruling would harm those large independents who normally purchased in lots above the 20,000-pound limit, and he estimated that the ruling would adversely affect a quarter of the independent dealers.[65]

Leigh was not the only one to point out that unintended consequences might result from a quantity limit. A Montgomery Ward spokesman claimed that the limit would not apply to the "override" system and therefore would actually favor the oil companies at the expense of other tire distributors.[66] B. F. Goodrich attorney Lowell Wadmond also noted that oil companies and chain stores could evade the rule by producing their own tires.[67] Thus, this small business measure might actually harm independent tire dealers.

Meanwhile, as the representatives of large manufacturers and distributors united against the proposed limit, seventeen of the smaller tire manufacturers gathered to discuss their response to the FTC's proposed discount rule. These companies formed an informal trade group, because they believed the Big Four dominated the Rubber Manufacturers Association. Nevertheless, they too felt threatened by the proposed limit, and J. P. Seiberling warned that the establishment of such a rule "could well be the beginning of the end of free enterprise in the USA."[68]

The arguments of the tire manufacturers failed to sway the FTC. On 4 January 1952, the commission issued Quantity Limit Rule 203-1, which established the discount ceiling on tire purchases. The commission linked the drop in the market share of independent dealers to the decline in the number of small tire manufacturers by arguing that sixty-three "large" buyers (defined as those purchasing at least $600,000 worth of tires annually) did most of their business with large tire manufacturers, thus forming a "bilateral oligopoly." The agency found that these large buyers paid approximately 30 percent less for their tires, and it asserted that this price discrimination threatened to "destroy the business of many small buyers." The FTC believed the quantity-limit rule would break up this bilateral oligopoly and halt the decline in the market share of independent dealers.[69]

Commissioner Lowell B. Mason vigorously dissented from the FTC's decision.[70] According to Mason, the FTC had denied the tire companies a fair hearing, because the commission would not reveal the data underlying its findings. The Big Four provided figures showing that they sold most of their tires to small purchasers, but the FTC did not bother to refute this evidence. On the other hand, the FTC based its own evidence on "fragmentary facts" gathered from questionnaires and four days of public hearings. Mason also cited the legislative history of the Robinson-Patman Act, which suggested that Congress was concerned with a situation where one or two buyers controlled an entire market.[71] In this case, however, sixty-three "large" buyers purchased less than 30 percent of all replacement tires—hardly an oligopoly. At any rate, Mason argued, the FTC defined a concentration of buyers in terms of their *annual* volume of purchases, but it applied the limit to *single* shipments.[72]

Mason's dissent anticipated the criticisms of many businesspeople, economists, and lawyers. Industry analysts feared the ruling would prevent manufacturers from passing their cost savings on to consumers. Others criticized the FTC for its sloppy handling of a case that promised to revolutionize business practices. Corwin Edwards concluded that "the evidence was slight, the diagnosis was slighter, and the exploration of possible alternatives substantially nonexistent."[73] One observer noted that "the implications of the Commission's new Rule are staggering," and *Business Week* expressed fear that the rule could set a dangerous precedent and "bring on a pricing revolution in many other industries."[74]

The FTC's decision divided the tire industry. A spokesman for the NAITD rejoiced at the news, declaring that it would "change the entire marketing structure" of the tire industry. George Burger predicted that the rule would "go far to destroy monopoly domination in rubber."[75] The tire manufacturers reacted with stunned disbelief. B. F. Goodrich attacked the order, describing it as "unsupported by facts, contrary to law, and detrimental to the interests of the Company, its customers, and the public." Goodrich joined Goodyear,

Firestone, and U.S. Rubber in filing a court complaint charging that the rule was invalid because the FTC had not issued it in accordance with the Administrative Procedure Act of 1946, a law that regulated the hearings and procedures of all federal agencies. The tire manufacturers also challenged the factual basis for the ruling and claimed that the FTC had denied them due process by not allowing them to cross-examine witnesses at the commission's hearings.[76]

Recent court decisions suggested that the tire companies would receive a favorable hearing. Before 1949, the Supreme Court had upheld FTC orders under the Robinson-Patman Act, but since then the Court had begun to sympathize with the concerns of business; indeed, Justice Robert H. Jackson described the act as "complicated and vague . . . almost beyond understanding."[77] In the early 1950s, the Court had overturned several FTC orders involving the Robinson-Patman Act. In 1950, for example, the FTC charged the Standard Oil Companies with attempting to use their buying power to extract illegal discounts on the purchase of tires, batteries, and accessories. Although these companies had acted in good faith to meet the price of a competitor, the FTC held that good faith did not justify price discriminations that "substantially lessened" competition. However, in *Standard Oil of Indiana* (1951) the Court applied the "rule of reason" and decided that good faith constituted a complete defense to charges of price discrimination, even if the alleged violations of the law lessened competition. Ironically, the good-faith provision of the Robinson-Patman Act proved to be the Achilles heel of a law intended to limit competition.[78]

Thus the tire manufacturers had reason to be optimistic about the outcome of their quantity-limit case. Initially, the district court hearing the case decided that it lacked jurisdiction over a matter it considered the proper concern of the FTC; but on 16 July 1953, the appeals court reversed this ruling and remanded the case to the lower court for a trial on the merits.[79] The FTC hoped to sustain the district court's ruling by appealing directly to the Supreme Court, but the solicitor general refused to grant the agency's request. Finally, in September 1955, the district court threw out the quantity-limit rule on the grounds that a single shipment limit had no logical relation to the FTC's finding that only a few buyers exceeded a certain level of *annual* sales. The FTC appealed the case, but the higher court upheld the decision. The FTC never again invoked this controversial clause of the Robinson-Patman Act.[80]

The quantity-limit case demonstrated the ability of organized interests to join together with members of Congress to influence the FTC's policymaking.

Organized tire dealers and their congressional allies, in particular, benefited from President Truman's appointment of small business advocates to the commission, which predisposed the agency to favor measures designed to aid small firms. Yet the commission was more than a passive instrument prodded by special interests; agency officials did debate the merits of a quantity limit on discounts. Eventually, the FTC's lawyers overcame the opposition of agency economists who considered a quantity limit detrimental to consumer welfare. But the lawyers failed to carefully draft a quantity-limit rule that might have survived a court challenge. They lost their case because of the logically inconsistent way in which they formulated a limit on discounts.

President Dwight D. Eisenhower and Antitrust

As the quantity-limit case worked its way through the courts, the Robinson-Patman Act came under attack from the executive branch of the government. When Dwight D. Eisenhower came to office in 1953, the legal community had reached a consensus that the antitrust laws needed revision. In an influential essay, law professor S. Chesterfield Oppenheim called for the establishment of a blue-ribbon panel to examine the effects of antitrust legislation; and in June 1953, Eisenhower's attorney general, Herbert Brownell, established the Attorney General's National Committee to Study the Antitrust Laws (AGNC). Chaired by Oppenheim and Stanley Barnes (assistant attorney general in charge of the Antitrust Division), the committee consisted of corporate lawyers and prominent economists (including Morris Adelman, George Stigler, and Alfred Kahn). In its final report, the AGNC called for stricter enforcement of the antitrust laws but also emphasized the anticompetitive nature of the Robinson-Patman Act and offered suggestions for how to make the law fit with "overall antitrust policy." The committee recommended abolition of the quantity-limit rule, which it described as "a crude form of price-fixing by administrative fiat," and supported legislation designed to strengthen the good-faith defense to charges of illegal price discrimination. The AGNC also criticized the strict accounting rules required for a cost-justification defense to charges of price discrimination. The great expense involved in meeting the FTC's accounting requirements meant that "only the most prosperous and patient business firm could afford pursuit of an often illusory defense"; for this reason, the AGNC asked the FTC to allow reasonable approximations of cost.[81]

Congressional small business advocates reacted strongly to these proposals to reform the "Magna Charta of small business." The chairman of the Senate

Small Business Committee, John Sparkman (D.-Ala.), denounced the AGNC and claimed that its findings represented "laissez-faire in full bloom" and "a shocking short-sale" of small business.[82] In late 1955, the House Small Business Committee also held hearings to attack the committee's findings. A spokesman for the NAITD (now known as the National Tire Dealers and Retreaders Association, or NTDRA) claimed that the AGNC's recommendations would weaken the position of independent tire dealers.[83] Wright Patman lashed back at the AGNC, characterizing it as "a group of . . . big corporation lawyers who are four-time losers in antitrust prosecutions," and declared that if enacted, the committee's recommendations would "wreck the Robinson-Patman Act."[84]

Patman also joined other Democrats on the committee in criticizing FTC chairman Edward Howrey's handling of the quantity-limit case. Before his appointment to the Federal Trade Commission, Howrey had represented Firestone on the case, and the Democrats claimed that as FTC chairman he had persuaded the solicitor general not to appeal to the Supreme Court. (Howrey denied the charge and later produced evidence that he had urged the solicitor general to appeal the case.) The issue split the House Small Business Committee along partisan lines as the Republicans charged the Democrats with launching an unfair attack on the president, his appointee, and the members of the AGNC, whom the Republicans described as "men of proven caliber and experience."[85]

Congressional Democrats mistakenly assumed that Eisenhower wanted to weaken the antitrust laws to favor big business at the expense of small business.[86] But in fact, Eisenhower favorably viewed antitrust enforcement as an alternative to direct regulation of industry, because he worried that as we "depend more and more upon the regulatory commission, we are departing from the system laid down in our Constitution."[87] During his presidency, the Justice Department prosecuted a record number of companies for antitrust violations, and for the first time the government made corporate executives serve jail time for their violations of the Sherman Act. The FTC also dramatically increased its Robinson-Patman complaints and set up a Division of Small Business to advise small business owners on antitrust matters.[88] In his second term, Eisenhower asked Congress to pass legislation designed to strengthen the antitrust agencies.[89] According to Eisenhower, corporate executives complained that the administration was "too harsh on big business," and he maintained that the strict enforcement of the antitrust laws resulted in a decline of political donations to the GOP.[90]

Nevertheless, this new antitrust campaign did not represent a full-scale assault on big business. *Business Week* noted that "the Republicans are making it easier for the businessman who is up on the FTC carpet." The agency demanded more evidence from its prosecutors, and in Robinson-Patman Act cases the commission required proof that an alleged price discrimination actually lessened competition. The FTC emphasized voluntary compliance and made extensive use of consent decrees and premerger clearances. In the rubber industry, for example, the FTC reached out-of-court settlements in several cases involving companies in the footwear and sponge markets.[91]

The tire industry, however, remained a target of antitrust prosecutors. As early as 1941, the Senate Small Business Committee had expressed its concern with "the tire manufacturer–oil company tie up," and after conducting hearings on the issue in 1955, the committee urged the FTC to take action.[92] In January 1956, the FTC declared the "override" system an unfair method of competition prohibited by the Federal Trade Commission Act, and it challenged commission arrangements between Goodyear and Atlantic Refining, B. F. Goodrich and Texaco, and Firestone and Shell Oil. The FTC charged the oil companies with coercing their dealers into carrying only their products. In the Goodyear case, the Seventh Circuit Court ruled in favor of the FTC, concluding that the "service station dealer is more of an economic serf than a businessman free to purchase the T.B.A. [tire, battery, or accessory] of his choice." Goodyear and Atlantic appealed the case to the Supreme Court, which upheld the FTC order. The courts likewise accepted the FTC's orders against the other tire and oil companies.[93]

The FTC also took industrywide action against unfair trade practices. In June 1959, the FTC charged fifteen tire companies and two of their trade associations with price-fixing violations of the Federal Trade Commission Act. The government charged the companies with collusive price leadership, identical bidding on government contracts, and deceptive advertising practices; yet the FTC added little to the evidence it had exhibited in the 1948 case. The tire manufacturers again pleaded no contest, and on 11 January 1962, the companies signed a consent decree whereby they agreed to adopt new price lists and discount schedules.[94]

Meanwhile, congressional small business advocates responded to the National Tire Dealer and Retreader Association's complaints that the tire manufacturers were opening retail outlets in response to renewed competition in the replacement market. (Between 1957 and 1961, the number of retail outlets operated by the Big Four increased 25 percent.)[95] In June 1959, the House Commerce Committee and a Senate subcommittee chaired by Hubert Humphrey (D.-Minn.) held hearings on "equal pricing" bills that would prohibit manufacturers from delivering products at a lower price to company-owned stores. Testifying in support of this legislation, a spokesman for the NTDRA claimed that "direct selling practices" constituted "unfair competition" because the manufacturers allegedly operated these outlets at a loss.[96] George Burger testified that company stores involved "not just competition" but "plain economic murder" of the independent tire dealers, and he cited a survey showing that all of B. F. Goodrich's dealers believed that the company's outlets undersold them.[97]

As the chief sponsor of this legislation, Hubert Humphrey argued that Congress should place the interests of small business above those of the consumer. If the lowest price to the consumer was all that mattered, Humphrey argued, then a few companies could run the entire economy by selling directly to the consumer. Thus, like many congressional legislators, Humphrey valued small business as a social institution but had little faith in the ability of small business owners to compete in the marketplace.[98]

The "equal pricing" bills met with opposition from the tire manufacturers and the Eisenhower administration. B. F. Goodrich's director of business research, Karl Nygaard, noted that his company and its rivals continued to rely on independent dealers for the distribution of tires. Nygaard denied charges of price discrimination and countered Burger's testimony by citing a Goodrich survey showing that independent dealers actually sold tires at a lower price than the company stores.[99] Speaking for the administration, Undersecretary of Commerce F. H. Mueller stated that this legislation was "diametrically opposed" to the antitrust laws because it would eliminate price competition. Similarly, FTC chairman Earl Kintner extolled the benefits to the consumer that resulted from "competing methods of distribution."[100] The small business advocates could not overcome this administration opposition; consequently, their measures died in committee.[101]

Under President Eisenhower, the FTC no longer based its policies on an automatic suspicion of big business motives. Yet contrary to the predictions of many critics, the FTC continued to actively pursue complaints of price discrimination against small business. The commission also responded to the pleas of small business owners by eliminating the commission arrangement between tire manufacturers and oil companies, thus affecting the distribution of nearly one-quarter of the tire market. But at the same time, administration officials were also concerned with the consumer welfare; therefore they opposed measures, such as the "equal pricing" bills, that limited price competition. In short, the Eisenhower administration adopted a middle-of-the-road approach to antitrust enforcement by attempting to balance the interests of small business, big business, and the consumer.

The Declining Significance of the
Robinson-Patman Act

The Eisenhower years marked the apogee of governmental activity on behalf of the independent tire dealers.[102] Over the next several years, Humphrey and others introduced legislation designed to limit vertical integration in the tire industry, but they were no more successful than their predecessors.[103] The small business advocates also continued to urge the FTC to use the Robinson-Patman Act to alter the marketing structure of the industry. On 19 June 1961, the act's silver anniversary, George Burger and the NTDRA joined the House Small Business Committee in looking forward to the next quarter century and expressed their hope that the government would continue "its current, stepped-up activity to enforce the Robinson-Patman Act."[104] President John F. Kennedy promised to act as vigorously as Eisenhower had, but the courts grew hostile and the FTC lacked the funds needed to enforce the law. Furthermore, during the late 1960s, the FTC became more concerned with merger cases and transferred staff from its Robinson-Patman division to its merger section.[105]

Proponents of the Robinson-Patman Act also faced an increasingly hostile intellectual climate. In 1968, a White House Task Force on Antitrust Policy condemned the act for its "unintended anticompetitive effects."[106] One year later, the administration of Richard M. Nixon and the ABA issued reports that were critical of the act. Nearly all economists favored the law's repeal, and this intellectual consensus influenced the policymaking of the FTC. (Harold Demsetz notes that "the absence of 'captors' encourages [the FTC] to be overly influenced by the scribbling of academics.")[107] Economists dominated the FTC, and during the 1970s they began to attack the Robinson-Patman Act; one FTC economist said, "You could put all pro-Robinson-Patman economists in a Volkswagen and still have room for a chauffeur"![108] The same critical attitude prevailed at the Justice Department. In 1975, the head of the Justice Department's Antitrust Division concluded that the only positive effect of the act was that it "provides a full employment program for antitrust lawyers and professors—and provides comic relief for law students."[109]

In the 1960s and 1970s, consumer activists also began to influence the federal government's antitrust policy. President Nixon hoped to gather the support of consumer groups by appointing opponents of the Robinson-Patman Act to the Federal Trade Commission; consequently, during his presidency, the FTC pursued a policy of "deliberate neglect." Between 1960 and 1973, the number of Robinson-Patman complaints issued by the FTC plummeted from 144 to one. Congressional small business advocates had few friends left in the Federal Trade Commission.

Finally, as a child of the Great Depression, the Robinson-Patman Act fell victim to the changed economic climate of the 1970s. In 1975, President Gerald Ford asked the Justice Department to study the question of whether repealing the act might help to restrain inflation. The House Small Business Committee hurriedly held hearings to defend the act; yet while Congress never repealed the law, presidents since then have appointed opponents of the act to the FTC. Thus the "Magna Charta of small business" remains a dead-letter law.[110]

The Robinson-Patman Act: An Appraisal

Those who study the political history of small business immediately confront a perplexing contradiction: for several decades, politicians sought federal aid for "free enterprise," claiming that the "independent" status of small business owners entitled them to government benefits. Yet the congressional champions of small business apparently were not aware of or bothered by this conflict between their stated goals and the means used to achieve them. The sponsors of the Robinson-Patman Act believed their legislation was a macroeconomic tool that would not only preserve small business but would also foster competition and benefit the consumer. In practice, however, the act limited competition, harmed small business, and threatened the interests of the buying public.

Those who supported the Robinson-Patman Act vehemently denied that their legislation would harm the consumer. Patman insisted that he sought only to eliminate unjustified discounts and thereby create a level playing field for small business. The early cases under the Robinson-Patman Act, however, demonstrated that chain stores earned their discounts. Proponents of the Robinson-Patman Act now had to choose between the interests of the consumer and those of small business. Eventually, they urged the FTC to establish a discount limit that clearly placed the interests of small business above those of the consumer. They resolved this apparent conflict by resorting to crisis rhetoric, arguing that small firms would soon perish at the hands of big business and that the consumer would be hurt in the long run if monopolies took over the retail sector of the economy. Yet despite a temporary loss in market share, independent dealers continued to prosper, and the tire trade remained competitive.

The FTC's interpretation of the Robinson-Patman Act imposed costs on the consumer in other ways. The agency prevented manufacturers from passing on cost savings to the consumer by limiting the cost-justification defense to charges of price discrimination. American companies also spent a considerable amount of time and money to comply with the act. (According to one estimate, the cost of compliance totaled $1.4 billion between 1936 and 1974.) Overall, studies have shown that the FTC's enforcement of the act probably led to higher consumer prices.[111]

The sponsors of the Robinson-Patman Act also denied that it conflicted with existing antitrust legislation; yet in all likelihood, the act fostered collusion by preventing the members of a cartel from cheating on the established monopoly price, since cheaters could be charged with price discrimination.[112] Thus, in his study of the Robinson-Patman Act, Frederick Rowe described the law as a "caricature of antitrust" because it led companies to violate the Sherman Act prohibition against price-fixing. Another writer wryly noted that the Robinson-Patman Act sent a confusing signal to businesspeople by encouraging them to "go out and compete but don't get caught at it."[113] Rather than clarifying the line between "fair" and "unfair" price competition, this complex and ambiguous act introduced a new element of uncertainty into the decision-making process of American business executives.

Many of these negative consequences ensued because small business advocates held to a mistaken economic theory that equated competition with the number of firms in an industry. Thus the president of the NAITD denied the anticompetitive nature of the World War II tire bills by claiming that "more independent retailers means more competition."[114] By the 1950s and 1960s, however, economists realized that concentrated industries could be competitive. For example, in 1962, Robert Knox completed his study of the tire industry and concluded that despite its high level of concentration, the industry "would fall toward the competitive end of any scale of classification."[115] According to Knox, the small business advocates simply exaggerated the market power of the largest tire manufacturers and distributors. In reality, the "bilateral oligopoly" so feared by the FTC actually preserved competition and kept the profits of manufacturers low.

Throughout the 1940s and 1950s, lobbyists for the NAITD claimed that competition from big business might soon result in the elimination of the small tire dealer, but their crisis rhetoric did not reflect reality. A 1957 opinion survey showed that tire dealers were optimistic about the future and opposed government regulation of their suppliers. Only 9 percent of the independent tire dealers surveyed favored regulation of suppliers, while 96 percent reported that they received "fairly good" or "very good" treatment from their suppliers.

The dealers favored tax cuts as the preferred form of government aid.[116] In 1964, Humphrey's subcommittee on retailing conceded that the oft-predicted crisis of small business had not come to pass. During the previous fifteen years, tire dealers had enjoyed significant sales increases, and the committee reported that "well-established TBA's [tire dealers] and their employees have fared quite well."[117] Despite the virtual demise of the Robinson-Patman Act, the tire dealers continued to fare well in the 1970s and 1980s. Independent dealers distributed a large share of imported tires and picked up additional market share as the oil companies abandoned full-service facilities in favor of self-service stations. Between 1964 and 1987, small tire retailers increased their market share from 39 percent to 68 percent—proof that minnows *could* compete with whales.[118] In short, market forces played a more important role than antitrust policy in determining the structure of the tire trade.

This history of the evolution of the Robinson-Patman Act shows that small business groups significantly influenced the politics of mid-twentieth-century America. In 1936, trade associations representing small business owners secured passage of the Robinson-Patman Act over the opposition of larger corporate interests. During the late 1930s, the NAITD persuaded the FTC to use its limited resources to pursue an investigation of the tire industry. Later, the NAITD and its allies in Congress pressured the FTC into using the quantity-limit clause in an attempt to eliminate the chain stores' competitive advantage. Thus, this study provides evidence to support the description of the FTC as an "antitrust pork barrel" agency influenced by pressure groups acting through congressional committees.[119]

The presence of ideologically minded small business advocates in Congress greatly contributed to the success of the organized tire dealers. Political scientist James Q. Wilson notes that in recent years "the cost of effective political access has . . . been lowered by the existence within government, especially in Congress, of people who are sympathetic to consumerist and environmental organizations." These policy entrepreneurs frequently exploit a scandal or crisis in order to secure passage of consumer and environmental legislation.[120] The same was true of those members of Congress who sympathized with the complaints of small tire dealers. The Goodyear-Sears case, for example, galvanized small business advocates and served as a focal point for anti-chain-store sentiment. The fear of an impending crisis also brought liberal and conservative small business advocates together during World War II in support of legislation designed to restructure the tire trade.

Yet politicians derived different meanings from the small business ideology. A populistic Patman hated big business and sought to punish the chain stores for their success. New Dealer James Murray sought to balance the economy by offering government aid to small business owners, farmers, workers, and other organized groups. Conservatives, on the other hand, accepted direct government aid to small business only during a wartime crisis. In peacetime, Republicans Taft and Eisenhower viewed the enforcement of the antitrust laws as an alternative to direct regulation of industry; consequently, they opposed positive measures designed to redistribute market share to independent tire dealers.

The independent tire dealers also failed to secure the passage of positive legislation because they did not enjoy the support of other small business owners. In fact, during World War II the tire dealers sought legislation that would have increased their market share at the expense of gas station owners and other small business people. Furthermore, as J. P. Seiberling noted, there simply were too few independent tire dealers to exert enough pressure on Congress to pass legislation that would dramatically alter existing business practices.

Organized tire dealers enjoyed greater success on the antitrust front; yet although the FTC responded to the complaints of tire dealers, the agency had its own bureaucratic imperative, which in general worked to the detriment of small business. The agency avoided expensive price-discrimination investigations and instead focused on "easy" cases involving the act's brokerage and advertising clauses. Between 1936 and 1961, the FTC issued nearly six hundred cease-and-desist orders under the Robinson-Patman Act, yet only 3 percent of these dealt with price discrimination. Furthermore, the FTC brought only a handful of its brokerage complaints against national firms.[121] As one analyst noted, from the perspective of big business the act's "pragmatic bite has often been far less than its analytical bark."[122]

Nonetheless, the Robinson-Patman Act was more than an ineffective piece of antitrust legislation. Robert Bork describes antitrust law as a "microcosm in which larger movements of our society are reflected."[123] The Robinson-Patman Act reflected a larger concern with the impact of big business on the American way of life. This concern also found expression in fair trade laws and, ultimately, in the creation of the Small Business Administration—subjects that will be examined in the remaining chapters of this book.

3

Fair Trade: The Politics of Price Maintenance, 1937–1975

During the Great Depression, as profits plunged and businesses failed, "competition" became a dirty word. Small business advocates characterized the low prices of the chain stores as "predatory price cutting" and "economic cannibalism" designed to destroy small firms. In this crisis atmosphere, congressional allies of small business had joined with independent grocers and tire dealers to secure the passage of the Robinson-Patman Act. At the same time, they also supported the National Association of Retail Druggists in its successful campaign to secure state legislation allowing manufacturers to maintain minimum prices on brand-name goods, a practice known as retail price maintenance or "fair trade." Advocates of fair trade hoped thereby to eliminate the price advantage of the chain store. In 1937, Congress exempted these fair trade agreements from the antitrust laws by passing the Miller-Tydings Act. The language of the "fair traders" echoed the rhetoric of a "just price" that harkened back to a medieval conception of economic virtue. The fair traders soon discovered, however, that they could not simply legislate virtue or higher profits. Consumer demand for lower prices resulted in new forms of mass marketing that undercut the practice of fair trade. Opposition from the executive branch and the courts also made it difficult for manufacturers to enforce their fair trade agreements. Finally, in 1975, Congress responded to a new economic environment by repealing the Miller-Tydings Act and ending the forty-year experiment with price-fixing.

The Origins of Fair Trade

In the late nineteenth century, America witnessed a mass-marketing revolution: manufacturers began using the railroad to distribute advertised brand-name products to the entire nation. Manufacturers still relied on independent retailers, however, and sought ways to encourage these merchants to carry their products. National advertising campaigns created consumer demand that a merchant could not ignore, but retailers still might choose not to carry a product if they thought they could make little profit on it. Moreover, small-town merchants sometimes convinced their customers to accept generic imitations of brand-name goods because they offered higher margins to the retailer—a practice manufacturers called "the substitution evil." Therefore, some manufacturers assigned exclusive territorial rights to individual merchants, thus providing them with a local monopoly and the hopes of higher profits.[1]

Other manufacturers attracted the business of independent merchants by maintaining minimum retail prices, a practice known as retail price maintenance (RPM). Small retailers found fair trade agreements attractive because they offered the prospect of high margins and eliminated price competition from mass retailers. Manufacturers also benefited from this marketing strategy in several ways. Use of the RPM strategy protected a manufacturer's goodwill by encouraging merchants to take the time to make consumers aware of a product's qualities. In addition, high profit margins allowed merchants to provide after-sales service. Manufacturers feared that without RPM, price-cutting retailers would act as "free riders" by taking advantage of the promotional activity of full-service merchants. For example, a consumer might visit the store of a full-service merchant to receive his or her advice on a certain brand-name product, then leave that store and purchase the product from a discounter. Fair-trading manufacturers believed that price-cutting affected consumer perception of quality. If retailers lowered the price of a product below the level suggested by the manufacturer, consumers might consider it a cheap commodity rather than a high-quality item. Also, if price-cutters used a manufacturer's product as a loss leader (an item sold below cost to attract customers into a store), small retailers might stop carrying it, and total sales of that item would drop.[2]

In the late nineteenth and early twentieth centuries, the courts generally upheld RPM agreements, but in the 1911 case *Dr. Miles Medical Company v. John D. Park & Sons*, the U.S. Supreme Court declared that they violated the Sherman Act's ban on price-fixing agreements. The Court held that a manufacturer relinquished control over its goods when it sold them to a wholesaler or re-tailer.[3] The Supreme Court also described the elimination of price competition as harmful to consumer welfare and declared that once a manufacturer has "sold its product at prices satisfactory to itself, the public is entitled to what-ever advantage may be derived from competition in the subsequent traffic."[4]

Manufacturers responded by orchestrating a public relations campaign in support of federal fair trade legislation. They formed the American Fair Trade League (AFTL) and enlisted the support of noted lawyer and activist Louis Brandeis, the "People's Lawyer." In a series of articles appearing in mass-circulation magazines, Brandeis extolled the benefits of fair trade and insisted that it ensured the survival of small business by preventing predatory price-cutting. Brandeis asserted that fair trade was "in the interest of the small man— the small manufacturer, the small producer, and the small retailer." He also promoted the notion of a "just" profit due merchants and warned that without fair trade, the country faced the "very great danger . . . of the retailer not making as much profit as he ought to."[5] Thus, although the AFTL represented only the manufacturers of trademarked goods, it exploited the symbolic ap-peal of small business by using independent retailers as a front for its campaign to restore fair trade. In 1915, a founder of the AFTL admitted that "we have been able to carry it so far as a retailers' fight. . . . The retailers have been in evidence and they are doing the obvious work, the work that is on the surface."[6]

Although it had the backing of many of the nation's largest manufacturers, federal fair trade legislation floundered in the 1910s and 1920s. But the anti-chain-store movement finally sparked congressional interest in the subject, and in 1929 Senator Arthur Capper (R.-Kans.) and Representative Claude Kelly (R.-Pa.) introduced a controversial bill to legalize RPM agreements. The two congressmen championed fair trade as a conservative measure designed to protect the interests of small business; yet their legislation had radical implica-tions. Capper, who had earlier secured similar legislation granting an anti-trust exemption to the cooperatives of small farmers (the Capper-Volstead Act of 1922), hoped to eliminate the price competition of chain stores and thereby make "free" enterprise free of failure. He declared, "If the profit system means that my profit comes from someone else's loss, then the profit system is wrong."[7]

Between 1929 and 1936, Congress debated the merits of fair trade, but the Capper-Kelly bill never became law, in large part because of opposition from the executive branch. In 1929, a Federal Trade Commission survey revealed widespread opposition to fair trade, with 72 percent of consumers reporting

their disapproval. Most retailers, wholesalers, and manufacturers favored legalization of fair trade, but many companies never adopted RPM because of the
difficulty in preventing price-cutting by mass retailers. Others abandoned RPM
because they found that distribution through chain stores increased their total
sales and profits. Two years later, the FTC completed its study of fair trade and
concluded that the government should not legalize retail price maintenance
because it threatened consumer welfare. A study by the National Recovery
Administration (NRA) reached a similar conclusion.[8]

The early history of the fair trade movement suggests the limits of big
business influence in the 1920s, a period often described by historians as a
"corporate-liberal" era during which policymakers sympathized with the concerns of corporate executives.[9] The nation's largest manufacturers had legitimate business reasons for favoring fair trade; nonetheless, they failed in their
efforts to legalize retail price maintenance. By promoting fair trade as a measure benefiting small businesses, these manufacturers recognized that politicians might condone price-fixing if it preserved the "backbone of democracy."
But it would still take a crisis situation before legislators decided to abandon
their scruples about price-fixing.

State Fair Trade Legislation, 1931–1937

During the 1930s, a powerful trade association representing small business
owners, the National Association of Retail Druggists (NARD), took over leadership of the fair trade movement and eventually secured the passage of state and
federal legislation legalizing RPM. The NARD had a long history of activism
dating back to its founding in 1898. Independent druggists had organized the
NARD to represent their interests, and in 1906 the group had used the threat of
a boycott to force manufacturers, wholesalers, and retailers to sign a pact
establishing fixed retail prices. However, in 1907 a federal court ruled that
this agreement violated the Sherman Act, and four years later, the U.S. Supreme Court struck down another NARD-sponsored agreement in the *Dr.
Miles* case. In *Dr. Miles*, the Court established a per se rule that banned all fair
trade agreements. Consequently, the NARD tried to overcome these adverse
court rulings by lobbying for state and federal fair trade legislation. With the
onset of the Great Depression, the NARD intensified its efforts to legalize fair
trade.[10]

The NARD is an exception to the rule that small businesses lacked the organization to be an effective pressure group. Several factors contributed to the

unusual success of the NARD. Like other organized groups of professionals, the druggists benefited from their mastery of their discipline.[11] Consumers valued pharmacists' knowledge and expertise, while manufacturers sought the favor of those in this tightly controlled profession. Also, the NARD faced little big business opposition in its industry, because during the depression, drug chains joined with the independents in seeking higher margins through fair trade. Most important, the leaders of NARD displayed political savvy and conducted a well-organized lobbying campaign. For example, rather than provoke an open public discussion of fair trade, NARD stifled debate by avoiding hearings and attaching bills as riders to unrelated legislation. The association also enlisted the support of retailer-legislators in state houses and in Congress. Yet despite these advantages, the NARD failed to convince lawmakers that small businesses needed fair trade legislation during the prosperous decades of the 1910s and 1920s.

The Great Depression changed the minds of legislators around the country. In their search for solutions to the crisis, some politicians and policymakers decided that RPM agreements might halt deflation by limiting price competition. Thus, in 1931, the druggists convinced California's lawmakers to enact the nation's first fair trade law. The original law proved ineffective, because it did not apply to merchants who refused to sign RPM agreements; therefore, in 1933, the legislature added a nonsigner clause making RPM agreements binding on all merchants within the state. Then, in December 1936, the floodgates of fair trade opened as the U.S. Supreme Court upheld Illinois's fair trade law. In *Old Dearborn Distributing Co. v. Seagram Distillers*, the Supreme Court decided that states could pass fair trade legislation to prevent predatory price-cutting and protect a manufacturer's goodwill. In contrast to its earlier rulings, the Court now held that a manufacturer maintained some degree of control over its products even after it sold them to a wholesaler or retailer. During the following year, twenty-eight states enacted measures modeled on the California statute, and by the end of that year a total of forty-two states had legalized fair trade. Many states also passed laws making it illegal to sell loss leaders.[12]

The passage of state fair trade legislation during the Great Depression demonstrated how a crisis situation can magnify the political influence of organized interest groups. In the years before the depression, proponents of fair trade included the nation's largest manufacturers and a well-organized group of small druggists, yet state legislators remained indifferent. During the Great Depression, however, politicians were willing to experiment with a form of price-fixing that they had refused to condone in more "normal" times. This new receptiveness to fair trade first became evident at the state level, but it soon affected the policymaking of the federal government.

Federal Fair Trade Legislation: The Miller-Tydings Act of 1937

In the space of a few years, advocates of RPM achieved an impressive series of victories at the state level, but fair trade failed to provide the relief sought by many small businesses. Most of the retail codes established under the NRA set minimum prices below the level desired by independent merchants. For example, members of the NARD felt entitled to a 50 percent margin of gross profit, but the code for their industry set minimum prices barely above cost.[13]

Throughout the country, independent merchants and manufacturers were complaining that the NRA discriminated against them, and in March 1934, President Franklin D. Roosevelt responded by appointing a National Recovery Review Board to investigate charges of monopolistic price-fixing under the NRA. Two critics of big business, lawyers Clarence Darrow and Lowell Mason, dominated this review board. Darrow and Mason made the NRA a scapegoat for the difficulties faced by small firms during the Great Depression. In their June 1934 report to the president, the Darrow Board's members concluded that minimum prices benefited independent retailers but harmed small manufacturers because many of them competed on the basis of price. Small manufacturers also had to pay higher prices for supplies under a regime of price maintenance. Thus, by pursuing a policy of price-fixing, the government found it could not aid one set of small business owners without harming another.[14]

Although the NRA failed to lift the country out of the Great Depression, it focused small merchants' attention on the need to organize and lobby for federal fair trade legislation. After securing fair trade legislation in nearly every state of the union, the NARD decided to temporarily abandon its efforts to pass a national fair trade law; instead, the druggists exploited growing states'-rights sentiment by seeking permissive legislation to exempt state fair trade laws from the Sherman Act and the Federal Trade Commission Act, a law that threatened the future of fair trade because it prohibited retail price-fixing in interstate commerce.[15]

In its campaign to secure an antitrust exemption for fair trade agreements, the NARD had influential allies in Congress. After the demise of the NRA in 1935, a lawyer for the NARD, Herbert Levy, drafted suitable legislation and presented it to his former law partner, Senator Millard Tydings (D.-Md.).[16] Tydings had a longstanding interest in small business (in 1929, he had introduced the Senate

Resolution calling for the Federal Trade Commission's investigation of chain stores), and his small-town upbringing colored his views. He noted with pride that "I was born, raised, and still live in a small country town," and he emphasized the important role that small business had played in the life of his community.[17] In January 1936, Tydings introduced the NARD bill in the Senate, and the Judiciary Committee held hearings on it in March. Like the Robinson-Patman Act, the bill clearly represented a special interest. Of the nine witnesses testifying in favor of the legislation, seven spoke for drug associations. On 1 June, after little debate, the Senate passed Tydings's bill, but Congress recessed before the House could consider it.[18]

Six months later, Tydings reintroduced his legislation, and Representative John E. Miller (D.-Ark.) offered a companion bill in the House. Tydings and Miller echoed the rhetoric of the anti-chain-store movement. Tydings argued that his bill would allow states to eliminate loss leaders, which he described as "the most potent weapon of monopoly, the surest means of killing off the small rival, the independent businessman." Likewise, Miller described small business as "the woof and fabric of our national life" and warned that chain stores had become "despotic powers" that threatened to monopolize retail trade. He hoped to "[bring] back common decency to the market place" by eliminating the practice of predatory price-cutting. Miller denied that his legislation would force a restructuring of the economy: it did not affect competition among manufacturers, he argued. Furthermore, his bill merely *permitted* manufacturers to establish retail price agreements; it did not *require* them to do so. Miller and Tydings both stressed that their legislation simply recognized a state's right to determine whether fair trade served the public interest.[19]

The Miller-Tydings bill met opposition from consumer advocates, mail-order companies, chain stores, and large department stores. Opponents argued that this legislation would limit price competition and thus increase the cost of living.[20] These critics of fair trade urged Congress not to enact a measure that would drain purchasing power from the pockets of consumers, thus stifling economic recovery.

By instituting its "Captain Plan," the NARD worked energetically to overcome this opposition. Under this plan the association placed "captains" (lobbyists) in every congressional district, while rank-and-file members of the NARD flooded their representatives with petitions and pleas for their support of the Miller-Tydings bills.[21] At the state level, the NARD had used such tactics to stifle debate and rush through legislation, but the association could not quiet those in Congress who believed that the Miller-Tydings bill represented a departure from the procompetitive intent of the antitrust laws. Thus, despite the bill's alleged benefits to small business, several congressional small business advocates resisted these demands for legalization of fair trade. Senate Majority Leader Joseph Robinson (D.-Ark.), coauthor of the Robinson-Patman Act, opposed the bill because he feared that small retailers might abuse their fair trade privileges. Robinson also expressed his concern that retail price-fixing might have contributed to a recent rise in prices.[22]

Meanwhile, in the House, Emanuel Celler (D.-N.Y.) emerged as the leading opponent of the Miller-Tydings bill. As a member of the House Judiciary Committee, Celler issued a minority report that was critical of fair trade legislation. He endorsed a provision of the bill eliminating loss leaders but steadfastly opposed the legalization of retail price maintenance. In the past, Celler noted, the NARD and other retail associations had coerced manufacturers into signing fair trade agreements, and he predicted that passage of the Miller-Tydings Act would encourage other retailers to violate the antitrust laws. Celler did not exaggerate the threat of coercion. In a widely publicized case, the Pepsodent Company announced that it would abandon fair trade in 1935, but the company reinstated its fair trade agreements and contributed $25,000 to the NARD after the druggists led a boycott of Pepsodent products.[23] Celler also warned that fair trade would weaken and "poison" small business because high margins would attract new competitors. Finally, although Celler had been an independent banker himself and was concerned with the fate of small business, he refused to endorse a measure that embodied a "profit by law idea"—a notion that violated the spirit of free enterprise.[24]

The Miller-Tydings bill also faced stiff opposition from the executive branch. The FTC had recently charged an association of distillers with having forced manufacturers to accept fair trade, and the commission's chairman, W. A. Ayres, feared that other groups would act in the same way if Congress passed this legislation. The Treasury, Labor, Agriculture, and Justice Departments also expressed this concern. The president, however, worried most about fair trade's inflationary potential. Roosevelt's feud with Senator Tydings, who had emerged as a vigorous opponent of the New Deal and its "alphabetical monstrosities," may also have motivated him to oppose this legislation. At any rate, in April 1937, Roosevelt persuaded congressional leaders to shelve their consideration of the Tydings bill and asked the FTC to investigate the cause of a recent increase in the cost of living.[25]

Tydings eventually succeeded in passing his legislation by attaching it as a rider to an appropriations bill for the District of Columbia. In July, he met with the attorney general and secured his support for the bill by adding a provision that prohibited horizontal price-fixing. Tydings's measure faced little opposition in Congress, perhaps because legislators feared the power of the NARD and recognized the popularity of the issue at that time. Consequently, on 23 July, Congress passed the appropriations bill with the rider attached. Emanuel Celler urged the president to veto the bill, but after much debate within his cabinet, Roosevelt reluctantly signed the bill into law. The president denounced the "vicious practice of attaching unrelated riders" and said that the Miller-Tydings Act "weakens the anti-trust laws" but that he "decided to sign the bill in the hope that it will not be as harmful as most people predict."[26]

By amending the Sherman Act, this legislation exempted retail price maintenance agreements from the antitrust laws. Although it became part of antitrust law, the Miller-Tydings Act did not authorize the federal government to police fair trade contracts; it left the responsibility for enforcement with the manufacturer. But the law had one defect: Tydings had neglected to incorporate a nonsigner clause allowing manufacturers to maintain minimum prices on goods sold to merchants who did not sign an RPM agreement. This oversight would later allow critics to successfully challenge fair trade agreements in the courts.

The Impact of Fair Trade, 1937–1941

The passage of the Miller-Tydings Act did not end the debate over fair trade. Proponents and critics of the law continued to wage a rhetorical war over the merits and demerits of retail price maintenance. Opponents, led by R. H. Macy's department store, publicized studies showing that consumers in fair trade states paid more for brand-name products. The American Fair Trade League (now known as the American Fair Trade Council, or AFTC) countered by conducting its own public relations campaign aimed at convincing consumers that fair trade guaranteed them quality and service. The council also claimed that consumers benefited from the elimination of loss leaders, which made it more difficult for unethical merchants to engage in the deceptive practice of "bait and switch."[27]

Fair trade advocates had triumphed in the political arena, but several factors confined the use of fair trade to less than 15 percent of total retail sales.[28] The return of prosperity in the late 1930s and the onset of war in Europe diminished the media's interest in fair trade, thus hampering the public relations efforts of the American Fair Trade Council. (In 1939, a survey of Michigan retailers revealed that many did not even know that the state had a fair trade law.)[29] State legislation limited the use of fair trade to products with brand-names or trademarks. Furthermore, these products had to be in "free and open competition" with similar goods on the market. Finally, as a marketing strategy, fair trade succeeded only in those industries that were dominated by a few manufacturers and had a trade association strong enough to enforce RPM agreements.

Manufacturers of luxury goods found it relatively easy to maintain minimum prices on their products; thus, RPM worked well in the distribution of drugs, cosmetics, tobacco, jewelry, and books.[30] Even in these fields, however, manufacturers found it difficult to prevent all price-cutting. Discounters evaded the stipulation of minimum prices by accepting trade-ins or by granting their customers rebates and bonuses. Mass-marketers also placed their own private labels in direct competition with fair trade products. A&P and other chains benefited from this marketing strategy, as cost-conscious consumers switched to private brands.[31]

Fair trade failed to serve as a panacea for the ills afflicting small business. Four years after the passage of the Miller-Tydings Act, small retailers had discovered that "a guaranty of margins is not a guaranty of sales."[32] Fair trade did not eliminate chain store competition; indeed, Congressman Celler's prediction that it would intensify competition became reality as mass-marketers sought the high margins promised by fair trade. Consequently, small retailers had to drop their prices to the stipulated minimum in order to remain competitive. This drawing of prices toward the minimum level set by the manufacturer hurt many merchants, because manufacturers still faced price competition and set prices so low that they provided an inadequate margin of profit for those small firms burdened with high operating costs. Thus, the National Association of Retail Grocers (NARG) complained that very few grocery manufacturers engaged in fair trade and that those that did set low minimum prices. Likewise, the NARD reported widespread dissatisfaction with the margins afforded druggists. Nor did fair trade save struggling businesses from bankruptcy. In fact, the failure rate in fair trade states exceeded the national average.[33]

Several factors also prevented trade associations such as the NARD from achieving complete political victory. The continued existence of a handful of states without fair trade laws provided the critics with ammunition, allowing them to show how retail price maintenance increased the cost of living. In the District of Columbia, the NARD's leaders refused to support legalization of fair trade because they feared that a backlash would occur if members of Congress had to pay higher prices.[34] Fair trade advocates also continued to face a hostile executive branch. In 1939, the FTC authorized a study of the economic effects of retail price maintenance, and during the next two years the commission investigated charges that druggists and liquor distributors coerced manufacturers into fair trade agreements.[35] Meanwhile, at the Justice Department, Attorney General Thurman Arnold opposed "the economic drug of [retail] price fixing." The consumer, he argued, should not be sacrificed for the benefit of small business owners.[36] In 1941, the Temporary National Economic Committee (TNEC), a government body investigating the "problem of monopoly," also published a study of small business in which the authors lambasted those who practiced fair trade, declaring it a "price-fixing, margin seeking measure that injures consumers" and "protects the inefficient" retailer at the expense of "the ambitious and resourceful merchants." In its final report, the TNEC called for the repeal of all fair trade legislation.[37] After America's entry into World War II, however, the president and Congress lost interest in the issue and deferred consideration of the TNEC's recommendations.

By allowing the states to determine whether fair trade was in the public interest, the Miller-Tydings Act appealed to growing states'-rights sentiment in Congress. But states'-rights sentiment did not allay the concerns of those opposed to fair trade. These critics continued to influence policymaking in the executive branch and urge Congress to repeal the Miller-Tydings Act. Sustained opposition from the Federal Trade Commission and the Justice Department ensured that the debate over fair trade would continue into the post–World War II years.

Challenges to Fair Trade, 1945–1951

During World War II and the immediate postwar period, manufacturers could maintain minimum retail prices because they enjoyed a seller's market. But in the late 1940s, renewed price competition led to widespread violations of fair trade agreements. At the same time, fair trade faced challenges from all three branches of the federal government. In December 1945, the Federal Trade Commission completed a six-year study of retail price maintenance and concluded that fair trade limited price competition. The FTC expressed concern that organized retailers had used boycotts and other forms of intimidation to force manufacturers into fair trade agreements. The commission again called for the repeal of the Miller-Tydings Act.[38]

Postwar inflation and the onset of a recession in 1949 also led President Truman to use antitrust suits as a macroeconomic tool to increase competition and lower prices. This policy represented a shift away from the depression-era concern with limiting competition through fair trade. Meanwhile, the chief congressional critic of fair trade legislation, Emanuel Celler, used his position as chairman of the Judiciary Committee to investigate ways to reform the antitrust laws. In March 1949, Celler met with representatives of the Federal Trade Commission, the Justice Department, and the Council of Economic Advisers to discuss how to "remove the anachronisms of the present laws," including the Miller-Tydings Act, which they unanimously agreed "was bad and should be repealed."[39] Subsequently, Truman gave his approval to Celler's proposal for an ongoing investigation of monopoly. During the next two years, Celler's investigations received widespread media attention, and his Antitrust Subcommittee provided a forum for those who wished to repeal statutes, such as the Miller-Tydings Act, that granted exemptions from the antitrust laws.[40]

These challenges to fair trade eventually affected judicial thinking on the matter. Throughout the 1930s and 1940s, the courts upheld the constitutionality of fair trade legislation; but in 1949, the Florida Supreme Court nullified the nonsigner clause of that state's fair trade law by declaring it an invalid use of police power and an unconstitutional delegation of legislative authority to private parties. The Florida court harshly criticized what it called "a price-fixing statute" and cited the FTC study as evidence that fair trade violated the public interest.[41] Two years later, a federal court ruled that the nonsigner clause of fair trade agreements did not apply to mail-order companies.[42] Then, on 21 May 1951, the U.S. Supreme Court stunned fair trade advocates by deciding that the nonsigner clause of RPM agreements did not apply to any goods in interstate commerce. In *Schwegmann Brothers v. Calvert Distillers*, Justice Robert H. Jackson described the legislative history of the Miller-Tydings Act as "unedifying and unilluminating." He concluded that because Congress failed to include a nonsigner clause, it had not intended to legalize the use of such clauses in transactions involving interstate commerce. Thus, the Miller-Tydings Act fell victim to the sloppy draftsmanship characteristic of fair trade legislation.[43] In effect, the *Schwegmann* case limited fair trade agreements to intrastate commerce, and in the months following the decision, mass-marketers took advantage of the situation by engaging in a fierce price war.[44]

Congress Resuscitates Fair Trade:
The McGuire Act of 1952

The NARD and AFTC tried to overturn the *Schwegmann* decision by presenting their case in the court of Congress. In October 1951, Representative John A. McGuire (D.-Conn.) introduced a bill drafted by the NARD to legalize the nonsigner clause and "restore the Miller-Tydings Act to the status it occupied prior to the Court decision." Because it amended the Federal Trade Commission Act instead of the Miller-Tydings Act, the McGuire bill went to the Interstate and Foreign Commerce Committee rather than to Emanuel Celler's Judiciary Committee.[45] The AFTC worried, however, that the McGuire bill would be placed under the jurisdiction of the FTC, a staunch opponent of fair trade. Therefore, the AFTC backed a bill introduced by Representative Eugene J. Keough (D.-N.Y.) that legalized the nonsigner clause by amending the Miller-Tydings Act. The Keough bill also allowed manufacturers to take violators of fair trade agreements into federal court, but by seeking an amendment to the Miller-Tydings Act, the AFTC took the risk that Emanuel Celler might table their legislation.[46]

As it turned out, Celler could not prevent his committee from approving this legislation. On 27 February 1952, the Commerce Committee approved the McGuire bill, and several weeks later the Keough bill emerged from the Judiciary Committee after surviving opposition from a three-man minority led by Emanuel Celler. In his minority report, Celler emphasized the extraordinary nature of the nonsigner clause, which forced the terms of a contract on those who were not party to it. Celler described how the Miller-Tydings Act encouraged the NARD and other trade associations to violate the antitrust laws and cited the Justice Department's repeated assertions that fair trade agreements fostered the formation of price-fixing cartels. Whereas supporters of fair trade emphasized the need to eliminate loss leaders, Celler did not "believe it proper to behead our economy in order to cure the headache of loss leaders." Instead, he offered a substitute bill that prohibited loss leaders without sanctioning retail price maintenance.[47]

The issue of fair trade divided congressional small business advocates. In February, the House Small Business Committee issued a balanced report recognizing "the complexity of the problem and . . . the weight of evidence on both sides of the issue." Fair trade advocates considered the nonsigner clause "majority rule applied to commercial practices." Critics, on the other hand, regarded it as "coercive, oppressive, unfair and undemocratic." The committee also found deep divisions within the public at large. Retail trade associations generally favored fair trade, while groups representing workers, farmers, and consumers opposed it. Ultimately, however, both the House and Senate Small Business Committees came out in support of legislation to legalize the nonsigner clause.[48]

In May, fair trade forces dropped the Keough bill after states'-rights representatives expressed their opposition to the provision allowing the federal courts to hear fair trade cases. In the subsequent debate over the McGuire bill, Emanuel Celler emerged as the only vocal critic of fair trade. Celler maintained that fair trade increased prices and did not provide small retailers with any real protection from the competition of chain stores. Furthermore, he argued, fair trade benefited large manufacturers of brand-name goods. Celler recognized that many representatives feared the power of the NARD, but he asked them to "not be afraid of the druggists," for he had always survived their attempts to unseat him.[49]

Celler's passionate critique of fair trade failed to sway his colleagues. McGuire emphasized the permissive nature of his legislation, noting that it placed no new responsibilities on the federal government. Like the Miller-Tydings Act, he said, his bill merely recognized a state's right to enact fair trade legislation. Others sought to protect small business from price competition. Allan Oakley Hunter (R.-Calif.) accepted the NARD's argument that "small business needs fair trade to survive" the "wild price cutting" sparked by the *Schwegmann* decision. Carl T. Durham (D.-N.C.) spoke from personal experience about the damage that the recent price war had done to his small store. Many other congressmen invoked the ideology of small business. Eugene J. McCarthy (D.-Minn.), for example, emphasized "the cultural benefits or values" represented by small business. McCarthy believed that the federal government should finally recognize small business as an interest group worthy of assistance and representation within the post–New Deal broker state. The government had come to the aid of farmers, he argued, but had left small business subject to the vagaries of the marketplace. In the end, these arguments convinced most of those present; and on 8 May, the House passed the McGuire bill by a lopsided vote of 196 to 10.[50]

The NARD then tried to rush the bill through the Senate without debate, but this move led Senator Paul H. Douglas (D.-Ill.) to ask, "Is this child going to be born without any statement as to the nature of the child? . . . I think perhaps there might be some doubt about the quality of the child itself."[51] Douglas's challenge sparked a two-day-long debate, as the "parents" of the child, led by Hubert Humphrey (D.-Minn.), came to its defense. Like his counterparts in the House, Humphrey emphasized the need to preserve the values embodied in small business. Sounding more like a preacher than a politician, Humphrey, an ex-druggist, asked the Senate to "put spiritual values above material values." He warned that without this legislation the economic landscape would become the province of "a few Frankensteins and giants."[52] The debate finally ended on 2 July, when the Senate passed the bill by a wide margin (64–16). As a sop to opponents, the Senate issued a resolution calling for further study of fair trade by the Senate Small Business Committee and a Joint Committee on Fair Trade Practices.[53]

The McGuire bill caused a great deal of consternation in the Truman administration. Emanuel Celler had the support of nearly the entire executive branch when he urged the president to veto the bill.[54] Except for the Commerce Department, every agency expressing an opinion opposed the measure.[55] Nevertheless, in the end, political considerations outweighed the economic arguments of those opposed to the bill. White House aide David Bell convinced Truman of the relative harmlessness of fair trade legislation and cited the widespread support it enjoyed among small business owners. On 14 July, Truman signed the bill into law but expressed his ambivalence. On the one hand, he stated, "I don't believe that the 'fair trade' laws are as harmful to competition as some have asserted"; on the other hand, he did not view fair trade as a panacea, and he called for the development of new measures to protect small business from "cutthroat competition."[56]

The McGuire Act did not eliminate all of the obstacles to the effective implementation of fair trade. Fair trade advocates secured passage of the McGuire Act by exploiting states'-rights sentiment, but the federal government's hands-off approach made it difficult for manufacturers to enforce their RPM agreements. The passive role played by the federal government also left fair trade advocates exposed to opposition at the state level. Furthermore, the McGuire Act did not change the attitude of the judicial and executive branches of government; nor did it eliminate chain store competition. These obstacles eventually led many manufacturers to abandon fair trade.

The Decline of Fair Trade, 1952–1961

Within a few years after the passage of the McGuire Act, fair trade fell into disuse in many industries. Between 1952 and 1954, the number of manufacturers participating in RPM agreements plummeted from 1,600 to 900. The products sold under fair trade agreements accounted for less than 7 percent of total retail sales.[57] By the end of 1955, the editors of *Life* magazine had said "Goodby to Fair Trade."[58] Competition from mass-marketers caused this rapid decline in the use of fair trade. Department stores and chain stores responded to fair trade by increasing their use of private brands. (Macy's carried 1,400 products under its own name.)[59] Most important, a new form of mass marketing emerged in the 1950s—the discount store. Discount stores, such as Zayres and E. J. Korvette, undersold their competitors by offering even fewer services than the chain stores and independents. These new stores found a home in suburban shopping centers that spread rapidly across America during this period. Fearing a loss of market share, established chains set up their own discount subsidiaries: in 1961–62, Woolworth created Woolco, and Kresge's opened its chain of Kmarts. Thus the "discount revolution" began to trans-form American retailing.[60]

In this competitive environment, manufacturers found it difficult to enforce their fair trade agreements. (Ironically, fair trade may have contributed to the growth of discount stores by providing them with a "yardstick" that could be used to measure savings.)[61] Several leading manufacturers, including General Electric and Westinghouse, cut off sales to discounters, but even they had to lower their prices in response to consumers' demands. Manufacturers in-curred a great deal of expense and bad publicity in pursuing legal actions against violators of their fair trade agreements; the Sheaffer Pen Company, for example, spent 4 percent of its sales revenue on legal expenses related to the enforcement of the company's RPM agreements.[62] The costs of enforcement limited the use of fair trade to the nation's largest manufacturers.[63] Manufac-turers also found it impossible to prevent the transshipping of their products to discount houses. Thus, in 1955, the Sheaffer Pen Company abandoned fair trade because "we found that Sheaffer merchandise still found its way into discount houses."[64]

Meanwhile, during the Eisenhower years, the antitrust agencies continued to attack fair trade. The Department of Justice published studies highlighting the disparity in prices between the District of Columbia and neighboring fair trade states.[65] In 1955, the Attorney General's National Committee to Study the Antitrust Laws called for repeal of the Miller-Tydings Act. That same year, the Federal Trade Commission refused to enforce the fair trade agreements of retail jewelers, stating that "it cannot seriously be suggested that price competi-tion is morally reprehensible."[66]

The McGuire Act had overturned the Supreme Court's decision in the *Schwegmann* case, but the Court's negative opinion of fair trade continued to influence the thinking of the lower courts.[67] The nearly unanimous opposi-tion of economists and legal scholars also contributed to a growing consensus that fair trade hurt the public interest. State courts began to strike down fair trade laws, usually by ruling that the nonsigner clause violated state constitu-tions.[68] By 1962, manufacturers could not enforce their fair trade agreements in twenty-four states.[69]

A series of U.S. Supreme Court decisions further weakened the position of fair traders. In the *McKesson-Robbin* case (1956), the Court declared wholesale price maintenance unconstitutional. The following year, in *Masters Mail Order Company v. Bissell Carpet and General Electric*, the Court held that mail-order companies could ship their products to fair trade states at below minimum prices. In 1960, the Supreme Court prevented manufacturers with wholesale divisions from imposing fair trade at the retail level (*U.S. v. Parke, Davis*). This ruling effectively destroyed fair trade in the drug industry, because most pharmaceutical manufacturers owned wholesale subsidiaries.[70]

Congressional small business advocates grew alarmed at the sudden collapse of fair trade in the 1950s. In 1956, the Senate Small Business Committee's Subcommittee on Retailing, chaired by Hubert Humphrey, came out with a study painting a pessimistic future for fair trade. Humphrey's subcommittee found widespread support for fair trade among manufacturers and retailers but also a concern that recent developments had weakened fair trade's status. The report concluded that fair trade would continue losing ground unless Congress took action.[71] Small business advocates became even more concerned with the fate of fair trade when General Electric and several of its competitors abandoned the practice in 1958. GE executives noted that recent court decisions had made it nearly impossible for the company to enforce its fair trade agreements. The company also cited difficulties in monitoring thousands of RPM agreements: between 1937 and 1958, GE had signed 30,000 fair trade contracts and brought over 3,000 lawsuits against those violating these agreements.[72]

In order to stem the tide of defections from the fair trade camp, Hubert Humphrey introduced several bills to legalize fair trade across the nation, rather than allowing the states to decide the matter. However, in passing the Miller-Tydings and McGuire Acts, Congress had washed its hands of a controversial issue and still preferred to leave that issue with state legislators. Humphrey and others submitted similar legislation in the 1960s, but Congress never seriously considered enacting a national fair trade law.[73]

Several factors contributed to the erosion of support for fair trade legislation in the late 1940s and 1950s. Once the anti-chain-store hysteria died down, most members of Congress lost interest in the issue. Although Congress did resuscitate fair trade by passing the McGuire Act, it did not act on stronger fair trade legislation. More important, the supporters of fair trade lost their case in the court of public opinion. A series of adverse court decisions and investigations by antitrust agencies gave the general impression that fair trade was little more than a price-fixing scheme aimed at gouging the consumer. Finally, consumers sealed the fate of fair trade when they refused to purchase products subject to RPM agreements. In short, except during the crisis years of the 1930s, when fair trade advocates enjoyed the support of Congress, a reluctant president, and the courts, small business advocates found it impossible to build a political consensus in favor of fair trade. They found it equally difficult to convince consumers that fair trade was in their best interest.

Congress Repeals Fair Trade:
The Consumer Goods Pricing Act

Like the Robinson-Patman Act, fair trade legislation eventually fell victim changing economic circumstances. During the 1970s, policymakers sought ways to halt inflation and promote the interests of consumers, and the antitrust agencies took advantage of this concern by citing studies showing that fair trade cost the buying public several billion dollars per year.[74] Finally, after nearly four decades of opposition to retail price maintenance, the Federal Trade Commission and the Justice Department secured a combination of state judicial and legislative victories that reduced the number of fair trade states to eleven by 1975.[75]

Congress also responded to the inflationary climate of the 1970s by changing its attitude toward fair trade. In January 1975, Senator Edward Brooke (R.-Mass.) introduced a bill to repeal the Miller-Tydings Act, describing his proposal as an "anti-inflationary measure." Barbara Jordan (D.-Tex.) introduced a similar bill in the House of Representatives. By repealing the Miller-Tydings Act, these bills reinstated the prohibition against the use of fair trade in interstate commerce. The legislation gathered bipartisan support in Congress, as consumer-minded liberals joined with market-oriented conservatives. President Gerald Ford also gave strong backing to the legislation and made it part of his W.I.N. ("Whip Inflation Now") program.

In the past, congressional critics of fair trade had spoken quietly for fear of antagonizing the NARD; now, even the staunchest advocates of fair trade, including Senator Humphrey, failed to show up to testify against repeal of the Miller-Tydings Act. In fact, according to one writer, the Senate Subcommittee on Antitrust "had a hard time finding people wanting to testify for retaining the system." In July, the House passed Representative Jordan's bill, and after very little debate, the Senate approved the measure. Then, on 12 December 1975, President Ford signed the Consumer Goods Pricing Act, thus ending a controversial chapter in American antitrust history.[76]

Fair Trade: A History of Failure

Since 1975, the Supreme Court has upheld the ban on retail price maintenance, but the repeal of the Miller-Tydings Act did not end the academic debate over fair trade, a debate likened to a "religious war" fought among true believers.[77] Both sides have fashioned elaborate theories to justify or condemn the practice of retail price maintenance but have provided very little empirical or historical evidence to support their claims. Proponents of fair trade, including Robert Bork and Richard Posner, emphasize the ways in which manufacturers can benefit from retail price maintenance. These scholars view retail price maintenance as a legitimate form of product promotion that can increase a company's sales and enhance distributive efficiency. According to this school of thought, retail price maintenance encourages retailers to sell and service a manufacturer's product. RPM also eliminates the problem of "free riders" who seek advice from full-service merchants but purchase products from discounters.

These scholars reject the current legal consensus that fair trade is a detriment to consumer welfare. Bork chides those who focus single-mindedly on the increased costs to the consumer while ignoring the value added in after-sales service. Posner points to the inconsistencies inherent in current antitrust policy, including the government's "indefensible" distinction between pricing restrictions (illegal) and territorial restrictions (legal). Both writers dismiss the threat of horizontal cartels, because they argue that the antitrust agencies could easily detect retail price-fixing conducted on an industrywide basis. They insist that the market can best judge the effectiveness of fair trade; therefore, Bork concludes, "every vertical restraint should be completely lawful."[78]

These arguments in favor of fair trade convinced the administration of Ronald Reagan to adopt a laissez-faire policy toward retail price maintenance in the 1980s.[79] Nevertheless, many legal scholars and antitrust officials remain skeptical of the theoretical defenses of fair trade. In 1984, FTC commissioner Patricia Bailey stated that "as a practical matter, the 'free-rider' problem might be characterized as the Loch Ness Monster of Antitrust—everyone's heard of it, but . . . nobody's ever seen it."[80] Former FTC official Benjamin Sharp has also stated that in his experience, fair trade springs from the desire of retailers to limit competition, not from the efficiency considerations of manufacturers. Sharp emphasizes the coercive nature of fair trade and notes that existing customers pay for the higher costs incurred in attracting new customers. Others have argued that manufacturers could ensure a high level of service by carefully selecting dealers or by simply inserting a service clause in their contracts with retailers.[81]

The historical record provides evidence for both sides of this debate. Bork and Posner assert that consumers can judge the merits of fair trade and, therefore, that the government should not have outlawed retail price maintenance. This may be true, but the market's harsh judgment of retail price maintenance suggests that Bork and Posner have exaggerated the potential benefits of fair trade. As a marketing strategy, retail price maintenance promised more than it could deliver. In 1937, a writer for *Retailing* predicted that

"Mrs. Consumer will say 'no' and that . . . will be the end of price mainte-nance."[82] Fair-trading manufacturers could fix prices on their own brand-name products, but they could not eliminate price competition from other manufacturers. Consumers made their preferences known in the marketplace by choosing products that were not subject to price maintenance. Consumer demand for lower prices led to the rapid growth in the number of private labels and discount houses. Enterprising discounters found ways to evade fair trade agreements, leading a *New York Times* writer to conclude that "no person or institution—not even the United States Supreme Court—can prevent the de-termined American shopper from buying some needed goods at a discount."[83] In short, manufacturers found it difficult to maintain minimum prices as the "discount revolution" swept across America in the 1950s.

Fair trade also failed to deliver the benefits promised to small business. The heterogeneous nature of the small business community made it impossible to develop a single solution to the problems faced by different types of firms. Ironically, by allowing companies to fix minimum prices, fair trade legislation made small retailers dependent on large manufacturers of brand-name prod-ucts.[84] Price maintenance could also harm one segment of small business while aiding another: the NRA experience showed that price maintenance benefited small retailers at the expense of small manufacturers. Policymakers made the mistake of assuming that all small businesses shared the same interests. Con-gressional small business advocates also discovered that fair trade had other unintended consequences. Emanuel Celler accurately forecast the future of fair trade when he warned "that what may be expected of legislation in 1937 may be far different when the record is cast up 23 years later."[85] Celler foresaw that small retailers would lose sales when the high margins on fair trade products attracted new competition. In other cases, manufacturers set minimum prices so low that they afforded no protection to small business.

The NARD successfully played on states' rights, but this strategy eventually backfired, as a "domino effect" led to the demise of fair trade. State courts began to nullify fair trade laws, thus weakening the position of fair traders in other states. Once the national consensus in favor of fair trade had broken down, many manufacturers abandoned the practice. In turn, the abandon-ment of fair trade by many states and businesses made it easier for opponents to repeal the remaining fair trade laws in the 1970s. In short, the absence of a federal fair trade law weakened the position of fair trading manufacturers, because these companies sold their brand-name products across the nation.

In the 1930s, congressional small business advocates had become disillu-sioned with antitrust legislation and departed from the antitrust tradition by passing laws, such as the Miller-Tydings Act, that were expressly designed to limit price competition. Sixty years later, however, one can conclude with Emanuel Celler that "the history of fair trade in the American economy has been a history of failure."[86] The failure of the fair trade laws and the Robinson-Patman Act led congressional small business advocates to seek positive assistance on behalf of small firms. Eventually, this shift in emphasis led to the creation of a permanent Small Business Administration.

4

Congressional Small Business Advocates:
The People behind the Politics

Who were the small business advocates, and why did they support small business legislation, given the general apathy of the small business community? This chapter examines the life experiences of those members of Congress who supported small business legislation in the 1930s, as well as those who would come to back the creation of federal small business agencies in the 1940s and 1950s. Most of these representatives sat on the Senate and House Small Business Committees created by Congress in 1940 and 1941. A biographical analysis of the politicians who sat on the Congressional Small Business Committees—altogether ninety congressmen between 1940 and 1961—demonstrates how personal interest and a belief in small business as a social institution held together an otherwise shaky coalition of congressional small business advocates.

Explanations of Congressional Interest
in Small Business

Previous writers have advanced several theories to explain congressional support for small business legislation. Several have argued that some legislators had small-town origins that made them suspicious of big business and monopoly. Thus, they note that in congressional debates, small business advocates extolled the small-town virtues of community spirit and civic responsibility displayed by local merchants. These writers also point out that politicians from the more rural regions of the South and West led the opposition to chain stores, viewing them as an outside threat to their small-town "way of life."[1] Other commentators note that some of these politicians were small business owners or served as lawyers for small businesses; therefore, they had a personal interest in legislation affecting small business.[2] Finally, some of those who have studied the politics of small business emphasize the political value of these committees. The staff on the Small Business Committees responded to the complaints of constituents and helped to foster good relations between these congressmen and the small business voters back home.

Apparently, a narrow political interest in small business did motivate most of those congressmen who served on the Small Business Committees. In 1962, C. Dale Vinyard conducted interviews with committee members and found that many believed that "the primary, if not the only function [of the committees], was political, to serve as a symbol of congressional recognition of small business." Members also used the committees' personnel as an adjunct to their own staff.[3] But most important, the committees handled the complaints of small business constituents who might be expected to vote for these congressmen in future elections. In the latter half of 1950, for example, the Senate Small Business Committee assisted 8,800 small business owners.[4] The committees' staff spent roughly half of their time on such case work. According to one congressional aide, "the concept that every problem solved is a potential vote for a candidate back home is ever-present."[5]

There were also congressmen whose interests sprang from their own careers as small business owners. For example, Senator Homer Capehart (R.-Ind.) became a self-made millionaire in the 1930s when he convinced the Wurlitzer Company to mass-produce jukeboxes. During World War II, Capehart sought military contracts for small businesses, including his own Packard Manufacturing Corporation.[6] Representative William S. Hill (R.-Colo.) owned a farm implement business and complained of manufacturers' moves to cut out middlemen in his line of trade.[7] Several congressmen offered both personal and political reasons for their support of small business legislation. Senator Hubert Humphrey (D.-Minn.), for example, combined a personal interest in small business with his desire to attract votes. In his memoirs, Humphrey wrote, "I wanted very much to serve on the Senate Select Committee on Small Business, partially out of my interest, which began in our drugstore, but also because I felt I needed some lines into the business community in Minnesota before my re-election campaign of 1954."[8]

The Congressional Small Business Advocates:
A Collective Biography

These explanations of congressional interest in small business offer only partial insight into the motivation of leading small business advocates. A collective
biographical analysis of the congressional Small Business Committees shows
that only about a quarter of the ninety members who served between 1940 and
1961 had small business backgrounds.[9] Most were lawyers; of these, it could not
be determined how many represented small business clients. This analysis also
calls into question the notion that these congressmen shared small-town origins or that they came primarily from the South. Some spent their formative
years in towns such as Garnett, Kansas, or Somerset, Kentucky, while others
came from Chicago, New York, or Los Angeles. Although southern politicians
played a key role in the anti-chain-store movement of the 1930s, that region of
the country was actually underrepresented. In fact, three northeastern states—
New York, Connecticut, and Pennsylvania—placed as many members on these
committees as the entire ex-Confederacy did.

Conventional descriptions of their voting records also fail to explain why
these congressmen backed small business. Admittedly, terms such as "liberal"
or "conservative" can conceal as much as they reveal. Nonetheless, it is helpful
to gain an understanding of how contemporaries viewed these small business
advocates. An examination of the political leanings attributed to some of these
congressmen shows representation of both the "liberal" viewpoint (twenty-
four members) and the "conservative" viewpoint (ten members). At various
times, the committees included those on the "left" end of the political spectrum (James Murray, Hubert Humphrey) and those on the "right" (Robert
Taft, Barry Goldwater).

The one element uniting these politicians was their common concern with
the survival of small business. The ideology of small business held together a
heterogeneous coalition of liberals, moderates, and conservatives. The members of this diverse group of congressmen espoused remarkably similar rhetoric and agreed on the necessity of preserving the "backbone" of democracy
and free enterprise, yet they had differing conceptions of the small business
ideology. An examination of the views of leading small business advocates will
reveal the conflicts, contradictions, and tensions inherent in their ideology.
The views of the leaders are especially important, since most of those who
served on the Small Business Committees considered it a minor legislative
assignment. Consequently, the few congressmen with a passionate interest in
small business had a disproportionate influence on the committees' work.[10]

Wright Patman: Neo-Antitruster

Wright Patman's biographer describes him as a politician with a singular concern with protecting "the little man." This concern sprang from his humble origins. Patman was born in a shack to a poor tenant-farm family, and his strict fundamentalist Baptist upbringing instilled in him a concern for applying the Golden Rule to politics and business. In 1928, he won a seat in Congress as the representative of a rural, poverty-stricken district in the northeastern corner of Texas. From the beginning, he opposed "greedy and selfish" Wall Street bankers, and over the years he garnered a reputation as "Mister Small Business" and the "last of the Populists."[11]

Throughout his long career as a congressman, Patman endeavored to strengthen the antitrust laws, but he also became convinced that antitrust legislation alone could not ensure the survival of small business. Whereas some antitrusters tried to increase competition to benefit the consumer, Patman wished to limit it in order to assist small business. Thus, like many other small business advocates, he argued for the necessity of anti-chain-store legislation on the grounds that the government needed to curb the "excesses of competition" to preserve small business; otherwise, large corporations would eliminate competition altogether by virtue of their market power. For the same reason, he campaigned long and hard for direct government aid to small business as a check against the power of large corporations.

Although many members of the Small Business Committees considered him overbearing and dictatorial (Senator Capehart characterized him as "almost a perfect demagogue"), Patman influenced the thinking of other prominent congressmen. He acted as a "legislative mentor" to Representative (later Senator) Estes Kefauver and worked closely with Senator John Sparkman, with whom he shared a common background and interests. Like Patman, Sparkman rose "from tenant farm boy to United States [congressman]" (his campaign slogan in 1946), and he shared Patman's populistic outlook. In fact, Sparkman wrote his master's thesis on the history of populism in Alabama.[12]

James Murray: Counterorganization

James E. Murray (D.-Mont.), founder and chairman of the Senate Small Business Committee, came from a very different background. As the member of a prominent Montana mining family, Murray was "one of the wealthiest" U.S. senators. A sense of *noblesse oblige* led Murray to seek government aid for those

Representative Wright Patman. Known as "Mr. Small Business," Patman spent nearly a half century in Congress championing the cause of small business. (Courtesy of the Library of Congress)

less fortunate than himself. Murray shared Patman's distrust of monopoly and believed that the Anaconda Copper Company (a corporation controlled by Rockefeller interests) had made his state an economic colony of the East. As a politician, he also recognized that his state consisted almost entirely of small businesses; therefore, in his successful 1934 bid for a Senate seat, he ran on a campaign promise that he would become the voice of small business in Washington.[13]

Republican senator Robert A. Taft (left) chats with Senator James A. Murray
(right), his Democratic colleague on the Senate Small Business Committee
(circa 1950). (Courtesy of Montana Historical Society, Helena)

Unlike Patman, Murray accepted the necessity of the "organizational revolution" that produced large bureaucratic organizations. According to the original Brandeisian ideology of small business, big business posed a threat to
democracy because it produced big government; but during the New Deal, a
new conception of "counterorganization" provided an alternative way of dealing with the threat of big business. As an advocate of counterorganization (or
"interest group liberalism"), Murray wanted to create a system of checks and
balances by organizing business people, workers, and farmers into countervailing power blocs. The successful organization of labor and farmers convinced Murray and others that they could gather small business people into a
cohesive interest group. Government coordination of interest groups would,
he believed, balance the economy and preserve a place for small business in an
organizational society. The failure of Murray and others to create a new pressure group of business owners may explain the fleeting interest most congressional legislators had in issues related to small business.[14]

Robert A. Taft: Public Use of Private Interest

Like Murray, Senator Robert A. Taft was born with a silver spoon in his mouth. As the son of President William H. Taft, he shared his father's antagonism toward monopoly. Like his father, Taft believed that a healthy small business sector guaranteed the survival of individual liberty and forestalled public demands for the nationalization of big business. Taft's admiration for his grandfather, a successful business owner, also contributed to his interest in the problems of small business.[15]

In contrast to some of his colleagues on the Small Business Committees, Taft had a rather sophisticated understanding of the place of small business in the modern American economy. Historian Thomas K. McCraw has criticized Louis Brandeis and his followers for failing to recognize the natural development of big business in certain capital-intensive industries.[16] McCraw describes how Brandeis's hatred for bigness blinded him to the new economic reality of a dual economy made up of "core" (large) and "peripheral" (small) firms. Taft, however, did realize that "certain industries must be conducted by large units."[17] He also recognized the persistence of small business and understood that "the growth of large companies . . . does not necessarily cut out the small company."[18] Anticipating the work of later writers, Taft emphasized the successes of small business, especially in the area of technological innovation and job creation.

Taft also differed from other small business advocates in the extent to which he believed the government should intervene on behalf of small firms. He accepted the need for antitrust legislation and government aid on behalf of disadvantaged groups but worried that excessive government control might threaten the freedom of individuals and businesses. Thus, he opposed direct government loans to small business, because "once you invite the government in, it is not unlikely to become a permanent guest."[19]

Taft preferred to rely on what economist Charles L. Schultze has called "the public use of private interest," or the use of incentives to encourage the private sector to engage in activity deemed to be in the public interest. For example, in 1944, as a member of the Senate Small Business Committee, Taft tried unsuccessfully to establish a program of government loan insurance that would "use our present processes of saving and capital investment." Loan insurance had "the advantage of removing the matter largely from political influence," a problem that revealed itself later in the scandals involving the Reconstruction Finance Corporation.[20] In addition, he favored deregulation and a repeal of the capital gains tax as ways to reduce the paperwork burden and encourage investment in small business.

Senator Joseph O'Mahoney (D.-Wyo.), chairman of the Temporary National Economic Committee (TNEC), shared Taft's desire to limit government interference in the private sector by relying on antitrust enforcement and the "public use of private interest." Like Taft, he opposed direct government aid to small business; instead, he favored a supply-side policy of encouraging investment in small business by cutting the taxes of high-income individuals. According to his biographer, O'Mahoney believed that "business would be stimulated, the public's purchasing power would be expanded, and the government's revenue would likewise be expanded." Most important, these indirect measures to benefit small business would not add to the national debt or create a large, meddlesome bureaucracy.[21]

Emanuel Celler: Orthodox Antitruster

Although he emerged as an opponent of federal anti-chain-store legislation, Emanuel Celler considered himself a small business advocate and was a staunch adversary of big business. Celler's interest in fighting monopoly sprang from his own confrontation with one of the nation's largest banks. Celler alleged that in 1930, when he tried to sell a small bank he owned, the Manufacturers Trust Company exerted its influence to prevent others from making bids; consequently, Celler had to accept an unfavorable offer from this bank. After that, Celler became so obsessed with his study of monopoly that he "could only see the picture of corporations before me as so many octopuses, reaching out to rake in more and more of the lesser fry."[22]

Celler's concern with the "lesser fry" never led him to depart from the proconsumer, procompetitive aim of the antitrust laws. In fact, his faith in the efficacy of antitrust prosecutions earned him a reputation as "Trustbuster Celler." Celler believed that by enhancing competition, the antitrust laws protected the interests of both the small business owner and the consumer. Thus he opposed the Robinson-Patman and Miller-Tydings acts, because both laws, he believed, limited competition and raised consumer prices.

Celler also differed from other small business advocates in his assessment of the chain store and its future impact on American society. Patman and other critics saw the chain store as purely a social "menace," but as early as 1929, Celler recognized that "the chain store is here to stay" because "the consumer seems well satisfied."[23] Like Taft and O'Mahoney, Celler doubted that anyone could predict the long-term effect of chain store competition; for that reason,

Representative Emanuel Celler. "Trustbuster Celler" emerged as the chief critic of anti-chain-store legislation because he believed it departed from the antitrust tradition of promoting competition. (Courtesy of the Library of Congress)

he counseled Congress to exercise restraint. He explained, "I am not omniscient. I have no 'cure all' up my sleeve. The problem is too new. Only time will bring a solution."[24]

The Ideological Origins of Small Business Politics

These brief biographical sketches offer insight into the dynamics of the small business ideology and its impact on the politics of small business. By its very nature, ideology oversimplifies reality by providing a basic understanding of "how the world works." A coherent ideology can bring together those who share a common vision of society but who disagree on particular issues. For example, congressional small business advocates agreed that democratic capitalism depended on a thriving small business sector. Yet their rhetoric obscured disagreements over the means used to preserve the "backbone of democracy." During times of perceived crisis, these disagreements receded into the background, but the return of peace and prosperity brought them back to the surface and caused splits in the small business advocates' congressional coalition.

The similarity in views espoused by Senator Taft, a "conservative," and Senators O'Mahoney and Celler, "liberals," suggests the inadequacy of the traditional liberal/conservative dichotomy. In his intellectual history of ideology, Thomas Sowell offers another way to approach the study of politics: by tracing the origins of political struggles to contrasting visions of society.[25] Those with a "constrained vision," such as Taft and O'Mahoney, believed that the knowledge needed to engineer society is beyond the grasp of policymakers, who cannot predict all of the consequences of their actions. As constrained visionaries, Taft and O'Mahoney emphasized freedom from government control and favored placing restraints on public policymakers. When at all possible, they preferred that the government conduct its public policy by acting indirectly through market processes. Like other congressional small business advocates, these constrained visionaries sought positive aid for small business, but only through indirect means (e.g., tax cuts, loan insurance).

On the other hand, "unconstrained visionaries," such as James Murray and Wright Patman, believe it is in the "public interest" to have policymakers directly intervene in the economy to achieve a social good. They maintain that policymakers can determine the public interest and have a moral duty to act on their knowledge of it. Unconstrained visionaries minimize the negative consequences of their actions and stress the positive freedoms that might result from their interventions in the marketplace. Thus, Murray, Patman, and other small business advocates sought direct government aid for small firms to achieve the positive good of increased small business opportunity.

Congressional small business advocates sometimes split along liberal/conservative lines when they debated the degree to which the federal government should intervene in the business sector of the economy; more often, though, they united or divided based on their contrasting visions of society and their differing interpretations of the small business ideology. One thing they did agree on, however, was the need to move beyond the reactive antitrust approach to the problems of small business. By the time the United States entered World War II, small business advocates were convinced that they would have to seek positive aid on behalf of small firms, while still maintaining their campaign to enforce the antitrust laws.

5

War and Peace: The Politics
of Small Business in the 1940s

On the eve of America's entry into World War II, Senator Joseph O'Mahoney (D.-Wyo.) warned that "if we let little business go down in a total effort to defend democracy we shall let the very foundation of democracy perish. The total effort will result in total government."[1] O'Mahoney was concerned that the growing concentration of defense contracts with large corporations would tie big business to big government and thereby leave small business out of the military buildup. This fear that big business might squeeze small manufacturers out of the war effort fueled demands for government assistance. With the antitrust laws suspended for the duration of the war, congressional small business advocates aggressively used crisis rhetoric to secure the creation of the Smaller War Plants Corporation (SWPC), the first federal agency to represent small manufacturers.

The brief and unsuccessful history of the SWPC highlights some of the problems faced by past policymakers who attempted to aid small business. The agency fell victim to bureaucratic rivalries, partisan politics and, above all, its inability to organize a heterogeneous community of small business owners into an effective pressure group. Although this chapter suggests the limitations of an industrial policy directed at the small business sector of the economy, it also challenges historians' gloomy assessment of the position of small manufacturers during World War II. Despite the shortcomings of the government's policies, small manufacturers adapted well to the wartime economy and viewed their postwar prospects with optimism; consequently, they did not respond to the crisis rhetoric of the small business advocates. The SWPC had no constituency; therefore, its congressional allies lacked the political support needed to transform it into a powerful, permanent agency.

FDR's Search for a Small Business
Constituency, 1938–1941

In the years just prior to World War II, politicians in both parties tried to organize small business owners and secure representation for them in the political process. In 1938, a Washington insider noted that "the successful politician with a nose for votes has made a new discovery. . . . He has found ready-made for his purposes a vast army" of disaffected small business owners.[2] After Congress passed the Robinson-Patman and Miller-Tydings Acts, President Franklin D. Roosevelt was one of those who jumped on the political bandwagon, hoping to capitalize on the growing interest in small business by incorporating small business owners into his New Deal coalition. Roosevelt was also responding to the criticism of corporate executives who had spoken out against his policies favoring organized labor and increased corporate taxation. The president sought to contain this business opposition by cultivating the support of small business owners. Thus, in the words of historian Ellis Hawley, the administration adopted a policy of " 'Save-Little-Business,' if not 'Kill-Big-Business.' "[3]

Roosevelt's overtures to small business failed to have the desired effect, however. In February 1938, Secretary of Commerce Daniel Roper sponsored a conference of small business people in Washington, D.C., but the delegates passed resolutions critical of the New Deal.[4] The executive committee of the conference demanded tax and spending cuts, stricter enforcement of the antitrust laws, an investigation of the National Labor Relations Board, and government-insured loans for small business.[5] In the aftermath of the conference, the Commerce Department received 3,700 letters from small business owners recommending various policy measures. Most of the correspondents sought government aid while denouncing government regulation, and Roper complained that "self help seems to be well nigh lacking" among these small business people.[6]

Initially, Republican members of Congress charged the administration with having "handpicked and railroaded" the delegates; but after the delegates attacked Roosevelt, conservatives took the opportunity to denounce the New Deal and its effect on small business. The Republicans denied Roosevelt's assertion that the interests of small business conflicted with those of big business, and they criticized the president for engaging in political gimmickry.[7]

The vehemence of the Republican attack revealed their concern that the president might attract the votes of an organized interest group of small business voters.

Yet although the conference spawned dozens of associations claiming to represent small business, in reality there was no common denominator uniting all small business owners. Most small business owners identified with their trade or industry rather than with the size of their company. Earlier studies of small business owners' responses to the New Deal found them divided by industry and by region. Similarly, in 1938, a Gallup poll revealed that small business owners agreed on few issues, and a contemporary described them as "the most confused group" in American politics. This lack of agreement limited the political influence of small business advocates. Between 1933 and 1942, Congress considered 390 bills to aid small business, but only twenty-six became law, and most of these were minor pieces of legislation providing assistance to small firms in a single line of trade.[8]

Charles Daughters, a Democratic small business activist and author of *Wells of Discontent*, an anti-chain-store tract, later lamented that "the Washington conference received a very bad press and left an unhealthy taste for small businessmen in the mouths of both the President and Mr. Roper."[9] In time-honored fashion, Roosevelt sought to save face by deferring the whole issue to a blue-ribbon commission. Thus, in April 1938, he called for an investigation of big business's impact on small business and the economy at large. Echoing the rhetoric of the small business advocates, Roosevelt associated the rise of big business in Germany with the emergence of fascism. In America, Roosevelt declared, monopoly had produced the Great Depression, and it threatened to "master our democratic government" unless Congress passed legislation to strengthen the antitrust laws and assist small business.[10]

Congress responded by creating the Temporary National Economic Committee (TNEC), which during the next three years published monographs critical of big business.[11] Overall, however, the TNEC offered a mixed bag to small business advocates. On the one hand, the TNEC's study of small business presented a positive assessment of chain stores and noted the "injurious" effects of chain taxes.[12] In its final 1941 report, the TNEC also expressed opposition to price-discrimination laws and called for the repeal of the Miller-Tydings Act. On the other hand, the committee recommended stricter enforcement of the antitrust laws and positive aid for "the Lilliputian members of the economic household."[13]

Although President Roosevelt was disappointed with the results of his small business conference, he still hoped to benefit politically by promoting public policies favoring small business. Roosevelt insisted on including a small business plank in the Democratic Party platform of 1940, because Senator Murray and others had convinced him that it "might add a million votes" in his campaign for reelection.[14] The heterogeneous nature of the small business community, however, meant that the Democrats could not count on a solid bloc of voters. Worse yet, the National Small Business Men's Association (NSBMA) had gained attention as a vocal critic of the administration. In 1940, Dewitt Emery, founder and president of the NSBMA, agreed to head a Small Business Division of the Republican National Committee.[15] Meanwhile, Charles G. Daughters worked to establish a rival pro-administration organization. Daughters decided that a congressional committee would best serve this purpose, and in July 1940, he persuaded Representative A. J. Sabath to introduce a House resolution calling for the creation of a special committee to study the problems of small business. At the same time, Daughters approached Senator James Murray (D.-Mont.) and asked him to lead the drive to create a Senate Small Business Committee. Murray accepted the task because he felt that Democratic small business advocates needed a forum to counter the rhetoric of NSBMA and other "front organizations" controlled by Republican interests.[16]

Throughout the summer of 1940, Murray held conferences between small business owners and government officials while trying to secure congressional support for his proposal to create a Senate Small Business Committee. Initially, many senators opposed the creation of a special committee because they felt that it would duplicate the TNEC, but Murray convinced them of the need to extend the TNEC's work into the next decade. Furthermore, Murray argued that farmers and workers had secured governmental representation and that "now is the time to do something for small business." Murray's proposal received the endorsement of Republican senators Robert Taft (R.-Ohio) and Arthur Capper (R.-Kans.), both of whom had a longstanding interest in issues affecting small business. His efforts finally paid off in October 1940, when the Senate voted unanimously to create a special small business committee. As chair of the new committee, Murray hoped to use his position to deflect Republican criticism of the administration's small business policies.[17]

Partisan politics also played a role in the creation of the House Small Business Committee. In the summer of 1941, House Republicans created their own unofficial small business committee, chaired by Charles Halleck (R.-Ind.). The leaders of the Democratic National Committee feared that the GOP would capitalize on the growing "dissatisfaction and resentment" of small business owners, many of whom felt they had not received a fair share of defense contracts. Therefore, in December 1941, the Democrats stole the thunder of the

Republicans by creating an official select committee on small business, chaired by Wright Patman (D.-Tex.).[18]

By the end of 1941, several attempts to organize small business owners had ended in failure because too much divided the small business community. Partisan politics had resulted in the creation of congressional committees claiming to speak for small business, but the lack of an organized pressure group of business owners meant that the members of these committees had to rely on the ideological appeal of small business and resort to crisis rhetoric in order to secure their legislation. These two elements, crisis and ideology, would continue to play an important role in defining the politics of small business during World War II.

The Creation of the Smaller War Plants Corporation

The creation of these congressional Small Business Committees occurred at a time when the war in Europe had intensified the concern many Americans had about the fate of small business. Both Murray and Patman feared that the war would undermine the position of small manufacturers because the conversion to a war economy created special problems for these firms. Small manufacturers suffered disproportionately from labor shortages, price controls, and a military bureaucracy that seemed to favor big business. President Roosevelt also lost interest in small business. Large manufacturers could quickly meet the demands of the war effort; therefore, in March 1942, the president ordered his attorney general to suspend all antitrust suits.[19]

The military's top brass expressed their sympathy for small business but argued that only the largest corporations could produce the materiel needed in the mobilization effort. Thus the head of the Services of Supply, General Brehon Somervell, declared that "all the small plants of the country could not turn out one day's requirements of ammunition." Similarly, Undersecretary of War Robert P. Patterson expressed the military's laissez-faire attitude toward small business with his remark that "we had to take industrial America as we found it."[20] This contention that the structure of American industry naturally favored big business outraged congressional small business advocates, who blamed the concentration of contracts on the influence of corporate lobbyists.

Throughout 1940 and 1941, the Small Business Committees tried to increase small manufacturers' share of military spending, but their efforts accomplished little. In October 1940, the National Defense Advisory Council (NDAC) created a short-lived Office of Small Business Activities. Several months later, the Office of Production Management (OPM) replaced the NDAC; and in September 1941, an executive order created a Division of Contract Distribution (DCD) within the OPM. The head of the DCD, Floyd B. Odlum, focused his efforts on those firms with fewer than twenty employees. These firms could not acquire the raw materials needed to convert to war production; for this reason, Odlum offered a plan to set aside 2 percent of all critical materials for their use. The officials at OPM rejected Odlum's plan, however, because they believed these firms were simply too small to meet most defense contracts.[21]

Congressional small business advocates sharply criticized the procurement agencies for their lack of concern with the survival of small business. In November 1941, the Senate Committee to Investigate the National Defense Program (also known as the Truman Committee) chastised the military for constructing new plants rather than using the existing capacity of small firms. The Truman Committee also criticized the OPM for failing to increase the production of raw materials and predicted that thousands of firms would fail unless Congress took immediate action.[22]

This growing concern about the fate of small manufacturers prompted action by government agencies eager to prevent congressional interference in their operations. The Department of Justice created a bureau to investigate the complaints of small firms, and in December 1941, the Department of Commerce, which claimed to represent all of the nation's businesses, set up its own Small Business Unit. This unit represented little more than a sop to Congress, however, since the Commerce Department merely shuffled personnel and limited the unit's activities to the publication of technical and managerial aids.[23]

Meanwhile, in Congress, as before the war, the political appeal of this issue crossed party lines. In a series of articles devoted to small business, the *Congressional Digest* abandoned its usual practice of offering opposing points of view because this issue was "all Pro and no Con."[24] Small business advocates tried to exploit the universal appeal of small business by introducing measures to reform the procurement process. Senator James Mead (D.-N.Y.) submitted legislation requiring the procurement agencies to use the idle capacity of small plants before financing the construction of new ones. In the House, Representative Jerry Voorhis (D.-Calif.) introduced a bill requiring large companies to subcontract out to small plants. But the military convinced congressional leaders that this type of legislation might interfere with war production, so these bills never made it out of committee.[25]

The crisis rhetoric of the congressional small business advocates reached a fever pitch after the Japanese bombed Pearl Harbor. One week after the attack,

Senator Murray warned that small business might be "wiped out" if the government did not offer assistance to struggling firms. Murray associated the preservation of small business with American war aims. He believed that America, a land of free enterprise, was fighting a war against collectivist Germany and Japan. Yet Murray also feared that the war would result in the collectivization of the American economy. In February 1942, his committee reported that fifty-six manufacturers had received three-quarters of all defense contracts, and it solemnly warned that the "death knell is ringing" for small manufacturers.[26]

Personal and political considerations also played a role in Murray's decision to act as an advocate for small business. As a member of a prominent Montana mining family, Murray sought legislation on behalf of western mining interests. He also lamented the depopulation of Montana that had resulted as workers migrated to industrial cities on the coasts. Along with Senator Harry S. Truman, Murray urged the military to redistribute defense production to the interior states. (In 1941, the TNEC reported that Montana had not received a single defense contract worth over $10,000.)[27] Thus, this sectional rivalry sparked congressional interest in small business, as states left out of the military buildup sought a larger share of defense dollars.

Murray believed that small manufacturers would not receive their "fair" share of government contracts until they secured representation within the federal government. Therefore, in February 1942, he introduced a bill to create a Smaller War Plants Division (SWPD) within the War Production Board, the central planning agency in the mobilization effort. (The WPB had replaced the OPM in January.) The head of the SWPD would sit on the WPB's board of directors and certify the capacity of small plants to carry out defense contracts. A separate Smaller War Plants Corporation would finance small-plant conversion to war production. The SWPC could also make loans, lease property, and acquire prime contracts on behalf of small firms. Murray hoped to counter big business influence within the WPB by establishing the SWPC as the small business person's lobbyist in Washington. If this act failed to save small business, Murray declared, America would succumb to totalitarianism. He also warned President Roosevelt that if the Democrats failed to create a small business agency, the Republicans would certainly exploit the issue in the next election.[28]

The chairman of the War Production Board, Donald Nelson, resented this encroachment on his authority and tried to make the SWPC a mere adjunct to his agency. As czar of the mobilization effort, Nelson demanded the power to appoint the SWPC's board of directors; and because Nelson enjoyed the support of the president, the Senate Small Business Committee reluctantly agreed to his request. In effect, this concession eliminated the independence of the proposed agency and left it dependent on the goodwill of WPB officials.[29]

Murray's bill also faced opposition from Jesse Jones, the secretary of commerce and chairman of the Reconstruction Finance Corporation (RFC), a federal lending agency. Jones insisted that "small business gets more attention than big business in the RFC" and argued that a new agency was unnecessary because the RFC already met the financial needs of small manufacturers. He offered a substitute bill placing the SWPC's lending powers within the RFC. After a heated debate in the Senate Banking and Currency Committee, Jones's proposal went down to defeat by a vote of eleven to seven. The committee then approved Murray's bill, and it passed the Senate unanimously on 1 April.[30]

Meanwhile, Wright Patman guided similar legislation through the House. His bill doubled the agency's capital to $200 million, granted antitrust immunity to production pools made up of small plants, gave the SWPC authority over essential civilian production, and set an expiration date of 1 July 1945. The Senate left it up to Patman to define "small" business. The members of the Senate Banking and Currency Committee had failed to come up with a definition of small business: according to James Hughes, they "tried to define it but could not do so." Murray felt comfortable leaving that determination up to the administrator of the SWPC. Finally, after a great deal of debate, Patman defined a small plant as one with fewer than five hundred employees.[31]

Because the SWPC remained subordinate to the WPB, Patman's bill faced little opposition from the military; for this reason, many representatives took the opportunity to make a symbolic gesture toward small business. Speaker after speaker declared that small business was the "backbone of democracy." Patman's bill sailed through the House, passing unanimously on 26 May. A conference committee accepted his amendments but lowered the SWPC's capital to $150 million. On 11 June, President Roosevelt signed the bill into law, creating the nation's first small business agency.[32]

The Small Business Committees had high hopes for the SWPC. Senator Murray expected it to act as an "aggressive agency" and claimed that its mere existence bolstered the morale of small manufacturers. According to Murray, the agency also served as a useful stepping-stone for the "ambitious future program" planned by the Small Business Committees. Although the act limited the SWPC's jurisdiction to manufacturing, the committees hoped to eventually expand it into an agency representing all types of small business.[33]

Nelson's actions would soon disappoint the small business advocates, however. He opposed relief measures that would interfere with the war effort, and

Franklin D. Roosevelt signs the bill creating the Smaller War Plants
Corporation, the first federal small business agency (11 June 1942). Senator
James A. Murray (left), Senator James Mead (right), and Representative Wright
Patman (center) look on. (Courtesy of UPI/Bettmann Archive)

he later complained of "too many plans to 'rescue' little business without
giving it a chance to rescue itself." Nelson limited the SWPC's assistance to
those firms contributing to military or essential civilian production.[34] Nelson's
choice for SWPC administrator also reflected his desire to place limits on the
new agency. In July, he appointed Lou Holland, deputy chairman of the WPB,
to head both the SWPC and SWPD. A Kansas City businessman and a close
personal friend of Senator Truman, Holland had successfully organized small-
plant production pools in the Kansas City area. Nonetheless, he proved to be
an ineffective administrator of this government agency. His lack of government experience, coupled with a wartime labor shortage, contributed to the
agency's difficulties in recruiting personnel. Consequently, the SWPC did not
approve its first loan until 24 September 1942 and did not assign regional loan
agents until 17 November.[35]

Holland sought the cooperation of the military by renouncing any use of the
SWPC's prime contracting power, which procurement officers regarded as an
intolerable infringement on their right to place contracts with the most quali-

fied firms. He also refused to accept the transfer of personnel from the DCD because they were on bad terms with the military's procurement officers. But Holland's nonconfrontational style of management won him few friends. In its coverage of the agency, *Business Week* reported that Holland "acts scared in a job no one envies him." Under Holland, the SWPC threatened no one and, like its predecessors, remained a paper tiger.[36]

Lou Holland's biographer, James W. Leyerzapf, speculated that "the Small Business act was motivated less by a sincere desire to help small business than it was by cynical political motives." He believes that Patman and Murray knew that the military could use its right of inspection to revoke the prime contracting power of the SWPC. If the military refused to let the SWPC manage prime contracts, the two congressmen could point to a conspiracy against small business; if, on the other hand, Holland refused to take prime contracts, they could clamor for a new administrator. Either way, Murray and Patman could make political hay out of the issue. But Leyerzapf overlooks the compromises Murray and Patman had to make in order to get their legislation passed by Congress. Given the constellation of forces arrayed against them, it is not surprising that the congressional small business advocates accepted a relatively weak SWPC, instead of nothing at all.[37]

Despite their disappointment with Holland's performance, the members of the congressional Small Business Committees did not initially criticize the SWPC, because they took a proprietary interest in the agency and wished to portray it in a positive light. The fall elections also diverted their attention from the agency.[38] In November, Patman offered a favorable progress report, noting Holland's success in securing the cooperation of the procurement agencies and reporting that the SWPC organization was "practically completed."[39] But this spirit of harmony did not last. As he campaigned for reelection, Murray warned of "the imminent destruction of thousands upon thousands of small plants" and declared that small manufacturers needed a "figurative oxygen tank" to survive wartime dislocations. Other congressmen expressed concern with securing aid for their districts. Representative Emanuel Celler (D.-N.Y.), for example, criticized the SWPC for doing "nothing for New York City."[40] Holland had also antagonized these small business advocates by refusing to hire their friends and constituents. Clearly, the SWPC's star was falling fast in Congress.[41]

Congressional dissatisfaction intensified in December, when the House Small Business Committee toured the South and discovered that the SWPC had no field offices there. Senator Murray described the SWPC's performance as "extremely discouraging," while Patman criticized Holland for refusing to take prime contracts. The Texas congressman insisted that Congress would appropriate an additional billion dollars if Holland requested it, but the budget-conscious administrator refused to do so.[42]

Holland responded by defending his administration and pointing to the $156 million in defense contracts that the SWPC had helped small plants to secure. He rejected the crisis rhetoric of Murray and Patman, citing the low number of loan applications as a sign that many small plants had successfully converted to war production. A Commerce Department study provided some basis for this optimism: it showed that very few manufacturers had failed. Apparently, most had overcome their early difficulties.[43]

The Small Business Committees ignored this good news and insisted that they represented a disaffected constituency of small manufacturers desperate for government assistance. At times, congressional criticism of the SWPC became shrill. Patman criticized the agency for its delays in loan processing, claiming that one of his constituents "became so nervous [waiting for his loan] . . . that he actually died"![44] In a letter to the president, Patman described the SWPC as "an absolute failure and a flop" and Holland as an incompetent who "does not have any more executive ability than a section foreman on a railway." Patman had no more faith in the SWPC staff, who he termed "a bunch of fifth raters."[45] Republican small business advocates joined in criticizing Holland. Representative Walter G. Ploeser (R.-Mo.), for example, considered the SWPC's performance "an insult to the intelligence of this Congress."[46]

President Roosevelt reacted to these complaints by searching for a new SWPC administrator. Initially, he suggested the "wild idea" of appointing Joseph Kennedy head of the SWPC, but Kennedy considered the SWPC's mission an impossible one, given the constraints placed on the agency.[47] Patman continued to pressure the president to name a new administrator; and on 19 January 1943, Roosevelt finally replaced Holland with Colonel Robert Wood Johnson, chief of army ordnance in New York. Murray, Patman, and the president had offered the post to Johnson in June 1942, but he had refused because he believed the SWPC was then in a "hopeless situation." By 1943, however, Johnson was heartened by the progress made by small manufacturers and was more optimistic about what he could achieve for these small firms.[48]

Although Johnson was a big businessman (the chairman of Johnson & Johnson), the Small Business Committees admired his work on behalf of small firms and believed he would act more aggressively than Holland.[49] The forced resignation of Holland, however, opened a rift between Truman and the other congressional small business advocates. In his typical fashion, Truman stuck with his friend and remained alone in his defense of Holland's management.

He viewed the appointment of Johnson as part of a WPB "conspiracy" to "break up" the agency and promised to "make Patman eat dirt" for his attacks on Holland.[50]

Several factors limited the effectiveness of the SWPC during its first six months of existence. First, the SWPC could not intervene in the procurement process without first securing the permission of WPB officials; thus the agency could do little more than inform small manufacturers of contract opportunities. Holland's stand-pat approach further dashed the Small Business Committees' hopes that the agency would actively lobby on behalf of small business owners. Finally, Holland's denial of the existence of a small business crisis antagonized members of the Small Business Committees because it undercut the basis of their support in Congress. As we shall see, this debate over the existence of a small business crisis continued even after Johnson replaced Holland as SWPC administrator.

Robert Johnson Revamps the Smaller War Plants Corporation

As SWPC administrator, Johnson immediately took steps to reorganize and strengthen his agency. The procurement agencies could not possibly contact all of the thousands of small plants in the country; therefore, Johnson decentralized the agency by creating fourteen regional boards of governors made up of local business owners. In addition, he authorized regional loan agents to make loans of up to $25,000 without home office approval, and he secured WPB approval for price differentials in favor of small manufacturers.[51]

Johnson experienced a great deal more difficulty in attracting personnel to the SWPC. The agency desperately needed more employees, so in March, Johnson persuaded Nelson to merge the SWPD with the SWPC. Although the SWPC thereby acquired four hundred additional employees, in Johnson's eyes the agency remained understaffed.[52] Johnson tried to hire employees from the War Production Board, but WPB officials blocked this "pirating of personnel." He recruited "dollar-a-year men" from large corporations, but red tape prevented many of them from working for the SWPC. Johnson also faced financial obstacles that prevented him from hiring additional employees. In 1943, Congress appropriated only $12 million of the $18 million he requested for operating expenses, leading Johnson to complain that Congress treated the agency as if it were a "static and senile bureau." According to Johnson's estimate, the SWPC needed 2,500 employees to fulfill its tasks, but by May the agency had only 1,100 on its payroll.[53]

Despite these difficulties, Johnson rejected the notion of a small business crisis. Surveys performed by the swpc revealed that fewer than 2,500 plants were "distressed" (i.e., operating at less than two-thirds of their prewar capacity), and Johnson channeled the swpc's limited resources to these firms. He assigned these plants to procurement agencies or prime contractors and persuaded the wpb to authorize higher prices if necessary to keep them in business. Johnson also used his corporate connections by working with the American Bankers Association and the National Association of Manufacturers. Together, they encouraged large corporations to subcontract out to smaller firms. Johnson emphasized, however, that the swpc could not "wet nurse" all of the nation's 165,000 small manufacturers, and he stressed that small firms would have to rely largely on their own resources.[54]

Johnson's policies outraged Senator Murray, who criticized him for adopting an "attitude of paternalism" by using his big business influence on behalf of small businesses.[55] The Montana senator continued to promote the idea of a small business crisis. He feared that if big business expanded its market share during the war, the United States would follow "the road to totalitarianism." Consequently, Murray's committee demanded a more aggressive lending policy, increased prime contracting, and a greater emphasis on civilian production.[56]

Johnson, in turn, complained that constant criticism from Congress hurt agency morale. He also noted that the wpb opposed the taking of prime contracts by the swpc; and since Chairman Nelson had to approve prime contracts, the agency simply could not act in this area. Nevertheless, Johnson retained his optimism about the future of small business, noting that very few plants were idle and that bankruptcy rates were below normal. Small firms had adjusted well to the wartime economy, largely without government aid, and Johnson concluded that small business was "in a stronger position now than it has been for a quarter of a century."[57]

Several surveys confirmed Johnson's optimism. Large corporations received most defense contracts, but small plants also enjoyed wartime prosperity. According to Dun and Bradstreet, business failures were at a twenty-year low. In March 1943, the Commerce Department reported that manufacturing failures had declined during the war; and in May, a Commerce Department official stated that the "outlook for small plants in the war economy grows steadily brighter."[58] Similarly, the *Executives' Defense Digest* reported, "Washington is impressed by the disappearance of complaints that small business isn't getting its share of war contracts." The Office of War Information (owi) reached a similar conclusion. The owi surveyed 3,500 plants with fewer than

125 employees and found that the product value of these plants had increased 16 percent since 1941. Two-thirds of their owners thought their situation was "more satisfactory" than it had been before the war, and only 5 percent feared the prospect of having to close down their operations. Conditions varied by industry and by plant size. Firms in the largest category (21–125 employees) were more satisfied than those in the smallest category (0–7 employees). Many firms reported labor and material shortages, but few complained of an inability to obtain defense contracts. Only 4 percent needed war production and could not secure any orders at all.[59]

Although the position of small business had improved since he took over the swpc, Johnson believed that he could not operate under a crisis mandate; and in September 1943, he resigned as chairman. Johnson complained that the agency was a "political football," and he criticized the Small Business Committees for their policy of "government by catastrophe." According to Johnson, congressional small business advocates used the swpc to distribute political pork to their constituents.[60] He further criticized them for unrealistically expecting the agency to serve all of the nation's small businesses. Johnson now thought that the government had become the problem, rather than the solution, to the difficulties of small business. For instance, he complained that "we started with time-consuming conferences about toilets"; apparently, the agency had exceeded its toilet quota and Johnson had had to witness "a solemn padlocking of our excess sanitary equipment"! He also complained of red tape, wage and price controls, and the intransigence of procurement officers. In short, the swpc had become "*an agency to defend small business from government*" (original italics).[61]

By the end of 1943, the swpc had lost much of the support of the congressional Small Business Committees. These committees had failed to convince the agency's first two administrators that small business faced a crisis situation, in large part because Holland and Johnson recognized the healthy state of small manufacturing. Publicly, congressional small business advocates continued to express hope that the agency might recover from its slow start; privately, though, they were extremely pessimistic about the agency's future.[62]

Maury Maverick's Administration

The aggressive policies pursued by Johnson's successor renewed their optimism. In January 1944, President Roosevelt appointed Maury Maverick to the chair of the swpc. Described as an "ardent New Dealer" and antitruster,

Maverick had served as a WPB administrator, as a congressman from Texas, and as one-time mayor of San Antonio. Contemporaries considered him "one of the most colorful figures in Washington."[63] Unlike Johnson, Maverick had no reservations about government aid to small business. He wholeheartedly accepted the small business ideology and defended government intervention in the economy. (He later asserted that "free enterprise is preserved by the Government.")[64] Maverick praised the Small Business Committees for demonstrating "the leadership of consciousness in Congress," and like his congressional allies, he hoped to expand the agency to serve wholesalers and retailers as well as manufacturers.[65]

Maverick moved beyond Johnson's "distressed plant" policy and declared that his agency would represent all of the nation's 165,000 small manufacturers. He reorganized the SWPC, launched a public relations blitz to highlight the agency's services, and liberalized the agency's loan policy by emphasizing a company's financial need rather than its credit rating. Maverick also proclaimed a global mission for small business, predicting that the United States would dominate the world economy and, therefore, that foreign trade might become a "big field for little business."[66]

Maverick tried to renew congressional concern for the fate of small business by joining with the Small Business Committees to warn of a reconversion crisis. As military production peaked in 1944, the committees feared the effect of contract cancellations on small firms. Small business advocates believed that big business would use its war-strengthened position to grab civilian markets; therefore, they argued that the government should allow small plants to reconvert from military to civilian production before large corporations did so. Donald Nelson also favored such a policy, and in June 1944, he allowed firms to reconvert on an individual basis. The military, however, blocked Nelson's plans for early reconversion, and full-scale reconversion did not take place until the end of the war.[67]

Nonetheless, in 1944, Congress passed several acts designed to speed eventual reconversion to civilian production, and under this legislation the SWPC gained new responsibilities. The Contract Settlement Act ordered the agency to help small firms with contract terminations. Under the Servicemen's Readjustment Act (the "GI Bill"), the agency could guarantee business loans to veterans. The Surplus Property Act authorized the SWPC to purchase military surplus and resell it to small firms. Finally, the War Mobilization and Reconversion Act ordered the procurement agencies to consult with the SWPC in reserving materials for the exclusive use of small plants.[68]

Postwar Planning for Small Business

Maverick tried to use the SWPC's new duties as justification for continuing the agency into the postwar period. He also emphasized the long-term credit needs of small business and asked Congress to make his agency a "permanent source of credit." He criticized the banks for demanding a higher rate of interest for small loans and argued that the government should step in to offer credit at below-market interest rates. (Actually, since 1934 the Reconstruction Finance Corporation and the Federal Reserve had been making loans to businesses, but the conservative lending policies of these agencies limited the amount of funds available to small firms.)[69] Some observers doubted whether small businesses really suffered from a credit crunch. In one survey of six hundred small firms, only nine reported difficulties in obtaining credit.[70] Nonetheless, Maverick insisted that many small businesses would fail unless Congress created a credit insurance program administered by the SWPC. He renewed his crisis rhetoric by citing an increase in mergers as a sign that large corporations were acquiring small firms "like so many bags of potatoes."[71] If Congress did not grant positive aid to small business, the economy would collapse, and "our democracy will then be whirling right, and left, and in a circle."[72]

Congress did not act on Maverick's proposal, but President Roosevelt provided him with a new opportunity to plead his case. In October 1944, Roosevelt declared that the American economy would have to generate 60,000,000 jobs to maintain full employment after the war, and Maverick suggested that small business could fill the gap.[73] Maverick argued that with SWPC assistance, small businesses might employ more people by increasing their participation in foreign trade. In early 1945, he traveled to Europe to survey small business opportunities, and this trip convinced him that France, England, and the Soviet Union were potential markets for the goods of small American firms. He hoped that the SWPC's foreign missions on behalf of small business might persuade Congress to continue the agency indefinitely.[74] But the Commerce Department had a long history of promoting the exports of small manufacturers. Now the SWPC hoped to take over this area of responsibility, and the SWPC's encroachment on their bureaucratic "turf" antagonized Commerce Department officials and later led them to call for the agency's elimination.[75]

The creation of a permanent SWPC required the active support of small business people. Maverick claimed that the agency spoke as the "voice" of small business and that it had "a good reputation in the field." But SWPC field directors reported that many manufacturers did not even realize the SWPC was a federal agency.[76] Furthermore, in early 1944, Maverick's assistant, C. W.

Fowler, surveyed the attitudes of seven hundred beneficiaries of SWPC aid, and the results disappointed agency officials. Two-thirds of the firms expressed appreciation, but one-third denied receiving any assistance at all (a testament to the agency's poor record-keeping).[77] The responses of many firms belied the crisis rhetoric of the SWPC. Powhatan Brass and Iron Works of West Virginia reported they could "sell more than we can produce." Similarly, the Thompson Pipe and Steel Company of Denver, Colorado, was "too busy to take on any additional work." Others remained completely unaware of the SWPC's services. The Carolina Underwear Company, for example, described the SWPC as "just another Department, Corporation or Bureau that we read about."[78]

The SWPC conducted further studies that disclosed the healthy state of small business. A survey of Michigan manufacturers revealed their optimism about the future. Fully 60 percent hoped to acquire surplus machine tools at the end of the war, and half expected to pay cash. A second nationwide survey of two hundred manufacturers showed them to be divided over the immediate need for federally funded scientific research. In another study, Connecticut manufacturers stated their opposition to government aid during the postwar reconversion period. A majority agreed that if Congress offered aid to business, it should distribute it through banks rather than a federal agency.[79]

The SWPC also tried to organize small business associations into regional "Small Business Councils," but an agency study revealed that only six of the associations remained active and that most of these were "promotional propositions" interested only in collecting membership dues. One group, the Conference of American Small Business Organizations (CASBO), claimed to represent all of the nation's small business owners, but an SWPC official reported that "the meetings are . . . too small to speak with authority for all small business."[80] Little had changed since President Roosevelt's unsuccessful attempt to organize small business in 1938.

Without the support of an organized interest group of small business owners, the SWPC could not survive the war; thus, agency officials desperately searched for a constituency. Maverick sought to cultivate the support of two groups of potential entrepreneurs: women and veterans. He believed that many of those women who had entered the workforce during the war would later be interested in starting small businesses of their own. In February 1945, Maverick reached out to this group by appointing the first woman to a SWPC regional board of governors.[81] At the same time, Maverick promoted the SWPC as an agency for returning veterans. An army survey revealed that at least 700,000 veterans planned to open businesses after the war. Forty-two percent needed to borrow most of their capital, and many others needed technical or managerial assistance. Maverick thought that his agency could provide an "industrial homestead" for these veterans by offering loans, technical advice, and surplus property. He hoped thereby to eventually establish a million veterans in business.[82] In practice, however, the agency contacted very few veterans. The SWPC could lend only to manufacturers, while most veterans wanted to open shops in the service or retail sectors, where capital requirements were lower. Furthermore, the SWPC held no monopoly on assistance to veterans; in fact, most returning GIs approached the Veterans Administration for financial assistance. Finally, demand for GI loans did not materialize until much later. Eventually, 1,000,000 veterans did take advantage of the GI bill to open their own businesses, but fewer than 50,000 had done so by the end of 1945.[83]

The lack of an organized constituency threatened the SWPC at a time when the agency faced growing opposition from conservative members of Congress who were concerned with the wartime growth of government. In December 1944, the first sign of opposition surfaced as the agency ran out of funds and Maverick requested an additional $200 million. His request stirred a debate over the merits of this troubled agency. Fred Crawford (R.-Mich.) denied that the SWPC represented small business and rejected the notion of a permanent SWPC. Crawford argued that subsidies to small business discriminated against those who did not receive aid. Frederick Smith (R.-Ohio) dismissed the agency as a "New Deal omnium-gatherum bureau." John McCormack (D.-Mass.) expressed his opposition to "wet-nursing programs" and agreed with Jessie Sumner (R.-Ill.) that a loan guarantee program operated by the Federal Reserve could substitute for the SWPC. Although Congress eventually approved Maverick's request for $200 million, this opposition did not bode well for the future health of the agency.[84]

Throughout 1944 and 1945, members of the Small Business Committees tried repeatedly to extend the life of the SWPC. In May 1944, Senator Murray introduced a bill to continue the agency until 1947. This legislation would have transformed the SWPC into an independent agency representing all types of small businesses, but the bill languished in committee. During the next year, Maury Maverick's congressional allies introduced a flurry of bills to extend the agency, but these measures met the same fate. Finally, as the war neared an end, the issue caused a split among congressional small business advocates. Two conservative members of the House Small Business Committee, Leonard Hall (R.-N.Y.) and Walter C. Ploeser, opposed Maverick's request because they feared it might add to the large budget deficits incurred during the war. Hall attacked Maverick for his policy of "bigger and bigger government," while Ploeser noted "an implied promise that we would discontinue it [the SWPC] at the close of the war." Eventually, in April 1945, those who favored a permanent SWPC secured a one-year extension, but the agency still lacked a clear-cut mission to carry it into the postwar period.[85]

Maverick continued to press for a permanent SWPC, but he now faced opposition from the Commerce Department, which reasserted its claim to represent all businesses, large and small.[86] Commerce Department officials had always viewed the SWPC as a rival; and in June 1945, they urged the president to merge the agency with the Commerce Department. Maverick tried to block this move "to gobble us up" by asking for another bill to extend and expand the SWPC.[87] He orchestrated nationwide meetings of small manufacturers and reported "an almost universal opinion" in favor of a permanent SWPC; but fewer than one hundred of the nation's manufacturers attended these meetings. Apparently, most small business owners did not care if the nation's only small business agency passed from the scene.[88]

Maverick's last-ditch efforts failed to save the agency. In October, President Truman sent him on a trip to the Far East to open up trade for small business, but the president hinted that Maverick's agency would not survive the war.[89] Truman did carry his concern for small business into the Oval Office, but he preferred to work toward this end through the Commerce Department and the Reconstruction Finance Corporation. Therefore, on 27 December 1945, as part of his policy of streamlining the government after the war, Truman abolished the SWPC effective 28 January 1946. Maverick considered the order unconstitutional and "political dynamite," but he relented in the interest of party unity. By executive order Truman transferred the SWPC's lending and surplus property powers to the RFC and all of its other functions to the Commerce Department. Thus the president finally put the agency out of its misery.[90]

The Record of the Smaller War Plants Corporation

Although the SWPC lasted less than four years, it marked an important turning point in the evolution of the federal government's policies toward small business. By World War II, congressional small business advocates had lost faith in the efficacy of antitrust legislation and had begun to focus on securing positive aid for small firms; the SWPC represented their first victory on this front. In the post–World War II years, they continued to follow this approach and eventually secured the establishment of a permanent Small Business Administration. The SWPC was the seed that grew into the present-day SBA.

Yet at the time, the lackluster performance of the SWPC dismayed its congressional supporters. The agency helped small manufacturers secure only $6 billion in defense contracts (just 3 percent of the wartime total), as well as loans and leases amounting to only $500 million. The swpc also handled twelve prime contracts worth approximately $35 million.[91]

Congressional small business advocates had hoped the agency would redistribute defense spending from big to small businesses; but in June 1946, the Senate Small Business Committee published an swpc survey revealing that the largest one hundred corporations received two-thirds of all prime contracts and that sixty-eight obtained two-thirds of R&D funding. Small manufacturers (those with fewer than five hundred employees) received 22 percent of the prime contracts and 7 percent of all subcontracts. Their share of manufacturing employment declined from 51 percent to 38 percent, while corporations with over 10,000 employees increased their share from 13 percent to 30 percent. The swpc also failed in its efforts to decentralize industry: the wartime placement of defense contracts and loans matched the regional distribution of manufacturing prior to the war.[92]

Big business reaped the benefits of reconversion as the government privatized publicly owned plants worth $17 billion. Large manufacturers operated most of these plants, and under the terms of their leases, the government gave them the first option to purchase. Consequently, eighty-seven companies received two-thirds of the value of these plants. The federal government sold all of its synthetic rubber facilities to the Big Four rubber companies and allowed U.S. Steel to purchase 71 percent of all the publicly built steel plants. The nation's largest corporations also purchased most of the surplus property sold by the government at the end of the war.[93]

Although large corporations benefited most from defense spending, small manufacturers also prospered in these years; indeed, the "crisis" of small business never materialized. Between 1939 and 1947, unincorporated manufacturers, typically small firms, increased their share of value-added output from 7.7 percent to 8.1 percent. The number of small manufacturers increased during the war, and in most industries the net profits of small manufacturers actually increased faster than those of the largest firms. The rate of return on investment was also higher in unconcentrated industries than in concentrated ones. Somehow these firms prospered, despite labor shortages and their loss of employees to larger corporations.[94]

In recent years, economists have emphasized the small firm's advantages in a rapidly changing economy.[95] But the historian Thomas S. Dicke has shown that the business press recognized the resiliency of small business as early as the 1920s and 1930s. This respect for the persistence of small business continued through the war years. Business writers noted small companies' flexibility and their ability to fill niches overlooked by large firms. Others cited cheap labor and "vertical disintegration" (subcontracting by large corporations) as the key to small business success. One writer expressed the general view that "there will always be big businesses: there will always be small businesses."[96]

In the postwar years, economists also challenged the notion that oligopolies would someday rule the economy. Studies showed that economic concentration had not increased in the recent past. Indeed, several studies showed a *decrease* in concentration during the war.[97] Before the war, the nation's most concentrated industries cut back on their civilian production as they shifted to the production of defense goods. Thus, although large firms clearly benefited from the defense buildup, they may have lost market share in the civilian sector, which also expanded during the war.[98] In addition, like defense firms today, many large corporations had trouble reconverting to civilian production.[99] To date, historians have focused on developments in the military sector, but they also need to explore how small manufacturers fared in consumer goods industries.

The Postwar Position of Small Business, 1946–1950

During the immediate postwar years, congressional small business advocates faced a hostile climate in terms of public opinion. The success of the American military-industrial machine restored the image of big business, and these years marked the high point for public approval of the large corporation. A 1950 poll revealed that 76 percent of Americans had a favorable opinion of big business. Not surprisingly, Americans were indifferent to the agenda of the antitrusters; in fact, only 8 percent could define the terms "monopoly" and "antitrust suit." Americans attributed the success of large corporations to smart management and organization rather than to unethical practices. In this age of the "organization man," young people sought the security of corporate careers and avoided the risks inherent in starting a small business. In their study of the "Class of '49," the editors of *Fortune* noted that "no longer is small business the promised land" for the younger generation.[100]

The pundits also ballyhooed big business. Several authors, including economist John Kenneth Galbraith and bureaucrat David Lilienthal, wrote paeans to the large corporation. During the 1930s, Lilienthal had been a Brandeisian admirer of small business, but he abandoned his "old dream: the independent man in his own little shop or business. It *was* a good dream. There is a new dream: a world of great machines" controlled by big business, "a social institution that promotes human freedom and individualism."[101] Both Lilienthal and

Galbraith believed that America's social and economic stability rested on a system of "countervailing powers" made up of Big Business, Big Labor, and Big Government. Galbraith also defended the nation's chain stores, arguing that they acted as a "countervailing power" in the economy by preventing manufacturers from arbitrarily setting high prices. Thus, in Galbraith's view, consumers benefited from the struggle between oligopsony (a few buyers) and oligopoly (a few sellers).[102]

This acceptance of big business diminished public support for small business legislation. During the Great Depression and World War II, small business advocates could plausibly argue that small business faced a crisis, but they lost this emergency rationale for aid during the prosperous postwar years. In 1950, columnist Peter F. Drucker wrote, "For the first time in more than seventy years the battle cry 'Down with Big Business!' has failed to raise the blood pressure of the American public." Consequently, the Democrats dropped their plans to make antitrust legislation an issue in the 1950 elections: "the public just wasn't interested."[103]

Although their gospel seemed hopelessly out of date, the Small Business Committees continued to preach the virtues of smallness as they agitated for a permanent small business agency. (The Commerce Department had an Office of Small Business, but this bureau had only twelve employees.) Between 1946 and 1949, members of these committees introduced bills to revive the SWPC or create a new agency, but in Congress their rhetoric fell on deaf ears.[104]

In the late 1940s, the Small Business Committees also tried unsuccessfully to organize small business owners into an effective pressure group. The smallest firms did not join organizations of any sort, while larger companies joined trade associations and chambers of commerce. Very few belonged to an all-inclusive small business association.[105] The organizations claiming to represent small business lacked any credibility in Washington. These associations exaggerated their importance by publishing wildly inflated membership figures and by reporting near unanimity among small business owners on a wide range of issues. For example, the American Association of Small Business reported that "the vote of our membership was 98% in favor of the Taft-Hartley bill."[106]

The positions taken by these associations sometimes conflicted with the agenda of the Small Business Committees. The more liberal associations, including the Little Business Men's League of America and the Small Business Association of New England, sought government aid, but the conservative associations believed that big government posed a threat to small business. The Conference of American Small Business Organizations "wanted less, not more, Government in business," and Congressman Charles Vursell praised this group for its opposition to "the present socialistic trend of government."[107] Likewise, the National Federation of Independent Business (NFIB) called for the enforcement of the antitrust laws but opposed the "Socialism and Communism" inherent in welfare legislation and direct aid to small business.[108]

While the Small Business Committees endured the criticisms of these associations, they confronted a more serious threat to their existence from conservatives in Congress. In 1946, Congress passed the Legislative Reorganization Act, which, in the name of governmental efficiency, called for the elimination of the special committees created during the war. The Senate Small Business Committee faced an additional challenge from those who criticized Murray for using the committee as a forum for legislation unrelated to small business. Conservatives accused Murray of having surrounded himself with radicals and communists bent on social experimentation. In 1947 and 1948, the newly appointed Republican chairman of the committee, Kenneth Wherry (R.-Nebr.), began "sweeping out the Moscow tinge" and the "Reds" on his staff, replacing them with representatives of the business community. At the same time, the Senate Banking and Currency Committee tried to replace Murray's committee with its own Small Business Subcommittee. The Democrats won back control of the Senate in 1948, and to prevent Murray from taking over as chairman again, the Republicans allowed the committee to expire in January 1949. One year later, the Senate reestablished it as a permanent Select Committee with an entirely new membership, including John Sparkman (D.-Ala.) as a less controversial chairman.[109]

Meanwhile, in the House of Representatives, small business advocates tried to discredit the conservative small business associations by charging that they were "fronts" for big business. These associations received funding from large corporations and, not surprisingly, emphasized the interdependence of big and small business. In 1950, the House Small Business Committee investigated the NSBMA and several other associations. The committee described the NSBMA as an "absolute fraud . . . financed by big-business money." The committee further claimed that the presidents of these associations were "professional promoters trading on the name of small business." The House Select Committee on Lobbying Activities conducted a separate investigation of the CASBO and concluded that it, too, was a front for big business. The committee cited a letter by CASBO chairman Fred Virkus stating that he sought support on matters "in which big business as such cannot come out in the open."[110]

In 1949, the House Small Business Committee also took steps to organize support for its small business legislation. The committee set up a broad front of trade associations, farm bureaus, and unions to act as the semiofficial spokesman for small business. This "Small Business-AntiMonopoly Conference" included representatives from nineteen associations, including the NFIB, the NARD, the CIO, and the American Farm Bureau Federation. Most of these groups had no direct interest in comprehensive small business legislation, however, and their endorsement of bills drafted by the House Small Business Committee carried little weight with other representatives.[111]

Partisan politics played a role in the unsuccessful attempt to form another small business organization, an idea proposed by the Washington-based Federation of Business Men's Associations (FBMA). Democratic National Committee leaders thought CASBO and the NSBMA were "violently pro-Republican and anti-Administration." The DNC tried to counter the rhetoric of these organizations by forming a confederation of trade associations to represent small business. The DNC's leaders backed FBMA's call for a national conference of trade association leaders in Washington, but this group never coalesced.[112]

Although they lacked an organized constituency, congressional small business advocates enjoyed the continued support of President Truman. In addition to promoting a renewed antitrust campaign, Truman sought to lend positive aid to small business. In May 1950, Truman proposed a five-point plan to provide financing for small business. Truman's program included short-term loan insurance; long-term financing through federally chartered investment companies; liberalization of RFC lending practices; a clearinghouse of technical information set up within the Commerce Department; and transfer of the RFC to the Commerce Department. Secretary of Commerce Charles Sawyer initiated this plan, and his agency would be responsible for administering it. A Small Business bill introduced by congressional small business advocates embodied the Truman plan. The members of the Small Business Committees hoped that with presidential backing they could push their bill through Congress, but as we shall see in the next chapter, the coming of the Korean War forced them to temporarily abandon their efforts to secure federal funds for all types of small businesses.[113]

The Politics of Small Business in the 1940s

In the first half of the 1940s, the growth of the federal government accelerated as a plethora of new agencies mobilized an unprecedented proportion of the nation's resources in support of a worldwide war effort. Between 1940 and 1944, government expenditures as a share of GNP increased from 18 percent to nearly 50 percent.[114] But numbers alone do not tell the entire story. Many scholars, including historians Alan Brinkley and Robert Higgs, have also noted how the war brought on ideological change. Since wartime spending seemed to end the Great Depression, policymakers became more receptive to the notion of Keynesian "pump-priming" as a way to stimulate the economy. The public also came to accept the ideology of a mixed economy, while businesses learned to seek opportunities within the public sector.[115]

As "ideological entrepreneurs," the members of the Small Business Committees successfully marketed their ideology to their colleagues in Congress and thereby secured the establishment of the Smaller War Plants Corporation. But the lack of an organized small business constituency limited the SWPC's success. In modern American politics, interest groups play an important role in determining the relative strength (or weakness) of government agencies; agencies that enjoy the backing of well-organized interests usually fare better than those that lack such support.[116] Thus, Ellis Hawley notes that successful interest groups possess both an "ideological rationale" and effective organization.[117] The small business ideology provided an emergency rationale for government aid, but small manufacturers remained unorganized, partly because the Small Business Committees failed to convince Holland and Johnson that a crisis existed. During their administrations, the contradictions inherent in the ideology became apparent. To what extent could "free enterprise" receive federal funds and remain "free"? Holland and Johnson stressed the self-reliance of small business owners and drew the line far short of the goals set by the Small Business Committees.

The heterogeneous nature of the small business population also defeated Maury Maverick's attempts to organize this group. None of the associations claiming to speak for small business truly represented this community. Trade associations of independent druggists and grocers occasionally testified in favor of legislation strengthening the SWPC, but they had no direct interest in the outcome. Finally, as we have seen, no group spoke for small manufacturers. The SWPC repeatedly tried but failed to organize them into an effective pressure group.

Small manufacturers prospered during the war and therefore did not respond to the crisis rhetoric of the small business advocates. Historians have assumed that this rhetoric reflected widespread disaffection among small manufacturers; however, this study of the SWPC suggests that small manufacturers were optimistic about the future.[118] Furthermore, they did not view themselves as having an interest separate from big business. They directed their hostility toward the government rather than large corporations. Throughout the war, small manufacturers complained of taxes, regulations, price controls, and the incompetence of the SWPC.[119] In short, the champions of small business gained a great deal of publicity from their crusade but failed to persuade small manufacturers that a government agency was in their best interest.[120]

This history of federal government policy toward small business revises the corporate-liberal interpretation of business-government relations during World War II. Gabriel Kolko and others have emphasized corporate influences on the wartime policy of the federal government.[121] On the one hand, it is clear that big business exerted a great deal of influence within the military-industrial complex during World War II. Procurement officers found it difficult, if not impossible, to acquire information on the thousands of small manufacturers scattered across the country, so they preferred to work with a few of the nation's largest industrial corporations. In the defense sector, the structure of American industry favored large corporations because they were concentrated in heavy industries. On the other hand, the close ties these firms had with the government placed constraints on them. They became enveloped in a web of regulations that may have lowered their profits and limited their flexibility. Small firms maintained their flexibility and could avoid regulations to move quickly to take advantage of profit opportunities in the civilian sector of the economy. There is evidence that this was the case during the Korean War; economic historians need to study whether this hypothesis explains the success of small manufacturers during World War II.[122]

Postwar developments provided evidence to support political scientist Harmon Zeigler's conclusion that "there is no small business interest."[123] Congressional small business advocates tried to fashion a small business lobby out of various interests—including trade associations, farm bureaus, and labor unions—but this loose federation could not speak for small business. Furthermore, none of the so-called small business associations truly represented all small businesses. Most small business owners remained politically apathetic and uninterested in joining any "small business lobby."

Zeigler accepted the Small Business Committees' argument that the conservative associations acted as "fronts" for big business because they emphasized the interdependence of large and small firms. But Zeigler mistakenly assumed that there was a monolithic community of big business executives opposed to government intervention in the economy. More recently, the historian Robert Collins has revealed deep divisions within those associations allegedly dominated by big business during the 1940s and 1950s.[124] Furthermore, the conservative associations' lack of hostility toward big business reflected the general climate of opinion. Polls showed that small business people, like the public at large, had a very favorable opinion of big business.[125]

During the post–World War II period, congressional small business advocates lacked the support of small business owners and faced the opposition of the conservative small business associations. Although President Truman offered his support to their cause, his attention would soon turn to foreign affairs. Thus Truman, like Roosevelt during World War II, would eventually abandon his commitment to small business legislation.

6

The Small Defense Plants Administration and the Creation of the Small Business Administration, 1951–1953

In the 1930s, Thurman Arnold described how antitrust legislation had become little more than a symbolic "preaching device" aimed at converting sinners in the business community.[1] The passage of federal anti-chain-store legislation did not alter this sense that antitrust laws had become irrelevant. By 1950, congressional small business advocates had lost much of their faith in the federal government's ability to challenge big business by invoking antitrust legislation. The House Small Business Committee lamented that "after 60 years of Sherman Act enforcement, concentration of economic power is greater than ever."[2] Therefore, in addition to their demands for stricter enforcement of the antitrust laws, the champions of small business continued to seek positive aid for small firms—including financial assistance and representation within the federal government—just as they had done during World War II. During the Korean War, they secured the creation of the Small Defense Plants Administration (SDPA) to help small manufacturers obtain military contracts. Like its World War II predecessor, however, the SDPA suffered from the opposition of other government agencies, partisan politics, and the lack of an organized constituency of small business owners. Finally, in July 1953, Congress abolished the SDPA and created the Small Business Administration (SBA), the first federal agency to represent all types of small businesses.

The Impact of the Korean War

On the eve of the Korean War, small business activists had joined President Truman in support of the Small Business Act, a bill designed to provide financial assistance to all types of small firms. Small business advocates expected quick passage for the act, but events changed course radically when the Communists invaded South Korea on 25 June 1950: Congress suspended its hearings on the bill and turned to the consideration of legislation to mobilize the economy in support of the war effort.

The Defense Production Act, which went into effect on 8 September 1950, activated the machinery of mobilization. This law gave the president the power to establish a system of priorities for the allocation of critical raw materials and authorized him to create wage and price controls to check inflation. Congress also gave the military's procurement agencies the authority to guarantee markets and prices when defense contractors faced undue risk. After the Chinese and North Koreans repelled a UN offensive in December, Truman declared a national emergency and issued an executive order establishing the Office of Defense Mobilization (ODM) as the chief policymaking and coordinating agency. Together with the Commerce Department's National Production Authority (NPA), the ODM indirectly planned industrial production by allocating basic raw materials, such as steel, copper, and aluminum.[3]

The Korean mobilization effort differed from the armament that took place during World War II. During World War II, the United States mobilized for a full-scale war at a time when industry had idle capacity; but in 1950, policymakers faced the prospect of a limited, long-term military mobilization superimposed on a civilian economy that was already operating at peak capacity. Therefore, the Truman administration pursued a "guns and butter" policy of trying to expand the economy in order to meet the military's needs while still maintaining a high standard of living.[4]

The Defense Production Act did not directly address how best to utilize the resources of small firms; it merely directed the president to encourage the participation of small manufacturers in the war effort. But several governmental agencies did respond to congressional concern in this area by providing assistance to small manufacturers. The Department of Commerce transferred its Office of Small Business to the National Production Authority, while the military's procurement agencies hired hundreds of specialists to work with small manufacturers. Despite this representation, many of those small manufacturers who sought military contracts could not secure them. Small firms producing nonessential goods could not obtain sufficient quantities of critical raw materials, nor did they have the physical resources and technical know-how to convert to military production. Moreover, the share of business suit-able for small-firm production was lower than it had been during World War II, because more procurement dollars went to the Air Force—the military branch with the highest demand for complex equipment that could usually only be produced by larger, more experienced firms.[5]

The Creation of the Small Defense
Plants Administration

In a repeat of the World War II experience, the congressional Small Business Committees feared the effect a concentration of contracts would have on the position of small firms; therefore, they sought to create a separate agency to represent small manufacturers. On 26 July 1950, the chairman of the Senate Small Business Committee, John Sparkman (D.-Ala.), introduced legislation to create a Small Defense Plants Corporation (SDPC), and Wright Patman (D.-Tex.) introduced a similar measure in the House. Their bills would have established a corporation with a $500 million revolving loan fund to finance small-plant construction, conversion, and expansion. Congress remained fo-cused on other aspects of mobilization, however, and this legislation died in committee.[6]

Nonetheless, Sparkman and Patman persisted in their efforts to establish a small business agency. In January 1951, they reintroduced their legislation and strengthened it by giving the SDPC the power to set aside contracts for small manufacturers. During World War II, Congress had placed the SWPC under the supervision of the War Production Board, and its subordinate status limited the agency's influence with the procurement agencies. Sparkman and Patman hoped to avoid this difficulty by making the SDPC an independent agency reporting directly to the president.[7]

The congressional Small Business Committees advanced several arguments in support of the SDPC. First, they charged that small manufacturers were not receiving a "fair" share of defense contracts: firms with fewer than five hun-dred employees received only a sixth of the defense contracts awarded in January 1951.[8] Small firms received a high percentage of advertised bids, but the military increasingly relied on negotiated purchases to speed up mobilization. The Senate Small Business Committee condemned the armed services for their "negativism" and lack of concern with the problems of small business.[9]

Members of the Small Business Committees also expressed their unhappi-ness with existing small business departments. The NPA's Office of Small Business had no lending authority and did nothing more than distribute information to small manufacturers. Small business advocates believed that big business dominated the Commerce Department, and for this reason, they doubted that agency's commitment to represent the interests of small manufacturers. (Maury Maverick, the former administrator of the SWPC, characterized the Commerce Department as "the biggest cemetery in the world" when it came to action on behalf of small firms.) For the same reason, they believed that small firms could not secure adequate financing through the Reconstruction Finance Corporation.[10]

History repeated itself as congressional proponents of small business resorted to crisis rhetoric reminiscent of their campaign to create the SWPC during World War II. Patman noted the dangers of delay and claimed that many small firms would fail without the assistance of a new agency. "Once again," he declared, "small business is facing a crisis."[11] Sparkman warned that "small business is on the way to extinction on a calamitous scale." He also took a new tack and played on the public's fear of an atomic holocaust, warning that "20 metropolitan areas . . . can be wiped out by atomic bombs in a single night's raid"; therefore, he argued, small manufacturers should receive a higher priority in the mobilization effort in order to decentralize industry in case of a nuclear attack. Thus, small business advocates adapted their old crisis-oriented arguments to reflect the fears of the nuclear age.[12]

The supporters of this legislation also resorted to cold war rhetoric to identify the fate of small business with American war aims. Representative Roy Riehlman (R.-N.Y.) noted the country's ideological competition with the Soviet Union and argued that the success of American small business provided a model for Third World nations. Representative Charles Halleck (R.-Ind.) described the cold war as a "great battle" between the "American competitive system" and the communist "slave nations." Others feared the threat of totalitarianism at home. One small business advocate, Senator Hubert Humphrey (D.-Minn.), asked his fellow senators, "Can our political democracy long endure if we permit the foundation of our economic democracy to crumble?"[13]

Finally, the sponsors of this legislation insisted that it had the full support of small business owners. Sparkman and Patman cited the endorsement of several small business associations and the unanimous approval of their legislation by the Small Business Committees. Other congressional legislators tried to sway their colleagues by noting the universal political appeal of small business. Senator Edward J. Thye (R.-N.Y.), for example, reminded other senators that, as a *New York Times* commentator put it, small business is "a politically significant area of our economy" that members of Congress should not ignore if they were interested in their own reelection.[14]

There was little overt opposition to this legislation in Congress, but within the Truman administration, Secretary of Commerce Charles Sawyer spoke against the proposal to create a small business agency. Sawyer, a self-described conservative Democrat, believed the federal government should play only a limited role in aiding small business. He rejected the crisis rhetoric of the Small Business Committees, noting that the number of small firms had increased substantially since World War II. Sawyer also maintained that his agency represented all businesses, large and small, and he opposed the creation of the SDPC because it would duplicate the work of the Commerce Department and thus add to the cost of government.[15] Acting as Truman's chief economic adviser, Sawyer initially succeeded in blocking congressional consideration of the bills introduced by Sparkman and Patman. He also sought an executive order recognizing the Commerce Department as the only agency representing small business, but the Truman administration eventually gave in to growing congressional sentiment in favor of a new small business agency. Recognizing political reality, one administration official advised the president to gain some political mileage from the issue: "the Sparkman-Patman bill is a good bandwagon," he argued, "and lots of people are getting aboard."[16]

In June 1951, acting on the president's advice, Sparkman and Patman created a small business agency by attaching an amendment to a bill extending the Defense Production Act. To achieve the creation of an independent agency, the two congressmen compromised by weakening provisions of their legislation. Their amendments created a Small Defense Plants Administration but reduced the size of the agency's revolving fund from $500 million to $50 million. (The SDPA could also recommend loans to the RFC up to a limit of $100 million.) The agency could attest to the credit and capacity of a firm but could not set aside contracts for small manufacturers; nor could the SDPA claim raw materials on behalf of small business, a power that had been used effectively by the SWPC during World War II. The agency could take prime contracts, but only on terms set by the military's procurement officers. Not surprisingly, the liberal small business associations were disappointed with the advisory nature of the agency. The president of the Small Business Association of New England (SBANE), for example, considered the SDPA too weak and "a waste of taxpayer's money."[17]

Perhaps because this legislation posed little threat to existing government agencies, Congress quickly acted on it. The Small Business Committees se-

cured lukewarm endorsements from the military and the Commerce Department, and on 30 July Congress passed the bill extending the Defense Production Authority and establishing the Small Defense Plants Administration.
President Truman signed the bill into law the next day, creating the first independent agency to represent small manufacturers.[18] The legislative history of
the SDPA, however, reveals a lack of congressional support for anything more
than a harmless temporary agency to represent small manufacturers during
the war. The opposition of the military and the Commerce Department had
blocked substantive measures and continued to plague the SDPA during its two
years of existence.

The Work of the Small Defense
Plants Administration

The SDPA encountered many of the same obstacles faced by the SWPC during
World War II. Like its predecessor, the SDPA operated without an administrator for several months because President Truman could not find a qualified
person willing to accept the job. In late September, Truman finally settled on a
close friend, Telford Taylor. A successful lawyer, Taylor had been associate
counsel for the Senate Interstate Commerce Committee (1935–39) and the
Federal Communications Commission (1940–42). During World War II he
served in the military's Intelligence Service and rose to the rank of brigadier
general. After the war, he became the chief U.S. prosecutor at the Nuremburg
trials. Taylor accepted the post of SDPA administrator as a favor to President
Truman. He had displayed no previous interest in small business, and he later
admitted that he did not come to the SDPA "of my own volition" and wished to
return to private practice as soon as possible. Several senators opposed Taylor's
nomination because he did not have a small business background. Nonetheless, despite his lack of experience and enthusiasm, the Senate confirmed
Taylor on 15 October by a vote of forty-one to twenty.[19]

Congress had given unanimous approval to the creation of the SDPA because
few politicians dared to "vote against small business"; but the minuscule sum
of $350,000 appropriated for the agency's administration reflected the shallow-
ness of congressional support. President Truman also gave only halfhearted
support to the agency, noting that it was inevitable that small manufacturers
would suffer during the war because civilian products were not essential to the
mobilization effort.[20] Thus, Taylor lacked the resources needed to organize his
agency, and by December he had set up no more than a "small skeletonic"
organization made up of several regional offices. The agency did not open its

first field office until February 1952. The agency remained overcentralized in part because, according to one official, Taylor and his deputy administrator spent "most of their time justifying their existence on the Hill and with other agencies."[21]

Initially, the SDPA found it difficult to define "small" business. During World War II, Congress had arbitrarily defined a small business as one with fewer than five hundred employees, but congressional small business advocates wanted a more flexible definition in order to exclude both firms that were dominant in their industry and those that were tied to larger corporations. Finally, in January 1953, the SDPA issued its own definition of small business. The agency considered a business "small" if it was independent and did not dominate its industry. The size of a small business varied by industry, but it could include a firm with as many as twenty-five hundred employees.[22] The military, however, refused to recognize the SDPA classification and continued to define a small business as one with fewer than five hundred employees. By narrowing the definition of small business, the military could thus limit the SDPA's interference in the procurement process.[23]

Mobilization planners continued to oppose the SDPA in other ways as well, greatly hindering its work. The House Small Business Committee had hoped Congress would appropriate funds from the agency's $50 million loan fund, but the head of the Office of Defense Mobilization, Charles E. Wilson, hampered the establishment of the agency by sending vague plans to Capitol Hill; consequently, Congress delayed appropriating funds until it knew how they would be spent. This delay exasperated congressional small business advocates. After reviewing the slow start of the SDPA, the House Small Business Committee concluded that "it is the old story of high purposes but inadequate means."[24]

Meanwhile, at the Commerce Department, Charles Sawyer opposed the transfer of staff and funds to the new agency. Sawyer considered Taylor "brilliant, persuasive and ambitious" but resisted his "grasp for power and personnel." In late October, Taylor and Sawyer engaged in "truce talks" in which Sawyer agreed to allow the SDPA to use his field service, but Sawyer continued to block the transfer of staff. In a testy letter to President Truman, the commerce secretary stated his opposition to a "raid on permanent agencies in an effort to build up temporary agencies." In December, he finally did agree to temporarily lend nine small business specialists to the SDPA. Officials at the SDPA complained, however, that the Commerce Department continued to consult with small manufacturers, in violation of an agreement reached between the two agencies.[25]

Sawyer was reportedly behind an unsuccessful move to abolish the SDPA in March 1952. The House Appropriations Committee denied Taylor's request for funds to continue operations through June, claiming that the SDPA duplicated the work of other agencies. The committee also rejected Taylor's request for a $10 million appropriation from the agency's revolving fund. Julian Gary (D.-Va.) argued that the abolition of the SDPA would actually benefit small business because it would lower government spending. Clare Hoffman (R.-Mich.) took the opportunity to state that "this New Deal administration should be kicked out" if it wasted money on agencies such as the SDPA. Others, including George Dondero (R.-Mich.), attacked Taylor's integrity, claiming that "left wingers" and communists had infiltrated his staff at the Nuremburg trials. Ultimately, Taylor used his personal influence with Speaker of the House Sam Rayburn, and the Appropriations Committee reinstated funding for the SDPA's administrative expenses. But the committee refused to approve the appropriation of money from the revolving fund.[26]

The SDPA survived on a shoestring budget and remained little more than an advisory body. Occasionally, other agencies did accept its advice. For example, the NPA agreed to set aside a special reserve of critical materials for small business hardship cases. The Renegotiation Board also declared that those prime contractors who offered subcontracts to small manufacturers would receive favorable treatment from the procurement agencies.[27]

Beyond this advisory role, the SDPA could do little to halt small manufacturers' declining share of military procurements. During fiscal year 1952, small manufacturers (defined as those with fewer than five hundred employees) received 17 percent of all procurement dollars, down from 25 percent in 1951. The Munitions Board estimated that 30 percent of all procurement contracts were "suitable" for production by small business, but small firms received less than 60 percent of these contracts.[28] In large part, this decline in small manufacturers' share of defense business resulted from the military's increasing emphasis on the purchase of complex aviation equipment. Although the Air Force's small business program received praise from the SDPA, only about 10 percent of Air Force contracts were suitable for production by small manufacturers. Small firms received only 6 percent of the procurement dollars spent by the Air Force; they did not receive the remaining share of "suitable" production because either their bids were too high or they could not meet delivery schedules. Thus, although today many economists argue that small firms are technological leaders, this did not seem to be the case in the 1950s, at least in the area of defense production.[29]

Neither Taylor nor his successor proved able to overcome the apathy of

Congress or the downright hostility of rival agencies. The apparent hopeless-
ness of the agency's mission frustrated Taylor, leading him to return to private
practice. In September, Taylor resigned as administrator of the SDPA, and
Deputy Administrator John Horne took his place. On his way out, Taylor
criticized the military for its lack of cooperation and asked Congress to pass
additional legislation to strengthen the agency. The SDPA continued to lack
strong congressional backing, however. Congress extended the agency for another year but appropriated only $1.5 million from the agency's loan fund.[30]
Horne was no more successful than Taylor had been in securing the cooperation of other governmental agencies; in fact, during his tenure the agency
developed new enemies within the RFC. Administrators of the RFC complained
that SDPA officials leaked loan recommendations and took "every opportunity
to try to build themselves up and justify their existence." Meanwhile, the
military continued to resist the SDPA's call for price differentials, because, in
the words of one official, they constituted a "political subsidy" that had no
place in the procurement process.[31]

In short, bureaucratic bickering and partisan politics hampered the SDPA's
effectiveness. The SDPA lacked financial support from Congress and continued
to face the opposition of existing government agencies and conservatives in
Congress. Thus, like its World War II predecessor, the SDPA remained a weak
reed for small manufacturers to lean on.

The Creation of the Small Business Administration

At the end of World War II, conservative Republicans concerned about the
federal government's huge debt had defeated measures to extend the SWPC into
the postwar period. A similar conflict between liberals and conservatives occurred at the end of the Korean War. The 1952 elections produced a Republican
presidency and Republican majorities in both houses of Congress for the first
time in twenty years. Throughout the war, the Republicans had criticized
Truman for amassing a large deficit, and they now promised to balance the
budget by abolishing government programs that competed with business.[32]

This new Republican majority in Congress made life difficult for the SDPA.
Republican criticisms of the agency surfaced in March 1953 when Congress
debated the SDPA's request for $825,000 in administrative expenses and $10
million from its loan fund. The House Appropriations Committee split along
ideological lines. The chairman of the committee, Glenn Davis (R.-Wis.),
reported that "one group of people support the theory that the only way you
can help small business is to create a Government agency . . . and the other . . .

believes the way to help small business is to cut the Government expenditures." Davis and his fellow conservatives hoped to "prevent this great mushrooming" of a government agency and thereby "take Government off the back of small business." After a great deal of debate, the agency's supporters overcame this opposition, and Congress appropriated the requested funds. Unless Congress extended the SDPA beyond its 30 June expiration date, however, the agency would not get the chance to spend the appropriated money.[33]

The Republicans had their eyes on a larger target: the Reconstruction Finance Corporation (RFC). Congress had created this lending agency during the Great Depression, and the RFC remained one of the largest agencies in the federal government during World War II. In peacetime, however, the RFC lost its emergency rationale, and critics called for its elimination. Instead of abolishing the agency, though, Congress simply cut its lending authority and restricted its activities.

The RFC survived, but it lacked a clear-cut mission and, according to *Business Week*, "turned to bailing out all kinds of businesses, a lot of them bad losers." Jules Abels, author of *The Truman Scandals*, sarcastically described how the RFC made "loans to concerns vital to our economy, such as a gambling casino, a rainbow trout fishery, night clubs, snake farms, . . . and a grower of cactus plants for sale in dime stores." In addition, it became known that several top Truman advisers had used their influence on behalf of certain corporations. These revelations led to renewed calls for the elimination of the RFC. In 1949, the Hoover Commission (a task force studying ways to make the federal government more efficient) recommended an end to all direct lending by the government because it "invites political and private pressure or even corruption." President Truman tried to avert criticism by offering to reorganize the RFC; but in February 1951, a Senate subcommittee chaired by J. William Fulbright (D.-Ark.) embarrassed the administration by disclosing further evidence of "favoritism and influence" in the RFC's lending operations. Soon thereafter, Senator Harry F. Byrd (D.-Va.), a longtime critic of the RFC, called for an end to what he described as "a useless nonessential agency with no real purpose to serve."[34]

The RFC's misbehavior made it an agency especially unpopular with Republicans; according to a Gallup poll, most Republican voters believed that Congress should abolish the RFC.[35] The Republicans capitalized on these scandals in the 1952 elections, and once in power, they immediately placed the RFC beneath their budget-cutting axe. President Dwight D. Eisenhower's chief economic adviser, Treasury Secretary George Humphrey, estimated that the liquidation of the RFC's assets would contribute "[up] to a billion dollars toward balancing the budget," but because the Republicans held only a slim majority in Congress, he regarded it as "politically essential" that the government continue to make loans to small business.[36] The administration's Government Reorganization Committee believed that a small business agency should be placed within the Commerce Department but recognized widespread congressional support for an independent SBA.[37]

Meanwhile, SDPA officials lobbied for a Small Business Administration to represent all small businesses, including manufacturers, retailers, wholesalers, and those in the service sector. Horne claimed that his agency had the "virtually unanimous" support of small business owners and that Congress should transform it into a powerful and permanent agency. However, in reality, the small business associations remained divided in their support of the SDPA. Several of the associations supported the establishment of the SBA, but the more conservative ones opposed the creation of any new small business agency. The nation's leading business organizations—including the American Bankers Association (ABA), the National Association of Manufacturers (NAM), and the U.S. Chamber of Commerce—also opposed the creation of a lending agency that competed with private banks.[38]

Although they lacked the unified support of the business community, congressional small business advocates joined the SDPA in seeking the creation of a peacetime small business agency. In February 1953, Senator Byrd introduced a measure to abolish the RFC, and in order to preserve a governmental source of loans for small business, Senators Capehart (R.-Ind.) and Thye (R.-Minn.) submitted bills to extend the SDPA to 30 June 1954. Then, in April and May, the chairmen of the Small Business Committees, Senator Thye and Representative William Hill (R.-Colo.), introduced legislation to create a permanent Small Business Administration.[39] In line with the Eisenhower administration's cost-consciousness, these bills provided the proposed agency with a loan fund of only $50 million and $100 million, respectively—far less than the RFC's $1 billion lending authority.[40]

Existing agencies tried to protect their bureaucratic turf and opposed the establishment of an independent small business agency. Thus, Treasury Secretary George Humphrey and Commerce Secretary Sinclair Weeks sought to control the SBA by securing representation on the agency's Loan Policy Board. Although Weeks endorsed the creation of a temporary SBA, he hoped to later incorporate the agency into his own Commerce Department.[41]

Democratic small business advocates faced a dilemma: they wanted to create a small business agency, but they viewed the administration's bill as a clever way to eliminate the RFC and SDPA while offering only a weak SBA as a sop to the Democrats. For years small business advocates had criticized the RFC for failing to lend adequate assistance to small business, but they now found themselves defending the agency as the last resort for small firms in need of financing. Wright Patman described the administration's bill as a "Trojan horse" designed to abolish the RFC. He called the SBA a "tiny RFC" with a lending authority "not nearly large enough to take the place of the RFC" and argued for the continuation of "such good organizations as the Small Defense Plants Administration and the RFC." Similarly, Hubert Humphrey preferred a true small business bill, "not a small business bill plus the obituary of the RFC." Senator Fulbright also expressed his dismay that his hearings might lead to the abolition of the RFC, when he had hoped that Congress would simply reform what he considered to be a fundamentally sound agency.

Others feared that the Treasury and Commerce Secretaries would dominate the SBA if they secured representation on the agency's Loan Policy Board. Senator Wayne Morse (R.-Ore.) expressed the concern that these "tools of big business" might use their position to limit governmental assistance to small business. Senators John F. Kennedy (D.-Mass.) and Lyndon B. Johnson (D.-Tex.) echoed this sentiment and called for the creation of a truly independent SBA. Johnson also accused the Republicans of making a "patronage grab" by creating the SBA, a charge repeated by Wright Patman.[42]

Congressional Republicans viewed the creation of the SBA as an inexpensive way to attract the votes of small business people. Representative Walter Ploeser (R.-Mo.) believed that by creating the SBA, Republicans could "refute the canard of the opposition" describing the GOP as the party of big business. Ploeser also took note of the "three million small businesses in this country which probably account for nine or ten million flexible, skeptical voters." Senator Robert A. Taft (R.-Ohio) agreed that such a measure was "particularly necessary since the Administration has appointed so many big businessmen to important jobs."[43]

The partisan nature of this congressional debate resulted in a stalemate; by July, the Senate and House had still not come to an agreement over their respective versions of legislation to create a small business agency. President Eisenhower finally ended the deadlock by voicing his support for a bill introduced by Senator Thye that eliminated the RFC and created a temporary SBA. Congress passed this legislation, and on 30 July 1953, Eisenhower signed the Small Business Act, creating the first peacetime small business agency.

The SBA represented a compromise between various interests. The secretaries of the Treasury and Commerce Departments secured representation on the agency's Loan Policy Board, which would also include the SBA administrator. Democratic small business advocates succeeded in increasing the lending authority of the SBA to $275 million. Of this amount, the SBA could spend $150 million on business loans, $100 million for the costs involved in taking prime contracts, and $25 million for disaster assistance (a function carried over from the RFC). The Democrats also insisted on a temporary SBA because they wished to retain the right to review and approve any extension of the agency. Unless Congress took further action to extend the agency, it would expire on 30 June 1955.[44] Nonetheless, one official predicted that "small business finally has an agency of its own in Washington and it will be mighty hard to get rid of."[45]

A Tale of Two Small Business Agencies

During the life of the SDPA, the federal government spent nearly $100 billion on defense contracts, but the SDPA secured very little of this largesse for small firms. In its final report to Congress, the agency estimated that it offered a total of $723 million in aid to small business, but half of this amount consisted of recommended awards accepted by the military. The SDPA approved $51 million in loans and sponsored tax depreciation certificates valued at $38 million. The agency took seven prime contracts worth $2.3 million and helped small firms secure $20 million in subcontracts.[46]

During World War II, small manufacturers' share of defense dollars increased over time, but during the Korean conflict, their share declined. While small firms (those with fewer than five hundred employees) accounted for 35 percent of prewar manufacturing employment, their share of procurement dollars declined from 21 percent to 16 percent between 1951 and 1953, as the military spent an increasing share of its budget on complex high-tech equipment.[47]

Despite this disappointing record, the oft-predicted crisis of small business never materialized. The Small Business Committees simply overemphasized the importance of military spending in the economy. Patman had said that "the hand that signs the defense contract rules our economy"; in fact, though, defense spending during the war represented only 18 percent of GNP.[48] Furthermore, the war effort did not directly affect most small manufacturers, because most small manufacturers produced consumer goods. During the Korean War, the government did not ration consumer goods, and allocation controls did not significantly affect small-firm production of these items. Moreover, many small firms avoided defense work because they found better opportunities in the civilian market and did not wish to face the regulatory maze that made the federal government "the worst customer in the world."[49] Thus, in 1953, the

Senate Small Business Committee conceded that "small business had a good year [in 1952] . . . strictly from a short-range bookkeeping point of view."[50] The economic historian Harold G. Vatter has studied the changing position of small manufacturing firms in the American economy, and he, too, concludes that these were "unusually good" years for small manufacturers as the number of business failures fell to a historic low.[51]

The history of the SDPA parallels that of the SWPC during World War II. Both agencies lacked congressional and presidential support. Congress unanimously approved the creation of these agencies, but the symbolic appeal of small business never translated into an effective legislative mandate. The lack of an organized pressure group of small business owners weakened the position of the Small Business Committees in Congress. The agency also lost presidential support as Presidents Roosevelt and Truman dropped their pro-small-business stance during wartime. In short, the SDPA, like its predecessor, remained a sop to a minority of small business activists in Congress.

During the Korean War, congressional small business advocates acted as ideological entrepreneurs by presenting the cold war as a battle between communism and free enterprise; yet their crisis rhetoric failed to mobilize its intended audience. They could not appeal to a disaffected constituency of small manufacturers, because most of these firms prospered during the war. Furthermore, the small business advocates no longer benefited from public hostility toward big business. They had cried "crisis" for decades, but the public now recognized that small business was here to stay.

The SDPA received bipartisan approval because Congress knew that mobilization favored big business and created special difficulties for small business. Thus, Republicans and Democrats accepted government aid on behalf of small business in order to redress an imbalance created by the government itself. At the end of the war, however, this spirit of consensus gave way to bitter partisan debate over the merits of the SDPA. This debate demonstrated that the small business ideology had different meanings for liberals and conservatives. Liberals sought substantial aid for small business, while conservatives stressed self-reliance and noted the inconsistency inherent in government aid for "free" enterprise. This atmosphere of bitter partisan politics carried over into the creation of the Small Business Administration and set the tone for years to come.

Scholars disagree over the meaning of the SBA's creation. Harmon Zeigler emphasizes the symbolic importance of the SBA, noting how Eisenhower used the agency to deflect Democratic criticism that his administration represented the interests of big business. The political scientist George Earl Green, on the other hand, has depicted the creation of the SBA as the realization of the small business community's desire for national representation.[52] However, Green wrongly assumed that the small business associations spoke for small business people at large, and he ignored those opposed to the SBA.

The SBA must be viewed in the context of Eisenhower's own political philosophy. Although committed to the principles of fiscal conservatism, Eisenhower made a point of supporting the creation or expansion of several social programs, including disability insurance, public housing, conservation projects, and small business assistance.[53] He accepted the existence of a limited welfare state and projected an image of caring centrism in order to cultivate a public image of the Republican Party as one that spoke "for all workers, for all farmers, for all businessmen, and all Americans everywhere."[54] Eisenhower's views reflected an era in which politicians eschewed the labels "liberal" or "conservative" and intellectuals spoke of an "end to ideology."[55]

Eisenhower's support for the SBA also reflected the workings of what Fred Greenstein has called Eisenhower's "hidden-hand presidency."[56] Publicly, Eisenhower championed the interests of small business, while privately, administration officials worked to limit the scope of the SBA in order to maintain a balanced budget. Political scientists often speak of a "bureaucratic imperative"—the notion that government bureaucrats seek to expand the scale and scope of their agencies.[57] In this case, however, the SBA provides a curious example of the bureaucratic imperative in reverse. Rather than augment their power by seeking greater responsibilities, SBA officials tried their best to see that the agency remained an insignificant part of the federal government. Yet the small business advocates in Congress kept up their campaign for a larger, more powerful agency. This tug-of-war continued through the remainder of the Eisenhower years and eventually resulted in the creation of a permanent Small Business Administration.

7

The Small Business Administration:
Push-and-Pull Politics, 1953–1961

Shortly before the inauguration of Dwight D. Eisenhower, the political scientist James MacGregor Burns predicted that "if the past is any guide, the relation between President Eisenhower and Congress is just as likely to be marked sooner or later by deadlock, intermittent guerrilla warfare, even hostility."[1] Burns had in mind a contentious coalition of conservatives in Congress, but he might as easily have referred to the coming conflict between the president and congressional small business advocates. During the Eisenhower years, the Small Business Administration embodied a struggle between a budget-conscious president and a Congress eager to increase government aid to small business. In a classic case of political "gridlock," the congressional Small Business Committees pushed an agenda designed to strengthen the SBA, while the president pulled back from his publicly proclaimed commitment to the agency. Eventually, this process of "push-and-pull" politics resulted in a significant increase in the size of the agency, as congressional small business advocates forced the president to acquiesce to some of their demands.

Despite this growth, the SBA still had only a limited impact on the economy. Nevertheless, as one administration official recognized, "the Small Business Administration is interesting for political reasons rather than economic ones."[2] The Republicans used the agency to deflect criticism that they represented corporate America. In addition, the Eisenhower administration turned the SBA into a patronage machine designed to reward loyal supporters of the Republican Party. Finally, the SBA served as a "safety valve" for small business while the administration pursued a "tight money" policy that limited opportunities for small businesses. In short, the Eisenhower administration reluctantly accepted the growth of the SBA because the agency served useful political purposes.

The Administration of William D. Mitchell

President Eisenhower's philosophy of government represented a mixture of liberalism and conservatism, and both elements served to weaken his support for the Small Business Administration. As a corporate liberal, Eisenhower emphasized voluntary cooperation among business, government, and labor.[3] Thus, although he supported the continuation of many New Deal programs, Eisenhower opposed government entry into the fields of finance and industry because such an entry would bring the government into competition, rather than cooperation, with business. At the same time, while he accepted a minimal welfare state, Eisenhower was a fiscal conservative whose "underlying ideology was strongly antigovernment."[4] The Republican president was wary of Keynesian theory and hoped to reduce the tax burden on businesses and individuals by maintaining a balanced budget, his top priority in domestic policymaking. According to historian John Sloan, Eisenhower also believed that balanced budgets were "necessary for democracy because demagogic politicians were tempted to cater to the demands of the present set of voters at the expense of the next generation."[5] Eisenhower's commitments to business-government cooperation and fiscal conservatism served to subordinate the needs of the SBA to the larger goal of achieving a balanced budget.

Eisenhower appointed an administrator of the SBA who shared his philosophy of government and whom he could rely on to limit the agency's demands for funding. Eisenhower chose William D. Mitchell, a former SDPA official and a lawyer for a small Colorado manufacturing firm.[6] Mitchell promised to pursue a policy of "self-help and cooperation" between business and government. Declaring that the SBA must "work with and not against the spirit of self-reliance," Mitchell refused to make direct loans to small businesses and requested an appropriation of only $50 million for the agency's loan fund. In fact, the Small Business Act required him to limit expenditures by seeking out banks that were willing to participate in the making of loans. Thus, under its "participation loan" program, the SBA supplied only part of each loan made to small businesses and backed the rest with a government guarantee. In this way, the SBA helped the Eisenhower administration achieve a balanced budget.[7]

The SBA's definition of small business did not fully satisfy small business advocates in Congress. The agency's enabling legislation defined a "small" business as "one which is independently owned and operated and which is not dominant in its field of operations."[8] Within the confines of these guidelines, the SBA administrator could use other criteria to define small business. The congressional Small Business Committees urged the SBA to adopt a relative definition because they hoped to check the growth of big business by providing assistance to firms far larger than the mom-and-pop establishments most Americans thought of as "small" business. In line with this way of thinking, the SBA varied its definition of small business by industry and trade. A "small" manufacturer could have as many as a thousand employees, while a small retailer could report annual sales as high as $1 million. However, much to the dismay of the Small Business Committees, for procurement purposes the SBA accepted the military's five-hundred-employee definition of small business, a classification used by the Department of Defense to limit the interference of the SBA.[9]

The Eisenhower administration's commitment to a balanced budget also conflicted with the congressional Small Business Committees' demands for government relief during a time of economic distress. Congress had created the Small Business Administration just as a recession began to weaken the small business sector of the economy. The end of the Korean War also adversely affected those small manufacturers who were dependent on military orders. Although the number of business failures remained historically low, the SBA admitted that cutbacks in defense had proved "disastrous" for these firms.[10] Congressional small business advocates demanded increased aid to small business in order to help them weather the recession. In his first State of the Union address, Eisenhower promised tax relief for small business, but he assigned a higher priority to achieving a balanced budget; therefore, contrary to the wishes of the Small Business Committees, he delayed repealing the wartime excess-profit tax—a levy that, according to one senator, "tends to crucify the small businesses."[11]

Meanwhile, under Mitchell, the SBA offered small business little assistance. In September, the agency's Loan Policy Board issued a statement limiting lending assistance to manufacturers engaged in military or essential civilian production. Thus, the SBA pulled back from its responsibility to represent all types of small business and instead limited itself to the activities once pursued by the SDPA. The overcentralized nature of the SBA also slowed the lending process down. By November, the regional offices of the agency had endorsed several dozen loans, but the Washington headquarters had not approved a single one.[12]

Wendell Barnes Takes Over

Congressional criticism of the SBA forced the Eisenhower administration to change its policy toward small business. In early November, the president replaced Mitchell with Wendell B. Barnes, a corporate lawyer and former state representative from Oklahoma who had served as Mitchell's general counsel. Barnes persuaded the Loan Policy Board to allow the agency to make loans to all types of small business. He decentralized the operations of the agency by authorizing the regional offices to make participation loans of up to $50,000 without having to wait for final approval from Washington.[13] President Eisenhower also made good on his promise of tax relief. In January 1954, he offered Congress a tax reform package containing several proposals designed to aid small business, including a liberalization of depreciation allowances and the simplified taxation of partnerships. Later that year, these proposals were embodied in the Tax Reform Act of 1954.[14]

Although congressional small business advocates had succeeded in pressuring the SBA into taking stronger action on behalf of small business, Barnes continued to follow the conservative lending policy of his predecessor. As the administrator of "a public agency using the taxpayers' funds," Barnes kept an ever-watchful eye on expenditures and limited the number of direct loans to small business.[15] He refused to risk money "to underwrite incompetence, or lend money to stave off inevitable failure." Like Mitchell, Barnes stressed the importance of "local self-help and community effort" and made it clear that the achievement of a balanced budget took precedence over the immediate interests of small business.[16]

The congressional Small Business Committees continued to criticize the SBA for its lack of initiative. In January 1954, the Senate committee completed an investigation of the agency's field operations in northern cities and reported "very disappointing" findings. The senators discovered "a disjointed organization, top-heavy in Washington." They complained that the SBA lacked the personnel and funds needed to assist the nation's four million small businesses. While Barnes publicly proclaimed the importance of grassroots activity, the committee found that in many towns "less than two percent" of the small businesses even knew of the SBA's existence.[17]

Throughout 1954, Barnes found himself on the defensive as congressional small business advocates demanded a more liberalized lending policy. As the Eisenhower administration restricted the money supply to restrain inflation, commercial banks made fewer loans to business, and Democratic critics charged that small firms could no longer secure the credit they needed. The

Democrats complained that the SBA failed to serve as an adequate "safety valve" during this period of "tight money." After one year of operation, the agency had lent small businesses only $35 million, mostly in the form of participation loans.[18] The average loan barely exceeded $60,000, an amount considered insufficient by many members of the Small Business Committees.[19]

Congressional small business advocates blamed the conservatism of the SBA on the domination of the Loan Policy Board by the secretaries of the Treasury and Commerce Departments. In May 1954, Representative Samuel W. Yorty (D.-Calif.) introduced legislation to eliminate the Loan Policy Board, increase the maximum loan amount, and grant permanent status to the agency; but the Eisenhower administration wished to retain control of the agency and opposed all such changes in the constitution of the SBA.[20]

In 1953, the Eisenhower administration had reluctantly agreed to create the SBA in order to get rid of the RFC. The Republicans now made the best of a bad situation by turning the agency into a patronage plum ripe for picking by GOP loyalists. Barnes reported with pride that his agency "employed 197 persons who have been recommended by the Republican National Committee, Republican congressional members, and Republican state organizations. These people constitute approximately 32 percent of the total percentage of SBA. . . . There is no other Federal agency which can approach this percentage of Republicans employed." In addition, the SBA hired nearly two hundred Republican attorneys as outside consultants. Barnes also noted how the agency's advisory boards served as an "effective political tool" because "Republican Senators and Congressmen generally understand that they may have as many appointments to these Boards as will serve their particular needs." The chairman of the Republican National Committee, Leonard Hall, praised Barnes for his ability to circumvent the civil service regulations, "which are presently such a handicap in employing Republicans." Hall proclaimed, "No Federal agency has worked as closely and as cooperatively with the Republican National Committee as has the SBA." The Republicans made no secret of their desire to distribute patronage. Stephen J. Spingarn, a Truman appointee to the Federal Trade Commission, later recalled that "the Republicans had been out of power for twenty years and there was tremendous pressure to 'Let's get those damned Democrats out of those jobs and get good Republicans in, and to hell with Civil Service Laws.'" Thus, the Republicans replaced the scandal-ridden RFC with an agency equally committed to political ends.[21]

Political considerations shaped nearly every aspect of the SBA's operations. Barnes spent much of his time on the political stump making speeches in defense of administration policies.[22] He defended the agency from its Democratic critics by denying that the Loan Policy Board hampered him in any way.[23] Barnes also took positive action when it seemed absolutely necessary to avert congressional criticism. During the 1953–54 recession he conceded that "small business in important industries is not faring well," and he responded to congressional alarm about that situation by seeking legislation to strengthen the agency.[24] In March 1954, he notified Eisenhower that the SBA lacked the funds and personnel needed to handle a flood of applications from small business owners. The SBA had taken on the combined responsibilities of the SDPA and RFC, yet the agency had only 545 employees, far fewer than the 2,300 persons once employed by the two former agencies. By stressing the "political aspects of this situation," Barnes secured Eisenhower's endorsement of legislation providing the agency with an additional $50 million.[25]

Despite this evidence of progress, congressional small business advocates remained unsatisfied with the performance of the SBA. In its final 1954 report, the House Small Business Committee declared that "the full legislative intent and objective of the Small Business Administration has as yet not been achieved." The committee pressed the SBA to act even more vigorously in the lending field and urged Barnes to overcome the "bickering and opposition" of the military's procurement officers.[26]

The debate over whether or not to extend the SBA beyond its June 1955 expiration date highlighted the agency's political importance. In December 1954, Secretary of Commerce Sinclair Weeks argued that his department represented all of the nation's businesses and urged the president to allow the SBA to expire on 30 June 1955.[27] Although Barnes agreed "in principle . . . to the eventual assignment . . . of the Small Business Administration to the Department of Commerce," he recognized "Congressional opposition" and the "realities of the political situation."[28] The Democrats had just regained control of both houses of Congress, and the Eisenhower administration knew that it could not secure the votes needed to eliminate the SBA.

In Congress, the SBA received bipartisan support from the members of the Small Business Committees, and in January 1955, Senator Thye introduced a bill to make the SBA a permanent agency. Thye cited the "splendid record" of the agency, which had shown "the proper regard for the taxpayers' money."[29] Congressional Republicans acknowledged the shortcomings of the agency but still favored giving it a renewed lease on life.[30] Meanwhile, the Democrats drafted legislation to extend the agency for two more years and strengthen it by eliminating the Loan Policy Board, increasing its lending authority, and raising the ceiling on loans.[31]

The SBA did have its critics. Several influential groups urged the president to

Wendell Barnes, administrator of the SBA, discusses the issue of small business and procurement with Assistant Secretary of Defense Thomas P. Pike (right) and Deputy Secretary of Defense Reuben B. Robertson Jr. (left). (U.S. Army photograph, courtesy of Dwight D. Eisenhower Presidential Library)

abolish the SBA in the interests of governmental economy. Representatives of the National Association of Manufacturers (NAM), the U.S. Chamber of Commerce, and the American Bankers Association (ABA) testified against an extension of the SBA.[32] A Hoover Commission Task Force also recommended termination, but the full commission supported a two-year extension of the agency because, according to an administration official, the commissioners did not want to "take action adverse to a program which *appears* to help small business and hence is politically unassailable" (original italics).[33]

In August, motivated by this political concern, Eisenhower signed a bill extending the life of the SBA for two years and doubling its authorization for business loans from $150 million to $300 million. Congress also authorized the SBA to raise the ceiling on loans to $250,000. In a provision directed at the military, Congress gave the SBA the power to make its own definition of small business binding on all other government agencies and also required the Defense Department to issue monthly reports on the share of contracts awarded to small firms.[34]

During the SBA's first two years, the agency failed to fulfill the expectations of its congressional sponsors. Members of the congressional Small Business Committees repeatedly expressed their dissatisfaction with the SBA's definition of small business and with the limits placed on lending assistance to small firms. This congressional criticism slowly forced the Eisenhower administration to increase its aid to small business. Moreover, with the return of a Democratic Congress in 1954, the Eisenhower administration could no longer entertain the thought of eliminating the SBA in the interests of governmental economy. Henceforth, the Democrats put the Republican president on the defensive by making a campaign issue out of his refusal to boost spending on SBA programs. This partisan debate over aid to small business came to a head in the election of 1956.

Election-Year Politics: 1956

In January 1956, the Senate Small Business Committee unanimously agreed to issue a report critical of the SBA.[35] This sense of unanimity did not last, however, as election-year politics shattered the notion of a unified coalition of small business advocates in Congress. In the coming months, the issue of small business and its fate under the Eisenhower administration became a political football tossed between Democrats and Republicans.

Throughout 1956, the Democrats repeatedly blasted the small business policy of the Eisenhower administration on the floor of Congress and in the mass media. In the House of Representatives, Wright Patman condemned what he called "a big business Administration" for its refusal to do more on behalf of a "forgotten man," the small business owner. Abraham Multer (D.-N.Y.) called for the elimination of the Loan Policy Board and an end to the administration's "tight money" policy.[36]

The Democratic National Committee (DNC) also tried to capitalize on the Eisenhower administration's apparent lack of concern for small business. In June, the DNC issued its candidates a fact sheet highlighting the relative decline of small business during Eisenhower's first term.[37] In addition, the DNC took up Senator Sparkman's suggestion to incorporate a strongly worded small business plank in the party platform. In their platform, the Democrats "severely condemn[ed] Republican discrimination" against small business and called for the "replacement of the weak and ineffective Republican conduct of the Small Business Administration."[38] As cochair of the DNC's Advisory Committee on Small Business, Sparkman joined with Wright Patman in issuing a press release lambasting the GOP for its adherence to trickle-down economics.

Sparkman and Patman claimed that the Tax Reform Act of 1954 benefited large corporations at the expense of small business and recommended the establishment of a steeply graduated corporate income tax designed to lift the tax burden from small businesses and place it on big business.[39]

In the presidential campaign, Democratic candidate Adlai Stevenson and his running mate—Estes Kefauver, a former member of the House Small Business Committee—promised to make the SBA a more powerful and effective voice for small business. Stevenson gathered support from the Independent Businessmen for Stevenson-Kefauver, a group set up to counter the rhetoric of Small Businessmen for Ike. Shortly before election day, these Democratic small business owners exploited the timely release of a study by the Public Affairs Institute, a think tank specializing in issues related to small business, which described the SBA as "only one-tenth as effective as [the] R.F.C." (as measured by total business loans). The pro-Stevenson business owners cited the PAI study and dismissed Eisenhower's business rhetoric as "nothing more than political drivel."[40]

Republican members of the Small Business Committees reacted to the Democratic onslaught by mounting a vigorous defense of Eisenhower's small business policies. Representative Roy Riehlman (R.-N.Y.) expressed his dismay at the partisan spirit displayed by the Democrats and told them, "Play all the politics you like, but do not play politics with small business." Riehlman reminded his Democratic colleagues that "the problems of small business did not arrive with Eisenhower" and criticized them for creating a "false issue of 'big business versus small business.'" Citing an increase in the number of firms, Riehlman argued that small business had shared in the general prosperity of recent years.[41] On the Senate side, Edward Thye noted the positive action taken by the Eisenhower administration, including its "outstanding record" of antitrust enforcement, its creation of the Small Business Administration, and its efforts to increase small manufacturers' share of military procurements.[42] Others, including Representative John E. Henderson (R.-Ohio), reminded voters that their party had eliminated the "scandal-ridden Reconstruction Finance Corporation" and replaced it with an agency that cooperated with business.[43]

As a politician, Eisenhower knew that "there are more small businesses than there are big businesses"; therefore, he emphasized the small business record of his administration and countered the criticisms of the Democrats by noting that "we—not they—created the Small Business Administration."[44] The Republicans emphasized this point throughout the campaign, and their party platform praised Eisenhower for creating "the very successful Small Business Administration."[45]

In June 1956, Eisenhower also sought political cover from the mounting criticism of his small business policy by establishing a Cabinet Committee on Small Business (CCSB) headed by Arthur F. Burns, chairman of the Council of Economic Advisers.[46] The CCSB recommended further tax relief for small business and an extension of the SBA beyond 1957. Burns argued that tax cuts would enlarge the national income in the long run and make up for the immediate loss of revenue. Yet the proposed cuts saved a small corporation a maximum of only $2,500, hardly enough to stimulate capital investment. Consequently, the business press considered the proposal a "politically motivated" sop to the Democrats, and a member of the committee later admitted that "the chief motive [in creating the CCSB] was a political one."[47]

Administration officials also defended Eisenhower's small business policy. In an address before a Small Businessmen for Ike group, a Commerce Department official accused the Democrats of engaging in demagoguery by preaching that "prosperity is very great but nobody is enjoying it."[48] But in its defense of Eisenhower, the Republican National Committee relied chiefly on the SBA, which according to RNC workers "had quietly been performing a task that proved that our administration is not Big Business minded."[49] During the campaign, Barnes presented the administration's case at numerous meetings of small business owners, leading Wright Patman to complain of his "political barnstorming." On the eve of the election, tempers flared in the House Small Business Committee as Patman released a telegram to the press asking the Republican members to use their influence with the Eisenhower administration to restrain Barnes. The Republicans refused to do so and countered by accusing Patman of using the committee for his own "unadulterated and unadorned political purposes."[50]

Although they publicly championed Eisenhower's small business policies, administration officials admitted privately that small business had lost ground in recent years. Arthur Burns attributed the decline to fundamental changes in the economy, including increased taxation, the advent of television advertising, and the growth of trade unions.[51] Although small business had begun to recover from the 1953–54 recession, Barnes conceded that the relative position of small business was still "not so good," and he blamed the situation on the restriction of the money supply. He persuaded the Loan Policy Board to liberalize the SBA's lending practices so that it might act as a "safety valve" as long as the administration pursued a "tight money" policy.[52] Consequently, in the last half of 1956 the SBA more than doubled the amount it lent to small business.[53]

Yet after Eisenhower's landslide victory in 1956, his administration pulled back on the promises made to small business during the campaign. In his second term, Eisenhower reacted to Democratic demands for increased spending on domestic programs by intensifying his efforts to achieve a balanced budget.[54] Consequently, Burns now worried that Eisenhower would not follow through on the CCSB's request for a tax cut and reminded the president that "from a political viewpoint, small business is a distinct sector of our economy."[55] Treasury Secretary George Humphrey admitted that the promise of a tax cut placed the administration in an "embarrassing position" because it needed to maintain current tax rates in order to balance the budget in 1957. Nevertheless, despite the political costs, Humphrey persuaded the president to reject Burns's request. Humphrey and Eisenhower both feared that if they supported a tax reduction for small business, other groups would rush in to demand similar cuts. Burns continued to press Eisenhower on the issue, but the president resisted offering a tax cut for small business because he said it would open the way for "the wails and screams of political demagogues and selfish interests."[56]

Following the election, the SBA became involved in another round of turf wars with rival agencies. Assistant Secretary of Commerce Frederick H. Mueller complained that the creation of the SBA had drained clients away from the Commerce Department. As a result, the public now considered his agency "the Department of 'Big Business.'" By abolishing the SBA, Mueller argued, the administration could remove this negative label from the Commerce Department. Mueller failed, however, to convince the administration that the political benefits outweighed the criticism that would result from the abolition of the SBA.[57]

The SBA also faced stiff opposition from the military, which resented the agency's interference in the procurement process. After 1955, small businesses' share of procurement dollars declined as the military continued to spend ever more on complex weapons systems. Procurement officers insisted that they could not aid small business without incurring unreasonable costs and delays in defense production. According to John Hamlin, a presidential aide and a former director of small business for the Department of Defense, the military reluctantly allowed the SBA to make nonbinding recommendations only "because it appeared to be an absolute political necessity." Since little could be done to aid small business in the defense sector, Hamlin suggested ways to cover up damaging statistics. He recommended that the SBA simply "discontinue the present series on 'share of prime contracts to small business,'" noting, "If we can't improve the statistics, we might at least stop supplying the opposition with this devastating ammunition."[58] The current director of small business, Joseph M. McKellar, also expressed his concern that the statistics on small business procurements are "going to lead us into political disaster," and he too suggested a change in "our reporting system whereby we can straighten the trend out and be of some assistance in getting a Republican Congress elected."[59] Yet the SBA, perhaps fearing a congressional reprimand, did not act on these suggestions; it continued to report the decline of small business in the defense sector.

Meanwhile, congressional small business advocates kept up their criticism of nearly every aspect of SBA operations. In January 1957, the House Small Business Committee lamented that the "SBA sees no problems and offers no solutions." The Senate Small Business Committee tried to fashion an economic crisis out of apparent prosperity by claiming that small business suffered from "Want in the Midst of Plenty." In the committee's opinion, general prosperity posed "the gravest threat" to small business because it strengthened the position of large firms and allowed them to acquire their smaller rivals. The senators chastised the SBA for not doing enough to improve the position of small business during this time of "crisis."[60]

Despite their misgivings about the SBA's current policies, the Small Business Committees remained committed to seeing the agency through the long haul. During 1957, members of both committees presented dozens of bills to strengthen the SBA and place it on a permanent footing. In January 1957, Senator Thye and Representative Thompson (D.-N.J.) introduced legislation to eliminate the Loan Policy Board and grant the agency permanent status. Over the course of the next few months, other congressmen introduced similar measures. Finally, in June, the House Banking and Currency Committee approved a bill that made the agency permanent, lowered the interest rate on loans, and increased the agency's lending authority.[61]

After receiving Eisenhower's approval, Wendell Barnes testified that the temporary nature of the agency made it difficult to attract personnel. Barnes also requested more money from Congress, stating that the onset of another recession had led many small businesses to seek government loans and that their demands would soon exhaust the SBA's loan fund.[62] However, although the president publicly proclaimed his support for a permanent Small Business Administration, his administration's commitment to this facet of the legislation came into question when the assistant secretary of commerce described the SBA as a "political gimmick" and offered his personal opinion "that there should be only one government department in business."[63]

Congressional debate centered on the proposal to eliminate the Loan Policy Board and replace it with an advisory board made up of the current members and several outside representatives of small business. All three members of the

Wright Patman discusses small business legislation with officials of the National
Small Business Men's Association (1957). (From "Cameramen," courtesy of
Lyndon B. Johnson Presidential Library)

board opposed such a move, as did the president. But many small business
advocates believed that the Treasury and Commerce Departments represented
big business and, therefore, that Congress should not allow them to dominate
a small business agency. The Commerce Department's repeated assertions that
the SBA should not even exist only strengthened small business advocates'
conviction that the board hampered the agency's operations. Democrats such
as Senator Joseph S. Clark (D.-Calif.) further charged that the Loan Policy
Board had allowed Eisenhower to flout the will of Congress by placing the
agency "under the control of people who do not want to see the program
succeed."[64]

The debate over this legislation also sparked a bitter brawl between Wright
Patman and the other members of the House Small Business Committee.
Patman stood alone in opposition to a permanent SBA: he considered the
agency's record "terrible" and "disgraceful." In a remarkable reversal of his past
views on the subject, Patman argued that the problems of small business were
"not chronic" and that the government should aid small business only during
a time of crisis. He also contended that the SBA duplicated the work of the

Commerce Department. Patman tried to convince the Democratic members of the committee that the Republicans favored a permanent SBA because it allowed them to continue using the agency for patronage purposes. Patman favored granting the SBA only a temporary extension, but every other member of the committee desired the creation of a permanent SBA, and they resented Patman's heavy-handed attempts to squash this legislation. Abraham Multer (D.-N.Y.) accused Patman of opposition for opposition's sake. The New York congressman acknowledged that Patman could change his mind on important issues, but he contended that "the reason ought not to be perversity."[65]

In the end, when it became clear that the House would pass the measure, Patman relented; and on 25 June 1957, the House voted 393–2 to grant permanent status to the SBA. The House also increased the agency's business loan fund to $500 million and eliminated the Loan Policy Board. The Senate did not have time, however, to consider the House bill before the 31 July expiration date of the SBA; instead, the senators agreed to a one-year extension, added $75 million to the loan fund, and postponed further action until the following year.[66]

As Congress resumed consideration of the House bill, the Eisenhower administration debated whether or not to support an act that increased the SBA's total lending authority to $650 million. Barnes pointed out that with participation loans the SBA could limit its expenditures; at any rate, spending by the agency amounted to less than 1 percent of the federal budget. The administration finally reached a consensus in favor of this legislation because, as one official put it, "it is good politics to be on the side of the numerous little fellows against the large fellows."[67] The administration still insisted on retaining the Loan Policy Board, however. Congress agreed to these terms; and on 18 July 1958, President Eisenhower signed an act creating the nation's first permanent small business agency.[68]

Small Business Investment Companies: The Government as Venture Capitalist

Congressional small business advocates had finally attained their cherished goal of a permanent SBA, but they had failed to wrest control of the agency away from the Loan Policy Board. Therefore, they now sought the establishment of a separate body to provide for the long-term credit needs of small business. Once again, however, presidential opposition resulted in a compromise measure that left the Small Business Administration in full control of the new program.[69]

For decades, small business advocates had expressed their concern over the so-called MacMillan Gap, named after a British politician who, in 1931, noted the credit gap created when a small firm has grown beyond its own resources but still is not large enough to issue stock at a reasonable cost.[70] As early as 1934, Adolf Berle recommended to Congress the creation of government credit banks to provide venture capital to these small firms.[71] Since then, the experts had debated whether a MacMillan Gap existed in the United States. Studies by the Commerce Department (1935), a congressional Subcommittee on Investment (1950), and the Federal Reserve (1952, 1955) found that many small firms could not secure long-term financing.[72] In 1957, at the urging of Wright Patman, the Federal Reserve further investigated the credit needs of small business. In April 1958, the Federal Reserve concluded that small manufacturers had suffered during the "tight money" years of 1955–57, and it estimated a MacMillan Gap of approximately $500 million per year. The chairman of the Federal Reserve emphasized the need for a new source of equity capital for small business.[73]

Others, however, disputed the notion of a gap between the supply and demand for long-term credit. Surveys conducted by the Commerce Department (1955), the Council of Economic Advisers (1957), and Dun & Bradstreet (1958) revealed no evidence of a MacMillan Gap. In its survey of fifteen thousand firms, the Commerce Department found that over half needed no outside financing at all and that a quarter could obtain all they needed. An additional 19 percent required loans, while only 1 percent sought equity investment. According to the Commerce Department, the problem lay not with an inadequate supply of investment capital but, rather, with the reluctance of small business owners to give up control of their enterprises by issuing stock to outsiders.[74] Although this issue remains controversial, later studies by economists have generally confirmed these findings.[75]

Whatever the economic reality, many small business advocates had become convinced of the need for government investment in small business. Consequently, in April 1958, Wright Patman and Senate Majority Leader Lyndon B. Johnson (D.-Tex.) introduced legislation to create an independent Small Business Investment Administration with a $250 million fund to lend money or purchase debentures from small business investment companies (SBICs). In turn, these SBICs would invest public and private funds in small firms with growth potential. Johnson and Patman emphasized the decentralized nature of their scheme. As directors of the SBICs, local business owners, rather than a Washington agency, would make all the investment decisions. The two Texas congressmen predicted that private capital would eventually take over the

SBICs and that there would then be no need for government investment. Wright Patman viewed it as "a way to help free enterprise help itself." Senator Fulbright (D.-Ark.) went even further: he foresaw an eventual end to all government financing of business, including the SBA's loan programs, and expressed his hope that "the Government may be able to work itself out of this [financial assistance] field."[76]

Conservative small business advocates, on the other hand, viewed direct government investment in the private sector as a threat to free enterprise, and they were skeptical of the claim that this intervention would be temporary. Three members of the Senate Small Business Committee (Homer Capehart, John W. Bricker, and Wallace Bennett) described the proposed bill as "the first step toward the socialization of an important segment of our free enterprise system." They argued that small business owners did not wish to relinquish control of their companies; thus, there had been no grassroots demands for additional equity capital. The conservatives also considered $250 million an "excessive" amount, given that the Chairman of the Federal Reserve had asked Congress to act "experimentally and on a small scale."[77]

The Eisenhower administration did not contest the principle of government investment in SBICs. On the contrary, Eisenhower hoped this spending program would stimulate the economy and lift it out of the recession. However, Eisenhower opposed the creation of an independent agency, and administration officials forced a compromise by demanding that Congress place the new organization within the SBA. Congress agreed; and on 21 August 1958, the president signed into law the Small Business Investment Act.

The act created within the SBA a Small Business Investment Division (SBID) with a $250 million revolving investment fund. The SBA could license SBICs and finance them with long-term, low-interest loans or by matching private investment with the purchase of subordinated debentures. The creators of the SBID hoped that low-interest loans and preferential tax treatment would attract investors seeking a high rate of return.[78] Congressional small business advocates had great expectations for what Neil Jacoby, a member of the Council of Economic Advisers, called the "fourth banking system" (after commercial banking, investment banking, and mortgage lending).[79]

Two weeks after creating this "fourth banking system," Congress and the president reached a compromise agreement on a tax package for small business. The Small Business Tax Revision Act offered a modest amount of tax relief by liberalizing various provisions of the tax code.[80] Thus, all in all, 1958 proved to be a banner year for the small business advocates: Congress created a permanent SBA, provided funds for venture capital investment in small business, and lowered the tax burden on small firms, and the SBA made a record total of $241 million in small business loans. Wright Patman could look back on the year and declare that the "last Congress has, I believe, done more for small business than any Congress, in history."[81] Never before had the federal government promised so much positive aid for small business.

The Small Business Administration: Success or Failure?

In the fall 1958 elections, the Democrats claimed credit for passing this small business legislation, and this claim may have contributed to their sweep of the Congress.[82] In the Eighty-sixth Congress (1959–61), the Democratic Party held large majorities in the Senate and in the House of Representatives.[83] Yet although they controlled Congress, the Democrats could not force President Eisenhower to abandon his commitment to a balanced budget. Eisenhower's fiscal conservatism continued to influence policymaking at the SBA. In December 1958, the deputy director of the Budget Bureau expressed his concern that the SBA had become "an uncontrollable program" and asked Barnes to tighten the agency's loan requirements. The SBA cooperated by directing its loan officers to "moderate demands for credit" in order to help the president maintain a balanced budget. Criticism from the Small Business Committees forced the SBA to reverse its official stand, but the agency continued to cut back on its lending assistance in 1959.[84]

By 1961, after nearly a decade of operation, the Small Business Administration had proved to be a disappointment to its congressional supporters. Presidential opposition prevented them from expanding the scope of SBA activities to the degree they desired. In his study of the agency, Harmon Zeigler emphasizes the president's reluctance to support the SBA and describes the agency as no more than a symbolic "sop" to the Democrats. According to Zeigler, the SBA provided no tangible benefit to small business, because its creation had actually resulted in an immediate reduction in financial aid to small firms.[85] It is true that as the nation's chief executive, Eisenhower focused on a few important policy concerns (principally foreign policy and the budget) and tried to fend off the pleas of special interests, including small business.[86] But Zeigler ignores the long-term effect of the political struggle between the Congress and the president. Constant pressure from the congressional Small Business Committees forced the administration to dramatically increase spending on small business. Between calendar years 1954 and 1960, the SBA increased its financial assistance to small business almost fourfold, from $58 million to $221 million.

During this seven-year period, the agency approved $1.05 billion in business loans. By comparison, the RFC's Small Loan Participation Program had provided only $151 million in loans to small business between 1947 and 1951.[87] In the 1960s, the SBA continued to grow; and by 1965, it had become a midsized agency, with nearly four thousand employees.[88] During the 1970s, the SBA increased its loan guarantee commitments from $450 million to $3.6 billion; and by the 1980s, the agency was guaranteeing nearly half of the intermediate and long-term credit extended to small business. The agency's growth during and after the Eisenhower years far exceeded the inflation rate, the growth in the business population, and the overall growth of the federal budget. In retrospect, these figures do not support Zeigler's contention that congressional pressure had "little tangible result."[89]

In his study of government bureaucracy, political scientist James Q. Wilson provides a useful framework for analyzing the operations of federal agencies. Wilson argues that agencies lacking an organized constituency can survive by taking advantage of "entrepreneurial" politics or by exploiting popular sentiment ("majoritarian" politics).[90] In the case of the SBA, the congressional Small Business Committees acted as political entrepreneurs by creating and sustaining the agency in the face of stiff opposition from the president, the Commerce Department, and the military. They did so by resorting to crisis rhetoric ("small business is doomed") and by playing on public sentiment for the "little guy."

Although congressional small business advocates succeeded in tangibly increasing the scale and scope of SBA activities, several factors, including the problem of bureaucratic rivalry, limited the agency's effectiveness. The SBA never achieved a sufficient degree of autonomy, because it antagonized the Commerce Department and the Department of Defense by encroaching on their perceived spheres of authority. The tension between these agencies continued into the post-Eisenhower period. In 1965, Congress tried to secure the independence of the agency by abolishing the Loan Policy Board. Two years later, however, President Johnson proposed a merger between the Commerce Department and the SBA. Although congressional small business advocates blocked this move, they could not eliminate the Commerce Department's thinly veiled hostility toward its younger rival.[91]

The large and heterogeneous nature of the small business community also made it difficult for the agency to set priorities. The Small Business Administration simply had too many potential clients. (A wit once defined a small business owner as "anyone who is less than eight feet tall"!)[92] Consequently, the agency spent its limited resources on a tiny fraction of the four million small businesses in the country. In the area of management assistance, for example, the SBA had fewer than one hundred counselors to serve the entire nation.[93]

The Eisenhower administration's policy of fiscal restraint limited the number of loans made by the SBA, but this conservative lending policy also restricted the agency's losses. Congressional small business advocates assumed that bankers had failed to recognize the creditworthiness of many small firms and that the government needed to correct this market failure. However, fiscal conservatives in the Eisenhower administration dismissed this notion of market failure. They predicted that if the SBA did not maintain strict credit standards, it would incur high losses on its loans to small business. Indeed, in the 1960s and 1970s, as its former fiscal restraint eroded, the SBA dramatically expanded its commitments; consequently, the default rate on SBA loans soared to between 25 percent and 40 percent, depending on the program being considered.[94]

The SBA was not very effective in promoting the welfare of marginal enterprises. By law, the agency could make loans only to small firms that were unable to find financing elsewhere; but agency funds still did not always reach truly needy small businesses. A spokesman for one trade association complained that "if you can get a loan from the SBA, you can certainly get it from a bank."[95] Indeed, an agency study of its loan operations in Connecticut between 1955 and 1959 revealed that a third of the loan recipients privately acknowledged that they could secure the same loan from a private bank, albeit at a higher rate of interest. An agency official concluded, "Our loans aren't reaching the risky type of business that really needs it so badly."[96]

After a slow start, the SBIC program experienced dramatic growth in its first five years, but it, too, disappointed small business advocates. During the first eighteen months of operation, the SBA spent only $10 million of the $150 million appropriated by Congress for investment in SBICs. A 1960 survey by the SBA revealed that the SBICs suffered from restrictive regulations and high operating costs.[97] In order to reduce these costs, Congress raised the ceiling on the permissible size of the SBICs, thus abandoning the original goal of aiding very small businesses. Investment in the SBICs then took off, and by mid-1962 it amounted to a total of $350 million.[98] Yet despite government subsidies and preferential tax treatment, the SBIC industry as a whole did not turn a profit until 1966, leading a former agency official to "question whether the whole exercise is worth the effort."[99] Senator William Proxmire, a leading advocate of small business, concluded that the program had been "of little or no help to the really small businesses" and called for its elimination.[100] In fact, the "fourth banking system" never closed the so-called MacMillan Gap. In 1983, twenty-five years after Congress created the program, SBICs invested a record $470 million in small business—an amount that still fell shy of the $500 million that small business advocates believed was needed to close the gap in 1957![101]

Despite the dramatic growth in the SBA's financial commitments during the Eisenhower years, the SBA as yet had only a limited impact on the small business sector of the economy. How, then, did small business fare during the early years of the agency? Democratic small business advocates painted a bleak picture of small business in the 1950s. In his review of the decade, Senator Sparkman expressed the view that "during the so-called fabulous fifties, the bright sun of business prosperity has been for them behind a dark cloud." Sparkman blamed much of the alleged decline of small business on the Eisenhower administration's policies for dealing with procurement, mergers, and monetary policy.[102]

Business writers at the time questioned this pessimism. One analyst wrote that "the reports of the death of small business have been greatly exaggerated," an opinion shared by those who studied the small business sector during these years.[103] Subsequent studies have revealed no significant change in the economic position of small business. During the 1950s, the business population continued to grow at the same rate as the increase in the working population.[104] For the most part, small establishments and firms lost little or no market share. Between 1954 and 1963, small establishments (defined as those with fewer than one hundred employees) in the service sector experienced a slight drop in their share of sales, from 79 percent to 77 percent, while the market share of small retail establishments declined from 89 percent to 88 percent. The small establishments' share of the value added in manufacturing remained the same, at 21 percent.[105] Small retail and service firms (defined as those with fewer than four units) lost a few percentage points of market share (measured by sales), but their relative decline was much steeper in the post-Eisenhower period. Moreover, they still reported an absolute increase in sales.[106] (Unfortunately, we do not have good data on the market share of small manufacturing firms.)[107] In sum, both big and small business prospered during these years. As one scholar put it, "The large firms have grown larger, and the small firms more numerous."[108]

Critics are fond of pointing out the many failings of the Small Business Administration. These critics note that although small businesses fared well during the 1950s, they did so largely without government aid. In her study of the SBA, Pearl Rushfield Willing describes its first quarter century of operations as "a record of scandals, inadequate management assistance and repetitive contract assistance to a limited number of small businesses, many of which did not 'graduate' from the nurturing provided by government contracts and did not become self-sustaining firms." In a similar vein, a *Fortune* writer characterized the agency as "an overgrown pest-plagued, bureaucratic weed."[109] In many respects, the SBA did fail in its mission to strengthen the small business sector; yet despite all its faults, the agency has survived forty years of repeated attacks by rival agencies and budget-cutting presidents, thus lending some support to Thurman Arnold's theory that bureaucracies "have the persistency of all living things. They tend to grow and expand. Even when their utility both to the public and their own members has disappeared, they still survive."[110]

Federal Government Policy
and Small Business

In just twenty-five years, congressional small business advocates successfully secured the passage of two major antitrust laws and the creation of three small business agencies, yet their legislation failed to redistribute much wealth to small business owners. In the end, these political entrepreneurs remained leaders without followers—self-appointed spokesmen for a small business community that never coalesced into an effective pressure group. This conclusion considers both their successes and failures, from the high hopes of the 1930s to the lowered expectations of the 1950s.

Political Economy: The Crisis Myth

"Crisis" may be the most overused term in a politician's vocabulary. From the constitutional crisis of the 1780s to the health care "crisis" of the 1990s, politicians have tried to create a sense of urgency and gather support for their programs by propagating the notion of an impending catastrophe. In the mid-twentieth century, congressional advocates of small business exploited the political potential inherent in the real or imaginary crises facing small business. This belief in a crisis united an otherwise diverse group of congressmen in support of small business legislation. Crisis rhetoric also overcame the reservations many congressmen had about the idea of government aid for "free" enterprise. Hence, during the Great Depression and World War II, liberals and conservatives agreed that small business people faced a crisis and needed federal aid. The return of peacetime prosperity did not alleviate their concern. In good times and bad, members of the Small Business Committees played on public sentiment for small business by resorting to crisis rhetoric.

The political scientist Theodore Lowi notes that crisis situations undermine the legitimacy of public authority and result in demands for the representation of previously unorganized and voiceless interests to restore a sense of legitimacy.[1] Thus, organization has become the sine qua non of politics. In his classic *Leviathan*, Thomas Hobbes described a powerful absolutist state able to subdue the various interests in society in order to prevent a "war of all against all"; the modern American leviathan, on the other hand, embraces these interests and attempts to organize new ones to quell disaffection with the regime. Ellis Hawley described this as the process of "counterorganization": "using the government to promote the organization of economically weak groups" in order to "balance" the economy and ensure the representation of all conceivable interests in the policymaking process.[2] During the Great Depression and World War II, the federal government encouraged the formation of organizations to represent farmers and workers. The heterogeneous nature of the small business community, however, undermined all attempts to "counterorganize" this group, thus demonstrating what Lowi calls "the myth of the group and the group will": the fallacious notion that special-interest organizations embody the general will of the diverse communities they seek to represent.[3]

Economic reality differed from the crisis rhetoric espoused by the champions of small business. Congressional small business advocates worked from an assumption of market failure, a belief that the American economy would grow increasingly concentrated and thereby fail to provide enough opportunities for those hoping to open their own small businesses. The small business advocates were not alone in their prediction of a rising tide of oligopoly. In their 1932 analysis of big business, *The Modern Corporation and Private Property*, lawyer Adolf Berle and economist Gardiner Means predicted that if then-current trends continued, the largest two hundred nonfinancial corporations would control the entire industrial sector of the American economy by 1969.[4] Contrary to these expectations, though, the level of economic concentration stabilized in the 1930s and later declined.[5] Congressional small business advocates also underestimated the ability of small firms to compete in the modern marketplace. Even during the spectacular rise of big business in the late nineteenth century, small companies continued to grow in absolute terms.[6] The emergence of large corporations did not mean the elimination of small business opportunities; on the contrary, in the first half of the twentieth century, the number of nonagricultural firms increased at a faster rate than the population at large.[7] During the crisis years of World War II, small manufacturers fared far better than expected, and independent tire dealers actually increased their market share. Again, in the 1950s, small business generally held its own. The persistence of small business belied the repeated prophecies that "the end is near."

Of course, it would be easy to justify this mistaken notion of a small business crisis on the grounds that Americans did witness a concentration of economic resources in the late nineteenth and early twentieth centuries. At the time, few people recognized the creation of what economists would now call a permanent "dual economy" made up of both large and small firms. Beginning in the 1930s, business writers and economists did comment on the persistence of small business and challenge the rhetoric of the Cassandras in Congress. Yet, intent on preserving the "backbone of democracy," the self-appointed advocates of "independent enterprise" simply ignored the signs of health in their small business patients.

Why did so many members of Congress maintain this belief in a small business "crisis" despite all the contrary evidence demonstrating that small firms could compete with large corporations? There are several possible explanations. Although the small business sector proved remarkably resilient in the face of dramatic changes in the economy (depression, war, the rise of chain stores, etc.), the losers were visible and vocal. During the Great Depression, for example, trade associations representing grocers and tire dealers attempted to use the government to halt their loss of market share to mass-marketers. Furthermore, politicians concerned with the health of small business lacked the support of a broad-based organization representing small business owners; therefore, they had to resort to crisis rhetoric to secure legislation favorable to their cause. Also, this generation of politicians came of age in the early twentieth century, when the rise of big business had already produced oligopolies in manufacturing. It is clear from the congressional debates over small business legislation that many representatives feared that big business might produce oligopolies in the retail and service sectors of the economy. Thus their mistaken perception of economic reality may have derived from events that had taken place in decades past.

The congressional small business advocates also offered faulty economic reasoning in support of their legislation. Motivated by conspiracy theories and a hatred of big business, the authors of the Robinson-Patman Act assumed that chain stores could not justify the volume discounts they received from manufacturers. When experience demonstrated that chain stores *could* justify these discounts, the Small Business Committees resorted to the quantity-limit rule to favor one group of business owners at the expense of the general population of consumers. In the case of fair trade, small business advocates argued that it would guarantee the survival of "independent" enterprise, when in fact they should have known that small merchants would find themselves dependent on the terms set by large manufacturers of brand-name goods.

Although congressional small business advocates did not intend to create these consequences, they ignored opponents, such as Emanuel Celler, who accurately forecast the negative results of their well-intentioned legislation. The failure of their policies substantiates economist Joseph D. Phillips's conclusion that "almost no laws have been enacted that enhance the position of the small firms."[8] Indeed, after several decades of agitation and activism, the small business advocates themselves recognized that their legislation had not worked as intended to improve the position of small business. Thus, in 1963, a congressional aide concluded his history of the Senate Small Business Committee by acknowledging that the "committee has not been altogether successful in protecting small business in the United States, even with all it has done."[9]

Nevertheless, the small business legislation passed in this era represented more than "a whole *history* of symbolic victories" with little or no tangible results.[10] Although the small business advocates experienced failure and frustration, they also achieved several remarkable legislative victories. The Robinson-Patman Act strengthened the Federal Trade Commission and gave it a new mission. During the following thirty years, the FTC cited this law in most of its antimonopoly complaints.[11] By securing passage of federal fair trade legislation, the congressional small business advocates overturned a long series of court decisions and allowed manufacturers to experiment with this marketing strategy for nearly forty years. Eventually, their creation of a permanent Small Business Administration also resulted in billions of dollars in low-interest loans for small firms. Although these laws did not always produce the desired results, this legislation was far from inconsequential.

As political entrepreneurs, congressional small business advocates enjoyed several advantages. The symbolic appeal of small business garnered them the support of other legislators. Politicians found it easy to vote for small business legislation if it did not seriously threaten other organized interest groups. The symbolism of small business also made it difficult for a politician to "vote against small business."[12] Consequently, Congress usually voted nearly unanimously to pass small business legislation.

The congressional champions of small business also enjoyed the support of several trade associations; in fact, these groups initiated the more important pieces of small business legislation. The United States Wholesale Grocers Association (USWGA) conceived the Robinson-Patman Act, and later the National Association of Independent Tire Dealers (NAITD) convinced the Federal Trade

Commission to enforce the law. Meanwhile, the National Association of Retail Druggists and the American Fair Trade League organized lobbying efforts in support of state and federal fair trade legislation. These four groups overcame the opposition of chain store interests by creating and maintaining disciplined lobbying organizations.

The Importance of Crisis and Ideology

In his history of American government in the twentieth century, Robert Higgs emphasizes the importance of crisis and ideology as contributors to the growth of the federal government. During periods of crisis, Higgs argues, the public demands action, and ideological entrepreneurs take advantage of the situation by proposing programs that will appeal to some disaffected constituency. Over time, the public comes to accept greater government intervention in their lives, thus paving the way for further expansions in programs originally created only to meet the nation's needs during a crisis.[13]

These two elements, crisis and ideology, played important roles in shaping the federal government's policies toward small business. It was not until the Great Depression that anti-chain-store legislation attracted widespread support in state legislatures, in Congress, and in the Oval Office. The creation of the Smaller War Plants Corporation and the Small Defense Plants Administration resulted from the perceived crisis confronting small manufacturers during World War II and the Korean War. Although Congress created the Small Business Administration in peacetime, contemporaries considered the SBA an outgrowth of the SDPA and the Reconstruction Finance Corporation, two agencies originally designed to meet the financial needs of businesses during times of crisis; in fact, the RFC has been called "the real father of the SBA." (In the early years, many of those who worked at the SBA were former employees of the RFC and SDPA.) The historical record also makes it clear that President Eisenhower would not have supported the creation of the SBA had it not been for his desire to eliminate the RFC.[14]

The Great Depression had a decisive impact on the small business ideology. As Ellis Hawley notes, the depression eliminated from serious consideration the last vestiges of laissez-faire thinking on matters of public policy.[15] Subsequently, politicians and policymakers sought statist solutions to the problems confronting the nation. Small business advocates moved beyond the limited intervention inherent in earlier antitrust legislation in search of more positive measures to improve the position of small business. From the 1930s onward, they took part in the politics of radical conservatism; by resorting to crisis rhetoric, they justified radical means in service of conservative ends (i.e., the preservation of small business as a social institution and "way of life"). Their efforts to limit volume discounts by invoking the Robinson-Patman Act's quantity-limit clause reflected their desire to preserve small business at all costs. The tire bill introduced during World War II represented another drastic attempt to augment the market share of independent dealers by granting them exclusive rights to tire distribution. Congressional small business advocates also moved beyond the negative antitrust approach by securing positive aid for small business, including financial assistance, tax relief, and representation within the federal government.

The same elements that accounted for the political successes of the small business advocates—crisis and ideology—also limited their influence. During each wartime crisis, Congress aided small businesses in order to redress the injuries inflicted by the government's own mobilization efforts. But in peace-time, the deficits created during the war became an issue splitting liberal and conservative small business advocates, and the congressional consensus in favor of assistance to small business gave way to bitter partisan debates over the budget.

The ideology of small business also necessitated concessions to the competi-tive ideal, and these compromises limited the effect of anti-chain-store legisla-tion. The "good-faith competition" clause of the Robinson-Patman Act ex-cused price-cutting that met the price of a competitor. State fair trade laws required RPM products to be in competition with similar goods not subject to retail price maintenance. These loopholes enabled discounters to find ways around the intent of these laws. In short, this legislation reflected the Ameri-cans' ambivalent feelings: as consumers, Americans desired the lower prices offered by large chain stores, but many still felt sentimental toward the small business owner. Thus, these antitrust laws embodied two conflicting aims: the promotion of competition and consumer welfare, and the preservation of small business.

The indifference of the general public further limited the influence of con-gressional small business advocates. Because they typically lack the support of an organized pressure group, ideological entrepreneurs must rely on public sentiment favorable to their cause. Although the ideology of small business retained some of its emotional appeal, American consumers "voted" for big business by purchasing the products of large corporations. Small business advocates could not convince consumers that the low prices offered by chain stores constituted a fatal threat to free enterprise or democracy; nor could they overcome the public's resistance to fair trade. By the 1950s, most Americans had come to terms with big business and were not overly concerned with the preservation of small business if it meant higher prices at the checkout counter.

The politics of administration also hampered the implementation of small business legislation. While the Federal Trade Commission vigorously enforced the Robinson-Patman Act, the commission believed that retail price maintenance conflicted with other antitrust laws. Along with the Justice Department, the FTC eventually succeeded in repealing state and federal fair trade legislation. During the Eisenhower years, partisan politics and the opposition of rival agencies also frustrated the congressional small business advocates as they sought to strengthen the Small Business Administration.

Implications: Business, Politics, and Policymaking in Modern America

This history of federal government policy toward small business challenges the notion put forth by "corporate-liberal" historians—including Gabriel Kolko, James Weinstein, Martin Sklar, James Livingston, and others—that Americans had reached a consensus over the issue of big business by the end of the Progressive Era. In their view, the election of Woodrow Wilson in 1912 and the subsequent passage of nonthreatening antitrust legislation represented a victory for corporate capitalism because it appeased small business owners and other disaffected groups. Sklar maintains that this legislation "ended the debate over the legitimacy of the large corporation—if nothing else, it took the trust question . . . 'out of politics.' "[16] This study shows, however, that although the issue of big versus small business no longer dominated the presidential agenda, it remained a live issue in Congress. Furthermore, although the debate over big business never again matched the heat of the 1912 presidential election, American presidents were still concerned about "doing something" for small business, if only to attract the votes of small business owners.[17]

Corporate-liberal historians differ in their interpretations of twentieth-century business-government relations. Sklar's work is the most difficult to categorize, in part because he attempts to have it both ways: on the one hand, he emphasizes corporate influences on policymaking in the Progressive Era (hence "corporate" liberalism), while admitting the many other influences that affected the course of legislation. Sklar writes that corporate liberalism "emerged not as the ideology of any one class, let alone the corporate sector of the capitalist class, but rather as a cross-class ideology expressing the interrelations of corporate capitalists, political leaders, intellectuals, proprietary capitalists, professionals and reformers, workers and trade-union leaders, populists, and socialists." This stretches the concepts of corporate capitalism and corporate liberalism so far that they lose all meaning. Consequently, Sklar's version of corporate liberalism does not differ substantively from a pluralist interpretation of this period.[18]

The more radical members of the corporate-liberal school argue that Progressive Era reforms led to the "the emergence of a modern ruling class" whose members acted as "trustees of the new social system."[19] This new class was, Weinstein argued, secure in its "loose hegemony over the political structure." Weinstein and Kolko argue that this corporate "hegemony" lasted well into the late twentieth century.[20] Yet from the 1930s through the 1950s, congressional small business advocates secured passage of legislation over the opposition of corporate interests, thus suggesting a continuing pluralistic character of politics in this period. Corporate liberals did play an important role in politics during and after the Progressive Era, but there was, in Alan Brinkley's words, a "persistence of disunity" with regard to the issue of big business. Brinkley notes that the "vaguely corporatist dream of an 'ordered economic world' " has "foundered—in large part, because of opposition from a decentralized, small-scale, localistic economic world that survives and thrives and displays considerable strength."[21] This history of "disunity" is not the whole story—corporate liberalism continued to influence policymakers—but it is an important part of the story and had been left largely untold by others.

This study of public policy toward small business also suggests the need to move beyond the broker-state model of politics in order to understand the federal government's growing involvement in the small business sector. For much of this century, social scientists worked within the broker-state framework and defined politics as the complex interplay of organized interest groups.[22] On the one hand, organizations representing small tire dealers, druggists, and grocers did play roles in securing legislation favorable to their interests. But this book has emphasized both the unorganized nature of the small business community as a whole and the importance of political entrepreneurs in Congress, who resorted to crisis rhetoric and the ideological appeal of small business to advance their agenda of change. In this respect, *Beyond the Broker State* adds to a growing body of literature demonstrating the importance of political entrepreneurship. Since the 1960s, policy entrepreneurs claiming to represent consumers and other unorganized interests have succeeded in passing legislation favorable to their cause. The rise of these policy entrepreneurs has prompted scholars to begin studying the dynamics of political entrepreneurship.[23] The legislative activity of the small business advocates represents an earlier expression of this phenomenon. In fact, one can draw valuable parallels between the small business advocates and the consumer activists. Both groups represented unorganized interests that are difficult to define. Furthermore, there was no sustained grassroots movement for legislation on behalf of small business owners or consumers. Like the consumer activists, congressional small business advocates enjoyed some success, but the absence of an organized group of business owners limited their influence and prevented them from securing legislation that would redistribute wealth to small business.

This history of public policy toward small business has implications for today's policymakers. Advocates of an interventionist industrial policy believe that they can enhance the performance of America's economy by coordinating organized interest groups of business, government, and labor.[24] Too often, however, interest-group bargaining has resulted in logrolling. The nature of modern American democracy, with its representation of many organized interests, limits the autonomy of policymakers. Any move toward an activist industrial policy—either toward freer markets or toward central planning—requires political restructuring; otherwise, policymakers will likely remain "prisoners in the House of Politics."[25] But any such restructuring should be based on the recognition that unorganized interests are at a disadvantage when it comes to the inevitable struggle to influence the policymaking process. For in the past, the heterogeneous nature of the small business community has prevented the organization of this group of business owners; therefore, small firms are likely to be left out of any industrial policy equation. Indeed, when they consider small business at all, most proponents of industrial policy argue that its benefits will trickle down to smaller firms.[26] It should not be surprising that most industrial policy proposals have focused on sectors where small firms are underrepresented (in comparison to their total share of the economy): exports, manufacturing, high-technology industries, and the military-industrial complex.[27]

The ideology of small business also poses an obstacle to the formulation of an effective industrial policy aimed at improving the performance of the American economy. Congressional small business advocates have influenced the federal government's policy by stressing the importance of small business as a social institution and at times have seemed to view small firms as special welfare cases, deserving of aid regardless of their ability to compete in the marketplace. The preservation of small business may or may not be a laudable goal, but it is bound to interfere with the economic decision-making of industrial policymakers.

There are a growing number of theorists who have resisted this preference for an industrial policy based on a triangle of big business, big labor, and big government. Economist Michael J. Piore and political scientist Charles F. Sabel have proposed the creation of a "yeomen democracy," a democratic-socialist polity with an economy made up of small firms. In their scheme, the government would be "responsible for creating conditions conducive to a republic of small holders" by preventing the creation of larger firms.[28] However, the historical inability of small business advocates to organize an effective pressure group suggests the improbability of ever realizing this neo-Brandeisian pipe dream. It is doubtful that policymakers could sustain a national consensus to reorganize society in favor of this one special interest.

The vast and diffuse nature of the small business population also makes it impossible for planners and policymakers to gather all the information they need to formulate an effective industrial policy.[29] During the early phases of the World War II and Korean War mobilization efforts, for example, planners preferred to work with a few large manufacturers and overlooked the potential of the thousands of smaller firms scattered across the nation. It is not surprising, then, that the SWPC became "an agency to defend small business from government." If the past is any indication, the "visible hand" of industrial policy is unlikely to shake the "invisible hand" that directs the economy's messy small business sector.

The interest-group liberalism inherent in industrial policymaking rests on the assumption that "organized interests are homogeneous and easy to define, sometimes monolithic."[30] Yet size is not a defining factor in the opinions of large or small businesses.[31] In fact, neither community of business people has ever represented a monolith. The diversity of viewpoints expressed by the so-called small business associations reflected the divisions among small business people. Several of these organizations favored vigorous enforcement of the antitrust laws, and some sought financial aid, while others opposed the granting of assistance to their competitors.[32] Each association appealed to a different segment of the small business community.

Critics of industrial policy point out that planners typically focus on the problems and prospects of yesteryear; indeed, the presence of entrenched, politically privileged groups encourages them to do so.[33] In this history, too, the advocates of small business resembled old generals fighting the last war (against big business) all over again. Their creation, the Small Business Administration, also focused on the past rather than the future. Some policymakers have considered the SBA a direct instrument of U.S. industrial policy. By targeting promising and productive firms, they have argued, the SBA can increase employment and enhance American competitiveness. But the SBIC program's poor historical performance does not bode well for the future success of an industrial policy directed at the small business sector of the economy.[34]

Finally, if history is any prologue to the future, policymakers will find it difficult to define "small" business, much less target tomorrow's winners. During World War II, tire dealers fought with gas station owners over the right to the title of "independent tire dealer." In the 1940s and 1950s, the military insisted on an arbitrary five-hundred-employee definition of small business, while members of the Small Business Committees sought assistance for "small" firms with thousands of employees. Very small firms, on the other hand, resented the government's expenditure of its limited resources on such large firms. Thus, the creation of small business programs encouraged rent-seeking and pitted business owner against business owner in an unfruitful struggle to determine the allocation of scarce resources.[35]

Although there are many reasons why small business advocates should be leery of a comprehensive industrial policy, recently some have become enamored with the notion that governmental assistance to small business may spur economic growth. Many now believe that small business has supplanted big business as the "locomotive of growth" in the economy. The current disenchantment with big business can be traced to the 1970s and early 1980s, when many large corporations stumbled in response to a changed economic environment. America's Fortune 500 corporations lost five million jobs between 1970 and 1984, while plant and firm size decreased worldwide.[36] Praise for big business has given way to extended criticism. In a 1993 cover story, the *Economist* attributed "the fall of big business" to an increasingly competitive global market and the introduction of computerized technology that lowered the optimum scale of efficiency. A number of studies purported to show how small businesses created most new jobs, generated a disproportionate number of technological innovations, and fostered a work environment where employees can participate in decision-making.[37] According to this new school of thought, the key to small business success in manufacturing is "flexible production": consumers are increasingly fashion-conscious, and small, flexible firms are best able to respond to their changing tastes. During the 1980s, the business press picked up on this theme and ran such articles as "The Rise and Rise of America's Small Firms" (*Economist*) and "Small Is Beautiful Now in Manufacturing" (*Business Week*).[38] By the end of the decade, "small was bountiful. Small was beautiful. Small was *in*."[39]

Politicians have responded to the new economics by jumping on the "small is beautiful" bandwagon. As always, the appeal of small business cuts across party lines. The writer Virginia Postrel has noted, "Just about everybody likes small business—liberals and conservatives, Democrats and Republicans, even aging Chinese Communists." Furthermore, "small business is, apparently, the opposite of the weather: Everybody praises it, and everybody does something about it."[40] Advocates of what Postrel calls "industrial policy with a populist face" have used the new understanding of small business economics to convince local and state governments to create development programs offering direct and indirect aid to small manufacturing firms.[41] At the federal level, new Manufacturing Technology Centers are providing technical and managerial assistance to small and medium-sized firms. Most of the efforts at small business promotion, however, have been concentrated at the local level, where small business owners have greater political influence.[42]

Has the situation of small business changed so much that history is no longer a useful guide for policymakers? Certainly small business has been transformed from the ugly duckling of the American economy into its "Prince Charming." The old Galbraithian notion of "big (business) is better" has given way in recent years to a "small is beautiful" philosophy. Yet if the history of small business teaches us anything, it is that we should be skeptical about such paradigm shifts. Indeed, many of the studies claiming to show the advantages of small business are deeply flawed.[43] Small business may not be the "locomotive of growth"; the verdict is still out. Furthermore, even if the small business sector does generate growth, policymakers still need to know which firms to target, because most will never experience appreciable growth. So far, the early evaluations of small business development programs have not been very promising.[44]

Should the government promote small business? During the 1950s, both the pundits and the public viewed the presumed trend toward big business as a good thing. Since that time we have lost faith in the large corporation, but we seem to have exchanged it for an equally naive belief in the progressive nature of small business. Yet, as critics of the "small is beautiful" philosophy point out, there still are advantages to bigness. Manufacturing productivity is probably related to firm size; concentrated industries have higher productivity growth rates than unconcentrated industries.[45] Small businesses are generally not as profitable as large corporations and cannot afford to be as philanthropic.[46] Large firms also offer higher wages and better benefits to their employees than do small firms, so the trend toward small business may not be good for American workers.[47]

If the critics of the small business gospel are correct, then we face a situation very similar to that of the 1950s. At that time, everyone "knew" that small business was an anachronism; yet small business was probably in better shape in the 1950s than it is now. Since the 1950s, small retail and service firms have lost ground, while small manufacturers may have gained a few percentage points of market share. Overall, small firms in the 1980s accounted for the same share of employment as they did in the 1950s, but their share of GNP was 38 percent (in 1982), down from 42.6 percent in 1958.[48] Once again, economic reality differs from political rhetoric.

The "small is productive" mantra has a bipartisan appeal. Government promotion of small business promises a solution to unemployment, a traditional concern of Democrats. Republicans have complained that large corporations are too willing to compromise with "big government"; members of the GOP now portray themselves as "the party of small business, not big business; of Main Street, not Wall Street."[49] But though they agree on the importance of small business, the two parties still disagree over the issue of government intervention in the economy: Democrats are more likely to favor direct aid to small business, while Republicans opt for indirect aid (e.g., tax preferences, enterprise zones).

Present-day advocates of small business face the same problem that plagued congressional champions of small business in the past: most small business owners lack any interest in politics and government. Administrators of small business development programs have been frustrated by the indifference of small business people. Many small business owners are simply too busy to concern themselves with government, even if it promises them benefits. The political scientist Benjamin Mokry concludes that the small business owner is "by nature independent and antibureaucratic, and may spend little time watching government actions."[50] Furthermore, many small business owners are hostile to government in general because they feel burdened by taxes and regulations.[51]

Today, politicians and policymakers continue to debate how to plot the future course of small business. A historical look backward provides not only a sobering lesson in the limitations of government aid to small business but also the hopeful realization that this social institution has proven to be remarkably resilient. The United States has not become a land made up entirely of "organization men." Many Americans are still driven by what Adam Smith called "the contempt of risk and the presumptuous hope of success."[52] Thus, the future economic landscape of America will, in all likelihood, be inhabited by millions of men and women pursuing a way of life that has survived the turbulence of the twentieth century.

NOTES

Abbreviations

EPL   Dwight D. Eisenhower Presidential Library (Abilene, Kansas)

FDRPL   Franklin D. Roosevelt Presidential Library (Hyde Park, New York)

FTC   U.S. Federal Trade Commission

HSTPL   Harry S. Truman Presidential Library (Independence, Missouri)

JPS   J. Penfield Seiberling Papers (Ohio Historical Society, Columbus)

LBJPL   Lyndon Baines Johnson Presidential Library (Austin, Texas)

NA   National Archives (Washington, D.C.)

TNEC   U.S. Congress, Senate, Temporary National Economic Committee

Introduction

1. Woodrow Wilson, address to Congress, 20 January 1914, in Henry Steele Commager, ed., *Documents of American History*, vol. 2, 9th ed., "The Federal Trade Commission Act," (Englewood Cliffs, N.J.: Prentice-Hall, 1973), 98.

2. "Does 'Small Business' Get a Fair Shake?," *Fortune*, October 1953, 164.

3. Drew R. McCoy, "Political Economy," in *Thomas Jefferson: A Reference Biography*, ed. Merrill D. Peterson (New York: Charles Scribner's Sons, 1986), 105–6; K. Austin Kerr, "Small Business in the United States during the Twentieth Century," unpublished paper presented at a conference titled "Comparative Enterprise Management: The Lessons of Business History," held in Budapest, Hungary, 13–15 June 1989. This belief in small business as "the backbone of democracy" was also a hallmark of the Republican Party on the eve of the Civil War; see Eric Foner, *Free Soil, Free Labor, Free Men: The Ideology of the Republican Party before the Civil War* (New York: Oxford University Press, 1970).

4. Irvin G. Wyllie, *The Self-Made Man in America: The Myth of Rags to Riches* (New Brunswick, N.J.: Rutgers University Press, 1954); Carl Bode, introduction to Horatio Alger Jr., *Ragged Dick and Struggling Upward*, ed. Carl Bode (1890, 1868; rpt. New York: Penguin, 1985), ix [quote]. The cultural status of business owners is discussed in Lewis A. Atherton, *The Frontier Merchant in Mid-America* (1939; rpt. Columbia: University of Missouri Press, 1971); Theodore P. Greene, *America's Heroes: The Changing Models of Success in American Magazines* (New York: Oxford University Press, 1970); Sigmund Diamond, *The Reputation of the American Businessman* (Cambridge: Harvard University Press, 1955); and Edward Kirkland, *Dream and Thought in the Business Community, 1860–1900* (Ithaca: Cornell University Press, 1956).

5. Andrew Carnegie, "The Road to Business Success: A Talk to Young Men," address to students at Curry Commercial College, 23 June 1885, in Carnegie, *Empire of Business* (New York: Doubleday, Page and Company, 1902), 14–15 [quote]; Carnegie, "The Common Interest of Labour and Capital," address to Workmen at Dedication of Carnegie Library, Braddock, Pennsylvania, January 1889, ibid., 72.

6. The standard work on the rise of big business is Alfred D. Chandler Jr.'s *The Visible Hand: The Managerial Revolution in American Business* (Cambridge: Belknap Press of Harvard University Press, 1977).

7. Thomas C. McCraw, *Prophets of Regulation* (Cambridge: Belknap Press of Harvard University Press, 1984), 77, 78.

8. Richard P. Adelstein, "'Islands of Conscious Power': Louis D. Brandeis and the Modern Corporation," *Business History Review* 63 (Autumn 1989): 615 [quote], 638, 642, 645; Louis Brandeis, "Shall We Abandon the Policy of Competition?" (1912 article), in Brandeis, *The Curse of Bigness* (New York: Viking, 1934), 105, 107 [quote]; Brandeis, dissenting opinion, *Liggett v. Lee* (1933), in ibid., 169; Melvin I. Urofsky, *A Mind of One Piece: Brandeis and American Reform* (New York: Charles Scribner's Sons, 1971), chap. 3 ("The Economist as Moralist"); McCraw, *Prophets*, chap. 3.

9. Joseph Cornwall Palamountain Jr., *The Politics of Distribution* (Cambridge: Harvard University Press, 1955), 210–13; Ellis W. Hawley, *The New Deal and the Problem of Monopoly: A Study in Economic Ambivalence* (Princeton: Princeton University Press, 1966), 254–61.

10. Hawley, *New Deal*, 274–75 [quote].

11. See, for example, Thurman Arnold, *The Bottlenecks of Business* (New York: Reynal & Hitchcock, 1940), 16; Emerson P. Schmidt, "The Role and Problems of Small Business," *Law and Contemporary Problems* 11, no. 1 (Summer–Autumn 1945): 205–19.

12. Wright Patman, "Small Defense Plants Corporation: Small Business at the Cross Roads," *Congressional Record* (28 June 1951), vol. 97, pt. 6, p. 7437.

13. Allan H. Meltzer and Scott F. Richard, "Why Government Grows (and Grows) in a Democracy," *The Public Interest* (Summer 1978): 111–18; Jonathan R. T. Hughes, *The Governmental Habit Redux: Economic Controls from Colonial Times to the Present* (Princeton: Princeton University Press, 1991), xiii [quote], 120 [quote]. According to the best available data, the government's share of GNP declined in only one period of modern American history: from 1870 to 1902 (Thomas E. Borcherding, "One Hundred Years of Public Spending, 1870–1970," *Budgets and Bureaucrats: The Sources of Government Growth*, ed. Thomas E. Borcherding [Durham, N.C.: Duke University Press, 1977], 32). See also Lance E. Davis and John Legler, "Government in the American Economy, 1815–1902: A Quantitative Study," *Journal of Economic History* 26 (December 1966): 514–52.

14. Richard M. Abrams, "Business and Government," in *Encyclopedia of American Political History: Studies of the Principal Movements and Ideas*, ed. Jack P. Greene (New York: Charles Scribner's Sons, 1984), 1:131.

15. These percentages are drawn from Robert Higgs, *Crisis and Leviathan: Critical Episodes in the Growth of American Government* (New York: Oxford University Press, 1987), 22–23, and U.S. Bureau of the Census, *Statistical Abstract of the United States: 1992* (Washington: GPO, 1992), 279, 428–29.

16. For an optimistic appraisal of government growth, see Harold G. Vatter and John F. Walker, *The Inevitability of Government Growth* (New York: Columbia University Press, 1990). Critics fear that capitalist nations will drift into some form of market socialism or fascism. See Joseph A. Schumpeter's *Capitalism, Socialism, and Democracy* (New York: Harper, 1942). See also Hughes, *The Governmental Habit Redux*, 118; Higgs, *Crisis and Leviathan*, 262; George Stigler, "Why Have the Socialists Been Winning?," *Essence of Stigler*, ed. Kurt R. Leube and Thomas Gale Moore (Stanford: Hoover Institution Press, 1986), 344–45; and Alan T. Peacock and Jack Wiseman, *The Growth of Public Expenditure in the United Kingdom* (Princeton: Princeton University Press, 1961), 149.

17. See Herbert Croly, *The Promise of American Life* (New York: Macmillan, 1909); Arthur M. Schlesinger Jr., *The Age of Jackson* (Boston: Little, Brown, and Company, 1945). Schlesinger defined American liberalism as "the movement on the part of the other sections of society to restrain the power of the business community" (ibid., 505).

18. According to "Director's Law of Public Expenditures" (named after economist Aaron Director), government programs tend to redistribute wealth from the rich and poor to the middle-class because that group constitutes a majority of voters (Thomas E. Borcherding, "The Sources of Growth of Public Expenditures in the United States," in *Budgets and Bureaucrats: The Sources of Government Growth*, ed. Thomas E. Borcherding [Durham, N.C.: Duke University Press, 1977], 57–58). For an elaboration of this theory of government growth, see Sam Peltzman, "The Growth of Government," *Journal of Law and Economics* 23 (October 1980): 209–87.

19. The journalist John Chamberlain coined the term "broker state" to describe the workings of modern American democracy; see Chamberlain, *The American Stakes* (New York: Carrick and Evans, 1940), chap. 1 ("Whose State?").

20. Ellis Hawley, "The Corporate Ideal as Liberal Philosophy in the New Deal," *The Roosevelt New Deal: A Program Reassessment Fifty Years Later*, ed. Wilbur J. Cohen (Austin, Tex.: The Lyndon B. Johnson School of Public Affairs, 1986), 85–105 [quote on 85]; Ellis Hawley, "The Discovery and Study of 'Corporate Liberalism,'" *Business History Review* 52 (Autumn 1978): 309–20; Louis Galambos and Joseph Pratt, *The Rise of the Corporate Commonwealth: U.S. Business and Public Policy in the Twentieth Century* (New York: Basic Books, 1988); Martin J. Sklar, *The Corporate Reconstruction of American Capitalism, 1890–1916: The Market, the Law, and Politics* (Cambridge: Cambridge University Press, 1988). For a survey of the literature dealing with group theory, see G. David Garson, *Group Theories of Politics*, vol. 61, Sage Library of Social Research (Beverly Hills, Calif.: Sage Publications, 1978); Grant McConnell, "Lobbies and Pressure Groups," *Encyclopedia of American Political History: Studies of the Principal Movements and Ideas*, 3 vols., ed. Jack P. Greene (New York: Charles Scribner's Sons, 1984), 2:764–76; and R. Jeffrey Lustig, "Pluralism," *Encyclopedia of American Political History: Studies of the Principal Movements and Ideas*, 3 vols., ed. Jack P. Greene (New York: Charles Scribner's Sons, 1984), 2:910–21.

21. Arthur F. Bentley, *The Process of Government: A Study of Social Pressures*, ed. Peter H. Odegard (1908; rpt. Belknap Press of Harvard University Press, 1967); David B. Truman, *The Governmental Process: Political Interests and Public Opinion* (New York: Knopf, 1951); Robert Dahl, *Who Governs?* (New Haven: Yale University Press, 1961);

Nelson Polsby, *Community Power and Political Theory* (New Haven: Yale University Press, 1963); L. Harmon Zeigler and G. Wayne Peak, *Interest Groups in American Society*, 2d ed. (Englewood Cliffs, N.J.: Prentice-Hall, 1972).

22. Theodore J. Lowi, *The End of Liberalism: The Second Republic of the United States*, 2d ed. (New York: Norton, 1979). For an early expression of this concern that organized elites subvert the public interest, see V. O. Key Jr., *Politics, Parties, and Pressure Groups* (New York: Thomas Y. Crowell, 1942), 169, 177, 179, and Floyd Hunter, *Community Power Structure: A Study of Decision-Makers* (Chapel Hill: University of North Carolina Press, 1953).

23. James M. Buchanan, *The Limits of Liberty: Between Anarchy and Leviathan* (Chicago: University of Chicago, 1975); George Stigler, "The Theory of Economic Regulation," *Essence of Stigler*, 243–64; James D. Gwartney and Richard L. Stroup, *Economics: Private and Public Choice*, 5th ed. (New York: Harcourt, 1990), 88–90, 96–97, 741–43.

24. See, for example, Gabriel Kolko, *The Roots of American Foreign Policy: An Analysis of Power and Purpose* (Boston: Beacon Press, 1969), chap. 1 ("The Men of Power"), and *The Triumph of Conservatism: A Reinterpretation of American History, 1900–1916* (Chicago: Quadrangle, 1963). David Lowery and William D. Berry survey theories of government growth in "The Growth of Government in the United States: An Empirical Assessment of Competing Explanations," *American Journal of Political Science* 27 (November 1983): 665–94.

25. For a "state-centered" interpretation of politics, see Eric A. Nordlinger, *On the Autonomy of the Democratic State* (Cambridge: Harvard University Press, 1981).

26. William A. Niskanen Jr., *Bureaucracy and Representative Government* (Chicago: Aldine-Atherton, 1971); James Buchanan, "Why Does Government Grow?," in *Budgets and Bureaucrats: The Sources of Government Growth*, ed. Thomas E. Borcherding (Durham, N.C.: Duke University Press, 1977), 14–18; Lowery and Berry, "The Growth of Government," 674; Herbert Stein and Murray Foss, *An Illustrated Guide to the American Economy: A Hundred Key Issues* (Washington, D.C.: AEI Press, 1992), 202–3; James Q. Wilson, *Bureaucracy: What Government Agencies Do and Why They Do It* (New York: Basic Books, 1989), 118, 195.

27. Peacock and Wiseman, *The Growth of Public Expenditure*, xxi–xxv [quote on xxi].

28. Higgs, *Crisis and Leviathan*, 20–34. Other scholars have also emphasized the importance of crisis; see William Leuchtenberg, "The New Deal and the Analogue of War," *Change and Continuity in Twentieth-Century America* (Columbus: Ohio State University Press, 1964), 81–143; Robert Nisbet, *Twilight of Authority* (New York: Oxford University Press, 1975), 178–86; Galambos and Pratt, *Rise of the Corporate Commonwealth*, 3, 100–126, 201–26; Hughes, *Governmental Habit Redux*, 225.

29. There is a vast body of literature discussing this "new class." See Schumpeter, *Capitalism, Socialism, and Democracy*; John Kenneth Galbraith, *The Affluent Society* (Boston: Houghton Mifflin, 1958) and *The New Industrial State*, 2d ed. (Boston: Houghton Mifflin, 1971), 295–97; George B. de Huszar, ed., *The Intellectuals: A Controversial Portrait* (Glencoe, Ill.: Free Press, 1960); Bruce Bruce-Briggs, ed., *The New Class?* (New Brunswick, N.J.: Transaction, 1979); Robert J. Brym, *Intellectuals and Politics* (London: Allen and Unwin, 1980); Friedrich A. von Hayek, ed., *Capitalism and the*

Historians (1954; rpt. Chicago: University of Chicago Press, 1967), and Hayek, *The Fatal Conceit: The Errors of Socialism* (Chicago: University of Chicago Press, 1988); Michael Novak, *The Spirit of Democratic Capitalism* (Lanham, Md.: Madison Books, 1982, 1991), 31–35, 186, 205–6; Robert L. Heilbroner, *Business Civilization in Decline* (New York: Norton, 1976); and George Stigler, "Economics or Ethics?," *Essence of Stigler*, 303–36.

30. For further discussion of political symbolism, see Murray Edelman, *The Symbolic Uses of Politics* (Urbana: University of Illinois Press, 1964), 22–43, and Charles D. Elder and Roger W. Cobb, *The Political Uses of Symbols* (New York: Longman, 1983), 115–21.

31. Higgs, *Crisis and Leviathan*, 15–16, 38–55. Political (or ideological) entrepreneurs typically represent unorganized interests, such as consumers or small business owners. Virginia Gray calls them "idea men" whose sustained commitment to a single idea or interest can eventually win them converts, even if they never succeed at grassroots organizing (Virginia Gray, "State Legislatures and Policy Innovators," in *Encyclopedia of the American Legislative System*, 3 vols., ed. Joel H. Silbey [New York: Charles Scribner's Sons, 1994], 3:1347–60).

32. Alfred D. Chandler Jr., *The Visible Hand: The Managerial Revolution in American Business* (Cambridge: Belknap Press of Harvard University Press, 1977). Chandler has also written a comparative history of big business in America, Great Britain, and Germany; see *Scale and Scope: The Dynamics of Industrial Capitalism* (Cambridge: Belknap Press of Harvard University Press, 1990). For other histories influenced by the work of Chandler, see McCraw, *Prophets*; Glenn Porter, *The Rise of Big Business in America, 1860–1910*, 2d ed. (New York: Thomas Y. Crowell, 1992); Glenn Porter and Harold Livesay, *Merchants and Manufacturers: Studies in the Changing Structure of Nineteenth-Century Marketing* (Baltimore: Johns Hopkins University Press, 1971); and Mansel G. Blackford and K. Austin Kerr, *Business Enterprise in American History*, 3d ed. (Boston: Houghton Mifflin, 1994).

33. Atherton, *The Frontier Merchant*; Theodore F. Marburg, *Small Business in Brass Fabricating: The Smith and Griggs Manufacturing Company at Waterbury* (New York: New York University Press, 1956); Martha Taber, *A History of the Cutlery Industry in the Connecticut Valley* (Northampton, Mass.: Smith College Studies in History, 1955); James Soltow, "Origins of Small Business: Metal Fabricators and Machinery Makers in New England, 1890–1957," *Transactions of the American Philosophical Society* 55 (December 1965): 1–58.

34. Philip Scranton, *Proprietary Capitalism: The Textile Manufacture at Philadelphia, 1800–1885* (Cambridge: Cambridge University Press, 1983) and *Figured Tapestry: Production, Markets, and Power in Philadelphia Textiles, 1885–1941* (Cambridge: Cambridge University Press, 1989); John Ingham, *Making Iron and Steel: Independent Mills in Pittsburgh, 1820–1920* (Columbus: Ohio State University Press, 1991); and Mansel G. Blackford, *Pioneering a Small Business: Wakefield Seafoods and the Alaskan Frontier* (Greenwich, Conn.: JAI, 1979), *A Portrait Cast in Steel: Buckeye International and Columbus, Ohio, 1881–1980* (Westport, Conn.: Greenwood, 1982), and *A History of Small Business in America* (New York: Twayne, 1992). For a collection of essays on small business history, see Stuart W. Bruchey, ed., *Small Business in American Life* (New York: Columbia University Press, 1980). Blackford surveys the literature in "Small Business in America: An Historiographic Review," *Business History Review* 65 (Spring 1991): 1–26.

35. Robert H. Wiebe, *The Search for Order, 1877–1920* (New York: Hill and Wang, 1967); Samuel Hays, *Conservation and the Gospel of Efficiency* (Cambridge: Harvard University Press, 1959); Kolko, *Triumph of Conservatism*; Sklar, *Corporate Reconstruction*, 425 [quote].

36. Hawley, *New Deal*.

37. Carl Ryant, "The South and the Movement against Chain Stores," *Journal of Southern History* 39 (May 1973): 207–22; David Horowitz, "The Crusade against Chain Stores: Portland's Independent Merchants, 1928–1935," *Oregon Historical Quarterly* 89 (Winter 1988): 341–68; Jim Heath, "American War Mobilization and the Use of Small Manufacturers, 1939–43," *Business History Review* 46 (Autumn 1972): 295–319.

38. Palamountain, *Politics*.

39. Harmon Zeigler, *The Politics of Small Business* (Washington: Public Affairs Press, 1961). Sumner Marcus and George Earl Green have written dissertations discussing the creation of the Small Business Administration in 1953. See George Earl Green, "The Small Business Administration: A Study in Public Policy and Organization" (Ph.D. diss., University of Colorado, 1965), and Sumner Marcus, "The Small Business Act of 1953: A Case Study of the Development of Public Policy Affecting Business" (D.B.A. diss., University of Washington, 1958). Addison Parris examines the operations of the Small Business Administration during the 1960s in *The Small Business Administration* (New York: Frederick A. Praeger, 1968).

40. John H. Bunzel, *The American Small Businessman* (New York: Knopf, 1962); Richard Hofstadter, "What Happened to the Antitrust Movement?: Notes on the Evolution of an American Creed," in *The Business Establishment*, ed. Earl F. Cheit (New York: John Wiley & Sons, 1964), 221. Some scholars claimed that both big and small business persons adhered to a "reactionary," antistatist ideology. See Francis X. Sutton, Seymour E. Harris, Carl Kaysen, and James Tobin, *The American Business Creed* (Cambridge: Harvard University Press, 1956), 216–17, 402–4.

41. Richard Hamilton, *Restraining Myths: Critical Studies of U.S. Social Structure and Politics* (New York: Sage, 1975), chap. 2 ("The Politics of Independent Business"), 33–98; Zeigler, *The Politics of Small Business*, 19; Ralph William Murphy, "Small Business Ideology: An In-Depth Study" (Ph.D. diss., University of Washington, 1978), 281.

For further discussion of the small business ideology, see Rowland Berthoff, "Independence and Enterprise: Small Business in the American Dream," *Small Business in American Life*, ed. Stuart W. Bruchey (New York: Columbia University Press, 1980), 28–48; Ross M. Robertson, "The Small Business Ethic in America," *The Vital Majority: Small Business in the American Economy: Essays Marking the Twentieth Anniversary of the U.S. Small Business Administration*, ed. Deane Carson (Washington: GPO, 1973), 25–38; C. Wright Mills, *White Collar: The American Middle Classes* (New York: Oxford University Press, 1965), 26–27, 32–33, 58, 329–31, 350; Kurt Mayer, "Small Business as a Social Institution," *Social Research* 14 (1947): 343–49; and Frank Bechhofer and Brian Elliott, "Persistence and Change: The Petite Bourgeoisie in Industrial Society," in *The Survival of the Small Firm*, ed. James Curran, John Stanworth, and David Watkins (Brookfield, Vt.: Gower, 1986), chap. 7.

42. Samuel P. Hays, "Political Choice in Regulatory Administration," in *Regulation in*

Perspective: Historical Essays, ed. Thomas K. McCraw (Cambridge: Harvard University Press, 1981), 125.

43. Zeigler, *The Politics of Small Business*, 23.

44. James Hughes, U.S. Congress, Senate, Banking and Currency Committee, Subcommittee on Small Business, *Conversion of Small Business*, hearings, 77th Cong., 2d sess., 11 March 1942, 273.

45. Wright Patman to H. E. Luedicke, 7 September 1955, folder "Small Business Committee, 1955–56," box 115-A, Wright Patman Papers (hereafter cited as Patman Papers), Lyndon Baines Johnson Presidential Library, Austin, Texas (hereafter cited as LBJPL).

46. Blackford, *A History of Small Business*, xi–xiii. Other scholars have also used arbitrary definitions in their studies of small business; see, for example, Joseph D. Phillips, *Little Business in the American Economy*, Illinois Studies in the Social Sciences, vol. 42 (Urbana: University of Illinois Press, 1958), 15.

47. Several other writers have also described the 1930s as the beginning of the so-called small business movement; see Zeigler, *Politics of Small Business*, 13; Thomas S. Dicke, "The Public Image of Small Business Portrayed in the American Periodical Press, 1900–1938" (M.A. thesis, Ohio State University, 1983), 70–71, 87.

Chapter One

1. "Chain Stores Are Rapped by Solon Patman," press release, *Texarkana Daily News*, 22 November 1933, folder 1, box 37-B, Patman Papers, LBJPL.

2. Richard Sylla, "The Progressive Era and the Political Economy of Big Government," *Critical Review* 5 (Fall 1991): 545. Many large corporations responded to this discrimination by appealing to the federal courts; see Tony A. Freyer, "The Federal Courts, Localism, and the National Economy, 1865–1900," *Business History Review* 53 (Autumn 1979): 343–65.

3. Census data indicated that "slaughtering and meatpacking was either the first or second most valuable U.S. industry from 1880 through 1910" (Gary D. Libecap, "The Rise of the Chicago Packers and the Origins of Meat Inspection and Antitrust," *Economic Inquiry* 30 [April 1992]: 246).

4. Libecap, "Rise of the Chicago Packers," 242–62.

5. Thomas K. McCraw, *Prophets of Regulation: Charles Francis Adams, Louis D. Brandeis, James M. Landis, Alfred E. Kahn* (Cambridge: Belknap Press of Harvard University Press, 1984), 78.

6. Christopher Grandy, "Original Intent and the Sherman Antitrust Act: A Reexamination of the Consumer-Welfare Hypothesis," *Journal of Economic History* 53 (June 1993): 359. See also William Letwin, *Law and Economic Policy in America: The Evolution of the Sherman Antitrust Act* (New York: Random House, 1965): 281; Tony Freyer, *Regulating Big Business: Antitrust in Great Britain and America, 1880–1980* (Cambridge: Cambridge University Press, 1992), 95–97.

7. Letwin, *Law and Economic Policy*, 15, 59; Hans B. Thorelli, *The Federal Antitrust*

Policy: Origination of an American Tradition (Baltimore: Johns Hopkins University Press, 1955), 570.

8. Robert H. Bork, *The Antitrust Paradox: A Policy at War with Itself* (New York: Basic Books, 1978), 61–63. Bork's "consumer-welfare" hypothesis has had a great influence on antitrust policy but has also sparked controversy among legal scholars. See, for example, Walter Adams and James W. Brock, *Antitrust Economics on Trial: A Dialogue on the New Laissez-Faire* (Princeton: Princeton University Press, 1991).

9. Libecap, "Rise of the Chicago Packers," 242–62; Grandy, "Original Intent," 359.

10. Thomas W. Hazlett, "The Legislative History of the Sherman Act Reexamined," *Economic Inquiry* 30 (April 1992): 263–76; Letwin, *Law and Economic Policy*, 87, 86 [quotes].

11. Jonathan R. T. Hughes, *The Governmental Habit Redux: Economic Controls from Colonial Times to the Present* (Princeton: Princeton University Press, 1991), 114 [quote]. See also Thorelli, *Federal Antitrust Policy*, 227.

12. Justice Rufus W. Peckham, *Bement v. National Harrow Company* (1902) opinion, quoted in Martin J. Sklar, *The Corporate Reconstruction of American Capitalism, 1890–1916: The Market, the Law, and Politics* (Cambridge: Cambridge University Press, 1988), 134.

13. Sklar, *Corporate Reconstruction*, 89–90; McCraw, *Prophets*, 78–79, 145. Some scholars reject the notion that the Sherman Act embodied some well-established common law tradition; see Bork, *Antitrust Paradox*, 20; Hughes, *Governmental Habit*, 113; Bruce Bringhurst, *Antitrust and the Oil Monopoly* (Westport, Conn.: Greenwood Press, 1979), 4–5; Letwin, *Law and Economic Policy*, 16, 51, 78–79; Freyer, *Regulating Big Business*, 97–98.

14. Alan Brinkley, "The Antimonopoly Ideal and the Liberal State: The Case of Thurman Arnold," *Journal of American History* 80 (September 1993): 567.

15. "Clayton Act," *The Guide to American Law: Everyone's Legal Encyclopedia*, 12 vols. (St. Paul, Minn.: West Publishing), 2:376.

16. Mansel G. Blackford, *A History of Small Business in America* (New York: Twayne Publishers, 1992), 33; McCraw, *Prophets*, 124.

17. McCraw, *Prophets*, 125, 150, 144 [quote].

18. Alfred D. Chandler Jr., *The Visible Hand: The Managerial Revolution in American Business* (Cambridge: Belknap Press of Harvard University Press, 1977), 225–29; Frank M. Mayfield, *The Department Store Story* (New York: Fairchild, 1949), 30–32; Susan Strasser, *Satisfaction Guaranteed: The Making of the Mass Market* (New York: Pantheon Books, 1989), 206–10; Jerome Gilbert Meyers, "Reactions of the Independent Retailer to the Evolution and Development of the Department Store, the Mail Order House, and Discount Operations" (M.B.A. thesis, Ohio State University, 1962), 7–11; Daniel J. Boorstin, *The Americans: The Democratic Experience* (New York: Random House, 1973), 101 [quote].

19. Mayfield, *Department Store Story*, 225.

20. Meyers, "Reactions of the Independent Retailer," 13 [quote].

21. Ibid., 14.

22. John P. Nichols, *The Chain Store Tells Its Story* (New York: Institute of Distribution, 1940), 127; Strasser, *Satisfaction Guaranteed*, 215; Ralph M. Hower, *History of*

Macy's of New York: 1858–1919 (Cambridge: Harvard University Press, 1943), 156; Chandler, *Visible Hand*, 229; Rowland Berthoff, "Independence and Enterprise: Small Business in the American Dream," in *Small Business in American Life*, ed. Stuart W. Bruchey (New York: Columbia University Press, 1980), 35; Stanley C. Hollander, "The Effects of Industrialization on Small Retailing in the United States in the Twentieth Century," in ibid., 225; Meyers, "Reactions of the Independent Retailer," 15, 18–20 [quote on 20].

23. Lewis A. Atherton, *Main Street on the Middle Border* (Chicago: Quadrangle, 1954), 230–31.

24. Boris Emmet and John E. Jeuck, *Catalogues and Counters: A History of Sears, Roebuck, and Company* (Chicago: University of Chicago Press, 1950), 17–22, 168; Richard S. Tedlow, *New and Improved: The Story of Mass Marketing in America* (New York: Basic Books, 1990), 265–74; Meyers, "Reactions of the Independent Retailer," 23–24; David L. Cohn, *The Good Old Days: A History of American Morals and Manners as seen through the Sears, Roebuck Catalogs, 1905 to the Present* (New York: Simon and Schuster, 1940), 545.

25. Emmet and Jeuck, *Catalogues*, 151–52.

26. Meyers, "Reactions of the Independent Retailer," 31.

27. Cohn, *The Good Old Days*, 510.

28. George Milburn, *Catalog* (New York: Harcourt, Brace, 1936), 187–88 [quote].

29. Cohn, *The Good Old Days*, 511.

30. Atherton, *Main Street*, 232–33; Strasser, *Satisfaction Guaranteed*, 217.

31. Cohn, *The Good Old Days*, 512; Louis E. Asher and Edith Heal, *Send No Money* (Chicago: Argus Books, 1942), 29 [quote].

32. Asher and Heal, *Send No Money*, 119.

33. Ibid., 72.

34. Emmet and Jeuck, *Catalogues*, 30.

35. Strasser, *Satisfaction Guaranteed*, 215–21; Tedlow, *New and Improved*, 203–4.

36. Joseph Cornwall Palamountain Jr., *The Politics of Distribution* (Cambridge: Harvard University Press, 1955), 6, 61, 159–69; "The Genesis of the Chain Store: Its Place in Our Mercantile History," *Congressional Digest* 9, no. 8–9 (August–September 1930): 193; Godfrey M. Lebhar, *Chain Stores in America, 1859–1962*, 3d ed. (New York: Chain Store Publishing Corporation, 1963), 395. The government defined a "chain store" as any company with four or more units. This definition encompassed multiunit department stores and mail-order houses, which accounted for approximately one-sixth of all "chain store" sales. U.S. Bureau of the Census, *Historical Statistics of the United States: Colonial Times to 1970*, 2 pts. (Washington: GPO, 1976), Series T 79–196, T 197–219.

37. Moody's Investors Service, "The Outlook for Chain Stores," 26 September 1930, no. 58, I-423–24; Institute of Distribution, *The Chain Store Is an American Asset: True or False?* (New York: Institute of Distribution, n.d.), 12. By 1974, cooperatives and voluntary chains made up over half of the supermarkets in operation (Stanley C. Hollander, "The Effects of Industrialization on Small Retailing in the United States in the Twentieth Century," in *Small Business in American Life*, ed. Stuart W. Bruchey [New York: Columbia University Press, 1980], 232).

38. Palamountain, *Politics*, 78.

39. U.S. Bureau of the Census, *Historical Statistics*, 1:11. In 1930, 53 percent of all Americans lived on farms or in small towns (defined as those with fewer than 10,000 people).

40. Godfrey M. Lebhar, "Does the Chain Store System Threaten the Nation's Welfare?," *Congressional Digest* 9, no. 8–9 (August–September 1930): 215.

41. J. Frank Grimes [president, Independent Grocers' Alliance of America], quoted in ibid., 218.

42. Palamountain, *Politics*, 163–64, 171, 182.

43. "The Lesson from California" [from the *Progressive Grocer*, December 1936], in *Chain Stores and Legislation*, ed. Daniel Bloomfield (New York: H. W. Wilson, 1939), 176–77; Institute of Distribution, *The Chain Store*, 5–14; Alan R. Raucher, "Dime Store Chains: The Making of Organization Men, 1880–1940," *Business History Review* 65 (Spring 1991): 140–43, 153; Thomas S. Dicke, "The Public Image of Small Business Portrayed in the American Periodical Press, 1900–1938" (M.A. thesis, Ohio State University, 1983), 57–58, 63.

44. Palamountain, *Politics*, 161–65; Lebhar, *Chain Stores*, 128, 130, 158, 137–44, 180. Chain taxes usually took the form of graduated license fees. The courts struck down some of these laws, but nineteen states still had them on the books in 1939 (Ellis W. Hawley, *The New Deal and the Problem of Monopoly: A Study in Economic Ambivalence* [Princeton: Princeton University Press, 1966], 261).

45. Thomas W. Ross, "Store Wars: The Chain Tax Movement," *Journal of Law and Economics* 39 (April 1986): 137; Thomas S. Dicke, *Franchising in America: The Development of a Business Method, 1840–1980* (Chapel Hill: University of North Carolina, 1992): 106–7. Groceries and filling stations reported the lowest profit margins in retail trade; see U.S. Bureau of the Census, "Retail Trade Margins, by Kind of Store: 1869–1947," in *Historical Statistics*, 2:848.

46. F. J. Harper, " 'A New Battle on Evolution': The Anti-Chain Store Trade-at-Home Agitation of 1929–1930," *Journal of American Studies* (Great Britain) 16 (1982): 413, 423; Carl Ryant, "The South and the Movement against Chain Stores," *Journal of Southern History* 39 (May 1973): 210; David Horowitz, "The Crusade against Chain Stores: Portland's Independent Merchants, 1928–1935," *Oregon Historical Quarterly* 89 (Winter 1988): 343, 359.

47. Palamountain, *Politics*, 58.

48. George V. Sheridan [executive director, Ohio Retailers Council], quoted in Lebhar, *Chain Stores*, 184–85.

49. Palamountain, *Politics*, 63–65, 73, 195–96.

50. Ibid., 188–93.

51. Tedlow, *New and Improved*, 290, 297–98.

52. Michael J. French, *The U.S. Tire Industry: A History* (Boston: Twayne, 1991), 54–55.

53. French, *U.S. Tire Industry*, 55–57; Michael French, "Manufacturing and Marketing: Vertical Integration in the U.S. Tire Manufacturing Industry, 1890–1980s," *Business and Economic History*, 2d ser., 18 (1989): 181–82.

54. French, "Manufacturing," 181–82; Robert Lee Knox, "Workable Competition in the Rubber Tire Industry" (Ph.D. diss., University of North Carolina at Chapel Hill,

1962), 317–19; French, *U.S. Tire Industry*, 55–57; Warren W. Leigh, *Automotive Tire Sales by Distribution Channels: 1926–1941 and 1946–47*, Study 5, Bureau of Business Research, p. 23, folder 21, box 24, J. P. Seiberling Papers, Ohio Historical Society (Columbus).

55. French, "Manufacturing," 180.

56. Knox, "Workable Competition," 317–19.

57. Palamountain, *Politics*, 197–98. For comments on the Goodyear-Sears case, see Joseph Robinson, *Congressional Record* (30 April 1936), vol. 80, pt. 5, p. 6429; John E. Miller, *Congressional Record* (4 May 1936), vol. 80, pt. 5, p. 6621; Representative George Sadowski (D.-Mich.), *Congressional Record* (14 May 1936), vol. 80, pt. 7, p. 7324.

58. W. H. Caven [Four States Grocer Company] to Wright Patman, 17 April 1935, folder 5 [quote], box 37C, Patman Papers, LBJPL; Wright Patman, interviewed by Joe B. Frantz, 11 August 1972, LBJPL Oral History Collection. For a history of the Patman committee's investigation, see Lebhar, *Chain Stores*, chap. 9 ("The 'Superlobby' Investigation").

59. Palamountain, *Politics*, 197–98; Ryant, "The South," 213; Wright Patman to Joseph T. Robinson, 22 June 1935, folder 1, box 244, Joseph Taylor Robinson Papers, University of Arkansas Library, Fayetteville; Wheeler Sammons, "Legislative History: Half the Verdict Is in on the Patman Act," in *Business and the Robinson Patman Law: A Symposium*, ed. Benjamin Werne (New York: Oxford University Press, 1938), 105; Cecil Edward Weller Jr., "Joseph Taylor Robinson and the Robinson-Patman Act," *Arkansas Historical Quarterly* 47 (1988): 35. Patman's bill received the endorsement of the NARD, the NARG, and the NAITD (National Conference of Independent Business Men to Franklin D. Roosevelt, 4 March 1936, Official File [OF] 2175, folder "National Conference of Independent Business Men," Franklin D. Roosevelt Presidential Library, Hyde Park, New York (hereafter cited as FDRPL).

60. Wright Patman, *Congressional Record* (27 May 1936), vol. 80, pt. 7, p. 8114.

61. Critics of the bill also viewed it as a price-fixing measure designed to replace the NRA. See Austin, "Prohibition of Price Discriminations," *Congressional Record* (29 April 1936), vol. 80, pt. 6, p. 6338.

62. Palamountain, *Politics*, 210–14; Patman, *Congressional Record* (20 April 1936), vol. 80, pt. 5, p. 5726; Patman, *Congressional Record* (27 May 1936), vol. 80, pt. 7, p. 8114; Patman, *The Robinson-Patman Act: What You Can and Cannot Do Under This Law* (New York: Ronald Press, 1938), 12, 20, 30.

63. Emanuel Celler, *Congressional Record* (23 April 1936), vol. 80, pt. 6, pp. 5976–78; Celler, *Congressional Record* (27 May 1936), vol. 80, pt. 6, p. 8108 [quote].

64. Palamountain, *Politics*, 228–29; "Alarmed by Patman Bill Victory," *Business Week*, 13 June 1936, 13. For a complete legislative history of the Robinson-Patman Act, see Palamountain, *Politics*, 188–231. Eleven states passed anti-price-discrimination laws within one year of the passage of the Robinson-Patman Act (U.S. Federal Trade Commission [hereafter cited as FTC], *Annual Report* [1937], 8).

65. Bork, *The Antitrust Paradox*, 63–64; Kenneth G. Elzinga, *Regulatory Change in an Atmosphere of Crisis: Current Implications of the Roosevelt Years* (London: Academic Press, 1979), chap. 4 ("The Robinson-Patman Act: A New Deal for Small Business"), esp. 64–66.

Chapter Two

1. U.S. Congress, Senate, Small Business Committee (hereafter cited as Senate Small Business Committee), *Problems of Independent Tire Dealers*, Staff Report, 83d Cong., 1st sess., 27 July 1953, Committee Print, p. 3.

2. Frederick M. Rowe, *Price Discrimination under the Robinson-Patman Act* (Boston: Little, Brown and Company, 1962), 535 [quote]; Robert H. Bork, *The Antitrust Paradox: A Policy at War with Itself* (New York: Free Press, 1978, 1993), 382 [quote].

3. Joseph Cornwall Palamountain Jr., *The Politics of Distribution* (Cambridge: Harvard University Press, 1955), 231; Wright Patman, testimony, U.S. Congress, House, Select Committee on Small Business (hereafter cited as House Small Business Committee), *Price Discrimination: The Robinson-Patman Act and Related Matters*, hearings, part 1, 84th Cong., 1st sess., 1 November 1955, 214 [quote].

4. Thurlow M. Gordon, "The Robinson-Patman Anti-Discrimination Act," in *Business and the Robinson-Patman Law: A Symposium*, ed. Benjamin Werne (New York: Oxford University Press, 1938), 64 [quote]. The sheer complexity of this legislation may have contributed to the high level of recidivism in Robinson-Patman cases; see William F. Shughart II and Robert D. Tollison, "Antitrust Recidivism in Federal Trade Commission Data, 1914–1982," chap. 12 in *Public Choice and Regulation: A View from Inside the Federal Trade Commission*, ed. Robert J. MacKay, James Miller III, and Bruce Yandle (Stanford: Hoover Institution Press, 1987), 263.

5. Edwin B. George, "Business and the Robinson-Patman Act: The First Year," in Werne, *Business and the Robinson-Patman Law*, 85, 91–98; Wright Patman, *The Robinson-Patman Act: What You Can and Cannot Do under This Law* (New York: Ronald Press, 1938).

6. "Goodyear-Sears Contract Is Ended," *Akron Beacon Journal*, 16 July 1936, 1; "Tire Trouble Gets Worse," *Business Week*, 26 September 1936, 28; Robert Lee Knox, "Workable Competition in the Rubber Tire Industry" (Ph.D. diss., University of North Carolina at Chapel Hill, 1962), 319; *Akron Beacon Journal*, 12 September 1936, 1; "Calls Tire Conference," *New York Times*, 11 January 1936, 7; "Trade Practice Rules for the Rubber Tire Industry, October 17, 1936," in U.S. Federal Trade Commission, *Trade Practice Rules, September 1, 1935, to June 30, 1945* (Washington: GPO, 1946), 36–41. Goodyear also suggested that labor unrest contributed to its decision to halt the production of Allstate tires. "Blames Unrest in Sears Move," *Akron Beacon Journal*, 22 July 1936, 13. The commission tried unsuccessfully to bring the Goodyear case under Section 2 as amended by the Robinson-Patman Act. The FTC appealed to the Supreme Court, which refused to hear the case (*F.T.C. v. Goodyear Tire and Rubber Company*, 1939).

7. "How FTC Got That Way," *Business Week*, 3 October 1936, 17–18; Federal Trade Commission, *Annual Report* (1937), 8; Federal Trade Commission, *Annual Report* (1938), 9.

8. Ellis W. Hawley, *The New Deal and the Problem of Monopoly: A Study in Economic Ambivalence* (Princeton: Princeton University Press, 1966), 284–93, 393 [quote].

9. Herbert Hovenkamp, *Enterprise and American Law, 1836–1937* (Cambridge: Harvard University Press, 1991), 360 [*Time* quote]; Gene M. Gressley, "Thurman Arnold, Antitrust, and the New Deal," *Business History Review* 38 (Summer 1964): 216; Tony

Freyer, *Regulating Big Business: Antitrust in Great Britain and America, 1880–1980* (Cambridge: Cambridge University Press, 1992), 209.

10. Hawley, *New Deal*, 300–301; Alan Brinkley, "The Antimonopoly Ideal and the Liberal State: The Case of Thurman Arnold," *Journal of American History* 80 (September 1993): 557–79; *Saturday Evening Post*, 12 August 1939, 7 [quote]. See also Wilson D. Miscamble, "Thurman Arnold Goes to Washington: A Look at Antitrust Policy in the Later New Deal," *Business History Review* 56 (Spring 1982): 1–15; and Thurman Arnold, *The Bottlenecks of Business* (New York: Reynal & Hitchcock, 1940).

11. Federal Trade Commission, *Annual Report* (1938), 9–10; "Price Law Looks Less Drastic," *Business Week*, 22 August 1936, 13–15.

12. "At Last: Some Light on R-P Law," *Business Week*, 24 July 1937, 13–14. This case also revealed the ways in which a company could evade the act. The FTC subsequently approved Bird's plans to sell only to mass-distributors on a flat-price basis. In a second case, involving the Kraft Cheese Company, the FTC accepted the company's defense that it had acted in good faith to provide the same discounts to all purchasers. The commission also found that Kraft's discount schedule, although not entirely cost-justified, did not lessen competition in the cheese market.

13. "FTC Will Enforce Brokerage Clause," *New York Times*, 5 September 1937, sec. F, p. 8; Benjamin Werne, "3 Years of Robinson-Patman: F.T.C. Invokes Every Phase and Wins All Appeals," *Printers' Ink*, 8 December 1939, 21; Rowe, *Price Discrimination*, 539–40.

14. U.S. Congress, Senate, Committee on Interstate Commerce, *Investigation by Federal Trade Commission of Methods used by Makers of Motor Vehicle Tires*, 75th Cong., 3d sess., 7 June 1938, S. Rept. 1994; Knox, "Workable Competition," 323; "Tire Makers Ready for Mr. Arnold," *Business Week*, 25 February 1939, 16–17; "U.S. Loses Tire Suit," *Business Week*, 9 March 1940, 36; *Rubber Age*, March 1941, 411.

15. "New Rubber Policy," *Business Week*, 27 May 1939, 26–27; U.S. Federal Trade Commission Records, Docket 3985; Francis Walker [chief economist], Memorandum for the Commission, 6 May 1939; James A. Horton [chief examiner], Memorandum for the Commission, 17 May 1939; Federal Trade Commission, Memorandum to Chief Counsel et al., 19 June 1939, Legal Docket Section Files, General Files 1914–1973, "U.S. Rubber," file 114–1, box 9; and W. T. Kelley, FTC General Counsel et al., "Memorandum for the Commission," 3 July 1947, file 203-1-3-1, all in RG 122, NA.

16. Wright Patman to Franklin D. Roosevelt, 24 April 1938, folder 2, box 37B, Patman Papers, LBJPL; Wright Patman to Franklin D. Roosevelt, 25 November 1938, Official File [OF] 288, folder "Chain Stores, 1937–1944," box 1, FDRPL; Wright Patman to Franklin D. Roosevelt, 11 May 1939, folder 2, box 37B, Patman Papers, LBJPL; Henry A. Wallace to R. L. Doughton [chair, House Ways and Means Committee], 2 April 1940, folder 1, box 37B, Patman Papers, LBJPL; Edward J. Noble [acting secretary of commerce] to Robert L. Doughton, 16 May 1940, folder 1, box 37B, Patman Papers, LBJPL; Wright Patman, "The Federal Chain Store Tax Should Become Law at This Session of Congress," *Congressional Record* (5 August 1939), vol. 84, pt. 11, p. 441; Emanuel Celler, "Confiscatory Chain-Store Tax Bill," *Congressional Record* (6 February 1939), vol. 84, pt. 11, p. 434; Carl Ryant, "The South and the Movement against Chain Stores," *Journal of Southern History* 39 (May 1973): 215 [Celler quote].

For a fuller discussion of the fight over Patman's "death tax," see Godfrey M. Lebhar, "The 'Death Sentence' Bill," *Chain Stores in America, 1859–1962*, 3d ed. (New York: Chain Store Publishing Corporation, 1963), chap. 12. Many writers in the business press argued that even if Congress passed Patman's "death sentence," consumers would simply turn to consumer cooperatives; see Godfrey Lebhar, "Chain Store Trends," in *Chain Stores and Legislation*, ed. Daniel Bloomfield (New York: H. W. Wilson, 1939), 27; "Shall We Curb the Chain Stores?" [1938 *Reader's Digest* article], in ibid., 31.

17. Hawley, *New Deal*, 320 [quote]; Merriner Eccles, quoted by Sumner T. Pike, 25 February 1941, testimony, U.S. Congress, Senate, Temporary National Economic Committee (hereafter cited as TNEC), *Final Report and Recommendations of the Temporary National Economic Committee* (Washington: GPO, 1941), 481. See also Hyo Won Cho, "The Evolution of the Functions of the Reconstruction Finance Corporation: A Study of the Growth and Death of a Federal Lending Agency" (Ph.D. diss., Ohio State University, 1953), 41–45; TNEC, *Problems of Small Business*, monograph No. 17, by John R. Cover et al. (Washington: GPO, 1941), 236–43; U.S. Commerce Department, Bureau of Foreign and Domestic Commerce, *Government Financial Aids to Small Business*, by Burt W. Roper (Washington: Department of Commerce, 1945), vii, 10–12.

18. F. J. Harper, " 'A New Battle on Evolution': The Anti-Chain-Store Trade-at-Home Agitation of 1929–1930," *Journal of American Studies* (Great Britain) 16 (1982): 425; "New Patman Bill Studied by Stores," *New York Times*, 21 November 1937, sec. 3, p. 9.

19. Palamountain, *Politics*, 168–69, 175–81; Ryant, "The South," 217.

20. U.S. Commerce Department, Bureau of Foreign and Domestic Commerce, *390 Bills: A Digest of Proposals Considered in Congress on Behalf of Small Business, 1933–1942*, by Burt W. Roper (Washington: GPO, 1943), 21; Palamountain, *Politics*, 185–86; Ryant, "The South," 219; Willard Thorp, "The Growth of Chains" [1938 *Dun & Bradstreet* article], in Bloomfield, *Chain Stores*, 19; "Antichain Weakness," *Business Week*, 22 July 1939, 32.

21. Harold G. Vatter, *The U.S. Economy in World War II* (New York: Columbia University Press, 1985), 57–59; John Morton Blum, *V Was for Victory: Politics and American Culture during World War II* (New York: Harcourt, 1976), 134–35; Franklin D. Roosevelt, memorandum to James F. Byrnes, 18 December 1942, OF 4735f, folder "WPB, SWPC, 1942" [quote], box 4, FDRPL.

22. Roper, *390 Bills*, 53; Senate Small Business Committee, *Small Business Problems: The Supreme Court in Relation to Small Business and the Sherman Act*, by Crichton Clarke, 77th Cong., 1st sess., 1941, Senate Committee Print 2, p. 25.

23. Senate Small Business Committee, *Small Business Problems*, 20.

24. Roper, *390 Bills*, 49, 187, 21, 308. S. 2315 provided RFC loans to those with tied-up inventory.

25. Senate Small Business Committee, *Small Business Problems of Tire and Rubber Manufacturers and Retailers*, 77th Cong., 1st sess., 1941, Committee Print 3; Roper, *390 Bills*, 50–51; George P. Comer [Department of Justice Antitrust Division, economic adviser], testimony, Senate Small Business Committee, *Tire Dealer and Rebuilder Problems*, hearings, 77th Cong., 2d sess., 3 March 1942, 310–11; James A. Murray, testimony, ibid., 308–9; George J. Burger, Burger Tire Consultant Service, Bulletin 389, 4 February 1949, folder 10, box 23, J. P. Seiberling Papers, Ohio Historical Society (hereafter cited as

JPS); U.S. Office of Price Administration, "Tire Return Plan for Dealers and Jobbers," folder "Small Business—Automobiles and Tires, 1942," box 796, Robert A. Taft Papers, Library of Congress.

This idea originated with George J. Burger, a small business advocate and ex−tire dealer. Burger was an independent tire dealer between 1909 and 1935. He served as the NAITD's president (1923−26) and secretary (1935−41). Burger claimed that his dismissal from the NAITD in 1941 resulted from "my 'over militant attitude' and my 'constant running to Washington for Government Aid against the tire manufacturers.'" He established his own consulting firm, the Burger Tire Consultant Service, in February 1941. See George J. Burger to Wright Patman, 30 January 1942, folder "Tire Bill—H.R. 315," Patman Papers, box 17D, LBJPL; "Progress of Legislative Fight for Preservation of America's Tire Independents," *National Independent*, September 1944, 4; George Burger, testimony, Senate Committee on Banking and Currency, *Distribution of Motor-Vehicle Tires*, hearings, 79th Cong., 2d sess., 2 July 1946, 8−9; George J. Burger, statement, 28 October 1946, in House Small Business Committee, *United States Versus Economic Concentration and Monopoly: An Investigation of the Effectiveness of the Government's Efforts to Combat Economic Concentration*, Staff Report to the Monopoly Subcommittee, 79th Cong., 2d sess., 27 December 1946, 202.

26. William Mark Hickey [NAITD president], testimony, Senate Small Business Committee, *Tire Dealer and Rebuilder Problems*, 336−38; J. P. Seiberling to Cecil A. Moore, 16 July 1942, folder 9, box 11, JPS; W. W. Marsh [NAITD executive secretary], testimony, House Small Business Committee, *Price Discrimination: The Robinson-Patman Act and Related Matters*, hearings, 84th Cong., 1st sess., 4 November 1955, 469 [quote]; Senate Small Business Committee, *Problems of Independent Tire Dealers*, Staff Report, 83d Cong., 1st sess., 27 July 1953, Committee Print 4.

27. J. P. Seiberling, testimony, Senate Small Business Committee, *Tire Dealer and Rebuilder Problems*, 450−51; J. P. Seiberling to J. P. Byrne, 9 February 1942, folder 9, box 11, JPS; "Seiberling Fair Trades Premium Products—Again Leads Fight to Protect Independent Dealer Profits!," January 1949 advertisement in *Tires, Battery and Accessory*, reprint in folder 24 ("Fair Trading, 1949"), box 23, JPS. The National Association of Retail Druggists (NARD) was the only other small business association to endorse this legislation.

28. J. P. Seiberling to Motor Supply Company, 31 January 1942, folder 9, box 11, JPS; J. P. Seiberling to Johnston G. Craig, 28 February 1942, folder 9, box 11, JPS; Burger Tire Consultant Service, pamphlet titled "Tire Conservation," folder 62, box 11, JPS; J. P. Seiberling to Burger, 4 August 1942, folder 63, box 10, JPS. Perhaps in deference to his friendship with Burger, J. P. Seiberling did not associate himself with the NAITD (J. P. Seiberling to George Burger, 25 November 1942, folder 63, box 10, JPS).

29. J. P. Seiberling to J. P. Byrne, 9 February 1942, folder 9, box 11, JPS. During the NRA period, Seiberling had also tried unsuccessfully to secure higher prices by uniting the small companies against the Big Four (J. P. Seiberling to J. W. Whitehead [Norwalk Tire and Rubber], July 18, 1934, folder 17, box 4, JPS).

30. John L. Collyer, testimony, Senate Small Business Committee, *Tire Dealer and Rebuilder Problems*, hearings, 5 March 1942, 447−48; Edwin J. Thomas, testimony, ibid., 468−70; Howard Hawkes [U.S. Rubber, general sales manager, tire division], testimony,

ibid., 465–67; Frank M. Judson [Sears, supervisor of tire division], testimony, ibid., 6 March 1942, 479–97.

31. George J. Burger, testimony, U.S. Congress, Senate, Committee on Judiciary, *Distribution of Motor Vehicle Tires*, hearings on S. 175, 83d Cong., 2d sess., 21 May 1954, 4; Senate Small Business Committee, "Utilization of Existing Stocks of Rubber Tires," *Congressional Record* (1 June 1942), vol. 88, pt. 4, pp. 4740–43.

32. Senate Small Business Committee, *Tire Dealer and Rebuilder Problems*, hearings, 6 March 1942, 492.

33. J. P. Seiberling to H. P. Klinger, 13 March 1942, folder 9, box 11 [quote]; J. P. Seiberling to Charles G. Daughters, 22 September 1942, folder 58, box 11 [quote]; J. P. Seiberling to George J. Burger, 30 July 1942, folder 63, box 10; J. P. Seiberling to Burger, 19 September 1942, folder 63, box 10; J. P. Seiberling to Jose R. Torres, 6 November 1942, folder 9, box 11; and J. P. Seiberling to C. H. Boyd, 22 December 1942, folder 9, box 11, all in JPS.

34. "Saving Tire Outlets," *Business Week*, 11 July 1942, 18–19; "Nine-Point Service Program Helps Goodyear Build Independent Dealers," *Sales Management*, 1 December 1945, 88–90; *Sales Management*, 1 December 1945, 99–102; A. F. Schalk Jr. [NAITD], "Significant Merchandising Trends of the Independent Tire Dealer," *Journal of Marketing* 12 (April 1948): 462–69; Warren W. Leigh, *Gross Margins and Net Profits of Tire Dealers, 1923–1948*, December 1949 (Akron, privately printed), 2, 27; Michael J. French, *The U.S. Tire Industry: A History* (Boston: Twayne Publishers, 1991), 77; "Firestone in Mail-order Business," *Printers' Ink*, 11 December 1942, 46.

35. "Saving Tire Outlets," *Business Week*, 11 July 1942, 18–19; Clifford Simpson [executive vice president, NAITD], testimony, Senate Small Business Committee, *Tire Dealer and Rebuilder Problems*, hearings, 78th Cong., 1st sess., 6 May 1943, 2645; William M. Jeffers [Director, Rubber Division of War Production Board], ibid., 8 April 1943, 2590.

36. *National Independent*, November 1943, p. 1, folder 49, box 12, JPS; C. C. Osmun [tire sales manager, Goodyear], testimony, Senate Small Business Committee, *Tire Dealer and Rebuilder Problems*, hearings, 13 May 1943, 2661; J. W. Keener [director of business research, B. F. Goodrich], testimony, ibid., 2695–2710. The tire manufacturers also used the company stores to test new products and sales techniques; see T. G. MacGowan [Firestone Tire & Rubber], "Trends in Tire Distribution," *Journal of Marketing* 10 (January 1946): 265–69.

37. Robert A. Taft to John L. Collyer [president, B. F. Goodrich Company], 29 April 1943; Robert A. Taft, memorandum, 1943; Robert A. Taft to J. J. Newman [vice president, Goodyear Tire], 1 November 1943; J. J. Newman, telegram to Robert A. Taft, 21 August 1943; Robert Taft, memorandum, "Rubber Tire Bill, S.1122," all in folder "Small Business Automobiles & Tires, 1943," box 796, Robert A. Taft Papers, Library of Congress.

38. J. P. Seiberling to H. P. Klinger, 13 March 1942, folder 9, box 11; J. P. Seiberling to George J. Burger, 5 June 1943, folder 23, box 12; J. P. Seiberling to T. H. Westgate [quote], 15 April 1942, folder 54, box 11, all in JPS.

39. J. P. Seiberling to George J. Burger, 13 September 1946, folder 32, box 16, JPS.

40. "The Future of the Independent Tire Dealer," address before annual convention

of the National Association of Independent Tire Dealers, Cincinnati, Ohio, 1 November 1949, folder 49, box 23, JPS.

41. J. P. Seiberling to George J. Burger, 4 November 1943, folder 23, box 12, JPS.

42. J. P. Seiberling to George J. Burger, 17 January 1945, folder 6, box 15, JPS.

43. John A. Danaher, testimony, Senate Banking and Currency Committee, *Distribution of Motor-Vehicle Tires*, hearings, 79th Cong., 2d sess., 23 July 1946, 20.

44. Robert A. Taft, testimony, ibid., 2 July 1946, 13 [quote]; Taft, testimony, ibid., 23 July 1946, 25–26.

45. Senate Small Business Committee, *Future of Independent Business: Progress Report of the Chairman*, 79th Cong., 2d sess., 2 January 1947, Print 16; Charles A. Welsh, "The Murray Report on Small Business," *Industrial and Labor Relations Review* 1 (October 1947): 96 [quote]; House Small Business Committee, *United States Versus Economic Concentration*, 2–4, 5 [quote], 6, 22, 26. The subcommittee relied on a study done by the Smaller War Plants Corporation; see SWPC, *Economic Concentration and World War II*, by John M. Blair, Harrison F. Houghton, and Matthew Rose (Washington: GPO, 1945), 172–77.

46. House Small Business Committee, *United States Versus Economic Concentration*, 12, 16–17. In response to the Kefauver report, the FTC investigated a number of industries and concluded that economic concentration had increased as a result of World War II and the postwar merger movement. Many economists challenged the commission's findings, however, and the agency later admitted that there had been no real increase in concentration between 1935 and 1947; see FTC, *Annual Report* (1948), 11; Senate Small Business Committee, *Monopolistic Practices and Small Business*, Staff Report to the Federal Trade Commission for the Subcommittee on Monopoly, 82d Cong., 2d sess., 31 March 1952, 20; FTC, *Report on Wartime Costs and Profits for Manufacturing Corporations, 1941 to 1945* (Washington: GPO, 1947); FTC, *Report on the Concentration of Productive Facilities, 1947: Total Manufacturing and 26 Selected Industries* (Washington: GPO, 1949); and FTC, *Report on Changes in Concentration in Manufacturing: 1935 to 1947 and 1950* (Washington: GPO, 1954). The subcommittee's Republican minority dissented from some of the report's recommendations ("Trusts Here Held Bid to Socialism," *New York Times*, 25 December 1946, 38).

47. Harry S. Truman, address before Washington College, quoted in "I Am Advocate of Small Business—Truman," *Commercial and Financial Chronicle*, 6 June 1946, 3091. Truman operated a haberdashery business between 1919 and 1921 ("Harry S. Truman," *Biographical Directory of the American Congress, 1774–1971* [Washington: GPO, 1971]).

48. Robert Lester Branyan, "Antimonopoly Activities during the Truman Administration" (Ph.D. diss., University of Oklahoma, 1961), 3 [quote].

49. Harry S. Truman, *Memoirs*, 2 vols. (Garden City, N.Y.: Doubleday, 1955), 1:165–66 [quote]. See also David McCullough, *Truman* (New York: Simon & Schuster, 1992), 232–33.

50. Senate Small Business Committee, *Monopolistic Practices*, 7 [quote]; House Small Business Committee, *Statistics on Federal Antitrust Activities*, 84th Cong., 1st sess., 1956, Committee Print 2; "FTC: Stronger and Tougher," *Business Week*, 3 June 1950, 24.

51. "Administration Maps Wider Field for FTC," *Business Week*, 1 June 1946, 7; Bran-

yan, "Antimonopoly Activities," 9–10; Craufurd D. Goodwin, "Attitudes toward Industry in the Truman Administration: The Macroeconomic Origins of Microeconomic Policy," chap. 3 in *The Truman Presidency*, ed. Michael J. Lacey (Cambridge: Cambridge University Press, 1989), 110; Robert Griffith, "Forging America's Postwar Order: Domestic Politics and Political Economy in the Age of Truman," chap. 2 in ibid., 76; Neil Fligstein, *The Transformation of Corporate Control* (Cambridge: Harvard University Press, 1990), 196; FTC, *Federal Trade Commission, 1945–1953* (Washington: GPO, 1953), 1–2 [quote]; George Stigler, "The Economic Effects of Antitrust Legislation," in *Essence of Stigler*, ed. Kurt R. Leube and Thomas Gale Moore (Stanford, Calif.: Hoover Institution Press, 1986). On the effects of the Celler-Kefauver Act, see John Frederick Bowen, "The Celler-Kefauver Act and Concentration in the Brewing Industry" (Ph.D. diss., Vanderbilt University, 1971), and Willard Fritz Mueller, *The Celler-Kefauver Act: The First 27 Years* (Washington: GPO, 1980).

52. B. F. Goodrich Company, Operations Council, minutes, 11 July 1946, in Record Book No. 11, p. 52, B. F. Goodrich Company headquarters; James B. Sharkey [general manager, NAITD] to Walter C. Ploeser, 21 July 1947, file 203-1-3-2-1, RG 122, NA; Branyan, "Antimonopoly Activities," 76; Fligstein, *Transformation*, 170, 197.

53. "Tire Industry Suit," *India Rubber World*, September 1947, 800–801.

54. B. F. Goodrich Company, Operations Council, minutes, 21 August 1947, in Record Book No. 13; B. F. Goodrich, Operations Council, minutes, 22 October 1948, in Record Book No. 14 [quote]; James B. Sharkey [general manager, NAITD], testimony, House Small Business Committee, *Monopolistic and Unfair Trade Practices*, hearings, 80th Cong., 2d sess., 19 November 1948, 1239–46; "$4,266,000 Damage Suit Filed by Tire Dealers Nears Settlement," *Rubber Age*, July 1952, 525; Knox, "Workable Competition," 324–26. The NAITD brought suit against Goodyear, Firestone, B. F. Goodrich, U.S. Rubber, Lee Rubber, and the RMA.

55. Rowe, *Price Discrimination*, 313–14; Walter C. Ploeser to Garland S. Ferguson [chairman, FTC], 3 July 1947, file 203-1-3-2-1, RG 122 [quote], NA; Patman, *The Robinson-Patman Act*, v; Everett MacIntyre to the Federal Trade Commission, 26 August 1949, file 203-1-6-1, RG 122, NA; Lowell Wadmond to Everett McIntyre, 20 August 1947, file 203-1-4-5-2, RG 122, NA; Corwin D. Edwards, *The Price Discrimination Law: A Review of Experience* (Washington: Brookings Institution, 1959), 270–73; House Small Business Committee, *Annual Report*, 80th Cong., 1st sess., 29 December 1948, H. Rpt. 2466, p. 32 [quote].

56. W. T. Kelley, FTC General Counsel et al., "Memorandum for the Commission," 3 July 1947, file 203-1-3-1, RG 122, NA.

57. Robert A. Katzmann, *Regulatory Bureaucracy: The Federal Trade Commission and Antitrust Policy* (Cambridge: MIT Press, 1980).

58. Corwin D. Edwards to the FTC, 28 April 1950; Everett McIntyre to the FTC, 26 August 1949; Everette McIntyre to the FTC, 1 May 1950, all in file 203-1-6-1, RG 122, NA; Wright Patman, *Complete Guide to the Robinson-Patman Act* (Englewood Cliffs, N.J.: Prentice-Hall, 1963), viii.

59. Wright Patman to Lowell B. Mason [acting chairman, FTC], 19 August 1949, file 203-1, RG 122, NA; Edwards, *The Price Discrimination Law*, 270–73.

60. *Goodyear, et al. v. F.T.C.*, U.S. District Court for the District of Columbia, 18 January 1950, in FTC, *Federal Trade Commission Decisions: Findings, Orders, and Stipulations*, 1 July 1949 to 30 June 1950, vol. 46 (Washington: Federal Trade Commission, 1952). Robert Knox notes that Congress inserted the quantity-limit clause to protect grocers, who purchased goods by the carload (Knox, "Workable Competition," 322). In establishing a carload limit on allowable discounts, the FTC also drew upon the experience of the Interstate Commerce Commission, which typically set rates by the carload. (The FTC stated that "the judgment of this Commission, like that of the Interstate Commerce Commission, is that discounts based on volume of transactions over a period of time are arbitrary and that those based on single transactions are not.") See John S. McGee, "The Decline and Fall of Quantity Discounts: The Quantity Limit Rule in Rubber Tires and Tubes," *Journal of Business* 27 (July 1954): 232.

61. "Tire Fire," *Business Week*, 4 February 1950, 21; FTC, *In the Matter of a Quantity-Limit Rule as to Replacement Tires and Tubes Made of Natural or Synthetic Rubber for Use on Motor Vehicles as a Class of Commodity*, 3 January 1952, FTC file no. 203-1, in Commerce Clearing House, "Quantity-Limit Rules of the Federal Trade Commission," *Trade Regulation Reports, 1952* (New York: Commerce Clearing House, 1952).

62. "Oil's Tire 'Deals' Called Harmful to Competition: FTC Inquiry Asked," *National Petroleum News*, 5 July 1950, 19 [quote].

63. "Tire Distribution by Oil Companies Key Issue in FTC Discount Hearing," *National Petroleum News*, 15 February 1950, 13–14; "Large Discounts Only Reason for Rivals' Success, Tire Dealers Say: Montgomery Ward Cites Distribution Economy, Favorable Location, as FTC Hearings Close," *National Petroleum News*, 22 February 1950, 19–20; House Small Business Committee, *Functional Operation of the Federal Trade Commission*, hearings, 80th Cong., 2d sess., 28 June 1950; "Oil's Tire 'Deals' Called Harmful to Competition: FTC Inquiry Asked," *National Petroleum News*, 5 July 1950, 19 [quote]; James B. Sharkey [general manager, NAITD], testimony, House Small Business Committee, *Monopolistic and Unfair Trade Practices*, 19 November 1948, 1218 [quote]; Warren W. Leigh, *Automotive Tire Sales by Distribution Channels: 1926–1941 and 1946–47*, Study 5, Bureau of Business Research, p. 23, folder 21, box 24, JPS.

64. "Large Discounts Only Reason for Rivals' Success, Tire Dealers Say," *National Petroleum News*, 22 February 1950, 19–20.

65. Leigh, *Automotive Tire Sales*, folder 21, box 24, JPS; Leigh, "The Quantity-Limit Rule and the Rubber Tire Industry," *Journal of Marketing* 17 (October 1952): 136–55; Leigh, *Gross Margins*.

66. "Montgomery Ward Says FTC Tire Rule Would Favor Large Oil Companies," *National Petroleum News*, 25 January 1950, 13–14. The FTC later stated that it would apply the discount limit to "overrides" and cost-plus contracts ("Tire Discount Limit Faces Court Test," *National Petroleum News*, September 1955, 75).

67. "Tire Distribution by Oil Companies Key Issue in FTC Discount Hearing," *National Petroleum News*, 15 February 1950, 13–14.

68. "Small Tire Firms Form Trade Group," *Akron Beacon Journal*, 16 November 1949, 1–2; J. P. Seiberling to George J. Burger, 30 November 1949, folder "George Burger," box 23, JPS. The group included Seiberling Rubber, Mohawk, Cooper, Dayton, McCreary,

Lee, Armstrong, Norwalk, Dunlop (Buffalo), Polson, Schenuitt, Carlisle, Durkee-Atwood, Webster, Cupples, Dismuke, Mansfield, and Gates ("Small Tire Firms," pp. 1–2, folder 21, box 24, JPS).

69. FTC, *In the Matter of a Quantity-Limit Rule*; FTC, *Annual Report* (1951), 10.

70. Mason had earlier served on the National Recovery Review Board (also known as the Darrow Board), a commission that issued a report critical of the NRA and its effect on small business. Contemporaries considered him an "antimonopoly Republican," but the business community generally approved of his appointment to the Federal Trade Commission (Branyan, "Antimonopoly Activities," 102).

71. The Senate committee managing the bill expressed its concern with domination by "a very few units of overshadowing size"; see Commerce Clearing House, "Quantity-Limit Rules of the Federal Trade Commission," *Trade Regulation Reports, 1952*. See also Representative John E. Miller (D.-Ark.), *Congressional Record* (4 May 1936), vol. 80, pt. 5, p. 6623.

72. "Minority Findings of Commissioner Mason," in FTC, *In the Matter of a Quantity-Limit Rule*; FTC, *Annual Report* (1951), 10.

73. Edwards, *The Price Discrimination Law*, 284.

74. John S. McGee, "The Robinson-Patman Act and Effective Competition" (Ph.D. diss., Vanderbilt University, 1952), 413 [quote]; "FTC Gets Tough on Discounts," *Business Week*, 12 January 1952, 126.

75. "FTC Orders Discount Ceilings," *New York Times*, 4 January 1952, 29; W. W. Marsh [executive secretary, NAITD], quoted in "FTC Ruling Confuses OPS, Wins Tire Dealer Support," *National Petroleum News*, 7 January 1952, 27.

76. B. F. Goodrich, *Annual Report* (1951), 4–5 [quote]; "F.T.C. Ruling Opposed," *New York Times*, 7 January 1952, 27; "Administrative Procedure Act," *Congress and the Nation, 1945–1964: A Review of Government and Politics in the Postwar Years* (Washington: Congressional Quarterly, 1965), 1657–58.

77. Louis W. Stern, *Legal Aspects of Marketing Strategy: Antitrust and Consumer Protection Issues* (Englewood Cliffs, N.J.: Prentice-Hall, 1984), 264. The quote is from *F.T.C. v. Ruberoid* (1952).

78. John Parkany, "Federal Trade Commission Enforcement of the Robinson-Patman Act, 1946–1952" (Ph.D. diss., Columbia University, 1955), 266–67. Congressional small business advocates tried to overturn the *Standard Oil* case, while supporters of the Court's decision tried to codify it into law. See "Price Differential," *Congressional Record* (4 May 1951), vol. 97, pt. 4, pp. 4845–47; "Pricing Practices," *Congressional Record* (1 August 1951), vol. 97, pt. 7, p. 9251; vol. 97, pt. 7, p. 9302; House Small Business Committee, *Progress Report*, 82d Cong., 1st sess., 7 January 1952, H. Rpt. 1228, pp. 65–66; Patman, "Robinson-Patman Act Under Attack," *Congressional Record* (3 August 1953), vol. 99, pt. 12, p. A5144; "Amendment to Robinson-Patman Act—Equality of Opportunity Bill," *Congressional Record* (16 February 1955), vol. 101, pt. 2, p. 1559; "Independent Tire Dealers," *Congressional Record* (28 March 1956), vol. 102, pt. 5, pp. 5775–76; "Amendment to Robinson-Patman Act—Equality of Opportunity Bill," *Congressional Record* (16 February 1955), vol. 101, pt. 2, p. 1559; "Proposed Merger Legislation," *Congressional Record* (27 July 1956), vol. 102, pt. 11, p. 15116; "Senator Wiley Appeals for Small-Business Bill," *Congressional Record* (21 July 1956), vol. 102, pt. 10, pp.

13801–2; "Price Bill Up to the Senate," *Business Week*, 7 July 1956, 29; House Small Business Committee, *Price Discrimination, the Robinson-Patman Act, and the Attorney-General's National Committee to Study the Antitrust Laws*, 84th Cong., 2d sess., 19 December 1956, H. Rpt. 2966, pp. 217–18; Joseph A. Seeley, "Current Legislative Proposals and Attitudes Concerning the Robinson-Patman Act," in *Symposium: Twenty Years of Robinson-Patman—The Record and Issues*, ed. Sigmund Timberg (New York: Federal Legal Publications, 1956), 31–50; House Small Business Committee, *Annual Report* (1959), 191.

The courts also ruled in favor of the tire companies when the FTC charged their footwear divisions with illegal price discrimination. See Albert E. Sawyer, *Business Aspects of Pricing under the Robinson-Patman Act* (Boston: Little, Brown and Company, 1963), 90–91; "Goodrich Cited by FTC," *New York Times*, 28 July 1949, 38; "Goodyear Denies F.T.C. Charges," *New York Times*, 25 October 1949, 47; "U.S. Examiner Backs Goodrich on Prices," *New York Times*, 24 December 1953, 26.

79. Patman, *Complete*, 81; Edwards, *The Price Discrimination Law*, 275–81. The court consolidated the complaints of fourteen tire manufacturers, thirty-five independent tire dealers, and twelve mass-distributors.

80. Patman, *Complete*, 81–82; Edwards, *The Price Discrimination Law*, 275–81; B. F. Goodrich, Authorizations Council, minutes, 28 November 1952, in Operations Council Record Book No. 20; *The B. F. Goodrich Company v. Federal Trade Commission, et al.*, United States District Court for the District of Columbia, 7 September 1955, in *Statutes and Court Decisions Pertaining to the Federal Trade Commission, 1949–1955*, comp. Harriette H. Esch, vol. 5 (Washington: GPO, 1957); *Federal Trade Commission, et al. v. The B. F. Goodrich Company, et al.*, 28 February 1957, Court of Appeals for the District of Columbia Circuit, in *Statutes and Court Decisions: Federal Trade Commission, 1956–1960*, comp. Harriette H. Esch, vol. 6 (Washington: GPO, 1961).

81. Theodore Philip Kovaleff, *Business and Government during the Eisenhower Administration: A Study of the Antitrust Policy of the Antitrust Division of the Justice Department* (Athens: Ohio University Press, 1980), 17–19, 22–23, 27 [quote]; Edwards, *The Price Discrimination Law*, 285 [quote]; S. Chesterfield Oppenheim and Glen E. Weston, *Unfair Trade Practices and Consumer Protection: Cases and Comments*, 3d ed. (St. Paul, Minn.: West Publishing, 1974), 897 [quote]; American Bar Association, *Antitrust Developments, 1955–1968: A Supplement to the Report of the Attorney General's National Committee to Study the Antitrust Laws, March 31, 1955* (Chicago: American Bar Association, 1968), 131.

82. Senate Small Business Committee, Weekly Staff Report, 26 February 1955, in U.S. Senate Committee Records, box 32, RG 46, NA.

83. Joseph Tacconelli [secretary, NTDRA], testimony, Senate Small Business Committee, *Report of the Attorney General's National Committee to Study the Antitrust Laws*, hearings, pt. 1, 84th Cong., 1st sess., 27–29 April 1955, 183–92.

84. Wright Patman, "Criticism of Report Made by Attorney General's Committee," *Congressional Record* (31 March 1955), vol. 101, pt. 3, pp. 4140–45; House Small Business Committee, *Price Discrimination, the Robinson-Patman Act, and the Attorney-General's National Committee to Study the Antitrust Laws*, 84th Cong., 2d sess., 19 December 1956, H. Rpt. 2966, pp. 1–9, 221–28, 304 [quotes on pp. 4, 304].

85. House Small Business Committee, *The Organization and Procedures of the Federal Regulatory Commissions and Agencies and Their Effect on Small Business*, Report to Subcommittee No. 1 on Regulatory Agencies, 84th Cong., 2d sess., 16 October 1956, 1, 52–53; "F.T.C. Head Defends Case Action," *New York Times*, 20 July 1955, 13. In September 1955, Howrey resigned from the FTC after the House Small Business Committee held hearings on the operation of the FTC.

86. Scholars have also portrayed Eisenhower as a champion of big business. See, for example, Stephen E. Ambrose, *Eisenhower: Soldier and President* (New York: Simon & Schuster, 1990), 221, 291. Leonard Hall, chairman of the Republican National Committee during Eisenhower's first term, later reminisced that "if Ike had any weakness that I know—a rich man meant a great deal to Ike" (Leonard Hall, Oral History 478, 19 May 1975, p. 40, Dwight D. Eisenhower Presidential Library, Abilene, Kansas [hereafter cited as EPL]).

87. Dwight D. Eisenhower, diary entry, 9 February 1953, in Dwight D. Eisenhower, *The Eisenhower Diaries*, ed. Robert H. Ferrell (New York: Norton, 1981), 229.

88. Kovaleff, *Business and Government*, 155–57; FTC, *Annual Report* (1955); Rowe, *Price Discrimination*, 538. For a study of the impact of antitrust enforcement on small business, see Laurence Ray Brown, "Development of Federal Antitrust Practices and Effect upon Small Business" (Ph.D. diss., George Washington University, 1968).

89. Eisenhower, "Letter to Jere Cooper, Chairman, House Committee on Ways and Means, Regarding Small Business," 15 July 1957, in *Public Papers of the Presidents of the United States: Dwight D. Eisenhower* (Washington: GPO, 1957), 543. Eisenhower requested that FTC orders under the Clayton Act be made final. He also asked Congress to give the FTC the power to issue a restraining injunction before filing a formal complaint in merger cases.

90. Eisenhower, "Televised Panel Discussion with a Group of Republican Women, San Francisco, California," 21 October 1958, in *Public Papers of the Presidents*, 768.

91. "Republicans Reshape the FTC," *Business Week*, 5 June 1954, 43–44; Kovaleff, *Business and Government*, 71; Sawyer, *Business Aspects of Pricing*, appendix B, p. 441; B. F. Goodrich Company, Operations Council, minutes, 11 July 1946, Record Book No. 11, p. 52; Talbot S. Lindstrom and Kevin P. Tighe, comps., *Antitrust Consent Decrees: Voluntary Antitrust Compliance Analysis and History of Justice Department Consent Decrees* (New York: Lawyers Co-operative Publishing Company, 1974), 707, 954. The House Small Business Committee criticized the FTC's use of consent decrees; see House Small Business Committee, *Law Enforcement Activities Affecting Small Business*, Report of Subcommittee on Law Enforcement and Subsidies Affecting Small Business, 85th Cong., 2d sess., 3 January 1959, H. Rpt. 2714.

92. Senate Small Business Committee, Weekly Staff Report, 14 January 1956, box 32, RG 46, NA.

93. "Tires and Accessories," *Newsweek*, 23 January 1956, 81; FTC, *Annual Report* (1956), 36; FTC, *Economic Report on the Manufacture and Distribution of Automotive Tires*, Staff Report (Washington: GPO, 1966), 39–40; *Goodyear v. F.T.C.* (1964), quoted in *In the Matter of The B. F. Goodrich Company and the Texas Company, Opinion of the Commission*, 14 January 1966, FTC Docket 6485-1-1, on pp. 7, 2, 11 in box 614, Docketed Case Files, RG 122, NA.

94. *In the Matter of The Rubber Manufacturers' Association, Inc., et al.*, Official Transcript of Proceedings, 27 June 1961, pp. 710–16, 726, in docket 7505-2-2, box 530, Docketed Case Files, Docket Section, RG 122, NA; *In the Matter of The Rubber Manufacturers' Association*, Docket 7505, Decision of the Commission, 6 January 1962, box 527, ibid.; Knox, "Workable Competition," 324–26.

95. French, *U.S. Tire Industry*, 95.

96. W. W. Marsh [executive secretary, NTDRA], testimony, Senate Small Business Committee, Subcommittee on Retailing, Distribution, and Fair Trade Practices, *Dual Distribution in the Automotive Tire Industry—1959*, hearings, pt. 1, 86th Cong., 1st sess., 17 June 1959, 13.

97. George Burger, testimony, House Committee on Interstate and Foreign Commerce, *Equal Pricing*, hearings on H.R. 2729, 86th Cong., 1st sess., 21 July 1959, 10. In 1954, the Burger Tire Consultant Service surveyed four thousand independent tire dealers. Seventy-seven percent of Goodyear dealers and 90 percent of Firestone dealers also complained of price discrimination in favor of the company stores. Burger frequently distributed biased questionnaires, however, so these figures should be treated with skepticism.

98. Hubert H. Humphrey, Senate Small Business Committee, Subcommittee on Retailing, *Dual Distribution*, 18 June 1959, 144, 147 [quote].

99. Karl Nygaard, testimony, Senate Small Business Committee, *Dual Distribution*, 19 June 1959, 331–48. Actually, between 1945 and 1959, the number of B. F. Goodrich stores increased only slightly, from 451 to 458.

100. F. H. Mueller, testimony, House Committee on Interstate and Foreign Commerce, *Equal Pricing*, 5; Earl Kintner, testimony, Senate Small Business Committee, Subcommittee on Retailing, *Dual Distribution*, 18 June 1959, 135.

101. The small business advocates also sought to impose excise and inventory taxes on tires delivered to manufacturers' outlets; see House Committee on Ways and Means, *Imposition of Tire Tax on Tires Delivered to Manufacturer's Retail Outlet*, 86th Cong., 2d sess., 15 August 1960, H. Rpt. 2093; House Committee on Ways and Means, *Imposition of Tire Tax on Tires Delivered to Manufacturer's Retail Outlet*, 87th Cong., 1st sess., 16 September 1961, H. Rpt. 1196; House Committee on Ways and Means, *Imposition of Tire Tax on Tires Delivered to Manufacturer's Retail Outlet*, 89th Cong., 1st sess., 27 September 1965, H. Rpt. 1096.

102. In the post-Eisenhower period, the most significant case against the tire companies began in 1973, when the Justice Department charged Goodyear and Firestone with attempting to establish a monopoly through predatory price-cutting. The government alleged that the two companies had cut prices in 1959–60, at a time when costs were rising, in an attempt to drive smaller companies out of business. In 1976, however, the Justice Department dropped the case after discovering that costs had not actually been rising at the time ("U.S. Ends Firestone and Goodyear Suits," *New York Times*, 3 March 1976, 1, 57).

103. During the 1960s, Representative Abraham Multer (D.-N.Y.) and Senator Lee Metcalf (D.-Mont.) introduced bills prohibiting manufacturers from operating retail outlets; see *Congressional Record* (29 August 1961), vol. 107, pt. 13, 17304; Abraham J. Multer, "Independent Tire Dealers Versus Factory Stores," *Congressional Record* (8 May

1961), vol. 107, pt. 13, A3165–66; *Congressional Record* (28 January 1963), vol. 109, pt. 1, 1173; Abraham J. Multer, "Tire Manufacturers 'Company Stores' Should Be Eliminated," *Congressional Record* (3 February 1965), vol. 111, pt. 24, A447–48; *Congressional Record* (19 January 1967), vol. 113, pt. 1, 1076; *Congressional Record* (9 May 1968), vol. 114, pt. 12, 12657.

104. "Silver Anniversary of the Robinson-Patman Act," *Congressional Record* (19 June 1961), vol. 107, pt. 8, 10708–15.

105. Alan Stone, *Economic Regulation and the Public Interest: The Federal Trade Commission in Theory and Practice* (Ithaca: Cornell University Press, 1977), 99–100.

106. Oppenheim and Weston, *Unfair Trade Practices*, 794.

107. Harold Demsetz, quoted in James Q. Wilson, "The Politics of Regulation," in *The Politics of Regulation*, ed. James Q. Wilson (New York: Basic Books, 1980), 393.

108. Robert A. Katzmann, "Federal Trade Commission," in ibid., 169.

109. Elzinga, "The Robinson-Patman Act," 67–68.

110. James Q. Wilson, *Bureaucracy: What Government Agencies Do and Why They Do It* (New York: Basic Books, 1989), 255; "Antitrust Chief Takes Firm Stand," *New York Times*, 23 January 1975, 47, 51; "Small Business Leaders Fight to Keep Robinson-Patman Act," *New York Times*, 28 July 1975, 1, 31; Wright Patman, House Small Business Committee, *Recent Efforts to Amend or Repeal the Robinson-Patman Act*, hearings, pt. 1, 94th Cong., 1st sess., 5 November 1975, 6 [quote]; House Small Business Committee, Subcommittee on Antitrust and Restraint of Trade Activities Affecting Small Business, *Impact of Federal Antitrust Enforcement Policies on Small Business*, hearings, 97th Cong., 2d sess., 9 September 1982.

111. Elzinga, "The Robinson-Patman Act," 74; Stone, *Economic Regulation*, 100.

112. Elzinga, "The Robinson-Patman Act," 72.

113. Rowe, *Price Discrimination*, 554; Thomas E. Sunderland, "The Robinson-Patman Act: Go Out and Compete But Don't Get Caught at It," *Chicago Bar Record* 34 (September 1953): 447.

114. L. E. Marlowe [president, NAITD], testimony, Senate Banking and Currency Committee, *Distribution of Motor-Vehicle Tires*, hearings, 23 July 1946, 51.

115. Knox, "Workable Competition," 408.

116. Opinion Research Corporation, *Dealers in Hot Competition: A Report of the Public Opinion Index for Industry* (Princeton, N.J.: Opinion Research Corporation, 1957), appendix, 11, 19.

117. Senate Small Business Committee, Subcommittee on Retailing, *Studies of Dual Distribution: The Automotive Tire Industry*, 88th Cong., 2d sess., 1964, Committee Print 1, pp. 13–27 [quote on p. 17].

118. French, *U.S. Tire Industry*, 113; Michael French, "Manufacturing and Marketing: Vertical Integration in the U.S. Tire Manufacturing Industry, 1890–1980s," *Business and Economic History*, 2d ser., vol. 18 (1989): 181. Between 1964 and 1987, the market share of the oil companies plummeted from 23 percent to 2 percent.

119. Robert L. Faith, Donald R. Leavens, and Robert D. Tollison, "Antitrust Pork Barrel," chap. 2 in *Public Choice and Regulation: A View from Inside the Federal Trade Commission*, ed. Robert J. MacKay, James Miller III, and Bruce Yandle (Stanford, Calif.: Hoover Institution Press, 1987), 15–29.

120. Wilson, "The Politics of Regulation," 386, 371.

121. Rowe, *Price Discrimination*, 539-40.

122. H. Thomas Austern, quoted in Parkany, "Federal Trade Commission Enforcement," 284. Economists have conducted few empirical studies of the act's effect on the position of small business. One study found that during the late 1930s the act may have contributed to the grocery chains' loss of market share but that it had little or no effect on other chain stores (Thomas W. Ross, "Winners and Losers Under the Robinson-Patman Act," *Journal of Law and Economics* 27 [October 1984]: 270-71).

123. Bork, *The Antitrust Paradox*, 10.

Chapter Three

1. Susan Strasser, *Satisfaction Guaranteed: The Making of the Mass Market* (New York: Pantheon Books, 1989), 83-84, 269-77.

2. Ibid. Between 1915 and 1917, manufacturers cited these considerations in a series of hearings held by Congress and the Federal Trade Commission; see Andrew N. Kleit, *Efficiencies without Economists: The Early Years of Resale Price Maintenance* (Washington: Federal Trade Commission Bureau of Economics, 1992), 28.

3. Louis W. Stern and Thomas L. Eovaldi, *Legal Aspects of Marketing Strategy: Antitrust and Consumer Protection Issues* (Englewood Cliffs, N.J.: Prentice-Hall, 1984), 327; Robert H. Bork, *The Antitrust Paradox: A Policy at War with Itself* (New York: Free Press, 1978, 1993), 33.

4. William H. Voelker, "Rise and Fall of 'Fair-Trade' Laws" (M.P.A. thesis, University of New Orleans, 1985), 17. By the time of *Dr. Miles* the Supreme Court had become influenced by neoclassical economic theory, which emphasized consumer welfare and was hostile toward price restraints; see Herbert Hovenkamp, *Enterprise and American Law, 1836-1937* (Cambridge: Harvard University Press, 1991), 341-43.

5. Strasser, *Satisfaction Guaranteed*, 282; Louis D. Brandeis, "On Maintaining Makers' Prices," *The Curse of Bigness* (New York, Viking, 1934), 125, 128; Brandeis (1915 article) quoted in *The Brandeis Guide to the Modern World*, ed. Alfred Lief (Boston: Little, Brown and Company, 1941), 219 [quote]; Brandeis (1912 article), in Lief, *The Brandeis Guide*, 219-20 [quote].

6. U.S. Federal Trade Commission (hereafter cited as FTC], *Report of the Federal Trade Commission on Resale Price Maintenance* (Washington: GPO, 1945), 45-46 [quote].

7. "Steps Taken by the Federal Government," in "Congress and the Chain Stores," *Congressional Digest* 9, no. 8-9 (August-September 1930): 196-97; Arthur Capper, speech before the American Fair Trade League, 4 April 1933, in Robert J. Bulkley, "The Fair Trade Movement," *Congressional Record* (14 April 1938), vol. 83, pt. 10, 1513 [quote]; Tony Freyer, *Regulating Big Business: Antitrust in Great Britain and America, 1880-1980* (Cambridge: Cambridge University Press, 1992), 166.

8. FTC, *Report on Resale Price Maintenance, General Economic and Legal Aspects*, pt. 1, 70th Cong., 2d sess., H. Doc. 546 (Washington: GPO, 1929), 11, 36, 62, 78; FTC, *Report on Resale Price Maintenance, Commercial Aspects and Tendencies*, pt. 2 (Washington: GPO,

1931), 157, 165, 170; U.S. National Recovery Administration, *Resale Price Maintenance Legislation in the United States*, by Harry S. Kantor with appendices by Anne Golden, Work Material No. 16 (November 1935), 4.

9. See, for example, Ellis W. Hawley, "Herbert Hoover, The Commerce Secretariat, and the Vision of an 'Associative State,'" *Journal of American History* 61 (June 1974): 116–40, and Kim McQuaid, "Corporate Liberalism in the American Business Community, 1920–1940," *Business History Review* 52 (Autumn 1978): 342–68.

10. Joseph Cornwall Palamountain Jr., *The Politics of Distribution* (Cambridge: Harvard University Press, 1955), 90, 94–100.

11. Brian Balogh discusses the political and organizational advantages of professionalism in "Reorganizing the Organizational Synthesis: Federal Professional Relations in Modern America," *Studies in American Political Development* 5 (Spring 1991): 119–72. For a brief survey of the literature on the growth of professional organizations, see Louis Galambos, "Technology, Political Economy, and Professionalization: Central Themes of the Organizational Synthesis," *Business History Review* 57 (1983): 486–90.

12. Palamountain, *Politics*, 235–41, 95, 103; Ellis W. Hawley, *The New Deal and the Problem of Monopoly: A Study in Economic Ambivalence* (Princeton: Princeton University Press, 1966), 256, 259; Voelker, "Rise and Fall," 5–6; Earl W. Kintner, ed., *The Legislative History of the Federal Antitrust Laws and Related Statutes*, pt. 1 (The Antitrust Laws) (New York: Chelsea House Publishers, 1978), 1:534; David B. Truman, *The Governmental Process: Political Interests and Public Opinion*, 2d ed. (New York: Knopf, 1971), 338; American Fair Trade Council, *Resale Price Maintenance by Means of Fair Trade Laws in Force April 1, 1942* (New York: The American Fair Trade Council, 1942), 7; Stanley C. Hollander, "The Effects of Industrialization on Small Retailing in the United States in the Twentieth Century," chap. 9 in *Small Business in American Life*, ed. Stuart W. Bruchey (New York: Columbia University Press, 1980), 228.

13. U.S. National Recovery Administration, Division of Review, *Restriction of Retail Price Cutting with Emphasis on the Drug Industry*, by Mark Merrell, E. T. Grether, and Summer S. Kittelle, Work Materials No. 57 (March 1936), 149.

14. Stephen J. Sniegoski, "The Darrow Board and the Downfall of the NRA," *Continuity* 14 (Spring/Fall 1990): 63, 68–69, 80; Hawley, *New Deal*, 124; Donald R. Brand, "Peripheral Businesses: The Disaffected Constituency," chap. 6 in *Corporatism and the Rule of Law: A Study of the National Recovery Administration* (Ithaca: Cornell University Press, 1988), 153–66. Surveys revealed that small manufacturers were more dissatisfied than small retailers with the NRA codes (Brand, *Corporatism*, 168n).

15. Hawley, *New Deal*, 188–89; Stanley C. Hollander, "United States of America," chap. 3 in *Resale Price Maintenance*, ed. B. S. Yamey (Chicago: Aldine Publishing, 1966), 68; Palamountain, *Politics*, 247–49.

16. Hawley, *New Deal*, 256–57.

17. "Steps Taken by the Federal Government," *Congressional Digest* 9, no. 8–9 (August–September 1930): 196–97; Millard E. Tydings, speech, 3 February 1938, in John E. Miller, "Fair-Trade Laws," *Congressional Record* (4 February 1938), vol. 83, pt. 9, 444.

18. Kintner, *Legislative History*, 462.

19. Millard E. Tydings, speech, 3 February 1938, in John E. Miller, "Fair-Trade Laws,"

Congressional Record (4 February 1938), vol. 83, pt. 9, 443; "Remarks of Rep. John E. Miller," 19 April 1937, in Kintner, *Legislative History*, 500–504.

20. Kintner, *Legislative History*, 462–63.

21. Palamountain, *Politics*, 243.

22. Nevin Emil Neal, "A Biography of Joseph T. Robinson" (Ph.D. diss., University of Oklahoma, 1958), 404–5.

23. Voelker, "Rise and Fall," 33.

24. "Report of the House Committee on the Judiciary," H. Rpt. 382, Minority Report [Emanuel Celler, Robert L. Ramsay], 11 March 1937, in Kintner, *Legislative History*, 483–89.

25. W. A. Ayres to Franklin D. Roosevelt, 14 April 1937, OF 277, folder "Antitrust Laws, January–April 1937," box 2, FDRPL; Hawley, *New Deal*, 257; Herbert Levy to Harry S. Truman, 12 December 1951, p. 2, folder "Fair Trade Laws—Correspondence, 1951–1955," box 38, Emanuel Celler Papers, Library of Congress (hereafter cited as Celler Papers); Holmes Alexander, "Millard E. Tydings: The Man from Maryland," chap. 6 in *The American Politician*, ed. J. T. Salter (Chapel Hill: University of North Carolina Press, 1938), 124 [quote]; Franklin D. Roosevelt to the President of the Senate, 24 April 1937, OF 277, folder "Antitrust Laws, January–April 1937," box 2, FDRPL; W. B. Bankhead to Franklin D. Roosevelt, 29 April 1937, PPF 4142, folder "William B. Bankhead," FDRPL. In November, the FTC authorized an investigation into the causes of inflation (FTC, resolution, 20 November 1937, OF 100, folder "F.T.C., 1937–1938," box 1, FDRPL).

26. "Senate Debate," 23 July 1937, in Kintner, *Legislative History*, 511; Emanuel Celler to Franklin D. Roosevelt, 6 August 1937, OF 277, folder "Antitrust Laws, August–December 1937," box 2, FDRPL; "Statement by President Franklin D. Roosevelt upon Signing H.R. 7472, August 18, 1937," in Kintner, *Legislative History*, 538.

27. "Costs of Price Fixing," *Business Week*, 16 October 1937, 55–56; American Fair Trade Council, *Resale Price Maintenance*, 2–4.

28. Estimates of the extent of fair trade varied from 4 to 20 percent of total retail sales. In 1941, the TNEC estimated that fair trade accounted for 15 percent of retail trade (Hilda Chiarulli Smith, "Resale Price Maintenance, 1940–1950" [Ph.D. diss., Syracuse University, 1955], 37).

29. U.S. Congress, Temporary National Economic Committee (hereafter cited as TNEC), *Problems of Small Business*, Monograph No. 17, by John R. Cover et al. (Washington: GPO, 1941), 164.

30. Smith, "Resale Price Maintenance," 38–39. For a list of the percentage of manufacturers engaged in fair trade by industry, see John Simon De Leeuw, "Fair Trade Developments, 1951–1961" (Ph.D. diss., University of Oklahoma, 1962), 26–27.

31. "Price Fixing Doesn't Stop Cutter," *Business Week*, 27 November 1937, 18–20; TNEC, *Problems of Small Business*, 201. For a discussion of how these problems plagued fair traders in the tire industry, see W. C. Behoteguy, "Resale Price Maintenance in the Tire Industry," *Journal of Marketing* 13 (January 1949): 315–20.

32. TNEC, *Problems of Small Business*, 201.

33. Edgar H. Gault, *Fair Trade with Especial Reference to Cut-Rate Drug Prices in Michigan*, Michigan Business Studies, vol. 9, no. 2 (Ann Arbor: University of Michigan,

1939), 41; FTC, *Report of the Federal Trade Commission on Resale Price Maintenance* (Washington: GPO, 1945), xxix–xxx; Smith, "Resale Price Maintenance," 184.

34. "FTC Will Probe 'Fair Trade,' " *Business Week*, 13 May 1939, 17.

35. FTC, *Report of the Federal Trade Commission on Resale Price Maintenance*, 1; Gilbert H. Montague, "The Fair Trade (Mess?)," *Business Management*, 15 March 1941, 33–34; "Fire at 'Fair Trade,' " *Business Week*, 25 March 1939, 26, 28.

36. Thurman W. Arnold, *The Bottlenecks of Business* (New York: Reynal & Hitchcock, 1940), 47 [quote].

37. TNEC, *Problems of Small Business*, 196, 195, 203; TNEC, *Final Report and Recommendations of the Temporary National Economic Committee* (Washington: GPO, 1941), 33.

38. Smith, "Resale Price Maintenance," 81; FTC, *Resale Price Maintenance: Summary and Conclusion* (Washington: GPO, 1945), lxiv.

39. Memorandum to Mr. Celler, 22 March 1949, bound minutes for subcommittee on antitrust, p. 1 [quote], box 53, Celler Papers; C. Murray Bernhardt, memorandum to Mr. Celler, 23 March 1949, p. 3 [quote], ibid.; "Summary Report of the Conference Relative to an Anti-Trust Inquiry on March 23, 1949," ibid.

40. Robert Lester Branyan, "Antimonopoly Activities during the Truman Administration" (Ph.D. diss., University of Oklahoma, 1961), 126–32.

41. De Leeuw, "Fair Trade Developments," 104, 112; Voelker, "Rise and Fall," 41 [quote].

42. Smith, "Resale Price Maintenance," 61.

43. Kintner, *Legislative History*, 540 [quote]; Smith, "Resale Price Maintenance," 60.

44. Smith, "Resale Price Maintenance," 188.

45. "Remarks of Rep. John A. McGuire," 17 October 1951, in Kintner, *Legislative History*, 562 [quote]; Richard Eric Johnson, "The McGuire Act and Its Effect on Resale Price Maintenance" (M.S. thesis, University of Pittsburgh, 1961), 16–17. In June and July, supporters and opponents of fair trade introduced several bills to legalize or outlaw retail price maintenance, but Congress recessed before considering their legislation (Johnson, "The McGuire Act," 16).

46. Smith, "Resale Price Maintenance," 63; Johnson, "The McGuire Act," 20.

47. U.S. Congress, House, Committee on the Judiciary, *Amending the Sherman Act with Respect to Resale Price Maintenance*, Minority Report [Celler, Jonas, Bakewell], 82d Cong., 2d sess., 13 March 1952, H. Rpt. 1516, 19–33.

48. U.S. Congress, House, Small Business Committee (hereafter cited as House Small Business Committee), *Fair Trade: The Problem and the Issues*, 82d Cong., 2d sess., 4 February 1952, H. Rpt. 1292, 1, 10, 14, 22–23; Johnson, "The McGuire Act," 20. The National Association of Retail Grocers (NARG), the United States Wholesale Grocers Association (USWGA), the National Retail Jewelers, and the Meat Dealers Protective Association spoke out in favor of fair trade. Groups opposed to this legislation included the American Farm Bureau Federation, the AFL and CIO, the National Housewives League, and Consumers Research, Inc.

49. *Congressional Record* (7 May 1952), vol. 98, 4898–4912.

50. John A. McGuire, *Congressional Record* (7 May 1952), vol. 98, 4901; John Dargavel [executive secretary, NARD], testimony, U.S. Congress, House, Committee on Interstate

and Foreign Commerce, Subcommittee on Federal Trade Commission, *Minimum Resale Prices*, hearings, 82d Cong., 2d sess., 4 February 1952, 9 [quote]; Allan Oakley Hunter, *Congressional Record* (7 May 1952), vol. 98, 4918; Carl T. Durham, ibid., 4923–24; Eugene J. McCarthy, ibid., 4925; Kintner, *Legislative History*, 552.

51. Kintner, *Legislative History*, 552.

52. Hubert H. Humphrey, *Congressional Record* (1 July 1952), vol. 98, 8822, 8741.

53. Kintner, *Legislative History*, 553.

54. Emanuel Celler to Harry S. Truman, 3 July 1952, Official File, folder "327 McGuire Bill," box 1013, Harry S. Truman Presidential Library, Independence, Missouri (hereafter cited as HSTPL).

55. Charles Sawyer [secretary of commerce] to Robert Crosser [chairman, House Committee on Interstate and Foreign Commerce], 2 February 1952, in Kintner, *Legislative History*, 574; James Mead [chairman, Federal Trade Commission] to Robert Crosser, in Kintner, *Legislative History*, 576; John Blair [economist, FTC], testimony, Senate Committee on Interstate and Foreign Commerce, *Resale Price Fixing*, hearings, 82d Cong., 2d sess., 2 June 1952, 36; H. Graham Morison [assistant attorney general, Antitrust Division of the Justice Department], testimony, House Committee on the Judiciary, *Study of Monopoly Power: Resale Price Maintenance*, hearings, 82d Cong., 2d sess., 13 February, 1952, 25; Leon H. Keyserling, John D. Clark, and Roy Blough [members, Council of Economic Advisers] to Harry S. Truman, 8 July 1952, Official File, folder "327 McGuire Bill," box 1012, HSTPL.

56. Harry S. Truman, press release, 14 July 1952, Official File, folder "H.R. 5767," box 1012, HSTPL.

57. Hollander, "United States," 80.

58. Voelker, "Rise and Fall," 34.

59. Ibid.

60. Godfrey M. Lebhar, *Chain Stores in America, 1859–1962*, 3d ed. (New York: Chain Store Publishing Corporation, 1963), 352–61.

61. Stewart M. Lee, *Consumers Look at Discount Houses* (Greeley, Colo.: Council on Consumer Information, 1958), 2.

62. "Fair Trade: The War's Not Over," *Business Week*, 7 November 1953, 43–44; U.S. Congress, Senate, Small Business Committee (hereafter cited as Senate Small Business Committee), Weekly Staff Report, 27 November 1954 and 31 December 1955, in Senate Committee Records, box 32, RG 46, NA; Hollander, "United States," 82.

63. Smith, "Resale Price Maintenance," 78; House Small Business Committee, *Sixth Annual Report*, 12 January 1956, 84th Cong., 2d sess., H. Rpt. 1368, 85.

64. De Leeuw, "Fair Trade Developments," 233.

65. "Fair Trade Faces Showdown," *Nation's Business*, March 1955, 37.

66. Theodore Philip Kovaleff, *Business and Government during the Eisenhower Administration: A Study of the Antitrust Policy of the Antitrust Division of the Justice Department* (Athens: Ohio University Press, 1980), 24–27; "FTC Won't Help Fair Traders," *Business Week*, 26 February 1955, 46 [quote].

67. Voelker, "Rise and Fall," 25.

68. De Leeuw, "Fair Trade Developments," 162–63.

69. Lebhar, *Chain Stores in America*, 116.

70. Johnson, "The McGuire Act," 71, 80; Thomas A. Rothwell [executive director, Marketing Policy Institute], statement in House Committee on the Judiciary, Subcommittee on Monopolies and Commercial Law, *Fair Trade*, hearings on H.R. 2384, 94th Cong., 1st sess., 25 March 1975, 28.

71. Senate Small Business Committee, Subcommittee on Retailing, Distribution, and Fair Trade Practices, *Fair Trade*, 84th Cong., 2d sess., 27 July 1956, S. Rpt. 2819, 8–22. Another survey reported similar results; see Opinion Research Corporation, *Dealers in Hot Competition: A Report of the Public Opinion Index for Industry* (Princeton, N.J.: Opinion Research Corporation, 1957), A-32–33.

72. Stewart Munro Lee, "Problems of Resale Price Maintenance," *Journal of Marketing* 23 (January 1959): 275; Senate Small Business Committee, Weekly Staff Report, 1 March 1958, box 32, RG 46, NA.

73. Senate Small Business Committee, Weekly Staff Report, 24 May 1958, box 32, RG 46, NA; Lebhar, *Chain Stores in America*, 116; Johnson, "The McGuire Act," 86.

74. In 1969, the Council of Economic Advisers estimated that fair trade cost consumers $1.5 billion per year. Later estimates placed the cost at between $2 billion and $6 billion. Lewis A. Engman [chairman, Federal Trade Commission], House Judiciary Committee, *Fair Trade*, hearings, 25 March 1975, 7; Voelker, "Rise and Fall," 8.

75. Voelker, "Rise and Fall," 8, 52.

76. Kintner, *Legislative History*, 939–40; House Committee on Judiciary, *Fair Trade*, hearings, 25 March 1975, 14–15; "Remarks of Sen. Edward W. Brooke Introducing S. 4203," 3 December 1974, in Kintner, *Legislative History*, 948; "White House Press Release, January 29, 1975," in Kintner, *Legislative History*, 953; Voelker, "Rise and Fall," 8, 51 [quote].

77. Thomas R. Overstreet Jr. and Alan A. Fisher, "Resale Price Maintenance and Distributional Efficiency: Some Lessons from the Past," *Contemporary Policy Issues* 3 (Spring 1985): 43.

78. Terry Calvani and James Langenfeld, "An Overview of the Current Debate on Resale Price Maintenance," *Contemporary Policy Issues* 3 (Spring 1985): 2–3; Stern and Eovaldi, *Legal Aspects of Marketing Strategy*, 326 [Posner quote]; Bork, *The Antitrust Paradox*, 288–98 [quote on 288].

One recent study found little evidence of collusion among those firms practicing retail price maintenance, but the author notes that there is an "empirical vacuum" in this area of research and that more work needs to be done to settle this question (Pauline M. Ippolito, "Resale Price Maintenance: Empirical Evidence from Litigation," *Journal of Law and Economics* 34 [October 1991]: 263–94).

79. Stern and Eovaldi, *Legal Aspects of Marketing Strategy*, 329; Voelker, "Rise and Fall," 53–58; Kleit, *Efficiencies without Economists*, 1.

80. Kleit, *Efficiencies without Economists*, 6. Mary E. Allender contends that manufacturers did not resort to the "free rider" argument until the 1980s. However, the legislative history of the Consumer Goods Pricing Act clearly states that "opponents were primarily service-oriented manufacturers who claimed retailers would not give adequate service unless they were guaranteed a good margin of profit." See Allender, "Why Did Manufacturers Want Fair Trade?," *Essays in Economic and Business History*,

ed. Edwin J. Perkins (Los Angeles: Economic and Business Historical Society, 1993), 11:218–30; and Kleit, *Efficiencies without Economists*, 58–59.

81. Calvani and Langenfeld, "An Overview," 4–6; B. S. Yamey, "Introduction: The Main Economic Issues," *Resale Price Maintenance*, ed. B. S. Yamey (Chicago: Aldine Publishing, 1966), 13–14.

82. A. L. Nassau, *Retailing*, 25 January 1937, 10–11.

83. Senate Small Business Committee, Weekly Staff Report, 29 August 1953, box 323, RG 46, NA.

84. In 1954, nearly two-thirds of all large manufacturers (defined as those with over $25 million in annual sales) engaged in fair trade, compared to only 1.4 percent of small manufacturers (those with annual sales under $1 million) (De Leeuw, "Fair Trade," 32).

85. "Report of the House Committee on the Judiciary," H. Rpt. 382, Minority Report [Celler, Robert L. Ramsay], 11 March 1937, in Kintner, *Legislative History*, 491.

86. House Committee on Interstate and Foreign Commerce, *Fair Trade, 1959*, hearings on H.R. 1253 and H.R. 768, 86th Cong., 1st sess., 18 March 1959, 222.

Chapter Four

1. C. Dale Vinyard, "Congressional Committees on Small Business" (Ph.D. diss., University of Wisconsin, 1964), 92–93; Daniel Bell, *The End of Ideology: On the Exhaustion of Political Ideas in the Fifties* (New York: Collier Books, 1960), 115; Carl Ryant, "The South and the Movement against Chain Stores," *Journal of Southern History* 39 (May 1973): 219.

2. "Does 'Small Business' Get a Fair Shake?," *Fortune*, October 1953, 164; Sumner Marcus, "The Small Business Act of 1953: A Case Study of the Development of Public Policy Affecting Business" (D.B.A. diss., University of Washington, 1958), 220.

3. Vinyard, "Congressional Committees," 102 [quote]. Many of these congressmen also sat on the Banking and Currency Committees and viewed the Small Business Committees as de facto subcommittees (ibid., 239).

4. Robert W. Coren et al., *Guide to the Records of the United States Senate at the National Archives, 1789–1989*, Bicentennial edition (Washington: U.S. National Archives and Records Administration, 1989), 218.

5. U.S. Congress, Senate, Small Business Committee, *History of the Small Business Committee in the United States Senate*, by V. A. Votaw, chap. 4, p. 9, and conclusion, p. 3 [quote], in Senate Committee Records, folder "History—Senate Small Business Committee," box 42, RG 46, NA. Others have also noted how the Small Business Committees served as "complaint bureaus." See, for example, Harvey C. Mansfield, "The Congress and Economic Policy," chap. 6 in *The Congress and America's Future*, ed. David B. Truman, 2d ed. (Englewood Cliffs, N.J.: Prentice-Hall, 1973), 174.

6. William B. Pickett, *Homer E. Capehart: A Senator's Life, 1897–1979* (Indianapolis: Indiana Historical Society, 1990), ix–x; Donald J. Mrozek, "Organizing Small Business during World War II: The Experience of the Kansas City Region," *Missouri Historical Review* 71 (1977): 180–81.

7. House Small Business Committee, *Monopolistic and Unfair Trade Practices: Problems of Small Business Resulting from Monopolistic and Unfair Trade Practices*, hearings, 80th Cong., 2d sess., 11 September 1948, 132.

8. Hubert H. Humphrey, *The Education of a Public Man: My Life and Politics*, ed. Norman Shorman (Garden City, N.Y.: Doubleday, 1976), 158–59.

9. The following biographical analysis was based on an examination of biographies, autobiographies, *Current Biography*, *Dictionary of American Biography*, *National Cyclopedia of American Biography*, *The Biographical Directory of Congress*, and *Political Profiles* (New York: Facts on File, 1976, 1978, 1980).

10. Vinyard described the committees as "personal vehicles" of the chairmen ("Congressional Committees," 107–8). The Senate Small Business Committee did not meet very often because of the difficulty in achieving a quorum for even its subcommittee work (Senate Small Business Committee, "Hearing on Eighth Annual Report," executive session, 28 January 1958, folder "Executive Meeting—January 28, 1958," box 9, RG 46, NA).

11. Janet Louis Schmelzer, "The Early Life and Early Congressional Career of Wright Patman, 1894–1941" (Ph.D. diss., Texas Christian University, 1978), 65 [quote], 10–11, 38, 54 [quote]; Vinyard, "Congressional Committees," 91 [quote], 109 [quote]; Ryant, "The South," 219; Jordan A. Schwarz, *The New Dealers: Power Politics in the Age of Roosevelt* (New York: Knopf, 1993), chap. 13 ("Wright Patman: The Last Brandeisian").

12. Pickett, *Homer E. Capehart*, 101 [quote]; Charles L. Fontenay, *Estes Kefauver: A Biography* (Knoxville: University of Tennessee Press, 1980), 112; Henry James Walker Jr., "A Political History of a Public Man: John Sparkman of Alabama" (M.A. thesis, University of Alabama, 1990), 3 [quote], 20. For biographical studies of Kefauver see Charles L. Fontenay, *Estes Kefauver: A Biography* (Knoxville: University of Tennessee Press, 1980); James B. Gardner, "Political Leadership in a Period of Transition: Frank G. Clement, Albert Gore, Estes Kefauver, and Tennessee Politics, 1948–1956" (Ph.D. diss., Vanderbilt University, 1978); Joseph Bruce Gorman, *Kefauver: A Political Biography* (New York: Oxford University Press, 1971); Estes Kefauver, *In a Few Hands: Monopoly Power in America* (New York: Pantheon Books, 1960).

13. *Current Biography*, 1945 ed., s.v. "Murray, James E." [quote]; Donald E. Spritzer, "New Dealer from Montana: The Senate Career of James E. Murray" (Ph.D. diss., University of Montana, 1980), 3–5; Donald E. Spritzer, *Senator James E. Murray and the Limits of Post-War Liberalism* (New York: Garland, 1985), 69, 81.

14. Ellis W. Hawley, *The New Deal and the Problem of Monopoly: A Study in Economic Ambivalence* (Princeton: Princeton University Press, 1966), 187–204, chap. 10 ("The Concept of Counterorganization"); Spritzer, "New Dealer," 5 [quote]. Small business advocates often cited the successful organization of farmers as a model for small business people; see, for example, Edward Thye, interviewed by Ed Edwin, 7 July 1967, Columbia Oral History Project, OH 22, p. 29 (copy at EPL).

15. James T. Patterson, *Mr. Republican: A Biography of Robert A. Taft* (Boston: Houghton Mifflin, 1972), 147, 191; Russell Kirk and James McClellan, *The Political Principles of Robert A. Taft*, A Project of the Robert A. Taft Institute of Government (New York: Fleet Press, 1967), 136.

16. Thomas C. McCraw, in *Prophets of Regulation* (Cambridge: Belknap Press of Harvard University Press, 1984), chap. 3 ("Brandeis and the Origins of the FTC").

17. Robert A. Taft, "The Sherman Antitrust Act," *National Independent*, March 1943, folder "Small Business—Automobiles, Tires, 1943–44," box 796, Robert A. Taft Papers, Library of Congress.

18. Robert A. Taft to Frank M. Folsom [president, Radio Corporation of America], folder "Small Business, 1951," box 1064, Robert A. Taft Papers.

19. Robert A. Taft, address before the Boston City Club, 14 January 1944, p. 4, folder "Small Business, 1944," box 795, Robert A. Taft Papers.

20. Ibid., 4–5; Charles L. Schultze, *The Public Use of Private Interest* (Washington: Brookings Institution, 1977).

21. Frank Alan Coombs, "Joseph Christopher O'Mahoney: The New Deal Years" (Ph.D. diss., University of Illinois, 1968), 217–19; Terry Gene Roice, "The Economic Philosophy of Senator Joseph C. O'Mahoney and the Concept of Federal Incorporation" (Ph.D. diss., University of Wyoming, 1971), 46–47, 509 [quote].

22. Emanuel Celler, *You Never Leave Brooklyn: The Autobiography of Emanuel Celler* (New York: J. Day Company, 1953), 144.

23. Emanuel Celler, "How a Congressman Views the Chain Stores," *Chain Store Review* (October 1929): 14.

24. Ibid., 62–63.

25. Thomas Sowell, *A Conflict of Visions: Ideological Origins of Political Struggles* (New York: Quill, 1987).

Chapter Five

1. Joseph O'Mahoney, "Save Little Business," NBC radio address (November 1941), quoted in Frank Alan Coombs, "Joseph Christopher O'Mahoney: The New Deal Years" (Ph.D. diss., University of Illinois, 1968), 385.

2. Nathaniel H. Engle [Commerce Department official], "Future of the Small Business Man" [November 1938 article], in *Chain Stores and Legislation*, ed. Daniel Bloomfield (New York: H. W. Wilson, 1939), 162.

3. Ellis W. Hawley, *The New Deal and the Problem of Monopoly: A Study in Economic Ambivalence* (Princeton: Princeton University Press, 1966), 348 [quote].

4. In 1935, Wright Patman urged the president to call a conference of small business associations in Washington, but the president's secretary, Marvin McIntyre, did not "think the movement sponsored by Patman would work very well," and the administration did not act on the suggestion (Wright Patman to Marvin H. McIntyre [assistant secretary to the president], 30 November 1935, and Marvin H. McIntyre to Franklin D. Roosevelt, 13 December 1935, both in OF 288, folder "Chain Stores, 1935–1936," box 1, FDRPL). For a colorful account of the boisterous proceedings of the 1938 conference, see John H. Bunzel, *The American Small Businessman* (New York: Knopf, 1962), 3–9.

5. Fred Roth et al. [Small Business Review Committee] to Franklin D. Roosevelt, 4 February 1938, OF 172A, folder "Small Business: January–February 1938," box 7, FDRPL.

Other groups at the conference issued separate but similar resolutions; see Edith Nourse Rogers, "Recommendations of Small-Business Men," *Congressional Record* (4 February 1938), vol. 83, pt. 9, 451.

6. Daniel C. Roper to Franklin D. Roosevelt, 24 February 1938, OF 172A, folder "Small Business: January–February 1938," box 7, FDRPL; Small Business Review Committee, *Final Report*, 19 March 1938, in ibid.

7. White (R.-Ohio), *Congressional Record* (2 February 1938), vol. 83, pt. 2, 1428–31, 1797–98; Robert Bacon (R.-N.Y.), "Small-Business Men Score New Deal and Its Work; Ask Tax Relief and Economy," *Congressional Record* (4 February 1938), vol. 83, pt. 9, 448.

8. Charles G. Daughters, *Relationship of Small Business and Democracy*, confidential report, 27 December 1942, section 4, p. 11, folder 62, box 11, JPS; Hawley, *New Deal*, 397; Bunzel, *The American Small Businessman*, 3–8; Roger S. Pepper, "Pressure Groups among 'Small Business Men' " (M.A. thesis, 1940; rpt. New York: Arno Press, 1979), 83–85 [quote]; U.S. Commerce Department, Bureau of Foreign and Domestic Commerce, *390 Bills: A Digest of Proposals Considered in Congress on Behalf of Small Business, 1933–1942*, by Burt W. Roper (Washington: GPO, 1943), 21.

9. Daughters, *Relationship*, section 4, "The Small Business Movement" [quote]; Charles G. Daughters, *Wells of Discontent: A Study of the Economic, Social, and Political Aspects of the Chain Store*, introduction by Wright Patman, John F. Dockweiler, and Gerald J. Boileau (New York: C. G. Daughters, 1937).

10. Franklin Delano Roosevelt, message to Congress, 29 April 1938, in U.S. Senate, TNEC, *Final Report and Recommendations of the Temporary National Economic Committee*, 76th Cong., 3d sess., transmitted to the Congress pursuant to Public Resolution No. 113 (Washington: GPO, 1941), 11–20; Hawley, *New Deal*, 488.

11. See TNEC, *Bureaucracy and Trusteeship in Large Corporations*, Monograph No. 11, by Marshall Dimock and Howard K. Hyde (Washington: GPO, 1940), 17–18, 67; TNEC, *Competition and Monopoly in American Industry*, Monograph No. 21, by Clair Wilcox (Washington: GPO, 1941), 315; TNEC, *Economic Power and Political Pressures*, Monograph No. 26, by Donald C. Blaisdell (Washington: GPO, 1941), 52, 187; TNEC, *Relative Efficiency of Large, Medium-Sized, and Small Business*, Monograph No. 13 (Washington: GPO, 1941), 12–14.

12. TNEC, *Problems of Small Business*, Monograph No. 17, by John R. Cover et al. (Washington: GPO, 1941), 176–79, 188, 202 [quote].

13. TNEC, *Final Report*, 24, 33, 31; TNEC, *Final Report of the Executive Secretary* (Washington: GPO, 1941), 302–8, 310 [quote]. Small business advocates often cited the TNEC studies; see Paul Lowry Brown, "The Economics of Small Business Enterprise" (Ph.D. diss., Ohio State University, 1944); Rudolph L. Weissman, *Small Business and Venture Capital: An Economic Program* (New York: Harper, 1945). For a critical study of the TNEC sponsored by the National Association of Manufacturers, see John Watson Scoville, comp., *Fact and Fancy in the T.N.E.C. Monographs: Reviews of the 43 Monographs Issued by the Temporary National Economic Committee*, Series "The Right Wing Individualist Tradition in America" (1942; rpt. New York: Arno Press, 1972).

14. Memorandum for Miss Barrows, 24 July 1940, OF 172, box 6, FDRPL.

15. Emery, an Akron printer, established the NSBMA in 1938 as an association in favor of "less and less regulatory legislation" (Daughters, *Relationship*, section 4).

16. A. J. Sabath, press release, 10 July 1940, in Daughters, *Relationship*, section 9, "Creation of the Senate Small Business Committee"; Charles G. Daughters to James E. Murray, 26 July 1940, *Relationship*, section 10; Donald E. Spritzer, *Senator James E. Murray and the Limits of Post-War Liberalism* (New York: Garland, 1985), 69−70; James E. Murray to Charles G. Daughters, 1 August 1940, in Daughters, *Relationship*, section 10.

17. James E. Murray to Alben Barkley, 1 October 1940, in Daughters, *Relationship*; Senate Small Business Committee, *History of the Small Business Committee in the United States Senate*, by V. A. Votaw, in Senate Committee Records, folder "History— Senate Small Business Committee," 4 [quote], box 42, RG 46, NA; C. Dale Vinyard, "Congressional Committees on Small Business" (Ph.D. diss., University of Wisconsin, 1964), 83−84, 90. Daughters became the chief assistant to Murray (Spritzer, *Senator James E. Murray*, 70).

18. Vinyard, "Congressional Committees," 85; Anonymous, Memorandum, Records of the Democratic National Committee, folder "Small Business," box 1174, FDRPL. Congress created a number of investigating committees before and during the war. In 1944, the Senate had twenty special committees, while the House of Representatives had thirty-one (Vinyard, "Congressional Committees," 86−87).

19. Harold G. Vatter, *The U.S. Economy in World War II* (New York: Columbia University Press, 1985), 57−59; John Morton Blum, *V Was for Victory: Politics and American Culture during World War II* (New York: Harcourt Brace Jovanovich, 1976), 134−35.

20. Donald Nelson, *Arsenal of Democracy: The Story of American War Production* (New York: Harcourt, Brace and Company, 1946), 178; "Small Businessmen are Confused Says Davis," *Commercial and Financial Chronicle*, 8 October 1942, 1268; Stuart Bruchey, *Enterprise: The Dynamic Economy of a Free People* (Cambridge: Harvard University Press, 1990), 476 [Somervell quote]; R. Elberton Smith, "The Army and Small Business," chap. 18 in *United States Army in World War II: The War Department: The Army and Economic Mobilization* (Washington: Office of the Chief of Military History, Department of the Army, 1959), 414.

21. Jim Heath, "American War Mobilization and the Use of Small Manufacturers, 1939−43," *Business History Review* 46 (Autumn 1972): 297−301; Floyd B. Odlum, "The Small Business Problem as Viewed by the O.P.M.," testimony before the Truman Committee, 21 and 27 October 1941, *Congressional Digest* 21 (February 1942): 50−58; Vatter, *U.S. Economy*, 58.

22. "Concerning Priorities and the Utilization of Existing Manufacturing Facilities," 17 November 1941 report, in "The Truman Committee Reports on Small Business," *Congressional Digest* 21 (February 1942): 43−47.

23. C. C. Fichtner, testimony, Senate Small Business Committee, 18 December 1941, in "The Department of Commerce Reports on Small Business," *Congressional Digest* (February 1942): 41−42; "New Unit to Aid Small Business," *Domestic Commerce*, 8 January 1942, 6; Harmon Zeigler, *The Politics of Small Business* (Washington: Public Affairs Press, 1961), 91−92.

24. *Congressional Digest* (February 1942): 39.

25. "Pending Measures for Relief of Small Business," *Congressional Digest* 21 (February 1942): 39−40; Senate Small Business Committee, *Small Business and Defense*, 77th

Cong., 1st sess., 20 September 1941, Committee Print 6. For other proposals to aid small business, see "Interim Recommendations of the Tolan Committee," Select House Committee Investigating National Defense Migration, 19 December 1941 report, *Congressional Digest* 21 (February 1942): 49; "Recommendations of the National Association of Manufacturers," *Congressional Digest* 21 (February 1942): 63–64; "Reed Urges Govt. to Aid Small Business," *Commercial and Financial Chronicle*, 2 July 1942, 25; Pierce Williams, "W.P.A. Official Makes Recommendations for Aid to Small Business," testimony before Truman Committee, 22 July 1941, *Congressional Digest* 21 (February 1942): 58–62.

26. James E. Murray, hearings, Senate Committee on Banking and Currency, Subcommittee on Small Business, *Small Business and the War Program*, hearings, pt. 1, 77th Cong., 1st Sess., 15 December 1941, 2–3; Murray, radio address, in "The Murray Committee's Approach to the Small Business Problem," *Congressional Digest* 21 (February 1942): 47–49; Vatter, *U.S. Economy*, 59. Murray's committee commissioned a study of the decline of small business in Germany; see Senate Small Business Committee, *The Fate of Small Business in Nazi Germany*, by A. R. L. Gurlan, Otto Kirchheimer, and Franz Neumann (Washington: GPO, 1943). German small business advocates also sought special privileges; see Emile Grunberg, "The Mobilization of Capacity and Resources of Small-Scale Enterprises in Germany," *Journal of Business* 14 (October 1941): 319–44; 15 (1942): 56–89.

27. TNEC, *Final Report*, 3; James Murray, "Conversion of Small Business Enterprises to War Production," *Congressional Record* (24 February 1942), vol. 88, pt. 8, A703–5. Donald J. Mrozek analyzes the wartime difficulties of midwestern small businesses in his "Organizing Small Business during World War II: The Experience of the Kansas City Region," *Missouri Historical Review* 71 (1977): 174–92.

28. The Small Business Act (P.L. 603; S. 2250): "An Act to mobilize the productive facilities of small business . . .," in Robert Wood Johnson, *"But, General Johnson": Episodes in a War Effort* (Princeton: Princeton University Press, 1944), 153–58; James E. Murray [quoting February 1942 report], House Committee on Banking and Currency, *Conversion of Small Business Enterprises to War Production*, hearings on S. 2250 and H.R. 6975, 77th Cong., 2d sess., 27 April 1942, 1–8; Murray, "Mobilization of Small Business for War Production," *Congressional Record* (31 March 1942), vol. 88, pt. 3, 3223; James E. Murray to Franklin D. Roosevelt, 23 March 1942, OF 4735f, folder "War Production Board, SWPC, 1942," box 4, FDRPL. Some small businessmen rejected Murray's gloomy prognosis; see Winthrop L. Carter, "Small Business *Can* Survive the War and Be Stronger Than Ever," *Printer's Ink*, 20 February 1942, 11–13.

29. Robert A. Taft, Senate Committee on Banking and Currency, *Conversion of Small Business Enterprises*, hearings on S. 2250, 77th Cong., 2d sess., 11 March 1942, 268.

30. Jesse Jones, ibid., 272–73; Senate Small Business Committee, Press Release, 20 March 1942, War Production Board Records, WPB 38.14, RG 179, NA; "Senate Approves Aid for Small Mfg. Plants," *Commercial and Financial Chronicle*, 9 April 1942, 1448; C. W. Fowler, "The Legislative Origins of the Smaller War Plants Corporation," in *Histories of the Smaller War Plants Corporation*, pp. 97–100, SWPC 71, box 1, RG 240, NA. As executive secretary of the Senate Small Business Committee, Fowler helped draft this legislation ("Biographical Sketches," SWPC 61, box 1, RG 240, NA).

31. "Promotion of Small Business," *Congressional Record* (25 May 1942), vol. 88, pt. 4,

4506–26; James E. Murray, testimony, House Banking and Currency Committee, *Conversion of Small Business*, hearings, 28 April 1942, 21; Hughes, *Conversion of Small Business*, 11 March 1942, 273.

32. Fowler, "Legislative Origins," 102–6.

33. Murray, House Banking and Currency Committee, *Conversion of Small Business*, 28 April 1942, 17; James M. Mead, ibid., 28 April 1942, 48; James E. Murray to Franklin D. Roosevelt, 2 July 1942, OF 4735f, folder "WPB, SWPC, 1942" [quote], box 4, FDRPL. Earlier, Murray admitted that "$100,000,000 will not go very far" but that nevertheless, he considered the SWPC an important "experiment" that offered hope of positive aid for small manufacturers (James E. Murray, "Mobilization of Small Business for War Production," *Congressional Record* [31 March 1942], vol. 88, pt. 3, 3270).

34. 1st Bimonthly Report of the War Production Board, 11 August 1942, 77th Cong., 2d sess., S. Doc. 244, 2–3. See also Donald Nelson, testimony, House Committee on Banking and Currency, *Conversion of Small Business*, 29 April 1942, 53–58; Nelson, *Arsenal*, 279 [quote].

35. WPB, *2d Bimonthly Report*, 11 October 1942, 77th Cong., 2d sess., S. Doc. 274, 1, 3–4; C. W. Fowler to Charles A. Murray, 22 October 1942, SWPC 34, box 1, RG 240, NA; Fowler, "Legislative Origins," 129–39.

36. James W. Leyerzapf, "The Public Life of Lou E. Holland" (Ph.D. diss., University of Missouri at Columbia, 1972), 111–13; "Little Man's Pal," *Business Week*, 10 October 1942, 20.

37. Leyerzapf, "The Public Life of Lou E. Holland," 127–28.

38. "Little Man's Pal," *Business Week*, 10 October 1942, 20–22. Murray highlighted his small business legislation in campaign literature; see "The Press of the Nation on Small Business—Editorial Comment Favorable," SWPC 34, box 1, RG 240, NA.

39. Patman, "Progress Report on Helping Small Manufacturers and Producers under Murray-Patman Act," *Congressional Record* (24 November 1942), vol. 88, pt. 10, A4074. See also Reid F. Murray (R.-Wis.), "Small Plants Getting Jobs Daily," *Congressional Record* (23 November 1942), vol. 88, pt. 10, A4053.

40. Murray, Senate Small Business Committee, *Problems of American Small Business*, hearings, pt. 10, 77th Cong., 2d sess., 13 October 1942, 1047; Murray, radio address, 29 September 1942, "The Preservation of Small Business in the War Emergency," *Congressional Record* (1 October 1942), vol. 88, pt. 10, A3487; Emanuel Celler, Senate Small Business Committee, *Problems of American Small Business*, 14 October 1942, 1128. See also Perry C. Magnus to William S. Shipley [SWPC director], inserted by Representative William T. Pheiffer (R.-N.Y.), "Idle Manpower and Idle Plants in New York City," *Congressional Record* (20 August 1942), vol. 88, pt. 5, 6914.

41. Leyerzapf, "The Public Life of Lou E. Holland," 123–24.

42. Patman, "A Preliminary Report of the Committee on Small Business of the House to the Speaker," *Congressional Record* (16 December 1942), vol. 88, pt. 10, A4438; Murray, Senate Small Business Committee, *Problems of American Small Business*, hearings, pt. 12, 15 December 1942, 1642; Patman, ibid., 1610, 1684; Wright Patman to Lou Holland, transcript of telephone conversation, 26 December 1942, SWPC 63, box 140, RG 240, NA.

43. Holland, testimony, Senate Small Business Committee, *Problems of American*

Small Business, 15 December 1942, 1641–51; Corrie Cloyes, "Small Business Specialists Give Senate Committee Manufacturers' Side of Wartime Picture," *Domestic Commerce*, 29 October 1942, 3–6.

44. Wright Patman to Senator Alben W. Barkley, 18 February 1943, swpc 26, box 12, RG 240, NA.

45. Wright Patman to Franklin D. Roosevelt, 16 December 1942, OF 4735f, folder "War Production Board, Smaller War Plants Corporation, 1942," box 4, FDRPL.

46. "Small Business Committee," *Congressional Record* (22 January 1943), vol. 89, pt. 1, 314.

47. Franklin D. Roosevelt to James F. Byrnes, 18 December 1942, OF 4735f, folder "WPB, SWPC, 1942," box 4, FDRPL; James F. Byrnes to Franklin D. Roosevelt, 14 January 1943, OF 4735f, folder "WPB, SWPC, January–June 1943," box 4, FDRPL.

48. Wright Patman to Donald Nelson, 12 January 1943, Records of the War Production Board, WPB 38.17C, RG 179, NA; Johnson, *"But, General,"* 28; James E. Murray to Franklin D. Roosevelt, OF 4735f, folder "War Production Board, SWPC, 1942," box 4, FDRPL; Johnson, *"But, General,"* 26 [quote]. The board of directors elected Johnson chairman on 18 February 1943 (swpc Board of Directors, minutes, swpc 1, box 1, RG 240, NA).

49. Patman, "Small Business Continues to Get Run-Around and Brush-Off by Smaller War Plants Corporation," *Congressional Record* (25 January 1943), vol. 89, pt. 9, A305; James E. Murray, "Has Small Business a Future?: What Do We Mean by Preserving Small Business?," address before Smaller Business Council of America, Cleveland, Ohio, 26 March 1943, *Vital Speeches*, 15 May 1943, 475.

50. Harry S. Truman, "Monopolistic Tendencies of the War Production Board—Aid for Small Business," *Congressional Record* (11 February 1943), vol. 89, pt. 1, 843, 851 [quote]; Leyerzapf, "The Public Life of Lou E. Holland," 130 [quote].

51. swpc, *7th Bimonthly Report*, 78th Cong., 1st sess., S. Doc. 98, 2; Johnson, *"But, General,"* 32–33; swpc, *8th Bimonthly Report*, 78th Cong., 1st sess., S. Doc. 134, 2–3. The reorganization was not altogether successful. The Detroit board of governors resigned in protest of continued interference from Washington ("Small Business' New Problem," *Business Week*, 16 October 1943, 15–17).

52. Donald M. Nelson to Johnson, 12 March 1943, WPB 38.14C, RG 179, NA.

53. Donald D. Davis [WPB operations vice chairman] to Colonel Robert Johnson, 8 April 1943, swpc 71, box 9, RG 240, NA; Johnson, *"But, General,"* 46, 51–52. According to an agency official, the swpc received the "less desirable" employees from other agencies, leading Johnson to view his staff as incompetent. Needless to say, Johnson's low opinion of swpc personnel did little to boost morale (C. W. Fowler, "History of the Administrative Policies of the Smaller War Plants Corporation," *Histories of the Smaller War Plants Corporation*, 150–54).

54. Robert Wood Johnson, address before the Economic Club of Detroit, 19 April 1943, "The Role of Big Business in Saving Small Business," *Congressional Record* (5 May 1943), vol. 89, pt. 10, A2190; Robert Wood Johnson, interview with A. N. Weckster, "Small Business Must Survive!," *Purchasing*, March 1943, 8; Johnson, *"But, General,"* 34–35; swpc, *8th Bimonthly Report*, 78th Cong., 1st sess., S. Doc. 134, 2; Robert Wood Johnson, WPB Minutes, 27 April 1943 (Historical Reports on War Administration, Doc.

Publ. 4), pp. 218–19, RG 179, NA; SWPC press release, 21 June 1943, SWPC 32, box 2, RG 240, NA; Walter Chamblin Jr. [executive director, NAM] to Colonel Robert Johnson, 13 April 1943, SWPC 26, box 11, RG 240, NA; Colonel R. W. Johnson to Board of Directors, 14 April 1943, SWPC 71, box 9, RG 240, NA; Robert Wood Johnson, *Spreading the Work: The Salvation of American Industry* (Washington: GPO, 1943), 3.

55. James E. Murray to General Robert W. Johnson, 19 July 1943, SWPC 26, box 11, RG 240, NA.

56. Murray, "Has Small Business a Future?," 473–77 [quote]; Senate Small Business Committee, *Small Business in War and Essential Civilian Production*, 78th Cong., 1st sess., 11 March 1943, S. Rpt. 12, pt. 2.

57. Johnson to James E. Murray, 30 August 1943, SWPC 26, box 11, RG 240, NA; Johnson to Murray, 26 August 1943, ibid.; Robert Wood Johnson to Murray, 25 September 1943, ibid. [quote]; Johnson, *"But, General,"* 71. The cumulative value of contracts secured with SWPC assistance increased from $87 million to $900 million (SWPC, *22d Bimonthly Report*, 37).

58. "True Facts about Business Failures—Effect of War on Small Business," *Congressional Record* (18 October 1943), vol. 89, pt. 12, A4346; Clay J. Anderson, "War Casualties in Manufacturing" [from *Domestic Commerce*, 25 March 1943], in Commerce Department, Bureau of Foreign and Domestic Commerce, Small Business Unit, *Small Business—A National Asset*, Economic Series no. 24, July 1943, 12, 11 [quote]. See also "How Small Business Is Faring in 1943," *Domestic Commerce*, November 1943, 12–20.

59. The smallest companies experienced a decline in sales, yet 59 percent of these firms described their business as "more favorable" than it had been before the war. The drop in sales for the smallest firms may have resulted from the conscription of small business owners or the lure of better opportunities in wage work. Thus, although the *average* sales figure declined, perhaps the surviving firms fared better (Office of War Information, Bureau of Special Services, Surveys Division, Memorandum No. 52, 17 May 1943, *Smaller Manufacturing Plants and Wartime Production, Part I: A Digest of the Findings*, SWPC 71, pp. 12, 22, 25, box 2, RG 240, NA; Howard R. Bowen, "Impact of the War upon Smaller Manufacturing Plants," *Survey of Current Business*, July 1943, 20–21; *Executives' Defense Digest*, 1 August 1943, excerpt, SWPC 32, box 12, RG 240, NA).

An army survey of small plants in New York City found that only 2.5 percent were "distressed" (Smith, "The Army and Small Business," 423).

60. "Johnson Resigns as Small Plants Head," *Commercial and Financial Chronicle*, 28 October 1943, 1714; Johnson, *"But, General,"* 76. Murray urged Johnson to adopt "a very liberal attitude toward financing of mining ventures," and by the end of the war, Murray's committee had interceded hundreds of times on behalf of various mining operations (Robert Wood Johnson to James E. Murray, 26 January 1943, SWPC 63, box 125, RG 240, NA; Senate Small Business Committee, *Senate Small Business Committee— Its Record and Outlook*, 79th Cong., 1st sess., 12 February 1945, S. Rpt. 47, 21).

61. Johnson, *"But, General,"* 74–76, 58, 55 [quote]; Johnson, "What Business Needs," *Saturday Evening Post*, 15 July 1944, 20 [quote].

62. Dan W. Eastwood [staff director, House Small Business Committee] to James Van Tassel [staff director, Senate Small Business Committee], 26 February 1944, SWPC 50, box 1, RG 240, NA.

63. "Maury Maverick," *Current Biography* (1944).

64. Maury Maverick, House Small Business Committee, *Financial Problems of Small Business*, hearings, pt. 2, 79th Cong., 1st sess., 23 May 1945, 1006.

65. "New WPB Position Given to Maverick: Ex-Congressmen Slated to Head Smaller War Plants Corporation," *New York Times*, 9 January 1944, 3; SWPC, *10th Bimonthly Report* (December 1943–January 1944), 78th Cong., 2d sess., S. Doc. 178, vol. 1; SWPC, *15th Bimonthly Report* (October–November 1944), 78th Cong., 2d sess., 3–4; "Maverick, Maury," *DAB* [quotes].

66. SWPC, *11th Bimonthly Report* (February–March 1944), vi, 3–21, 30, 9. For an analysis of the SWPC's organizational structure, see W. Darlington Denit, "The Area Administrative Offices of the Smaller War Plants Corporation," *Public Administration Review*, Winter 1946, 25–29.

67. SWPC, *10th Bimonthly Report*, v–vi; Maverick, "How Shall We Reconvert: Small Business Must Get the Breaks," *Saturday Evening Post*, 16 September 1944, 14, 44; Vatter, *U.S. Economy*, 60, 64; Blum, *V Was for Victory*, 129; "War Leaders Testify at Length: Fight to Aid Small Business Faces Test," *Iron Age*, 4 May 1944, 106–8. For a discussion of the reconversion debate, see Jack W. Peltason, "The Reconversion Controversy," *Public Administration and Policy Development: A Case Book*, ed. Harold Stein (New York: Harcourt, 1952), 215–83.

68. U.S. Commerce Department, Bureau of Foreign and Domestic Commerce, *187 Bills: A Digest of Proposals Considered in Congress on Behalf of Small Business, 1943–1944*, by Burt W. Roper (Washington: GPO, 1946), 96–100, 106–13. The Small Business Committees sponsored the Surplus Property Act (House Small Business Committee, *The Surplus Property Problem from the Viewpoint of Small Business*, 78th Cong., 2d sess., 9 March 1944, H. Rpt. 1245; Senate Small Business Committee, *Problems of Surplus Property Disposal*, Preliminary Report, 78th Cong., 2d sess., 21 July 1944, Senate Subcommittee Print 1).

69. SWPC, *13th Bimonthly Report* (June–July 1944), 78th Cong., 2d sess., S. Doc. 234, 3; SWPC, *17th Bimonthly Report* (February–March 1945), 78th Cong., 2d sess., 10; Maverick to James E. Murray, 15 November 1944, SWPC 63, box 125, RG 240, NA; Hawley, *New Deal*, 320. See also Hyo Won Cho, "The Evolution of the Functions of the Reconstruction Finance Corporation: A Study of the Growth and Death of a Federal Lending Agency" (Ph.D. diss., Ohio State University, 1953), 41–45; TNEC, *Problems of Small Business*, monograph No. 17, by John R. Cover et al. (Washington: GPO, 1941), 236–43; U.S. Commerce Department, Bureau of Foreign and Domestic Commerce, *Government Financial Aids to Small Business*, by Burt W. Roper (Washington: Department of Commerce, 1945), vii, 10–12.

70. A. D. H. Kaplan, *Small Business: Its Place and Problems* (New York: McGraw, 1948), 149. See also Theodore H. Smith, "Small Retailer Credit Sources," *Law and Contemporary Problems* 11, no. 1 (Summer–Autumn 1945): 274–80.

71. SWPC, *16th Bimonthly Report* (December 1944–January 1945), 78th Cong., 2d sess., 17.

72. SWPC, *16th Bimonthly Report*, ii; *14th Bimonthly Report* (August–September 1944), 78th Cong., 2d sess., S. Doc. 246, iii.

73. Wright Patman, "Accomplishments of Committee on Small Business of the

House," *Congressional Record* (9 January 1945), vol. 91, pt. 10, A74. As early as October 1943, Secretary of Commerce Henry A. Wallace had noted the role small business could play in achieving full employment after the war ("We Must Save Free Enterprise," *Saturday Evening Post*, 23 October 1943, 12).

In 1945, the Bureau of Labor Statistics predicted that employment would increase in sectors of the economy dominated by small business (e.g., construction, trade, services); SWPC, *18th Bimonthly Report* (April–May, 1945), 2–4. Economists were divided in their forecasts of postwar conditions, with some expecting a return to prewar conditions and others predicting full employment and a sharp increase in exports; see Julius Hirsch, "Fact and Fantasies Concerning Full Employment," *American Economic Review*, vol. 34, no. 1, supplement, pt. 2 (March 1944): 118–27; "Discussion," ibid., 128–33; and Theodore N. Beckman, "Large versus Small Business after the War," ibid., 94–106. See also Michael Sapir, "Review of Economic Forecasts for the Transition Period," *Studies in Income and Wealth* 11 (1949): 275–351.

74. Senate Small Business Committee, *Senate Small Business Committee—Its Record*, 6, 18; Maverick, *Report on France: A Descriptive and Factual Statement*, 2 April 1945, SWPC 71, box 11, RG 240, NA; Maverick, *Report on Trip to England* [report to the board of directors and staff], SWPC 71, box 11, RG 240, NA; Maury Maverick, speech before Subcommittee on Foreign Trade of the Senate Small Business Committee, 21 May 1945, in John M. Blair, "Small Business after the War," *Histories of the Smaller War Plant Corporation*, Exhibit 1, 4–5; "American Technological Assistance Will Be Offered Friendly Nations," *Steel*, 26 March 1945, 68.

Maverick's trips abroad came under fire from SWPC director S. Abbot Smith, who resigned in February 1945, complaining that Maverick had completely ignored the day-to-day management of the agency ("Dissension in Ranks of Smaller War Plants Corp. Top Management," *Steel*, 5 March 1945, 101–2).

75. For an excellent discussion of the Commerce Department's relationship with small manufacturers, see William H. Becker, *The Dynamics of Business-Government Relations: Industry and Exports, 1893–1921* (Chicago: University of Chicago, 1982).

76. SWPC, *13th Bimonthly Report*, 4 [quote]; Maverick to Jesse Robison, 29 April 1944, SWPC 12, box 2, RG 240, NA.

77. In July 1943 Johnson asked C. W. Fowler to "develop a flow of commendatory comment" from small firms. These letters were sent to the Small Business Committees in a bound volume entitled *500 Letters Illustrating the Nature of the Services Performed by the Smaller War Plants Corporation* (Robert Wood Johnson to James E. Murray, 25 September 1943, SWPC 26, box 12, RG 240, NA). Fowler also provided the committees with a list of eight thousand beneficiaries of SWPC aid. Many congressmen wrote to these firms and received "negative and critical" comments on the performance of the SWPC (C. W. Fowler to Maury Maverick, memorandum, 24 February 1944, SWPC 33, box 1, RG 240, NA).

78. Eininger [vice president, Powhatan Brass and Iron] to C. W. Fowler, 15 January 1944; G. H. Garrett [general manager, Thompson Pipe and Steel] to C. W. Fowler, 30 November 1943; N. C. English [Carolina Underwear] to C. W. Fowler, 29 November 1943, all in SWPC 33, box 1, RG 240, NA.

79. SWPC, *14th Bimonthly Report*, 24; E. H. Little to Alfred C. Fuller [chair, Manufac-

turing Committee of the Connecticut War Council], 15 June 1944, SWPC 77, box 1, RG 240, NA; SWPC, *Industry Opinion on Proposed Science Legislation* [survey made by the Smaller War Plants Corporation for the Subcommittee on War Mobilization of the Senate Committee on Military Affairs], 18 October 1945 (Washington: GPO, 1945).

An earlier study of small manufacturing firms in New Jersey found them more optimistic about their postwar prospects than big business (Johnson, *"But, General,"* 133). A Commerce Department survey of small retailers revealed that they were also opposed to direct government aid (William T. Hicks and Walter F. Crowder, "Small Retail Store Births and Deaths," in Commerce Department, Bureau of Foreign and Domestic Commerce, Small Business Unit, *Small Business—A National Asset*, Economic Series no. 24 [July 1943]: 27).

80. Jesse Robison to Maury Maverick, 1 March 1944, SWPC 12, box 2, RG 240, NA; H. P. Warhurst to J. Russell Boner, preliminary report, 27 January 1944; Carl E. Bolte, report on Conference of American Small Business Organizations, 11 February 1944; Shelby C. Davis to Ray H. Haun [American Business Congress], 6 March 1944; H. Paulman to Victor Fabian [report on Little Businessman's League of America], 28 February 1944; Lloyd K. Moody to Granville B. Fuller [report on Smaller Business Association of New England], 7 March 1944; R. G. Brown, report on National Small Businessmen's Association, 11 February 1944, SWPC 77, box 1, RG 240, NA. A National Federation of Small Manufacturers was formed in 1940, but it was apparently defunct by 1944 ("Small Manufacturers Federation Formed," *Oil, Paint and Drug Reporter*, 8 January 1940). The SWPC had a file on all small business associations (Lou E. Holland to Fred M. Wilson, 29 September 1942, SWPC 63, box 46, RG 240, NA).

81. "Bids Women Turn to Small Business," *New York Times*, 12 August 1944, 8; "First Woman on Board of Governors of SWPC," *New York Times*, 28 February 1945, 17.

82. SWPC, *16th Bimonthly Report*, 6–9; C. W. Fowler, "The Mature Program of the Smaller War Plants Corporation as Developed by Chairman Maury Maverick," *Histories of the Smaller War Plants Corporation*, 260; SWPC, *18th Bimonthly Report* (April–May 1945), 25–27; SWPC, *Smaller War Plants Corporation Will Help Veterans* (Washington: GPO, 1945), 1; SWPC, *19th Bimonthly Report* (June–July 1945), 22.

83. Ralph Coburn [SWPC district manager], testimony, House Small Business Committee, *Financial Problems of Small Business*, hearings, 19 April 1945, 79th Cong., 1st sess., pt. 1, 242–43; SWPC, *19th Bimonthly Report*, 10; Frank Gervasi, "Cradle of Free Enterprise," *Collier's*, 16 March 1946, 27; Stanley Lebergott, *The Americans: An Economic Record* (New York: Norton, 1984), 472.

84. House Committee on Banking and Currency, *To Increase the Capitalization of the Smaller War Plants Corporation by $200,000,000*, hearings on S. 2004, 78th Cong., 2d sess., 22 November 1944, 21–50; "Increase in Capital Stock of Smaller War Plants Corporation," *Congressional Record* (1 December 1944), vol. 90, pt. 7, 8689–8707; "Practices and Objectives of SWPC Sharply Questioned by Committee," *Steel*, 11 December 1944, 92–94; Roper, *187 Bills*, 100.

85. "Amendment of Smaller War Plants Act—Report of the Special Committee to Study Problems of American Small Business," *Congressional Record* (12 May 1944), vol. 90, pt. 4, 4370–75; House Committee on Banking and Currency, *Extending the Life of Smaller War Plants Corporation*, 79th Cong., 1st sess., 12 February 1945, S. Rpt. 45;

House Committee on Banking and Currency, *1945 Continuance of the Smaller War Plants Corporation*, hearings on H.R. 8, 79th Cong., 1st sess., 27 March 1945, 5; Roper, *187 Bills*, 15, 20; House Small Business Committee, *Financial Problems of Small Business*, hearings, pt. 2, 79th Cong., 1st sess., 23 April 1945, 1005, 1017 [Hall, Ploeser quotes]; "War Plants Corporation to Go On," *New York Times*, 28 April 1945, sec. III, 3.

86. Commerce officials emphasized the interdependence of big and small business, and during the war, they had created a "Big Brother" program whereby corporate executives offered advice to small business owners. See "Department Promotes 'Big Brother' Movement," *Domestic Commerce*, 3 September 1942, in *Small Business—A National Asset*, 29; "Help for Small Manufacturers," *Domestic Commerce*, February 1945, 12, 21; Jesse H. Jones, "Freedom of Enterprise for Small Business," in Roper, *390 Bills*, 2–3; Jesse H. Jones, "Nation's Need of Small Business Stressed by Commerce Secretary," *New York Times*, 28 March 1943, sec. III, 5; Senate Committee on Commerce, *Providing for an Assistant Secretary of Commerce for Small Business*, hearings on S. 356 and S. 883, 78th Cong., 1st sess., 27 May 1943, 22.

87. Maury Maverick to James E. Murray, 2 July 1945, SWPC 63, box 125, RG 240, NA [quote]; Maury Maverick to Wright Patman, 9 October 1945, SWPC 63, box 140, RG 240, NA.

88. Maverick to Harry S. Truman, 11 June 1945, SWPC 63, box 140, RG 240, NA; Maverick to Wright Patman, 9 October 1945, SWPC 63, box 140, RG 240, NA; SWPC, *Small Plants Speak for Themselves: A Special Report to the Small Business Committees of the Senate and House of Representatives* (4 October 1945), SWPC 71, box 11, RG 240, NA.

89. Richard B. Henderson, *Maury Maverick: A Political Biography* (Austin: University of Texas Press, 1970), 249–50.

90. Executive Order 9665 (27 December 1945), *Federal Register*, vol. 10, no. 252, 15365–67; Maverick to Charles B. Henderson [RFC chairman], 9 January 1946; Maverick to Harry S. Truman, memorandum, 8 January 1946, SWPC 63, box 64, RG 240, NA [quote].

The RFC received the bulk of the SWPC's assets ($177 million); see U.S. Treasury Department, *Final Report on the Reconstruction Finance Corporation*, Pursuant to Section 6(c) Reorganization Plan No. 1 of 1957 (Washington: GPO, 1959), 167.

91. SWPC, *22d Bimonthly Report*, 39, 37, 41, 9. The SWPC also left a literary legacy: Maury Maverick coined the term "gobbledygook" to describe the impenetrable jargon of agency officials; see *Current Biography*, 1945 ed., s.v. "Maverick, Maury."

92. SWPC, *Economic Concentration and World War II*, by John M. Blair, Harrison F. Houghton, and Matthew Rose (Washington: GPO, 1945), 29–33, 46–49, 54, 64, 314, 318; SWPC, *22d Bimonthly Report*, 19. David Mowery challenges the SWPC's assertion that small firms did not benefit from R&D spending; see Mowery, "Industrial Research and Firm Size, Survival and Growth in American Manufacturing, 1921–1946: An Assessment," *Journal of Economic History* 43 (December 1983): 977–80.

93. Vatter, *U.S. Economy*, 64–65; Louis Cain and George Neumann, "Planning for Peace: The Surplus Property Act of 1944," *Journal of Economic History* 41 (March 1981): 129–35.

94. F. C. Dirks, "Wartime Earnings of Small Business," *Federal Reserve Bulletin* 31 (January 1945): 16–26; Emerson P. Schmidt, "The Role and Problems of Small Busi-

ness," *Law and Contemporary Problems* 11, no. 1 (Summer–Autumn 1945): 205–19; "How Tough Is It for Small Business?," *Business Week*, 29 December 1951, 80–81; Vatter, "The Position of Small Business in the Structure of American Manufacturing, 1870–1970," in *Small Business in American Life*, ed. Stuart W. Bruchey (New York: Columbia University Press, 1980), 154–60; Vatter, *U.S. Economy*, 66; FTC, *Report on Wartime Costs and Profits for Manufacturing Corporations, 1941 to 1945* (Washington: GPO, 1947): 15; George J. Stigler, *Capital and Rates of Return in Manufacturing Industries* (Princeton: Princeton University Press, 1963), 67–68. Although the total number of small firms declined by 324,000 during the war, most of these losses occurred in the retail and service sectors of the economy. The small business population had become artificially inflated during the Great Depression as the nation saw unemployed "white collar men turn retailers." Moreover, the decline in the number of small firms did not mean that all of these companies failed. In September 1944, the Commerce Department reported a wartime shrinkage in the business population of 500,000, but 541,000 firms changed status (reorganized, sold out, etc.). See Bruchey, *Enterprise*, 476; Carl W. Dipman, "Mortality of Retail Stores," in *Chain Stores and Legislation*, ed. Daniel Bloomfield (New York: H. W. Wilson, 1939), 129 [quote]; "Vital Statistics of Small Business," *Banking*, September 1944, 130.

95. See, for example, David L. Birch, *Job Creation in America: How Our Smallest Companies Put the Most People to Work* (New York: Free Press, 1987), 6; Steven Solomon, *Small Business USA: The Role of Small Companies in Sparking America's Economic Transformation* (New York: Crown Publishers, 1986).

96. Thomas S. Dicke, "The Public Image of Small Business Portrayed in the American Periodical Press, 1900–1938" (M.A. thesis, Ohio State University, 1983); Charles Cortez Abbott, "Small Business: A Community Problem," *Harvard Business Review* 24 (1945): 191; Graham Hunter, "The Truth about the 'Squeeze' on Small Business," *Forbes*, 15 December 1948, 22; Rudolph Jones, "The Relative Position of Small Business in the American Economy since 1930" (1952 article), in *The Survival of Small Business*, ed. Vincent P. Carosso and Stuart Bruchey (New York: Arno Press, 1979), 34–35; Joseph Steindle, "Small and Big Business: Economic Problems of the Size of Firms" (1945 article), in ibid., 59–61; C. Hartley Grattan, "Small Business, I Love You," *Harper's Magazine*, February 1946, 145–50.

97. George J. Stigler, "Competition in the United States," in *Five Lectures on Economic Problems* (1949; rpt. Freeport, N.Y.: Books for Libraries, 1969), 53–54; G. Warren Nutter, *The Extent of Enterprise Monopoly in the United States, 1899–1939: A Quantitative Study of Some Aspects of Monopoly* (Chicago: University of Chicago, 1951), 44–48; M. A. Adelman, "The Measurement of Industrial Concentration," *Review of Economics and Statistics*, November 1951, 275–77; Jones, "The Relative Position of Small Business," 34–35; Soloman Fabricant, "Is Monopoly Increasing?," *Journal of Economic History* 13 (1953): 93; A. D. H. Kaplan, *Big Enterprise in a Competitive System* (Washington: Brookings Institution, 1954), 126–27; Edward S. Mason, "A Review of Recent Literature," in *Economic Concentration and the Monopoly Problem* (Cambridge: Harvard University Press, 1957), 28–31; Henry Einhorn, "Competition in American Industry, 1939–1958," *Journal of Political Economy* 74 (1966): 506–11.

The Commerce Department reported a decline in the market share of the largest two hundred manufacturers (as measured by sales, 1939–46); see Hunter, "The Truth," 22. In 1964, Morris Adelman reported that corporations with assets greater than $100 million experienced a decline in their share of manufacturing assets from 41.5 to 38.7 percent (1942–46). A study by the Federal Trade Commission (*Economic Report on Mergers*, 1969) revealed that the two hundred largest corporations' share of manufacturing assets declined from 45.1 to 45.0 percent (1941–47) (Cain and Neumann, "Planning for Peace," 132–33). Recent studies confirm a decline in aggregate concentration since the 1930s; see Yale Brozen, *Concentration, Mergers, and Public Policy* (New York: Macmillan, 1982), 26–27, 312; James D. Gwartney and Richard L. Stroup, *Economics: Private and Public Choice*, 5th ed. (New York: Harcourt, 1990), 546. Economist Arthur B. Laffer has also found no change in the level of vertical integration in American industry (Laffer, "Vertical Integration by Corporations, 1929–1965," *Review of Economics and Statistics* 51 [1969]: 91–93).

98. Between 1942 and 1945, personal consumption expenditures increased from $161 billion to $183 billion in constant (1958) dollars; U.S. Bureau of the Census, *Historical Statistics of the United States: Colonial Times to 1970*, pt. 2 (Washington: GPO, 1976), Series F47–70. Robert Higgs questions this data and argues that real personal consumption did not increase during the war. If accurate, his findings only underscore the need to further research the reasons for small manufacturers' satisfaction with the state of the wartime economy. See Robert Higgs, "Wartime Prosperity?: A Reassessment of the U.S. Economy in the 1940s," *Journal of Economic History* 52 (March 1992): 50–52.

99. See Ann Markusen and Joel Yudken, *Dismantling the Cold War Economy* (New York: Basic Books, 1992), for a discussion of the difficulties faced by firms attempting to convert to civilian production. In his study of Platt Brothers, a small Connecticut manufacturer, Matthew W. Roth found that this company fared better in reconversion than rival firms who became dependent on military orders (Roth, *Platt Brothers and Company: Small Business in American Manufacturing* [Hanover, N.H.: University Press of New England, 1994], 213).

100. Burton R. Fisher and Stephen B. Whithey, *Big Business as the People See It: A Study of a Socio-Economic Institution* (Ann Arbor: University of Michigan, 1951), xii, 57–58; Richard Hofstadter, "What Happened to the Antitrust Movement?: Notes on the Evolution of an American Creed," in *The Business Establishment*, ed. Earl F. Cheit (New York: John Wiley & Sons, 1964), 136–39. Historian Louis Galambos argues that Americans came to accept big business by 1940; see Louis Galambos, *The Public Image of Big Business in America, 1880–1940: A Quantitative Study in Social Change* (Baltimore: Johns Hopkins University Press, 1975).

101. David Eli Lilienthal, *Big Business: A New Era* (New York: Harper, 1953), 142–43, ix [quote], 204 [quote]. The historian Walter Prescott Webb underwent a similar change of heart; see Edward S. Shapiro, "Walter Prescott Webb and the Crisis of a Frontierless Democracy," *Continuity* 8 (1984): 43–61.

102. John Kenneth Galbraith, *American Capitalism: The Concept of Countervailing Power* (Boston: Houghton-Mifflin, 1952), 118, 146. Of course, opposition to big business did not entirely disappear. For a catalog of the criticisms directed at big business in this period, see David A. Glover, *The Attack on Big Business* (New York: Columbia University Press, 1954).

103. Peter F. Drucker, "How Big Is Too Big?," *Harper's Magazine*, July 1950, 23.

104. Zeigler, *Politics*, 98; Senate Committee on Banking and Currency, *Establishment of Permanent Small Business Finance Corporation*, hearings on S. 1320, 79th Cong., 2d sess., 25 July 1946, 5–14; Murray, "Federal Small Business Corporation," *Congressional Record* (25 July 1947), vol. 93, pt. 8, 10172; Senate Small Business Committee, *Future of Independent Business: Progress Report of the Chairman*, 79th Cong., 2d sess., 2 January 1947, Committee Print 16, pp. xiii–xiv; Charles A. Welsh, "The Murray Report on Small Business," *Industrial and Labor Relations Review* 1 (October 1947): 96; H.R. 6015 (Lane), *Congressional Record* (25 March 1948), vol. 94, pt. 3, 3574; H.R. 6250 (Rogers), *Congressional Record* (14 April 1948), vol. 94, pt. 4, 4474; H.R. 461 (Lane), *Congressional Record* (3 January 1949), vol. 95, pt. 1, 22. Patman criticized the Commerce Department for the "pitifully small" staff of its Office of Small Business (Patman to Albert W. Schindler [undersecretary of commerce], 20 February 1946, SWPC 50, box 1, RG 240, NA). Patman's committee urged the RFC and Commerce to take SWPC staff, but the two agencies refused to do so (House Small Business Committee, *Study and Investigation of the National Defense Program*, pt. 6 [22 January 1946], 1676, 1694).

105. C. J. Judkins, "Do Associations Represent the Small Business Firm?," *Domestic Commerce*, July 1946, 15–20.

106. John Henderson to Senator Burnet R. Maybank, 1 January 1950, box 44, folder "Small Business—General," RG 46 (Senate Banking and Currency Committee), NA. See also Andrew F. Schoeppel, *Congressional Record* (5 July 1950), vol. 96, pt. 16, A4914; National Federation of Independent Business (NFIB), *Attitudes of Independent Business Proprietors toward Antitrust Laws, 1943 to 1963* (San Mateo, Calif.: National Federation of Independent Business, 1963); Robert Lester Branyan, "Antimonopoly Activities during the Truman Administration" (Ph.D. diss., University of Oklahoma, 1961), 188; Bunzel, *The American Small Businessman*, 78.

107. Fred A. Virkus to Burnet R. Maybank, 27 June 1950, in Senate Committee Records, Banking and Currency Committee, Correspondence, 81A-F4, tray 152, folder "Small Business," RG 46, NA; Anonymous to Walter Cosgriff (RFC), 10 August 1950, in ibid.; Charles W. Vursell, "Problems of Government," *Congressional Record* (30 March 1950), vol. 96, pt. 14, 2382.

108. NFIB, *Attitudes*; National Federation of Independent Business, *An Achievement Report to Independent Business and Professional People of Anytown U.S.A. on Defense Activities*, Senate Small Business Committee, box 19, folder "Geo. J. Burger," RG 46, NA.

109. Zeigler, *Politics of Small Business*, 81–83; George Earl Green, "The Small Business Administration: A Study in Public Policy and Organization" (Ph.D. diss., University of Colorado, 1965), 12; Spritzer, *Senator James E. Murray*, 91–92 [quote]; Votaw, *History of the Small Business Committee*, chap. 3, pp. 1–2, 6–7; Vinyard, "Congressional Committees," 96, 100; Alben Barkley, "Appointment of Members of the Senate Small Business Committee, April 10, 1950," excerpts from the *Congressional Record*, Records of the Senate Small Business Committee, box 2, folder "History—Senate Small Business Committee," RG 46, NA.

110. House Small Business Committee, *Small Business Organizations: Four Case Studies of Organizations Purporting to Represent Small Business*, H. Rpt. 1675, 81st Cong., 2d

sess., 21 February 1950; House Select Committee on Lobbying Activities, *Conference of American Small Business Organizations*, H. Rpt. 3232, 26 December 1950, 3, 22. Shortly before the House Small Business Committee released its report, the NSBMA filed a lawsuit charging the NFIB with libel for publishing material that called the NSBMA a "phoney" organization bankrolled by big business. In 1952, the NSBMA won ninety-nine cents in damages. See George Burger, "National Small Business Men's Association Gets 99¢ Verdict against National Federation of Independent Business in Federal District Court, March 18, 1952, Case Number 531–50," folder 49, box 27, JPS.

111. House Small Business Committee, *Final Report*, 81st Cong., 2d sess., 1 January 1951, H. Rpt. 3237, 108.

112. Bob Black to Jack Redding [DNC, director of public relations], 14 April 1950 [quote], Senate Select Committee on Small Business, box 19, folder "American Small Business," RG 46, NA; Robert I. Black to Theodore J. Kreps, 19 May 1950, in ibid.; "Washington Businessmen and Businesswomen Spearhead National Small Business Movement," Senate Small Business Committee, 1950, folder "American Small Business," box 19, RG 46, NA.

In 1946, a dissident member of the CASBO urged the Democrats to form a new "Administration supporting body" (Thomas F. Maloney to General Harry H. Vaughan, 1 May 1946, OF 172, folder "1946," box 648, HSTPL).

113. "Problems of Small Businesses," *Congressional Quarterly Almanac* (1950), 652; "Small Business: Big Bundle," *Business Week*, 13 May 1950, 24–25; "Truman's Death Knell for RFC," *Business Week*, 13 May 1950, 25; "President's Plan to Provide More Capital for Business," *U.S. News and World Report*, 12 May 1950, 54; Wright Patman, "Small Business," *Congressional Record* (11 May 1950), vol. 96, pt. 5, 6946; House Small Business Committee, *Final Report*, H. Rpt. 3237, 81st Cong., 2d sess., 1 January 1951, 7; Charles Sawyer, *Concerns of a Conservative Democrat* (Carbondale: Southern Illinois University Press, 1968), 192, 359n. For an analysis of Truman's plan, see Peter F. Drucker, "The Care and Feeding of Small Business," *Harper's Magazine*, August 1950, 74–79.

114. Robert Higgs, *Crisis and Leviathan: Critical Episodes in the Growth of American Government* (New York: Oxford University Press, 1987), 22.

115. Alan Brinkley, "The New Deal and the Idea of the State," in *The Rise and Fall of the New Deal Order, 1930–1980*, ed. Steve Fraser and Gary Gerstle (Princeton: Princeton University Press, 1989), 100–109; Higgs, *Crisis and Leviathan*, 196–236.

116. Theodore J. Lowi examines the dynamics of interest-group liberalism in *The End of Liberalism: The Second Republic of the United States*, 2d ed. (New York: Norton, 1979).

117. Hawley, *New Deal*, 189.

118. Heath, "American War Mobilization," 295; Blum, *V Was for Victory*, 128.

119. A. B. ZuTavern, "Red Tape Strangles Small Business," *American Business*, September 1944, 38–39; "NACM Locals Respond to Appeal for Assistance by SWPC," *Credit and Financial Management*, October 1943, 24; "What's Ahead for Small Business: How Government Can Help," *Modern Industry*, 15 April 1944, 145–48; National Conference of State University Schools of Business, comp., *Report on Problems and Attitudes of Small Business Executives: Result of a National Survey in Feb. 1945* (n.p.); Richard H. Keehn and Gene Smiley, "Small Business Reactions to World War II Government Controls," *Essays in Economic and Business History* 8 (1990): 303–16.

120. Between 1941 and 1946, the Senate Committee published forty-seven prints and fourteen reports and held 185 days of hearings (George Earl Green, "The Small Business Administration," 61).

121. Gabriel Kolko, *Roots of American Foreign Policy: An Analysis of Power and Purpose* (Boston: Beacon Press, 1969).

122. Berlie Loren Lunde, "The Role of Small Business in Defense Production with Special Reference to Air Force Contracts" (M.B.A. thesis, University of Pittsburgh, 1956): 12; "How Tough Is It for Small Business?," *Business Week*, 29 December 1951, 80–81; "Small Firms Aren't Losing Out," *Business Week*, 8 March 1952, 64–66; "Little Business Holds Its Own," *Business Week*, 16 June 1951, 144.

123. Zeigler, *Politics of Small Business*, 66.

124. Robert Collins, *The Business Response to Keynes, 1929–1964* (New York: Columbia University Press, 1981).

125. Richard Hamilton, "The Politics of Independent Business," in *Restraining Myths: Critical Studies of U.S. Social Structure and Politics* (New York: Sage Publications, 1975), 58.

Chapter Six

1. Thurman W. Arnold, *The Folklore of Capitalism* (New Haven: Yale University Press, 1937), 212.

2. House Small Business Committee, *Final Report*, 81st Cong., 2d sess., 1 January 1951, H. Rpt. 3237, 106.

3. Roderick L. Vawter, *Industrial Mobilization: The Relevant History* (Washington: National Defense University Press, 1983), 15–22; Allan R. Millett and Peter Maslowski, *For the Common Defense: A Military History of the United States of America* (New York: Free Press, 1984), 488–90; Joseph Z. Reday [lieutenant commander, U.S. Naval Reserve], "Industrial Mobilization in the U.S.," *U.S. Naval Institute Proceedings* (October 1953): 1065–75. For a more complete description of the Korean mobilization effort, see "Mobilization Plans for Industry," *Army Information Digest* 6, no. 2 (1951): 11–21.

4. Vawter, *Industrial Mobilization*; Peter F. Drucker, "This War Is Different," *Harper's Magazine*, November 1950, 19–27.

5. George L. Noble Jr. and Hugh G. Francis [army ordnance officials], "The Role of Small Business in Defense Mobilization Planning," *Federal Bar Journal* 13 (April–June 1953): 227–32.

6. "Small Business Defense Plants Act of 1950," *Congressional Record* (26 July 1950), vol. 96, pt. 8, 1163–65; Wright Patman, "Small Business Defense Plants Act of 1950," *Congressional Record* (28 August 1950), vol. 96, pt. 17, A6199–6200; Senate Small Business Committee, *Report*, 82d Cong., 1st sess., 15 January 1951, S. Rpt. 2:38.

7. John Sparkman, "Small Defense Plants Corporation," *Congressional Record* (17 January 1951), vol. 97, pt. 1, 357–58; Wright Patman, "Small Defense Plants Act Introduced," ibid., 410–16.

8. "Statement by Senator Lehman on Small Defense Plants" [statement of Sen.

Warren G. Magnuson, Harley M. Kilgore, Herbert H. Lehman, Hubert Humphrey, and John J. Sparkman], *Congressional Record* (28 June 1951), vol. 97, pt. 6, 7381.

9. Senate Small Business Committee, *Participation of Small Business in Military Procurement*, 82d Cong., 1st sess., 21 June 1951, S. Rpt. 469, 32.

10. Maury Maverick, testimony, House Small Business Committee, Subcommittee No. 1, *Problems of Small Business Relating to the National Emergency*, hearings, 82d Cong., 1st sess., 2 May 1951, 2052; House Small Business Committee, *Final Report*, 1 January 1951, 5.

11. Wright Patman, "Small Defense Plants Act Introduced," *Congressional Record* (17 January 1951), vol. 97, pt. 1, 413.

12. John Sparkman, " 'Let's Put More Plants to Work on Defense!,' " *Sales Management*, 1 June 1951, 88. See also Wright Patman, "Small Defense Plants Act of 1950," *Congressional Record* (28 August 1950), A6199–6200; Statement by Senator Sparkman and Representative Patman, "Small Defense Plants Corporation," *Congressional Record* (17 January 1951), vol. 97, pt. 1, 357; Maverick, testimony, House Small Business Committee, *Problems of Small Business*, hearings, 2 May 1951, 2056. Beginning in 1953, the military did make industrial decentralization part of its preparations for a possible nuclear attack (Vawter, *Industrial Mobilization*, 40–41).

13. Riehlman, *Congressional Record* (2 February 1951), vol. 97, pt. 1, 877–78; Charles A. Halleck, testimony before House Banking and Currency Committee, 8 June 1951, inserted in "Bipartisan Action Will Reactivate Small Defense Plants Corporation," *Congressional Record* (11 June 1951), vol. 97, pt. 13, A3443; Hubert Humphrey, "Utilization of Small Business Enterprises in National Defense Program," *Congressional Record* (12 March 1951), vol. 97, pt. 2, 2268.

14. Patman, "Small Business Defense Plants Act of 1950," *Congressional Record*, A6199–6200; House Small Business Committee, *Final Report*, 1 January 1951, 4; Senate Small Business Committee, *Report*, 15 January 1951, 82d Cong., 1st sess., 6; Howard D. Williams [president, SBANE], testimony, House Small Business Committee, *Problems of Small Business Related to the National Emergency*, 25 April 1951, 1739–40; Edward J. Thye, "Small Business Is Hit by Defense Rationing," *Congressional Record* (17 May 1951), vol. 97, pt. 12, A2822–23 [insertion of 13 May *New York Times* article by Joseph Loftus].

15. Charles Sawyer, *Concerns of a Conservative Democrat* (Carbondale: Southern Illinois University Press, 1968), 192, 225–26.

16. Richard E. Neustadt to Charles S. Murphy, 11 June 1951, in folder "Small Business," box 6, Files of David D. Lloyd, HSTPL. Patman's bill had 261 cosponsors, "the largest [group] ever to join in sponsoring a bill" (House Small Business Committee, *Progress Report*, 82d Cong., 1st sess., 7 January 1952, H. Rpt. 1228, 53).

17. Wright Patman, testimony, House Banking and Currency Committee, 8 June 1951, inserted in Abraham J. Multer, "Bipartisan Action Will Reactivate Small Defense Plants Corporation," *Congressional Record* (11 June 1951), vol. 97, pt. 13, A3442–43; John Sparkman, *Congressional Record* (28 June 1951), vol. 97, pt. 6, 7378–80; Patman, "Small Defense Plants Administration," *Congressional Record* (30 July 1951), vol. 97, pt. 15, 9153–55; Telford Taylor, transcript, "Meeting of Small Manufacturers [Washington, D.C., 20 January 1952]," pp. 27–29, folder "Hearings—Small Manufacturers Meeting,"

box 17, Small Defense Plants Administration Records, RG 309, NA; John Sparkman to
Burnet R. Maybank, Sen. 82A-F4, "Small Business," Banking and Cur-
rency Committee Correspondence, Senate Committee Records, RG 46, NA; Howard D.
Williams [quote] and Ralph R. West [Small Business of America], testimony, Senate
Banking and Currency Committee hearings, 10 July 1951, pp. 19, 37, Tray 113, Sen. 82A-
F4, Banking and Currency Committee Correspondence, RG 46, NA.

18. "Defense Production Act Amendments of 1951," *Congressional Quarterly Almanac*
(1951): 438-39.

19. Harry S. Truman to Frazier Reams, 26 September 1951, OF, folder "3174," box 1751,
HSTPL; "Defined—But Leaderless," *Business Week*, 15 September 1951, 24; Telford Taylor,
testimony, Senate Banking and Currency Committee, hearings on nomination of Tel-
ford Taylor, 9 October 1951, 13–14, Senate Committee Records, RG 46, NA; "Defense
Production Act Amendments of 1951," *Congressional Quarterly Almanac* (1951): 690;
New York Times, 10 December 1951, 12 [quote]; Telford Taylor, "All Business Needs
Small Business," *Purchasing*, March 1952, 70–72.

20. Harry S. Truman to Telford Taylor, 5 January 1952, in SDPA, *1st Quarterly Report*,
14 January 1952, 33.

21. Telford Taylor, press conference, 13 December 1951, folder "Speeches and Statements" [quote], box 12, RG 309, NA; SDPA, *7th Quarterly Report*, 31 August 1953, Reports
and Statistics 5, 31, box 28, RG 309, NA; Allan L. Willard [regional director, SDPA at
Seattle] to Harry E. Pontius [director, Office of Field Operations, SDPA], 21 July 1952
[quote], folder "House Small Business Committee," box 2, RG 309, NA.

22. House Small Business Committee, *Review of Small Business*, 82d Cong., 2d sess.,
H. Rpt. 2513, 4–5; SDPA, press release, 15 January 1953, folder "Small Business Committee," box 3, RG 309, NA.

23. John E. Horne to Edward J. Stewart [regional director, SDPA at Boston], 19
January 1953, folder "Federal Agencies—Air Corp," box 9, RG 309, NA.

24. "Delay in Establishment of Small Defense Plants Administration," *Congressional
Record* (17 September 1951), vol. 97, no. 9, 11467–68; "Small Business vs. The Pentagon,"
Business Week, 16 February 1952, 25; House Small Business Committee, *Progress Report*,
7 January 1952, 60 [quote].

25. Charles Sawyer to Frederick J. Lawton [director, Bureau of the Budget], 8 August
1951, folder "Commerce," box 9, RG 309, NA; William D. Carey to Arnold Miles, memorandum, 24 October 1951, ibid.; Charles Sawyer to Harry Truman, 17 December 1951,
ibid.; Sawyer, *Concerns of a Conservative Democrat*, 227; Casper H. Citron to Harry E.
Pontius, 25 September 1952, folder "Commerce," box 9, RG 309, NA.

26. *New York Times*, 8 March 1952, 19; "Fast Action Asked on Plants Agency," *New
York Times*, 12 March 1952, 44; *Business Week*, 5 April 1952, 22; "Booklet Revised on
Procurement," *New York Times*, 15 March 1952, 20; "Third Supplemental Appropriation
Bill, 1952," *Congressional Record* (12 March 1952), vol. 98, no. 2, 2187–98; Clare E.
Hoffman, "Small Business and Defense Orders," *Congressional Record* (5 March 1952),
vol. 98, no. 9, A1705–6.

27. SDPA, *2d Quarterly Report*, 15 April 1952, 3, 15–16.

28. Ibid., 7, 32–33; SDPA, *3d Quarterly Report*, 15 July 1952, 9; House Small Business
Committee, *Review of Small Business*, 161.

29. Senate Small Business Committee, *Military Procurement*, 82d Cong., 2d sess., 2 July 1952, S. Rpt. 2070, 15; "How the Air Force Aids Small Business," *Aviation Week*, 18 August 1952, 21–25; House Small Business Committee, *Review of Small Business*, 161; John M. Carmody [engineering consultant, SDPA] to William C. Brittian [Munitions Board, DOD], 12 September 1952, folder "Federal Agencies—Air Corp," box 9, RG 309, NA.

30. Telford Taylor, "Special Report on the SDPA and Its Future," 15 September 1952, folder "Speeches, Lectures and Statements," box 11, RG 309, NA; Telford Taylor, press conference, 16 September 1952, folder "Information 12—Speeches, Lectures and Statements," box 11, RG 309, NA; SDPA, *3d Quarterly Report*, 1. Horne had earlier worked as an administrative assistant to the chairman of the Senate Small Business Committee (SDPA, *Weekly Bulletin*, 15 September 1952).

31. H. Sanford Saari to Buskie [director of OLAM, RFC], 14 November 1952, Reconstruction Finance Corporation Records, folder "SDPA" [quote], box 48, RG 234, NA; G. F. Buskie to H. Sanford Saari [loan agency manager, RFC], 15 December 1952, ibid.; Charles H. Swisher [Office of Contract Procurement] to W. Campbell [chairman, Working Committee VI, DPA], 29 October 1952, box 2, RG 309, NA.

32. *Congressional Quarterly Almanac* (1952): 772; Representative Shephard J. Crumpacker (R.-Ind.), "The Effect of Controls on Small Business," *Congressional Record* (2 February 1951), vol. 97, no. 1, 896–97; Senator Hugh Butler, "Interference of Government in Private Business," *Congressional Record* (12 July 1951), vol. 97, no. 13, A4313. For a study of the Republican Party during the Korean War, see Ronald Caridi, *The Korean War and American Politics* (Philadelphia: University of Pennsylvania Press, 1968).

33. "Small Defense Plants Administration," *Congressional Record* (12 March 1953), vol. 98 no. 2, 2211–23 [quote on p. 2212].

34. "Truman's Death Knell for RFC," *Business Week*, 13 May 1950, 25 [quote]; Hyo Won Cho, "The Evolution of the Functions of the Reconstruction Finance Corporation: A Study of the Growth and Death of a Federal Lending Agency" (Ph.D. diss., Ohio State University, 1953), 173–83, 220–62, 270–76; Addison W. Parris, *The Small Business Administration* (New York: Frederick A. Praeger, 1968), 14 [Abels quote], 16–17 [Byrd quote].

35. "R.F.C.," 7 May 1951, in George H. Gallup, *The Gallup Poll: Public Opinion, 1935–1971*, 2 vols. (New York: Random House, 1972), 2:981.

36. George Humphrey to Sherman Adams, 28 February 1953 [quote], in folder "Reconstruction Finance Corporation, 1953," Central Files, box 228, EPL; George Humphrey to Sherman Adams, 2 March 1953, ibid.; "Humphrey, George M.," *Profiles: The Eisenhower Years*, ed. Eleanora W. Schoenebaum (New York: Facts on File, 1980): 295.

37. "Small Business Agency," *Congressional Record* (28 May 1953), vol. 99, pt. 11, A3042 [*New Orleans Picayune* article, 8 April 1953].

38. SDPA, *5th Quarterly Report*, 15 January 1953, folder "Reports and Statistics 5" [quote], box 28, RG 309, NA; Y. Brynildssen [acting administrator, SDPA], statement, Senate Banking and Currency Committee, hearings on S.753, 27 March 1953, folder "Small Business Committee," box 2, RG 309, NA; George Earl Green, "The Small Business Administration: A Study in Public Policy and Organization" (Ph.D. diss., University of Colorado, 1965), 11–12; CASBO, Fourteenth Annual Conference of Small Business

Organizations, Resolution on Small Business Problems, 24 March 1953, Sen. 83 A-F4, Banking and Currency Committee Correspondence, folder "Small Business," Tray "Silver Purchase Act to War Damage," RG 46, NA; "$$ for Small Business," *Congressional Quarterly Weekly Report*, 11 September 1953, 1143–47; J. M. Carmody to Brynildssen, 6 April 1953, folder "Meetings," box 17, RG 309, NA; Harmon Zeigler, *The Politics of Small Business* (Washington: Public Affairs Press, 1961), 106.

The Smaller Manufacturers Council in Pittsburgh nearly split apart over this issue (SDPA, *6th Quarterly Report*, 15 April 1953, folder "Reports and Statistics 5," box 28, RG 309, NA).

39. SDPA, *Weekly Bulletin*, 23 February 1953; SDPA, *Weekly Bulletin*, 9 March 1953; Zeigler, *Politics of Small Business*, 105; Cho, "Evolution," 272.

40. Senate Small Business Committee, *History of the Small Business Committee in the United States Senate*, by V. A. Votaw, chap. 5, pp. 16–17, in folder "History—Senate Small Business Committee," box 42, RG 46, NA.

41. Sinclair Weeks to Jesse P. Wolcott [chair, House Banking and Currency Committee], in House Banking and Currency Committee, *Creation of Small Business Administration*, hearings on H.R. 5141, 83d Cong., 1st sess., 18 May 1953, 91–92.

42. "Defense Production Act Amendments, 1953," *Congressional Record* (17 June 1953), vol. 99, no. 5, 6695–96; Wright Patman, "Extension of Defense Production Act—Very Important Vote Coming Up," *Congressional Record* (22 June 1953), vol. 99, no. 5, 7032; "Temporary Economic Controls—Conference Report," ibid., 6942–58; Patman, "Small Business Act of 1953—Reconstruction Finance Corporation Liquidation Act," *Congressional Record* (27 July 1953), vol. 99, no. 8, 10007; Fulbright, "Creation of Small Business Administration," *Congressional Record* (20 July 1953), vol. 99, pt. 7, 9212–13; Hubert Humphrey, ibid., 9219.

43. Walter Ploeser to Robert A. Taft, 19 February 1953, folder "Small Business," box 1273, Robert A. Taft Papers, Library of Congress; Robert A. Taft to Walter C. Ploeser, 28 February 1953, ibid.

44. American Enterprise Association, "Analysis of S. 1523," 22 May 1953, AEA Report No. 55, Sen. 83A-F4, Banking and Currency Committee Correspondence, Tray "Silver Purchase Act-War Damage," folder "Small Business," RG 46, NA; Parris, *The Small Business Administration*, 18–23; "Small Business Act of 1953," *Congressional Record* (5 June 1953), vol. 99, pt. 5, 6156; "Creation of Small Business Administration," *Congressional Record* (20 July 1953), vol. 99, pt. 7, 9208–22; Senate Small Business Committee, *Small Business Administration: Title II of Small Business Act of 1953*, 83d Cong., 1st sess., 10 August 1953, Committee Print 2. Harmon Zeigler provides a detailed legislative history of the Small Business Act in his *Politics of Small Business*, 104–11. See also Marcus, "The Small Business Act," 143–89. For a first-hand history of the origins of the SBA, see Norman W. Stevenson, memorandum to Senator Wallace F. Bennett, "Congressional Intent in the Establishment of the Small Business Administration," 28 May 1954, Sen. 83A-F4, Banking and Currency Committee Correspondence, folder "Small Business," RG 46, NA.

45. "Mitchell of SDPA," *Newsweek*, 24 August 1953, 64.

46. SDPA, *7th Quarterly Report*, 31 August 1953, pp. 2–5, box 28, RG 309, NA.

47. SDPA, *8th Quarterly Report*, 8–10; John H. Bunzel, *The American Small Business-man* (New York: Knopf, 1962), table 14 ("Small Business Share of Defense Contracts, 1951–9"), p. 288.

48. Patman, "Small Defense Plants Corporation: Small Business at the Cross Roads," *Congressional Record* (28 June 1951): 7437 [quote]; Herbert Stein and Murray Foss, *An Illustrated Guide to the American Economy: A Hundred Key Issues* (Washington: The AEI Press, 1992), 205.

49. Berlie Loren Lunde, "The Role of Small Business in Defense Production with Special Reference to Air Force Contracts" (M.B.A. thesis, University of Pittsburgh, 1956), 12; "Small Firms Aren't Losing Out," *Business Week*, 8 March 1952, 64 [quote].

50. Bert G. Hickman, *The Korean War and United States Economic Activity, 1950–1952* (New York: National Bureau of Economic Research, 1955), 2, 32–33; Reday, "Industrial Mobilization," 1069; Senate Small Business Committee, *Annual Report*, 83d Cong., 1st sess., 2 March 1953, S. Rpt. 49, 1 [quote]. Several surveys of local small business conditions offered a mixed picture. A survey of New York City machine and metalworking companies revealed a high level of idle capacity, but a survey of conditions in northwestern Ohio indicated that small firms were prospering from the continued high demand for civilian goods. In late 1951, a Commerce Department survey of 250 companies showed that 65 percent accumulated all their necessary capital from internal sources. Fifteen percent of manufacturers and 5 percent of retailers failed to get all the capital they desired (Commerce and Industry Association of New York, "Survey of New York City Machine and Metal Working Plants," 13 March 1952, folder "Surveys and Studies," box 7, RG 309, NA; Northwestern Ohio Industrial Council, 29 March 1951, box 24, RG 309, NA). *Business Week* surveys indicated that small firms had adjusted well to the realities of wartime mobilization. *Business Week* noted that because of their size, many could evade government regulations and controls that limited the flexibility of larger corporations; see "How Tough Is It for Small Business?," *Business Week*, 29 December 1951, 80–81; "Small Firms Aren't Losing Out," *Business Week*, 8 March 1952, 64–66; "Little Business Holds Its Own," *Business Week*, 16 June 1951, 144.

51. Vatter, "The Position of Small Business," 157; *Nation's Business*, April 1954, 66–67; Small Business Administration, *1st Semi-Annual Report*, 67.

52. Green, "The Small Business Administration," 5–6, 15, 77.

53. John W. Sloan, *Eisenhower and the Management of Prosperity* (Lawrence: University Press of Kansas, 1991), 71.

54. Dwight D. Eisenhower, "Radio and Television Address Delivered at a Rally in the Syria Mosque, Pittsburgh, Pennsylvania," 27 October 1958, in *Public Papers of the Presidents of the United States: Dwight D. Eisenhower* (Washington: GPO, 1958), 807.

55. Daniel Bell, *The End of Ideology: On the Exhaustion of Political Ideas in the Fifties* (New York: Collier Books, 1960), 397–99.

56. Fred I. Greenstein, *The Hidden-Hand Presidency: Eisenhower as Leader* (New York: Basic Books, 1982).

57. See, for example, William A. Niskanen Jr., *Bureaucracy and Representative Government* (Chicago: Aldine-Atherton, 1971).

Chapter Seven

1. James MacGregor Burns, *New York Times Magazine*, 4 January 1953, reprinted in Joan Coyne MacLean, ed., *President and Congress: The Conflict of Powers*, The Reference Shelf, vol. 27, no. 1 (New York: H. W. Wilson Company, 1955), 15.

2. Anonymous [Wendell Barnes?], "Background Report: Small Business Administration," 1 May 1958, p. 1, folder 258 (5), Central Files, box 917, EPL.

3. Robert Griffith, "Dwight D. Eisenhower and the Corporate Commonwealth," *American Historical Review* 87 (February 1982): 89–90, 100–103; Kim McQuaid, *Big Business and Presidential Power: From FDR to Reagan* (New York: William Morrow, 1982), 174–75.

4. Lance T. LeLoup and Steven A. Shull, *Congress and the President: The Policy Connection* (Belmont, Calif.: Wadsworth Publishing Company, 1993), 79.

5. John Sloan, *Eisenhower and the Management of Prosperity* (Lawrence: University Press of Kansas, 1991), 71.

6. "William D. Mitchell," *New York Times*, 31 July 1953, 10; biographical sketch of William D. Mitchell, folder "Small Business Administration (1)," Central Files, box 916, EPL.

7. Senate Small Business Committee, Weekly Staff Report, 15 August 1953, Senate Committee Records, box 32, RG 46, NA; Senate Small Business Committee, Weekly Staff Report, 29 August 1953 [quote]; William D. Mitchell to C. J. Rogers [governor of Wyoming], n.d., folder "Small Business Administration (1)," Central Files, box 916, EPL; SBA, *1st Semi-Annual Report*, 31 January 1954, 55.

8. Senate Small Business Committee, *Small Business Administration: Title II of Small Business Act of 1953*, 83d Cong., 1st sess., 10 August 1953, Committee Print 1.

9. Harmon Zeigler, *The Politics of Small Business* (Washington: Public Affairs Press, 1961), 117–18; SBA, *1st Semi-Annual Report*, 8–9.

10. SBA, *1st Semi-Annual Report*, 11 [quote], 16–17, 21.

11. Eisenhower, "Annual Message to the Congress on the State of the Union," 2 February 1953, in Dwight D. Eisenhower, *Public Papers of the Presidents of the United States: Dwight D. Eisenhower* (Washington: GPO, 1953): 21; Senate Small Business Committee, *History of the Small Business Committee in the United States Senate*, by V. A. Votaw, chap. 5, p. 5, folder "History—Senate Small Business Committee," box 42, RG 46, NA; "Extension of Excess-Profits Tax," *Congressional Record* (15 July 1953), vol. 99, no. 7, 8851–73 [quote by Senator George, 8872].

12. "Small Business . . .," *Business Week*, 10 July 1954, 29.

13. "Small Business . . .," *Business Week*, 7 November 1953, 31; "Small Business," *Business Week*, 10 July 1954, 29; biographical sketch of Wendell Burton Barnes, folder "Small Business Administration (1)," Central Files, box 916, EPL; SBA, *1st Semi-Annual Report*, 56.

14. Senate Small Business Committee, Weekly Staff Report, 23 January 1954, box 32, RG 46, NA.

15. SBA, "Public Statement of Loan Policy: Explanation of Loan Procedures," December 1953, Loan Policy Board minutes, SBA Law Library, Washington, D.C.

16. SBA, *1st Semi-Annual Report*, 31 January 1954, 4–5.

17. Senate Small Business Committee, "Observations on and Reactions to Small Business Administration Field Offices," 1954, pp. 2–5, folder "Small Business Administration (1)," Central Files, box 916, EPL.

18. Senate Small Business Committee, Weekly Staff Report, 15 May 1954, box 32, RG 46, NA; Wright Patman, "Small-Business Administration Not Effective—Small-Business Man Asks for Bread, Given a Stone," *Congressional Record* (30 June 1954), vol. 100, pt. 7, 9411; SBA, *2d Semi-Annual Report*, 31 July 1954, 46.

19. Senate Small Business Committee, Weekly Staff Report, 24 April 1954, box 32, RG 46, NA.

20. Samuel W. Yorty, "Small Business Act Needs Improvement," *Congressional Record* (29 March 1954), vol. 100, pt. 3, 4034–35; Senate Small Business Committee, Weekly Staff Report, 21 May 1954, box 32, RG 46, NA.

21. Wendell Barnes, "Progress Report of the Small Business Administration," 12 July 1954, folder 258 (2), box 917, Central Files, Official File, EPL; interview of Stephen J. Spingarn, 20–29 March 1967, Oral History, HSTPL, p. 596.

22. Senate Small Business Committee, *Report of Small Business Administration*, hearings, 15 February 1954, p. 30, folder "Report of SBA—February 15, 1954 (not printed)," box 15, RG 46, NA.

23. Senate Small Business Committee, Weekly Staff Report, 15 May 1954, box 32, RG 46, NA.

24. SBA, *2d Semi-Annual Report*, 31 July 1954, 14.

25. Wendell B. Barnes to Sherman Adams, 27 March 1954, folder "Small Business Administration (1)," Central Files, box 916, EPL; Senate Small Business Committee, Weekly Staff Report, 24 April 1954, box 32, RG 46, NA.

26. House Small Business Committee, *Final Report*, 83d Cong., 2d sess., 28 December 1954, H. Rpt. 2683, 4, 26.

27. Sinclair Weeks, memorandum for the president, 18 December 1954, folder "Small Business Administration," Central Files, box 66, EPL.

28. Wendell B. Barnes, memorandum for the president, 22 December 1954, folder "Small Business Administration," Central Files, box 66, EPL.

29. Senate Small Business Committee, Weekly Staff Report, 8 January 1955, box 32, RG 46, NA.

30. Senate Small Business Committee, *Annual Report*, 84th Cong., 1st sess., 30 March 1955, S. Rpt. 120, 16; Representative William S. Hill et al., "Amending the Small Business Act of 1953," *Congressional Record* (2 August 1955), vol. 101, pt. 10, 13039–45.

31. Senate Small Business Committee, Weekly Staff Report, 15 January 1955, box 32, RG 46, NA; Abraham J. Multer, press release, 11 July 1955, Records of the Small Business Administration, RG 309, NA; Accession 58–361, folder Legal 5 (January 1955), box 8, and Accession #60A-920, folder "Legal 6—Legislation," box 10, both in RG 309, NA; "Small Business Agency," *Congressional Quarterly Almanac* (1955): 469.

32. Senate, Small Business Committee, Weekly Staff Report, 14 May 1955, box 32, RG 46, NA; "Small Business Agency," *Congressional Quarterly Almanac* (1955): 470.

33. U.S. Commission on Organization of the Executive Branch of Government, Task Force on Lending Agencies, *Report on Lending Agencies*, February 1955, 71; Anonymous, "Background Report," 10 [quote].

34. Senate Small Business Committee, 6 August 1955, box 32, RG 46, NA; "Small Business Agency," *Congressional Quarterly Almanac* (1955): 468–70; Abraham J. Multer to Wendell B. Barnes, 14 September 1955, Accession #60A-920, box 10, RG 309, NA.

35. Senate Small Business Committee, *6th Annual Report*, 84th Cong., 2d sess., 12 January 1956, S. Rpt. 1368; "Administration's Treatment of Small Business Scored," *Business Week*, 14 January 1956, 108.

36. Wright Patman, 18 January 1956, quoted in "Is the Present Federal Small Business Policy Inadequate?," *Congressional Digest*, December 1956, 300 [quote]; Wright Patman to Dwight D. Eisenhower, 22 September 1956, folder 5 [quote], box 90-B, Wright Patman Papers, LBJPL; Abraham Multer, 24 April 1956, quoted in "Is the Present Federal Small Business Policy Inadequate?," *Congressional Digest*, 312.

37. Democratic National Committee, fact sheet, "The Fate of Small Business under the GOP," 15 June 1956, folder "Dr. Arthur F. Burns, 1956–1957 (2)," box 9, Ann Whitman File, Administrative Series, EPL. A Republican analyst conceded that small business had lost ground during the recent recession but attributed the decline to factors other than government policy (Frank E. Norton to R. J. Saulnier, 20 September 1956, folder "Democratic Party Critiques re Small Business, 1956," box 11, Records of the Council of Economic Advisers, EPL).

38. Senate Small Business Committee, Weekly Staff Report, 18 August 1956, box 32, RG 46, NA.

39. John Sparkman and Wright Patman, "The Tax Squeeze on Small Business—Tax Favoritism for Big Business," press release, 30 October 1956, folder "Democratic Party Critiques re Small Business," box 11, Records of the Council of Economic Advisers, EPL.

40. Independent Businessmen for Stevenson-Kefauver, press release, 28 October 1956, folder "Democratic Party Critiques re Small Business, 1956" [quote], box 11, Records of the Council of Economic Advisers, EPL; Wilfred Lumer, *Small Business at the Crossroads: A Study of the Small Business Retreat of 1953–1955* (Washington: Public Affairs Institute, 1956), 20. The founder of the Public Affairs Institute was the director in charge of the TNEC investigation and later became the director of the Senate Small Business Committee. He established the PAI to continue the work of the TNEC (Lumer, *Small Business*, iii).

41. Roy Riehlman, "Facts and Figures—A Correction of Distortions and Omissions," *Congressional Record* (9 May 1956), vol. 102, pt. 8, 7839–41.

42. Edward Thye, 7 February 1956, quoted in "Is the Present Federal Small Business Policy Inadequate?," *Congressional Digest*, December 1956, 301.

43. John E. Henderson, 27 July 1956, quoted in "Is the Present Federal Small Business Policy Inadequate?," *Congressional Digest*, 313.

44. Dwight D. Eisenhower, "Televised Panel Discussion with a Group of Republican Women, San Francisco, California," 21 October 1958, in Eisenhower, *Public Papers*, 768; Eisenhower, "Address at the Hunt Armory in Pittsburgh, Pennsylvania," 9 October 1956, in ibid., 873.

45. Senate Small Business Committee, Weekly Staff Report, 25 August 1956, box 32, RG 46, NA.

46. Dwight D. Eisenhower, "Letter to Arthur F. Burns, Chairman, Council of Eco-

nomic Advisers, Appointing Him Chairman of Cabinet Committee on Small Business," 1 June 1956, in Eisenhower, *Public Papers*, 947. The CCSB also included the heads of the SBA, the Department of Defense, the Commerce Department, the Labor Department, the Office of Defense Mobilization, and the Housing and Home Finance Agency.

47. Jim Hagerty, memorandum for the president, 1 January 1957, pp. 1–2 [quote], folder "Dr. Arthur F. Burns, 1956–1957 (1)," box 9, Ann Whitman File, Administrative Series, EPL; Rolles B. Kadesch, "Meeting to Plan Ways of Publicizing the White House Committee on Small Business," 14 August 1956, Council of Economic Advisers, Office of the Chairman, 1953–1960: CCSB—Personnel Matters, folder "C.C.S.B.—Publicity, 1956–1957," box 8, EPL; Paul Donham, "Whither Small Business?," *Harvard Business Review* 35 (March–April 1957): 80 [quote]; Anonymous, "Background Report."

48. Philip A. Ray [general counsel, Commerce Department], address before Small Business for Ike, Rochester, New York, 25 October 1956, folder "Monopolies and Trusts," box 1101, Central File, EPL.

49. E. Burke Wilford to Sherman Adams, 15 February 1956, folder "Small Business Administration, 1956," box 1303, Central File, EPL.

50. William S. Hill et al., telegram to Wright Patman, 23 October 1956, folder "Small Business, 1956," box 62, Sidney R. Yates Papers, HSTPL; Wright Patman, telegram to William S. Hill et al., 25 October 1956, ibid.; Wright Patman, press release, "Reports of House Small Business Committee," 27 October 1956, folder "Small Business Committee, 1955–1956," container 115, Patman Papers, LBJPL.

51. Minutes, Cabinet Meeting, 27 July 1956, pp. 1–2, folder "Cabinet Meeting of July 27, 1956," box 7, Ann Whitman File, Cabinet Series, EPL.

52. Minutes, Cabinet Meeting, 16 May 1956 [quote], folder "Cabinet Meeting of May 16, 1956," box 7, Ann Whitman File, Cabinet Series, EPL; SBA Loan Policy Board, minutes, 5 April 1956, SBA Law Library, Washington, D.C.

53. SBA, *7th Semi-Annual Report*, 31 December 1956, 1.

54. Sloan, *Eisenhower*, 50–53.

55. Arthur F. Burns to Dwight D. Eisenhower, 31 December 1956, folder "Dr. Arthur F. Burns, 1956–1957 (1)," box 9, Ann Whitman File, Administrative Series, EPL.

56. George Humphrey and Dan Throop Smith, "Draft of Treasury Recommendations Concerning Tax Proposals for Small Business," 18 December 1956, folder "C.C.S.B.—Tax Proposals re Small Business, 1955–1957," Records of the Council of Economic Advisers, EPL; Dwight D. Eisenhower to Arthur F. Burns, 3 January 1957, folder "Dr. Arthur F. Burns, 1956–1957 (1)," box 9, Ann Whitman File, Administrative Series, EPL; Dwight D. Eisenhower to Arthur F. Burns, 15 May 1958 [quote], folder "Dr. Arthur F. Burns, 1958–59 (1)," box 9, Ann Whitman File, Administrative Series, EPL.

57. Frederick H. Mueller to Sherman Adams, 3 December 1956, folder 258 (3), box 917, Central Files, Official File, EPL.

58. John Hamlin to Dr. Gabriel Hauge [administrative assistant to the president], 1 May 1957, folder "John H. Hamlin: Records, 1956–1959," box 5, Records of John H. Hamlin, EPL.

59. Joseph M. McKellar [director of small business, Department of Defense], memorandum for Mr. McGuire, 7 May 1957, folder "John H. Hamlin: Records, 1956–1959,"

box 5, Records of John H. Hamlin, EPL. Small manufacturers expressed their views of the military procurement process in Albert N. Schrieber, Sumner Marcus, Robert A. Suterrmeister, and Edward G. Brown, *Defense Procurement and Small Business: A Survey of Practices and Opinions of Small Business Firms Selling to Defense Programs* (Seattle: University of Washington Press, 1961).

60. House Small Business Committee, *Final Report*, 84th Cong., 2d sess., 3 January 1957, H. Rpt. 2970, 125; Senate Small Business Committee, *7th Annual Report*, 85th Cong., 1st sess., 1 February 1957, S. Rpt. 46, 9, 3.

61. Edward Thye, "Permanent Status for Small Business Administration," *Congressional Record* (7 January 1957), vol. 103, pt. 1, 264; Frank Thompson Jr., "The President Finally Decides Small Business Is Here to Stay," *Congressional Record* (13 March 1957), vol. 103, pt. 3, 3612; "Small Business Agency," *Congressional Quarterly Almanac* (1957): 677.

62. Senate Small Business Committee, Weekly Staff Report, 18 May 1957, box 32, RG 46, NA.

63. Ibid., 25 May 1957.

64. "Small Business Act," *Congressional Record* (25 June 1957), vol. 103, pt. 8, 10201–46; Senator Clark, testimony, Senate Committee on Banking and Currency, Subcommittee on Small Business, *Credit Needs of Small Business*, hearings, 85th Cong., 1st sess., 11 June 1957, 411; Carl F. Oechsle [Commerce Department official], ibid., 282–88; Wendell Barnes, 13 June 1957, ibid., 333; Laurence B. Robbins [assistant secretary of treasury], 18 June 1957, ibid., 449.

65. Wright Patman, "Small Business Act," *Congressional Record* (25 June 1957), vol. 103, pt. 8, 10202, 10229, 10241, 10245; Wright Patman to Abraham J. Multer, 23 May 1957, folder "Small Business Committee #1," container 115-B, Patman Papers, LBJPL; Abraham J. Multer to Wright Patman, 28 May 1957, folder 5, container 90-B, Patman Papers, LBJPL. Years later, in interviews with C. Dale Vinyard, House Small Business Committee members vividly recollected how this dispute tore the committee apart; see C. Dale Vinyard, "Congressional Committees on Small Business" (Ph.D. diss., University of Wisconsin, 1964), 188.

66. Senate Small Business Committee, Weekly Staff Report, 29 June 1957; Senate Small Business Committee, Weekly Staff Report, 10 August 1957, box 32, RG 46, NA; "Small Business Agency," *Congressional Quarterly Almanac* (1957): 677–79.

67. "Small Business Administration: 1958: Legislative Program," folder "Staff Notes, December 1957," box 29, Ann Whitman File, Diary Series, EPL; Republican Legislative Meeting, 4 December 1957, folder "Legislative Leaders Meetings, 1957 (5)," box 2, Ann Whitman File, Legislative Meeting Series, EPL; Anonymous, "Background Report."

68. Senate Small Business Committee, Weekly Staff Report, 14 June 1958, box 32, RG 46, NA; "The Small Business Administration Made Permanent," *Congressional Record* (3 July 1958), vol. 104, pt. 10, 13017; SBA, *11th Semi-Annual Report* (31 December 1958): 29. The act also increased the maximum SBA share of any loan to $350,000 and lowered the maximum rate of interest from 6 to 5.5 percent. For a complete legislative history, see "Small Business Agency," *Congressional Quarterly Almanac* (1958): 257–58.

69. Harmon Zeigler, "Small Business in the Political Process" (Ph.D. diss., University of Illinois at Urbana-Champaign, 1960), 235; George Earl Green, "The Small Business

Administration: A Study in Public Policy and Organization" (Ph.D. diss., University of Colorado, 1965), 171–72; Vinyard, "Congressional Committees," 238.

70. Samuel L. Hayes and Donald H. Woods, "Are SBICs Doing Their Job?," *Harvard Business Review* 41 (March–April 1963): 10.

71. Ellis W. Hawley, *The New Deal and the Problem of Monopoly: A Study in Economic Ambivalence* (Princeton: Princeton University Press, 1966), 321. The chairman of the Federal Reserve proposed a similar measure in 1940 (U.S. Congress, Senate, Temporary National Economic Committee [TNEC], *Problems of Small Business*, Monograph No. 17, by John R. Cover et al. [Washington: GPO, 1941], 278).

72. Senate Small Business Committee, *Small Business Investment Act of 1958*, 85th Cong., 2d sess., June 1958, S. Rpt. 1652, 3–4; House Small Business Committee, *Annual Report*, 85th Cong., 2d sess., 3 January 1959, H. Rpt. 2718, 31–33.

73. Donald Earl Vaughn, "Development of the Small Business Investment Company Program" (Ph.D. diss., University of Texas at Austin, 1961): 36–44. See also Kermit L. Culver, "Small Business Investment Companies," chap. 4 in *The Vital Majority: Small Business in the American Economy: Essays Marking the Twentieth Anniversary of the U.S. Small Business Administration*, ed. Deane Carson (Washington: GPO, 1973), 61–64.

74. Vaughn, "Development," 29–30; Henry W. Briefs to R. J. Saulnier, 20 August 1957, folder "C.C.S.B.—The Economic Position of Small Business, August 1956," box 9, Records of the Council of Economic Advisers, EPL; Donham, "Whither Small Business?," 77.

75. See Irving Schweiger, "Adequacy of Financing for Small Business since World War II," *Journal of Finance* 13 (September 1958): 323–47; G. L. Bach and C. J. Huizenga, "The Differential Effects of 'Tight Money,' " *American Economic Review* (March 1961): 75–83. For a survey of the literature and a contrary view, see Deane Carson and Ira O. Scott Jr., "Differential Effects of Monetary Policy on Small Business," chap. 11 in Carson, *The Vital Majority*, 197–235.

76. House Small Business Committee, *Annual Report*, 3 January 1959, 34–35; Vaughn, "Development," 46; Wright Patman, memorandum, 28 August 1958 [Fulbright quote], folder 18, box 109C, Patman Papers, LBJPL; "Small Business Investment Act of 1958," *Congressional Record* (9 June 1958), vol. 104, pt. 8, 10506, 10521 [quote].

77. Senate Small Business Committee, *Small Business Investment Act of 1958*, Minority Report (Capehart, Bricker, Bennett), 85th Cong., 2d sess., 4 June 1958, S. Rpt. 1652, 19–21.

78. Don Rogers to Senator [Homer] Capehart, 23 May 1958, folder "Small Business Memoranda," Tray Sen 85A-F4 (Correspondence), Small Business Subcommittee, Senate Banking and Currency Committee, RG 46, NA; Memorandum to Senator Johnson, n.d., ibid.; Vaughn, "Development," 47; House Small Business Committee, *Annual Report*, 3 January 1959, 35; Hayes and Woods, "Are SBICs Doing Their Job?," 10.

79. Carolyn Nell Hooper, "Public Policy toward Small Business: Implications for Efficient Utilization of Resources" (Ph.D. diss., University of Texas at Austin, 1968), 179.

80. Cabinet Committee on Small Business, *Second Progress Report*, 31 December 1958, folder "C.C.S.B.—Second Progress Report, December 31, 1958," box 9, Records of the Council of Economic Advisers, EPL.

81. Wright Patman, memorandum, 28 August 1958, folder 18, box 109C, Patman

Papers, LBJPL. Wendell Barnes also described 1958 as the "high water mark" for small business legislation (Senate Small Business Committee, Weekly Staff Report, 13 September 1958, box 32, RG 46, NA).

82. Paul M. Butler [chairman, Democratic National Committee] to Fellow Democrats, n.d., folder "Policy: Democratic National Committee," U.S. Senate, 1949–1961: Papers of the Democratic Leader, box 392, Lyndon Baines Johnson Papers, LBJPL. Senator Edward Thye blamed his own defeat on Eisenhower's apparent lack of concern for small business owners and farmers (Edward Thye, interview with Ed Edwin, 7 July 1967, pp. 26–31, OH 22, Columbia Oral History Project, EPL).

83. "1st Time in History: 3rd Straight Opposition Congress," *Congressional Quarterly Almanac* (1958): 728–29.

84. Deputy Director [name illegible], Bureau of the Budget to Wendell B. Barnes, 9 December 1958, RG 309, NA; Senate Small Business Committee, *Review of Small Business Administration Activities, 1959–1960*, 87th Cong., 1st sess., S. Rpt. 30, 5–6.

85. Zeigler, *Politics of Small Business*, 112, 126.

86. For an analysis of Eisenhower's management style, see John W. Sloan, "The Management and Decision-Making Style of President Eisenhower," *Presidential Studies Quarterly* 20 (Spring 1990): 295–313.

87. SBA, *3d Semi-Annual Report*, 31 January 1955, 29; SBA, *14th Semi-Annual Report*, 24 October 1960, 27, 54, 58; SBA, *15th Semi-Annual Report*, 16 January 1961, 31, 62, 68; U.S. Treasury Department, *Final Report on the Reconstruction Finance Corporation* (Washington: GPO, 1959), 73. The RFC discontinued the Small Loan Participation Program in 1952. In that year, the RFC provided a total of $162 million in financial assistance to businesses and various government agencies (p. 47).

88. Addison W. Parris, *The Small Business Administration* (New York: Frederick A. Praeger, 1968), 3.

89. Elisabeth Holmes Rhyne, *Small Business, Banks, and SBA Loan Guarantees: Subsidizing the Weak or Bridging a Credit Gap?* (New York: Quorum Books, 1988), 18, 3; Zeigler, *Politics of Small Business*, 126. Between 1954 and 1961, the SBA's participation in business loans and SBICs increased 281 percent, surpassing increases in the consumer price index (11 percent), the business population (21 percent), and federal expenditures (38 percent). Between 1961 and 1988, the agency's participation in business financing (including loan guarantees and direct investments) rose from $221 million to $4.36 billion, an increase of 1,874 percent. By comparison, consumer prices increased by 296 percent, and federal spending grew by 988 percent. These growth rates were calculated from data in U.S. Bureau of the Census, *Statistical Abstract of the United States: 1992* (Washington: GPO, 1992), Nos. 498, 740; U.S. Bureau of the Census, *Historical Statistics of the United States: Colonial Times to 1970*, 2 pts. (Washington: GPO, 1976), Series E 135–66, V 1–12, Y 339–42; and SBA, *Annual Report* (1988), 49, 51–52.

90. James Q. Wilson, *Bureaucracy: What Government Agencies Do and Why They Do It* (New York: Basic Books, 1989), 77–84. See also Jameson W. Doig and Erwin C. Hargrove, "'Leadership' and Political Analysis," chap. 1 in *Leadership Innovation: A Biographical Perspective on Entrepreneurs in Government*, ed. Jameson W. Doig and Erwin C. Hargrove (Baltimore: Johns Hopkins University Press, 1987).

91. Parris, *Small Business Administration*, 90–91; Wilson, *Bureaucracy*, 126.

92. Pearl Rushfield Willing, "A History of the Management Assistance and Educational Programs of the Small Business Administration from 1953 to 1978" (Ph.D. diss., New York University, 1982), 474.

93. Parris, *Small Business Administration*, 149.

94. Rhyne, *Small Business*, 3–4, 8. Very few statistics are available on the performance of SBA borrowers. In 1967, the SBA reported its positive findings from an initial study of the financial reports of twenty thousand borrowers, but the agency never published its data. See Robert C. Moot [administrator, SBA], testimony, Senate Small Business Committee, SBA's Financial Assistance Programs, hearings, 90th Cong., 1st sess., 25 August 1967, 3–14. Published studies of the SBA's loan portfolio are much more critical; see Richard Klein, "SBA's Business Loan Programs," *Atlanta Economic Review* 28 (September–October 1978): 28–37; Barry P. Bosworth, Andrew S. Carron, and Elisabeth H. Rhyne, *The Economics of Federal Credit Program* (Washington: Brookings Institution, 1987); and Rhyne, *Small Business*.

95. Zeigler, *Politics of Small Business*, 123.

96. Parris, *Small Business Administration*, 109 [quote].

97. Vaughn, "Development," 97–98, 196.

98. Charles M. Noone and Stanley M. Rubel, *SBICs: Pioneers in Organized Venture Capital* (Chicago: Capital Publishing Company, 1970), 41–47.

99. Parris, *Small Business Administration*, 160. In 1966, the industry reported a 2.4 percent rate of return on investment, less than the interest paid on government bonds (Hooper, "Public Policy," 203). The SBICs became more profitable in the late 1960s, but in 1970, the authors of a study examining the SBIC industry still concluded that "this industry performance has not been particularly impressive to date" (Noone and Rubel, *SBICs*, 109). Similarly, in 1980, Roland I. Robinson asserted that "a very rough judgment might lead to the conclusion that, in spite of the strong support by the SBA, and the great tax advantages, the system had not, in total, returned a profit to its investors" (Robinson, "The Financing of Small Business in the United States," in *Small Business in American Life*, ed. Stuart W. Bruchey [New York: Columbia, 1980], 296).

100. Hayes and Woods, "Are SBICs Doing Their Job?," 194, 198. Proxmire characterized the SBA as a "medium-size or even a big business administration" (William Proxmire, *Can Small Business Survive?* [Chicago: Henry Regnery, 1964]).

101. John D. Aram and Jeffrey S. Coomes, "Public Policy and the Small Business Sector," *Policy Studies Journal* 13 (June 1985): 692–99. By comparison, a single over-the-counter mutual fund raised almost $400 million in 1968 (Noone and Rubel, *SBICs*, 122).

102. John J. Sparkman, *Ten-Year Record of the Select Committee on Small Business, United States Senate, 1950–1960: Statement by Senator John Sparkman* (Washington: GPO, 1959), 3.

103. Paul Donham, "Whither Small Business?," 73 [quote]. See W. Arnold Hosmer, "Small Manufacturing Enterprises," *Harvard Business Review* 35 (November–December 1957): 111–22; Eugene C. McKean, *The Persistence of Small Business: A Study of Unincorporated Enterprise* (Kalamazoo, Mich.: W. E. Upjohn Institute for Community Research, 1958); J. Jewkes et al., *Sources of Invention* (London: Macmillan, 1958); Arnold C. Cooper, "R&D Is More Efficient in Small Companies," *Harvard Business Review* 42 (May–June 1964): 78–82.

104. Edward Hollander et al., *The Future of Small Business* (New York: Frederick A. Praeger, 1967), 100.

105. Hooper, "Public Policy," 36, 39, 40, 42.

106. The Census Bureau gathered firm-size data based on the number of units rather than on the number of employees per firm. In 1963, small firms accounted for 70 percent of total retail sales, down from 76 percent in 1954 (their sales increased 32 percent). Small firms collected 78 percent of the receipts in services, down from 83 percent (they reported an absolute increase in receipts of 78 percent). Calculated from "Table 1: Single Units and Multiunits," in U.S. Department of Commerce, Bureau of the Census, *1963 Census of Business*, vol. 1, *Retail Trade: Summary Statistics* (Washington: GPO, 1966), and "Table 1: Single Units and Multiunits," ibid., vol. 6, *Selected Services: Summary Statistics* (Washington: GPO, 1966).

107. During this period, there was surprisingly little change in the distribution of payroll, value added by manufacture, and capital expenditures among manufacturing establishments. See U.S. Bureau of the Census, "Manufactures—Summary, by Employee Size-Class: 1947 to 1963," *Statistical Abstract of the United States: 1970* (Washington: GPO, 1970), No. 1122.

The Census Bureau broke its firm data into two categories: single-plant firms and multiplant firms. Harold Vatter uses the single-plant category as a proxy for "small business" and reports that between 1954 and 1963, the single-plant firms' share of manufacturing employment declined from 39 percent to 32 percent (Vatter, "The Position of Small Business in the Structure of American Manufacturing, 1870–1970," *Small Business in American Life*, ed. Stuart W. Bruchey [New York: Columbia University Press, 1980], 158–59). This proxy is unsatisfactory. In 1963, single-plant firms averaged only twenty employees. These were *very* small manufacturers, far smaller than the firms most small business advocates had in mind. (The SBA defined a "small" manufacturing firm as one with up to one thousand employees, depending on the industry.) Multiplant firms (Vatter's proxy for medium and large businesses) averaged only 240 employees per establishment; thus, this category undoubtedly contained many small firms.

108. Gideon Rosenbluth, quoted in Edward Hollander, *The Future of Small Business*, 3–4.

109. Willing, "A History," 457, 28.

110. Thurman W. Arnold, *The Folklore of Capitalism* (New Haven: Yale University Press, 1937): 355.

Conclusion

1. Theodore J. Lowi, *The End of Liberalism: The Second Republic of the United States*, 2d ed. (New York: W. W. Norton, 1979), 61.

2. Ellis W. Hawley, *The New Deal and the Problem of Monopoly: A Study in Economic Ambivalence* (Princeton: Princeton University Press, 1966), 187.

3. Lowi, *End of Liberalism*, 55.

4. Adolf A. Berle Jr. and Gardiner C. Means, *The Modern Corporation and Private Property* (New York: Commerce Clearing House, 1932), 40–41.

5. The virtual demise of A&P, the "Frankenstein monster" loathed by critics of the chain store, also brings into question the extent to which large firms can insulate themselves from competitive forces. See Richard S. Tedlow, *New and Improved: The Story of Mass Marketing in America* (New York: Basic Books, 1990), chap. 4 ("Stocking America's Pantries: The Rise and Fall of A&P").

6. Harold Livesay, "Lilliputians in Brobdingnag: Small Business in Late-Nineteenth-Century America," in *Small Business in American Life*, ed. Stuart W. Bruchey (New York: Columbia University Press, 1980), 343–47; Harold G. Vatter, "The Position of Small Business in the Structure of American Manufacturing, 1870–1970," in ibid., 147.

7. In 1949 there were twenty-six firms per thousand people, up from twenty-one in 1900 (Rudolph Jones, "The Relative Position of Small Business in the American Economy since 1930" [1952 article], chap. 2 in *The Survival of Small Business*, ed. Vincent P. Carosso and Stuart Bruchey [New York: Arno Press, 1979], 34–35).

8. Joseph D. Phillips, *Little Business in the American Economy*, Illinois Studies in the Social Sciences, vol. 42 (Urbana: University of Illinois Press, 1958), 111.

9. U.S. Congress, Senate, Small Business Committee, *History of the Small Business Committee in the United States Senate*, by V. A. Votaw, conclusion, p. 2, folder "History—Senate Small Business Committee," Senate Committee Records, box 42, RG 46, NA.

10. Lawrence M. Friedman, "Law and Small Business in the United States: One Hundred Years of Struggle and Accommodation," in Bruchey, *Small Business in American Life*, 310 (original italics).

11. Alan Stone, *Economic Regulation and the Public Interest: The Federal Trade Commission in Theory and Practice* (Ithaca: Cornell University Press, 1977), 95.

12. Votaw, *History of the Senate Small Business Committee*, chap. 5, p. 15.

13. Robert Higgs, *Crisis and Leviathan: Critical Episodes in the Growth of American Government* (New York: Oxford University Press, 1987).

14. Addison W. Parris, *The Small Business Administration* (New York: Frederick A. Praeger, 1968), 8 [quote], 11.

15. Hawley, *New Deal*, 52.

16. Gabriel Kolko, *The Triumph of Conservatism: A Reinterpretation of American History, 1900–1916* (Chicago: Quadrangle, 1963); James Weinstein, *The Corporate Ideal in the Liberal State, 1900–1918* (Boston: Beacon Press, 1968); Martin J. Sklar, *The Corporate Reconstruction of American Capitalism, 1890–1916: The Market, the Law, and Politics* (Cambridge: Cambridge University Press, 1988), 425 [quote]; James Livingston, *Origins of the Federal Reserve System: Money, Class, and Corporate Capitalism, 1890–1913* (Ithaca: Cornell University Press, 1986).

17. One might also question the degree to which Woodrow Wilson was a "corporate liberal" unconcerned with the fate of small business. See Alan L. Seltzer, "Woodrow Wilson as 'Corporate Liberal': Toward a Reconsideration of Left Revisionist Historiography," *The Monopoly Issue and Antitrust, 1900–1917*, vol. 2 of *Business and Government in America since 1870: A Twelve-Volume Anthology of Scholarly Articles*, ed. Robert F. Himmelberg (New York: Garland, 1994), 249–78.

18. Sklar, *Corporate Reconstruction*, 35 [quote]. I would have to agree with Robert Higgs's view that "one may well wonder how, in light of the many caveats he makes, he

can cling to his own interpretation" (Higgs, "Origins of the Corporate Liberal State," *Critical Review* 5 [Fall 1991]: 488). Ellis Hawley has noted the same contradiction between Sklar's pluralism and his " 'ruling class' analysis" (Hawley, "Remarks Concerning Martin J. Sklar's *The Corporate Reconstruction of American Capitalism, 1890–1916*," *Business and Economic History*, 2d ser., 21 [1992]: 40). Sklar does, however, make an important contribution to our understanding of economic thought and judicial interpretations of antitrust law in this period; his *Corporate Reconstruction* is required reading for anyone interested in business-government relations during the late nineteenth and early twentieth centuries.

19. Livingston, *Origins of the Federal Reserve*, 233 [quotes].

20. Weinstein, *Corporate Ideal*, 3 [quote].

21. Alan Brinkley, "Writing the History of Contemporary America: Dilemmas and Challenges," *Daedalus* (1984): 135. Others have also pointed out the evidence of disunity beyond 1914. See Hawley, "Remarks," 41; Higgs, "Origins," 484–92; and Gerald Berk, "Corporate Liberalism Reconsidered," *Journal of Policy History* 3 (1991): 81–82. In a recent essay, Sklar discusses "some new considerations that have since arisen or taken firmer shape in my own thinking." He now concedes the persistence of disunity:

> Property and market relations, modes of thought, political movements, and cultural patterns associated with the proprietary-competitive stage of capitalism . . . remained or became widespread, influential, and strongly represented in national politics, in Congress, and at the state and local levels of politics and government. They continually exerted a large impact, moreover, in party politics, in the electoral arena, and in legislative activity at the national, state, and local levels. Throughout this period and well beyond it, the large corporations lacked anything near full legitimacy in the minds of a considerable segment of the people and their political representatives. (Sklar, "Studying American Political Development in the Progressive Era, 1890s–1916," chap. 2 in *The United States as a Developing Country: Studies in U.S. History in the Progressive Era and the 1920s* [Cambridge: Cambridge University Press, 1992], 68.)

22. See, for example, Arthur F. Bentley, *The Process of Government: A Study of Social Pressures*, ed. Peter H. Odegard (1908; rpt. Cambridge: Belknap Press of Harvard University Press, 1967); David B. Truman, *The Governmental Process: Political Interests and Public Opinion* (New York: Knopf, 1951); L. Harmon Zeigler and G. Wayne Peak, *Interest Groups in American Society*, 2d ed. (Englewood Cliffs, N.J.: Prentice-Hall, 1972).

23. For a discussion of political entrepreneurs in the Congress of the 1970s and 1980s, see Loomis Burdett, *The New American Politician: Ambition, Entrepreneurship, and the Changing Face of Political Life* (New York: Basic Books, 1988). On the role of entrepreneurs within government bureaucracies, see Jameson W. Doig and Erwin C. Hargrove, eds., *Leadership and Innovation: A Biographical Perspective on Entrepreneurs in Government* (Baltimore: Johns Hopkins University Press, 1987); Eugene Lewis, *Public Entrepreneurship: Toward a Theory of Bureaucratic Political Power: The Organizational Lives of Hyman Rickover, J. Edgar Hoover, and Robert Moses* (Bloomington: Indiana University Press, 1980). Mark Nadel examines consumer activists inside and outside the government in *The Politics of Consumer Protection* (Indianapolis: Bobbs-Merrill, 1971).

24. Proponents of an activist industrial policy usually address the problem of accountability by recommending the establishment of an advisory body made up of key business, labor, and government officials. Policymaking would entail bargaining among these groups. See, for example, Robert B. Reich, *The Next American Frontier* (New York: Times Books, 1983), 276; Lester Thurow, *The Zero-Sum Solution: Building a World-Class American Economy* (New York: Simon and Schuster, 1985), 264–65; Irving S. Shapiro with Carl B. Kaufmann, *America's Third Revolution: Public Interest and The Private Role* (New York: Harper and Row, 1984), 136, 146–47. Otis Graham maintains that a genuine industrial policy is marked by the absence of interest-group bargaining, but he offers no plan for cutting through the gridlock of special interests. Graham advocates grassroots democracy as the solution to the problem of accountability, but such efforts in the past (e.g., the "community action" projects of the 1960s) have merely added new special interests to the mix of groups clamoring for government assistance. Both sides of the controversial debate over industrial policy are presented in his *Losing Time: The Industrial Policy Debate* (Cambridge: Harvard University Press, 1992). See also Michael L. Wachter and Susan M. Wachter, *Toward a New U.S. Industrial Policy?* (Philadelphia: University of Pennsylvania Press, 1981); and Chalmers Johnson, ed., *The Industrial Policy Debate* (San Francisco: ICS Press, 1984).

25. Robert Nisbet, *Twilight of Authority* (New York: Oxford University Press, 1975), 242. Nisbet uses this phrase in a somewhat different context to describe the increasing politicization of modern life.

26. "Would Industrial Policy Help Small Business?," *Business Week*, 6 February 1984, 72 [quote]. See also Walter Adams and James W. Brock, "Industrial Policy: The Neoliberal Vision," chap. 25 in *The Bigness Complex: Industry, Labor, and Government in the American Economy* (New York: Pantheon Books, 1986), 351–63.

27. Advocates of industrial policy frequently tie a nation's standard of living to its ability to compete in the global marketplace. See, for example, Lester Thurow's *Head to Head: The Coming Economic Battle among Japan, Europe, and America* (New York: Morrow, 1992) and Ira C. Magaziner and Mark Patinkin, *The Silent War: Inside the Global Business Battles Shaping America's Future* (New York: Vintage, 1990). Despite recent gains, American small businesses play a relatively unimportant role in international trade. See Lincoln Armstrong, "Small Business Overseas Marketing," chap. 19 in *The Vital Majority: Small Business in the American Economy: Essays Marking the Twentieth Anniversary of the U.S. Small Business Administration*, ed. Deane Carson (Washington: GPO, 1973), 365–84; U.S. President's Commission on Industrial Competitiveness, *Global Competition: The New Reality*, 2 vols. (Washington: GPO, January 1985), 1:41; George S. Vozikis and Timothy S. Mescon, "Stages of Development and Stages of the Exporting Process in a Small Business Context," chap. 6 in *Small Business in a Regulated Economy: Issues and Policy Implications*, ed. Richard J. Judds, William T. Greenwood, and Fred W. Becker (New York: Quorum Books, 1988); U.S. Department of Commerce, Bureau of the Census, *Manufacturing: Analytical Report Series: Selected Characteristics of Manufacturing Establishments that Export: 1987* (Washington: GPO, 1992); and "Helping Small- and Medium-Sized Businesses," *Business America* 115, no. 9 (September 1994): 40–51.

28. Michael J. Piore and Charles F. Sabel, *The Second Industrial Divide: Possibilities for*

Prosperity (New York: Basic Books, 1984), 305. See also Charles Sabel and Jonathan Zeitlin, "Historical Alternatives to Mass Production: Politics, Markets and Technology in Nineteenth-Century Industrialization," *Past and Present* 108 (1985): 134–56; Gerald Berk, "Corporate Liberalism Reconsidered," *Journal of Policy History* 3 (1991): 70–84; James Livingston, "A Reply to Gerald Berk," ibid., 85–89; David Vogel, "A Reply to Gerald Berk," ibid., 90–93.

29. The economist Friedrich von Hayek has discussed this informational problem extensively; see Hayek, "Competition as a Discovery Procedure," "The Impossibility of Socialist Calculation," and "The Uses of Knowledge in Society," in *The Essence of Hayek*, eds. Chiaki Nishiyama and Kurt R. Leube (Stanford, Calif.: Hoover Institution Press, 1984). See also Charles R. Morris, "It's *Not* the Economy, Stupid," *Atlantic Monthly*, July 1993, 49–62.

30. Lowi, *End of Liberalism*, 71.

31. On the diversity of opinion among big business executives, see Robert Collins, *The Business Response to Keynes, 1929–1964* (New York: Columbia University Press, 1981).

32. Paradoxically, the staunchest critics of the sba's loan programs have been small business associations, because according to Elisabeth Rhyne, "thriving small businesses do not wish to invite stronger competition by giving weaker firms government-backed loans" (Rhyne, *Small Business, Banks, and* sba *Loan Guarantees: Subsidizing the Weak or Bridging a Credit Gap?* [New York: Quorum Books, 1988], 22). See also Sumner Marcus, "The Small Business Act of 1953: A Case Study of the Development of Public Policy Affecting Business" (D.B.A. diss., University of Washington, 1958), 215.

33. For a discussion of the inherent conservatism of "interest-group liberal" regimes, see Lowi, *The End of Liberalism*.

34. Also, since its creation in 1953, the sba's lending division has focused its efforts on assisting businesses in already competitive sectors of the economy. Perhaps because the agency already experiences high default rates on its business loans, it has been reluctant to take on additional risks by venturing into unknown territory. See Barry P. Bosworth, Andrew S. Carron, and Elisabeth H. Rhyne, *The Economics of Federal Credit Programs* (Washington: Brookings Institution, 1987), 88; Rhyne, *Small Business*, 9; Richard Klein, "sba's Business Loan Program," *Atlanta Economic Review* 28 (September–October 1978): 35–36.

35. This problem continues to plague the sba. In 1984, the sba's general counsel acknowledged that agency staff members spend a great deal of time "hassling out tough questions such as where you draw the line on size" ("Would Industrial Policy Help?," 72).

36. Peter F. Drucker, *Innovation and Entrepreneurship: Practice and Principles* (New York: Perennial Library, 1985), 2–3; Steven Solomon, *Small Business USA: The Role of Small Companies in Sparking America's Economic Transformation* (New York: Crown Publishers, 1986), 191 [quote], 29; Bo Carlsson, "The Evolution of Manufacturing Technology and Its Impact on Industrial Structure: An International Study," *Small Business Economics* 1 (1989): 21–37; Werner Sengenberger and Gary Loveman, *Smaller Units of Employment: A Synthesis Report on Industrial Reorganization in Industrialized Countries*, rev. ed. (Geneva: International Institute for Labour Studies, 1988), 9–10.

37. David L. Birch, *Job Creation in America: How Our Smallest Companies Put the Most People to Work* (New York: Free Press, 1987); Zoltan J. Acs and David B. Audretsch, "Innovation, Market Structure, and Firm Size," *Review of Economics and Statistics* 69 (November 1987): 567–74; Zoltan J. Acs, "Flexible Specialization Technologies, Innovation, and Small Business," chap. 2 in *Small Business in a Regulated Economy: Issues and Policy Implications*, ed. Richard J. Judd, William T. Greenwood, and Fred W. Becker (New York: Quorum Books, 1988).

38. "The Rise and Rise of America's Small Firms," *Economist*, 21 January 1989, 73–74; "Small is Beautiful Now in Manufacturing," *Business Week*, 22 October 1984, 152–56.

39. Bennett Harrison, *Lean and Mean: The Changing Landscape of Corporate Power in the Age of Flexibility* (New York: Basic Books, 1994), 38 [quote].

40. Virginia Postrel, "Populist Industrial Policy," *Reason* (January 1994): 4.

41. Ibid., 6; Graham, *Losing Time*, 194–95.

42. William L. Waugh Jr. and Deborah McCorkle Waugh, "Economic Development Programs of State and Local Governments and the Site Selection Decisions of Smaller Firms," chap. 7 in Judd, Greenwood, and Becker, *Small Business in a Regulated Economy*, 111–26; Robert E. Berney and Ed Owens, "A Model for Contemporary Small Business Policy Issues," chap. 14 in ibid., 209; Richard J. Judd and Barbra K. Sanders, "Regulation, Small Business, and Economic Development: A Historical Perspective on Regulation of Business," chap. 15 in ibid., 221–29; Donald F. Kuratko, "Small Business Challenging Contemporary Public Policy: A Coalition for Action," chap. 8 in ibid., 134–35; and Harrison, *Lean and Mean*, 17, 236–38.

43. David L. Birch first popularized the notion that small firms create the most new jobs (see his *Job Creation in America*), but he has many critics. See Harrison, *Lean and Mean*, especially Part 2 ("Reassessing the Idea That Small Firms Are the Economic Development Drivers"); Gary Loveman and Werner Sengenberger, "Introduction: Economic and Social Reorganization in the Small and Medium-Sized Enterprise Sector," in *The Re-Emergence of the Small Enterprises: Industrial Restructuring in Industrialized Countries*, ed. Werner Sengenberger, Gary Loveman, and Michael J. Piore (Geneva: International Institute for Labour Studies, 1990); Sylvia Nasar, "Myth: Small Business as Job Engine," *New York Times*, 25 March 1994: C1–C2; Anne G. Perkins, "Job Creation: Does Small Business Really Have an Edge?," *Harvard Business Review* (May/June 1994): 12; Steven J. Davis, John Haltiwanger, and Scott Schuh, "Small Business and Job Creation: Dissecting the Myth and Reassessing the Facts," NBER Working Paper No. 4492 (Cambridge, Mass.: National Bureau of Economic Research, 1993).

44. Harrison, *Lean and Mean*, 244. See also Benjamin W. Mokry, "Encouraging Small Business Startups: An Alternative to Smokestack Chasing?," chap. 10 in Judd, Greenwood, and Becker, *Small Business in a Regulated Economy: Issues and Policy Implications*, 164–65.

45. Steven A. Lustgarten, "Firm Size and Productivity Growth in Manufacturing Industries," chap. 9 in Judd, Greenwood, and Becker, *Small Business in a Regulated Economy*, 141–54; Solomon, *Small Business USA*, 152–53.

46. Philip M. Van Auken and R. Duane Ireland, "Divergent Perspectives on Social Responsibility: Big Business versus Small," chap. 12 in Judd, Greenwood, and Becker, *Small Business in a Regulated Economy*, 181–86.

47. U.S. Bureau of the Census, "Employee Benefits in Medium and Large Private Establishments, 1991 and Small Private Establishments, 1990," No. 670 in *Statistical Abstract: 1993* (Washington: GPO, 1993); Solomon, *Small Business USA*, 67; Harrison, *Lean and Mean*, 11–12, 20; Sengenberger, *Smaller Units*, Table 11 ("Average Wages by Enterprise Size"), 66.

48. Harrison, *Lean and Mean*, 44–45; Mansel G. Blackford, *A History of Small Business in America* (New York: Twayne Publishers, 1992), 107; Berney and Ownes, "A Model," 217.

49. Haley Barbour [chairman of the Republican National Committee], quoted in Richard I. Kirkland Jr., "The New GOP to Big Business: Drop Dead!," *Fortune*, 6 February 1995, 50. See also David Samuels, "Tinkers, Dreamers, and Madmen: The New History According to Newt," *Lingua Franca*, January/February 1995, 38–39.

50. Mokry, "Encouraging Small Business Startups," 164 [quote]. See also "An Empirical Investigation of Export Promotion Programs," *Columbia Journal of World Business* 21 (Winter 1986): 13–20.

51. A survey of small business executives revealed their negative attitudes toward many government agencies, including the National Labor Relations Board, the Equal Employment Opportunity Commission, the Occupational Safety and Health Administration, and the Office of Federal Contract Compliance Programs (Herbert R. Northrup and Evelyn M. Erb, "Employment Disincentives and Small Business: A Pilot Study," chap. 4 in Judd, Greenwood, and Becker, *Small Business in a Regulated Economy*, 68).

52. Adam Smith, *The Wealth of Nations*, with introduction by Andrew Skinner (1776; rpt. New York: Penguin Books, 1980), 211.

BIBLIOGRAPHY

Archival Materials

Celler, Emanuel. Papers. Library of Congress, Washington, D.C.

Council of Economic Advisors, Office of the Chairman. Records, 1953–60. Dwight D. Eisenhower Presidential Library, Abilene, Kansas.

Eisenhower, Dwight D. Papers. Dwight D. Eisenhower Presidential Library, Abilene, Kansas.

B. F. Goodrich Company. Executive and Operating Committee Records, 1936–62. Akron, Ohio.

Hamlin, John H. Papers. Dwight D. Eisenhower Presidential Library, Abilene, Kansas.

Johnson, Lyndon Baines. Papers. Lyndon B. Johnson Presidential Library, Austin, Texas.

Patman, John William Wright. Papers. Lyndon B. Johnson Presidential Library, Austin, Texas.

Robinson, Joseph Taylor. Papers. University of Arkansas Library, Fayetteville, Arkansas.

Roosevelt, Franklin D. Papers. Franklin D. Roosevelt Presidential Library, Hyde Park, New York.

Seiberling, J. Penfield. Papers. Ohio Historical Society, Columbus, Ohio.

Taft, Robert A. Papers. Library of Congress, Washington, D.C.

Truman, Harry S. Papers. Harry S. Truman Presidential Library, Independence, Missouri.

U.S. Small Business Administration. Records, 1953–61. Law Library, Washington, D.C.

Yates, Sidney R. Papers. Harry S. Truman Presidential Library, Independence, Missouri.

Records in the National Archives, Washington, D.C.

Record Group 40: Department of Commerce

Record Group 46: U.S. Congress, Senate
  Small Business Committee
  Banking and Currency Committee

Record Group 122: Federal Trade Commission

Record Group 144: Temporary National Economic Committee

Record Group 153: U.S. Congress, House of Representatives
  Banking and Currency Committee
  Judiciary Committee
  Interstate and Foreign Commerce Committee
  Ways and Means Committee

Record Group 179: War Production Board
Record Group 234: Reconstruction Finance Corporation
Record Group 240: Smaller War Plants Corporation
Record Group 309: Small Defense Plants Administration
   Small Business Administration

Oral Histories

Hall, Leonard. Interviewed by David Horrocks on 19 May 1975. OH 478, Dwight D.
   Eisenhower Presidential Library.
Patman, Wright. Interviewed by Joe B. Frantz on 11 August 1972 and 4 February 1976.
   Lyndon B. Johnson Presidential Library.
Spingarn, Stephen J. Interviewed by Jerry Hess, 20–29 March 1967. Harry S. Truman
   Presidential Library.
Thye, Edward. Interviewed by Ed Edwin on 7 July 1967. Columbia Oral History Proj-
   ect, OH 22, Dwight D. Eisenhower Presidential Library.

Published Government Documents

Congressional Hearings and Reports

U.S. Congress. House of Representatives. Committee on Banking and Currency. *Con-
   version of Small Business Enterprises to War Production*. Hearings on S. 2250 and
   H.R. 6975, 77th Cong., 2d sess., 27 April 1942.
——. *Creation of Small Business Administration*. Hearings on H.R. 5141, 83d Cong., 1st
   sess., 18 May 1953.
——. *Extending the Life of Smaller War Plants Corporation*. 79th Cong., 1st sess., 12
   February 1945, S. Rpt. 45.
——. *1945 Continuance of the Smaller War Plants Corporation*. Hearings on H.R. 8,
   79th Cong., 1st sess., 27 March 1945.
——. *To Increase the Capitalization of the Smaller War Plants Corporation by
   $200,000,000*. Hearings on S. 2004, 78th Cong., 2d sess., 22, 24 November 1944.
U.S. Congress. House. Committee on Interstate and Foreign Commerce. *Equal Pric-
   ing*. Hearings on H.R. 2729, 86th Cong., 1st sess., 21–22 July 1959.
——. *Fair Trade, 1959*. Hearings on H.R. 1253 and H.R. 768, 86th Cong., 1st sess., 16–
   20, 23–25 March 1959.
——. Subcommittee on Federal Trade Commission. *Minimum Resale Prices*. Hearings,
   82d Cong., 2d sess., 4–8, 14–15, 20 February 1952.
U.S. Congress. House. Committee on Judiciary. *Amending the Sherman Act with Re-
   spect to Resale Price Maintenance*. 82d Cong., 2d sess., 13 March 1952, H. Rpt. 1516.
——. Subcommittee on Monopolies and Commercial Law. *The Celler-Kefauver Act:
   The First 27 Years*. By Willard Fritz Mueller. Washington: GPO, 1980.
——. *Fair Trade*. Hearings on H.R. 2384 [Consumer Goods Pricing Act of 1975], 94th
   Cong., 1st sess., 25 March, 10 April 1975.

——. *Study of Monopoly Power: Resale Price Maintenance.* Hearings, 82d Cong., 2d sess., 13–15, 18, 20–22, 25, 27 February 1952.

U.S. Congress. House. Committee on Ways and Means. *Imposition of Tire Tax on Tires Delivered to Manufacturer's Retail Outlet.* 86th Cong., 2d sess., 15 August 1960, H. Rpt. 2093.

——. *Imposition of Tire Tax on Tires Delivered to Manufacturer's Retail Outlet.* 87th Cong., 1st sess., 1961, H. Rpt. 1196.

——. *Imposition of Tire Tax on Tires Delivered to Manufacturer's Retail Outlet.* 89th Cong., 1st sess., 27 September 1965, H. Rpt. 1096.

U.S. Congress. House. Select Committee on Lobbying Activities. *Conference of American Small Business Organizations.* 81st Cong., 2d sess., 1950, H. Rpt. 3232.

U.S. Congress. House. Select Committee on Small Business. *Amending Federal Trade Commission Act with Respect to Resale Price Maintenance.* 82d Cong., 2d sess., 1952, H. Rpt. 1516.

——. *Annual Report* [various titles]. 1942–61.

——. *Fair Trade: The Problem and the Issues.* 82d Cong., 2d sess., 4 February 1952, H. Rpt. 1292.

——. *Final Report.* 81st Cong., 2d sess., 1 January 1951, H. Rpt. 3237.

——. *Financial Problems of Small Business.* Hearings, pt. 1, 79th Cong., 1st sess., 19 April 1945.

——. *Functional Operation of the Federal Trade Commission.* Hearings, 81st Cong., 2d sess., June 26–28, 1950.

——. *Law Enforcement Activities Affecting Small Business.* Report of Subcommittee on Law Enforcement and Subsidies Affecting Small Business, 85th Cong., 2d sess., 3 January 1959, H. Rpt. 2714.

——. *Monopolistic and Unfair Trade Practices: Problems of Small Business Resulting from Monopolistic and Unfair Trade Practices.* Hearings, 80th Cong., 2d sess., September–24 November 1948.

——. *The Organization and Procedures of the Federal Regulatory Commissions and Agencies and Their Effect on Small Business.* Report to Subcommittee No. 1 on Regulatory Agencies, 84th Cong., 2d sess., 16 October 1956.

——. *Price Discrimination: The Robinson-Patman Act and Related Matters.* Hearings, pt. 1–3, 84th Cong., 1st sess., 31 October–17 November 1955.

——. *Price Discrimination, the Robinson-Patman Act, and the Attorney-General's National Committee to Study the Antitrust Laws.* 84th Cong., 2d sess., 19 December 1956, H. Rpt. 2966.

——. *Progress Report.* 81st Cong., 2d sess., 2 February 1950, H. Rpt. 1576.

——. *Progress Report.* 82d Cong., 1st sess., 7 January 1952, H. Rpt. 1228.

——. *Recent Efforts to Amend or Repeal the Robinson-Patman Act.* Hearings, pt. 1, 94th Cong., 1st sess., 5, 6, 11, 12, 19 November 1975.

——. *Review of Small Business.* 82d Cong., 2d sess., 1952, S. Rpt. 2513.

——. *Small Business Organizations: Four Case Studies of Organizations Purporting to Represent Small Business.* 81st Cong., 2d sess., 21 February 1950, H. Rpt. 1675.

——. *Statistics on Federal Antitrust Activities.* Staff Report to the Select Committee on Small Business. 84th Cong., 1st sess., 1956, Committee Print.

——. *Study and Investigation of the National Defense Program.* Hearings, pt. 6, 79th Cong., 2d sess., 22 January 1946.

——. *The Surplus Property Problem from the Viewpoint of Small Business.* 78th Cong., 2d sess., 9 March 1944, H. Rpt. 1245.

——. *United States versus Economic Concentration and Monopoly: An Investigation of the Effectiveness of the Government's Efforts to Combat Economic Concentration.* Staff Report to the Monopoly Subcommittee, 27 December 1946.

——. Subcommittee No. 1. *Problems of Small Business Relating to the National Emergency.* Hearings, 82d Cong., 1st sess., 2 May 1951.

U.S. Congress. Senate. Committee on Banking and Currency. Subcommittee on Small Business. *Conversion of Small Business Enterprise to War Production.* Hearings on S. 2250, 77th Cong., 2d sess., 1942.

——. *Credit Needs of Small Business.* Hearings, 85th Cong., 1st sess., 23 May, 3–6, 10, 11, 13, 18, 20 June 1957.

——. *Distribution of Motor-Vehicle Tires.* Hearings, 79th Cong., 2d sess., 2, 23 July 1946.

——. *Establishment of Permanent Small Business Finance Corporation.* Hearings on S. 1320, 79th Cong., 2d sess., 25 July 1946.

——. *Nomination of Telford Taylor.* Hearings, 82d Cong., 1st sess., 9 October 1951.

——. *Small Business and the War Program.* Hearings, pt. 1, 77th Cong., 1st sess., 15–19 December 1941.

U.S. Congress. Senate. Committee on Interstate Commerce. *Investigation by Federal Trade Commission of Methods Used by Makers of Motor Vehicle Tires.* 75th Cong., 3d sess., 7 June 1938, S. Rpt. 1994.

——. *Providing for an Assistant Secretary of Commerce for Small Business.* Hearings on S. 356 and S. 883, 78th Cong., 1st sess., 27 May 1943.

——. *Resale Price Fixing.* Hearings, 82d Cong., 2d sess., 2–5 June 1952.

U.S. Congress. Senate. Committee on Judiciary. *Distribution of Motor Vehicle Tires.* Hearings on S. 175, 83d Cong., 2d sess., 21 May 1954.

U.S. Congress. Senate. Select Committee on Small Business. *Annual Reports* [various titles]. 1941–61.

——. *Fair Trade.* 84th Cong., 2d sess., 27 July 1956, S. Rpt. 2819.

——. *Future of Independent Business: Progress Report of the Chairman.* 79th Cong., 2d sess., 2 January 1947, Print 16.

——. *History of the Small Business Committee in the United States Senate.* By V. A. Votaw. In Senate Committee Records, box 42, folder "History—Senate Small Business Committee," Record Group 46, National Archives.

——. *Military Procurement.* 82d Cong., 2d sess., 2 July 1952, S. Rpt. 2070.

——. *Monopolistic Practices and Small Business.* Staff Report to the Federal Trade Commission for the Subcommittee on Monopoly of the Senate Select Committee on Small Business, 31 March 1952.

——. *Participation of Small Business in Military Procurement.* 82d Cong., 1st sess., 21 June 1951, S. Rpt. 469.

——. *Problems of American Small Business.* Hearings, 77th Cong., 2d sess., 15 December 1942.

——. *Problems of Independent Tire Dealers*. Staff Report, 83d Cong., 1st sess., 27 July 1953, Committee Print.

——. *Problems of Surplus Property Disposal*. Preliminary Report, 78th Cong., 2d sess., 21 July 1944, Senate Subcommittee Print 1.

——. *Report of the Attorney General's National Committee to Study the Antitrust Laws*. Hearings, pt. 1, 84th Cong., 1st sess., 27–29 April 1955.

——. *Review of Small Business Administration Activities, 1959– 1960*. 87th Cong., 1st sess., 1961, S. Rpt. 30.

——. *Senate Small Business Committee—Its Record and Outlook*. 79th Cong., 1st sess., 12 February 1945, S. Rpt. 47.

——. *Small Business Administration: Title II of Small Business Act of 1953*. 83d Cong., 1st sess., 10 August 1953, Committee Print.

——. *Small Business Administration's Financial Assistance Programs*. Hearings, 90th Cong., 1st sess., 25 August 1967.

——. *Small Business and Defense*. 77th Cong., 1st sess., 20 September 1941, Committee Print No. 6.

——. *Small Business Investment Act of 1958*. 85th Cong., 2d sess., 1958, S. Rpt. 1652.

——. *Small Business in War and Essential Civilian Production*. 78th Cong., 1st sess., 11 March 1943, S. Rpt. 12, pt. 2.

——. *Small Business Problems: The Supreme Court in Relation to Small Business and the Sherman Act*. By Crichton Clarke. 77th Cong., 1st sess., 1941, Senate Committee Print No. 2.

——. *Small Business Problems of Tire and Rubber Manufacturers and Retailers*. 77th Cong., 1st sess., 1941, Committee Print 3.

——. Subcommittee on Retailing, Distribution, and Fair Trade Practices. *Dual Distribution in the Automotive Tire Industry—1959*. Hearings, pt. 1, 86th Cong., 1st sess., 17–19 June 1959.

——. Subcommittee on Retailing, Distribution, and Marketing Practices. *Studies of Dual Distribution: The Automotive Tire Industry*. 88th Cong., 2d sess., 1964, Committee Print.

——. *Tire Dealer and Rebuilder Problems*. Hearings, 77th Cong., 2d sess., 3–6 March 1942.

——. *Tire Dealer and Rebuilder Problems: II*. Hearings, 78th Cong., 1st sess., 5, 7, 8 April, 6, 13 May 1943.

U.S. Congress. Senate. Temporary National Economic Committee. *Bureaucracy and Trusteeship in Large Corporations*. Monograph No. 11. By Marshall Dimock and Howard K. Hyde. Washington: GPO, 1940.

——. *Competition and Monopoly in American Industry*. Monograph No. 21. By Clair Wilcox. Washington: GPO, 1941.

——. *Economic Power and Political Pressures*. Monograph No. 26. By Donald C. Blaisdell. Washington: GPO, 1941.

——. *Final Report and Recommendations of the Temporary National Economic Committee*. Washington: GPO, 1941.

——. *Final Report of the Executive Secretary*. Washington: GPO, 1941.

——. *Problems of Small Business*. Monograph No. 17. By John R. Cover, Nathanael H.

Engle, Earl D. Strong, Peter R. Nehemkis Jr., William Saunders, Harold Vatter, and Harold H. Wein. Washington: GPO, 1941.

——. *Relative Efficiency of Large, Medium-Sized, and Small Business*. Monograph No. 13. Washington: GPO, 1941.

——. *Trade Association Survey*. Monograph No. 18. By Charles Albert Pearce. Washington: GPO, 1941.

Executive Agencies

U.S. Bureau of the Census. *Historical Statistics of the United States: Colonial Times to 1970*. 2 pts. Washington: GPO, 1976.

U.S. Commerce Department. Bureau of Foreign and Domestic Commerce. *Government Financial Aids to Small Business*. By Burt W. Roper. Washington: Department of Commerce, 1945.

——. *187 Bills: A Digest of Proposals Considered in Congress on Behalf of Small Business, 1943–1944*. By Burt W. Roper. Washington: GPO, 1946.

——. *Small Business—A National Asset*. Economic Series No. 24 (July 1943).

——. *390 Bills: A Digest of Proposals Considered in Congress on Behalf of Small Business, 1933–1942*. By Burt W. Roper. Washington: GPO, 1943.

U.S. Commission on Organization of the Executive Branch of the Government (Hoover Commission). Task Force on Lending Agencies. *Report on Lending Agencies*. February 1955.

U.S. Congress. *Biographical Directory of the American Congress, 1774– 1971*. Washington: GPO, 1971.

U.S. Federal Trade Commission. *Annual Report*. 1936–64.

——. *Chain Stores*. Washington: GPO, 1935.

——. *Economic Report on the Manufacture and Distribution of Automotive Tires*. Staff Report. Washington: GPO, 1966.

——. *Federal Trade Commission Decisions: Findings, Orders, and Stipulations*. 1 July 1949 to 30 June 1950. Vol. 46. Washington: Federal Trade Commission, 1952.

——. *Federal Trade Commission, 1945–1953*. Washington: GPO, 1953.

——. *In the Matter of a Quantity-Limit Rule as to Replacement Tires and Tubes Made of Natural or Synthetic Rubber for Use on Motor Vehicles as a Class of Commodity* [FTC File No. 203-1], 3 January 1952. In Commerce Clearing House, "Quantity-Limit Rules of the Federal Trade Commission," *Trade Regulation Reports, 1952*. New York: Commerce Clearing House, 1952.

——. *Report of the Federal Trade Commission on Resale Price Maintenance*. Washington: GPO, 1945.

——. *Report on Changes in Concentration in Manufacturing: 1935 to 1947 and 1950*. Washington: GPO, 1954.

——. *Report on the Concentration of Productive Facilities, 1947: Total Manufacturing and 26 Selected Industries*. Washington: GPO, 1949.

——. *Report on Resale Price Maintenance, Commercial Aspects and Tendencies*. Part 2. Washington: GPO, 1931.

——. *Report on Resale Price Maintenance, General Economic and Legal Aspects*. 70th Cong., 2d sess., 1929, H. Doc. 546, pt. 1.

——. *Report on Wartime Costs and Profits for Manufacturing Corporations, 1941 to 1945.* 6 October 1947. Washington: GPO, 1947.

——. *Resale Price Maintenance: Summary and Conclusion.* 13 December 1945. Washington: GPO, 1945.

——. *Trade Practice Rules: September 1, 1935, to June 30, 1945.* Washington: GPO, 1946.

U.S. National Recovery Administration. Division of Review. *Resale Price Maintenance Legislation in the United States.* By Harry S. Kantor. Appendices by Anne Golden. Work Material No. 16 (November 1935).

——. *Restriction of Retail Price Cutting with Emphasis on the Drug Industry.* By Mark Merrell, E. T. Grether, and Summer S. Kittelle. Work Materials No. 57 (March 1936).

U.S. Office of War Information. Bureau of Special Services. Surveys Division. *Smaller Manufacturing Plants and Wartime Production, Part I: A Digest of the Findings.* Memorandum No. 52, 17 May 1943. In Smaller War Plants Corporation Records, Record Group 240, National Archives.

U.S. President. Executive Order 9665 (27 December 1945). *Federal Register*, vol. 10, no. 252, pp. 15365–67.

U.S. Small Business Administration. *Annual Reports.* 1954–61.

——. *Semi-Annual Reports.* January 1954–December 1961.

U.S. Small Defense Plants Administration. *Quarterly Reports.* 14 January 1952–31 August 1953.

——. *Weekly Bulletin.* 1952–53.

U.S. Smaller War Plants Corporation. *Bimonthly Reports.* 1942–46.

——. *Economic Concentration and World War II.* By John M. Blair, Harrison F. Houghton, and Matthew Rose. Washington: GPO, 1946.

——. *Histories of the Smaller War Plants Corporation.* In Records of the Smaller War Plants Corporation, Record Group 71, National Archives.

——. *Industry Opinion on Proposed Science Legislation.* A Survey made by the Smaller War Plants Corporation for the Subcommittee on War Mobilization of the Committee on Military Affairs. United States Senate. 18 October 1945. Washington: GPO, 1945.

——. *Smaller War Plants Corporation Will Help Veterans.* Washington: GPO, 1945.

——. *Small Plants Speak for Themselves: A Special Report to the Small Business Committees of the Senate and House of Representatives.* 4 October 1945. In Records of the Smaller War Plants Corporation, Record Group 240, National Archives.

U.S. Treasury Department. *Final Report on the Reconstruction Finance Corporation.* Pursuant to Section 6(c) Reorganization Plan No. 1 of 1957. Washington: GPO, 1959.

U.S. War Production Board. *1st Bimonthly Report.* 77th Cong., 2d sess., 11 August 1942, S. Doc. 244.

——. *2d Bimonthly Report.* 77th Cong., 2d sess., 11 October 1942, S. Doc 274.

Newspapers and Periodicals

Akron Beacon Journal
Aviation Week

Burger Tire Consultant Service Bulletin
Business Week
Commercial and Financial Chronicle
Congressional Digest
Congressional Quarterly Almanac
Congressional Quarterly Weekly Report
Current Biography
Dictionary of American Biography
Forbes
Fortune
Gallup Poll
Harper's Magazine
Harvard Business Review
India Rubber World
Modern Tire Dealer
NAITD Dealer News
National Cyclopedia of American Biography
National Independent
National Petroleum News
Nation's Business
New York Times
Printer's Ink
Purchasing
Rubber Age
Trade Regulation Reporter
U.S. News and World Report

Books, Articles, and Dissertations

Abbott, Charles Cortez. "Small Business: A Community Problem." *Harvard Business Review* 24 (1945): 191.

Abrams, Richard M. "Business and Government." In *Encyclopedia of American Political History: Studies of the Principal Movements and Ideas*, 3 vols., ed. Jack P. Greene, 1:126–46. New York: Charles Scribner's Sons, 1984.

Acs, Zoltan J. "Flexible Specialization Technologies, Innovation, and Small Business." In *Small Business in a Regulated Economy: Issues and Policy Implications*, ed. Richard J. Judd, William T. Greenwood, and Fred W. Becker, chap. 2. New York: Quorum Books, 1988.

Acs, Zoltan J., and David B. Audretsch. "Innovation, Market Structure, and Firm Size." *Review of Economics and Statistics* 69 (November 1987): 567–74.

Adams, Walter, and James W. Brock. *Antitrust Economics on Trial: A Dialogue on the New Laissez-Faire*. Princeton: Princeton University Press, 1991.

——. *The Bigness Complex: Industry, Labor, and Government in the American Economy*. New York: Pantheon Books, 1986.

Adelman, M. A. "The Measurement of Industrial Concentration." *Review of Economics and Statistics* 33 (November 1951): 275–77.

Adelstein, Richard P. " 'Islands of Conscious Power': Louis D. Brandeis and the Modern Corporation." *Business History Review* 63 (Autumn 1989): 614–56.

Alexander, Holmes. "Millard E. Tydings: The Man from Maryland." In *The American Politician*, ed. J. T. Salter, chap. 6. Chapel Hill: University of North Carolina Press, 1938.

Allender, Mary E. "Why Did Manufacturers Want Fair Trade?" *Essays in Economic and Business History* 11 (1993): 218–30.

Ambrose, Stephen E. *Eisenhower: Soldier and President.* New York: Simon & Schuster, 1990.

American Bar Association. *Antitrust Developments, 1955–1968: A Supplement to the Report of the Attorney General's National Committee to Study the Antitrust Laws, March 31, 1955.* Chicago: American Bar Association, 1968.

American Fair Trade Council. *A Practical Guide to Fair Trade Laws.* New York: The American Fair Trade Council, 1949.

———. *Resale Price Maintenance by Means of Fair Trade Laws in Force April 1, 1942.* New York: The American Fair Trade Council, 1942.

Aram, John D., and Jeffrey S. Coomes. "Public Policy and the Small Business Sector." *Policy Studies Journal* 13 (June 1985): 692–99.

Armstrong, Lincoln. "Small Business Overseas Marketing." In *The Vital Majority: Small Business in the American Economy: Essays Marking the Twentieth Anniversary of the U.S. Small Business Administration*, ed. Deane Carson, chap. 19. Washington: GPO, 1973.

Arnold, Thurman. *The Bottlenecks of Business.* New York: Reynal & Hitchcock, 1940.

———. *The Folklore of Capitalism.* New Haven: Yale University Press, 1937.

Asher, Louis E., and Edith Heal. *Send No Money.* Chicago: Argus Books, 1942.

Atherton, Lewis A. *The Frontier Merchant in Mid-America.* 1939. Rpt., Columbia: University of Missouri Press, 1971.

———. *Main Street on the Middle Border.* Chicago: Quadrangle, 1954.

Austern, H. Thomas. *Antitrust in Action: Some Recent Developments in Antitrust Enforcement.* New York: New York University of Law, 1960.

Bach, G. L., and C. J. Huizenga. "The Differential Effects of 'Tight Money.' " *American Economic Review* 51 (March 1961): 75–83.

Balogh, Brian. "Reorganizing the Organizational Synthesis: Federal Professional Relations in Modern America." *Studies in American Political Development* 5 (Spring 1991): 119–72.

Bechhofer, Frank, and Brian Elliott. "Persistence and Change: The Petite Bourgeoisie in Industrial Society." In *The Survival of the Small Firm*, 2 vols., ed. James Curran, John Stanworth, and David Watkins, vol. 1, chap. 7. Brookfield, Vt.: Gower, 1986.

Becker, William H. *The Dynamics of Business-Government Relations: Industry and Exports, 1893–1921.* Chicago: University of Chicago, 1982.

Beckman, Theodore N. "Large versus Small Business after the War." *American Economic Review* 34, no. 1, supplement, pt. 2 (March 1944): 94–106.

Behoteguy, W. C. "Resale Price Maintenance in the Tire Industry." *Journal of Marketing* 13 (January 1949): 315–20.

Bell, Daniel. *The End of Ideology: On the Exhaustion of Political Ideas in the Fifties.* New York: Collier Books, 1960.

Bentley, Arthur F. *The Process of Government.* Ed. Peter H. Odegard. 1908. Rpt., Cambridge: Belknap Press of Harvard University Press, 1967.

Berk, Gerald. "Corporate Liberalism Reconsidered." *Journal of Policy History* 3 (1991): 70–84.

Berle, Adolf A., Jr., and Gardiner C. Means. *The Modern Corporation and Private Property.* New York: Commerce Clearing House, 1932.

Berney, Robert E., and Ed Owens. "A Model for Contemporary Small Business Policy Issues." In *Small Business in a Regulated Economy: Issues and Policy Implications*, ed. Richard J. Judd, William T. Greenwood, and Fred W. Becker, chap. 14. New York: Quorum Books, 1988.

Berthoff, Rowland. "Independence and Enterprise: Small Business in the American Dream." In *Small Business in American Life*, ed. Stuart W. Bruchey, chap. 1. New York: Columbia University Press, 1980.

Birch, David L. *Job Creation in America: How Our Smallest Companies Put the Most People to Work.* New York: Free Press, 1987.

Blackford, Mansel G. *A History of Small Business in America.* New York: Twayne Publishers, 1992.

———. *Pioneering a Small Business: Wakefield Seafoods and the Alaskan Frontier.* Greenwich, Conn.: JAI, 1979.

———. *A Portrait Cast in Steel: Buckeye International and Columbus, Ohio, 1881–1980.* Westport, Conn.: Greenwood, 1982.

———. "Small Business in America: An Historiographic Review." *Business History Review* 65 (Spring 1991): 1–26.

Bloomfield, Daniel, ed. *Chain Stores and Legislation.* New York: H. W. Wilson, 1939.

Blum, John Morton. *V Was for Victory: Politics and American Culture during World War II.* New York: Harcourt Brace Jovanovich, 1976.

Boorstin, Daniel J. *The Americans: The Democratic Experience.* New York: Random House, 1973.

Borcherding, Thomas E. "One Hundred Years of Public Spending, 1870–1970." In *Budgets and Bureaucrats: The Sources of Government Growth*, ed. Thomas E. Borcherding, chap. 2. Durham, N.C.: Duke University Press, 1977.

———. "The Sources of Growth of Public Expenditures in the United States." In *Budgets and Bureaucrats: The Sources of Government Growth*, ed. Thomas E. Borcherding, chap. 3. Durham, N.C.: Duke University Press, 1977.

Bork, Robert H. *The Antitrust Paradox: A Policy at War with Itself.* New York: Basic Books, 1978.

Bosworth, Barry P., Andrew S. Carron, and Elisabeth H. Rhyne. *The Economics of Federal Credit Programs.* Washington: Brookings Institution, 1987.

Bowen, John Frederick. "The Celler-Kefauver Act and Concentration in the Brewing Industry." Ph.D. diss., Vanderbilt University, 1971.

Brand, Donald R. "Peripheral Businesses: The Disaffected Constituency." In *Corpora-*

tism and the Rule of Law: A Study of the National Recovery Administration, chap. 2. Ithaca: Cornell University Press, 1988.

Brandeis, Louis. *The Curse of Bigness*. New York: Viking, 1934.

Branyan, Robert Lester. "Antimonopoly Activities during the Truman Administration." Ph.D. diss., University of Oklahoma, 1961.

Brinkley, Alan. "The Antimonopoly Ideal and the Liberal State: The Case of Thurman Arnold." *Journal of American History* 80 (September 1993): 557–79.

———. "Writing the History of Contemporary America: Dilemmas and Challenges." *Daedalus* (1984): 121–41.

Brooks, Robert C. "One of the Four Hundred and Thirty-Five: Maury Maverick, of Texas." In *The American Politician*, ed. J. T. Salter, chap. 8. Chapel Hill: University of North Carolina Press, 1938.

Brown, Laurence Ray. "Development of Federal Antitrust Practices and Effect upon Small Business." Ph.D. diss., George Washington University, 1968.

Brown, Paul Lowry. "The Economics of Small Business Enterprise." Ph.D. diss., Ohio State University, 1944.

Brozen, Yale. *Concentration, Mergers, and Public Policy*. New York: Macmillan, 1982.

Bruchey, Stuart W., ed. *Small Business in American Life*. New York: Columbia University Press, 1980.

Buchanan, James M. *The Limits of Liberty: Between Anarchy and Leviathan*. Chicago: University of Chicago, 1975.

———. "Why Does Government Grow?" In *Budgets and Bureaucrats: The Sources of Government Growth*, ed. Thomas E. Borcherding, chap. 1. Durham, N.C.: Duke University Press, 1977.

Bunzel, John H. *The American Small Businessman*. New York: Knopf, 1962.

Cain, Louis, and George Neumann. "Planning for Peace: The Surplus Property Act of 1944." *Journal of Economic History* 41 (March 1981): 129–35.

Calvani, Terry, and James Langenfeld. "An Overview of the Current Debate on Resale Price Maintenance." *Contemporary Policy Issues* 3 (Spring 1985): 1–7.

Caridi, Ronald J. *The Korean War and American Politics: The Republican Party as a Case Study*. Philadelphia: University of Pennsylvania Press, 1968.

Carlsson, Bo. "The Evolution of Manufacturing Technology and Its Impact on Industrial Structure: An International Study." *Small Business Economics* 1 (1989): 21–37.

Carson, Deane, and Ira O. Scott Jr. "Differential Effects of Monetary Policy on Small Business." In *The Vital Majority: Small Business in the American Economy: Essays Marking the Twentieth Anniversary of the U.S. Small Business Administration*, ed. Deane Carson, chap. 11. Washington: GPO, 1973.

Celler, Emanuel. "How a Congressman Views the Chain Stores." *Chain Store Review* 2 (October 1929): 14, 60–63.

———. *You Never Leave Brooklyn: The Autobiography of Emanuel Celler*. New York: J. Day Company, 1953.

Chamberlain, John. *The American Stakes*. New York: Carrick & Evans, 1940.

Chandler, Alfred D., Jr. *The Visible Hand: The Managerial Revolution in American Business*. Cambridge: Belknap Press of Harvard University Press, 1977.

Cho, Hyo Won. "The Evolution of the Functions of the Reconstruction Finance Corporation: A Study of the Growth and Death of a Federal Lending Agency." Ph.D. diss., Ohio State University, 1953.

Cohn, David L. *The Good Old Days: A History of American Morals and Manners as seen through the Sears, Roebuck Catalogs, 1905 to the Present*. Foreword by Sinclair Lewis. New York: Simon & Schuster, 1940.

Collins, Robert. *The Business Response to Keynes, 1929–1964*. New York: Columbia University Press, 1981.

Coombs, Frank Alan. "Joseph Christopher O'Mahoney: The New Deal Years." Ph.D. diss., University of Illinois, 1968.

Cooper, Arnold C. "R&D Is More Efficient in Small Companies." *Harvard Business Review* 42 (May–June 1964): 78–82.

Culver, Kermit L. "Small Business Investment Companies." In *The Vital Majority: Small Business in the American Economy: Essays Marking the Twentieth Anniversary of the U.S. Small Business Administration*, ed. Deane Carson, chap. 4. Washington: GPO, 1973.

Dahl, Robert. *Who Governs?* New Haven: Yale University Press, 1961.

Daughters, Charles G. *Wells of Discontent: A Study of the Economic, Social, and Political Aspects of the Chain Store*. Introduction by Wright Patman, John F. Dockweiler, and Gerald J. Boileau. New York: C. G. Daughters, 1937.

Davis, Lance E., and John Legler. "Government in the American Economy, 1815–1902: A Quantitative Study." *Journal of Economic History* 26 (December 1966): 514–52.

Davis, Steven J., John Haltiwanger, and Scott Schuh. "Small Business and Job Creation: Dissecting the Myth and Reassessing the Facts." NBER Working Paper No. 4492. Cambridge, Mass.: National Bureau of Economic Research, 1993.

De Leeuw, John Simon. "Fair Trade Developments, 1951–1961." Ph.D. diss., University of Oklahoma, 1962.

Denit, W. Darlington. "The Area Administrative Offices of the Smaller War Plants Corporation." *Public Administration Review* (Winter 1946): 25–29.

Diamond, Sigmund. *The Reputation of the American Businessman*. Cambridge: Harvard University Press, 1955.

Dicke, Thomas S. *Franchising in America: The Development of a Business Method, 1840–1980*. Chapel Hill: University of North Carolina Press, 1992.

———. "The Public Image of Small Business Portrayed in the American Periodical Press, 1900–1938." M.A. thesis, Ohio State University, 1983.

"Does 'Small Business' Get a Fair Shake?" *Fortune*, October 1953, 163–65, 196–200.

Doig, Jameson W., and Erwin C. Hargrove. " 'Leadership' and Political Analysis." In *Leadership and Innovation: A Biographical Perspective on Entrepreneurs in Government*, ed. Jameson W. Doig and Erwin C. Hargrove, chap. 1. Baltimore: Johns Hopkins University Press, 1987.

Donham, Paul. "Whither Small Business?" *Harvard Business Review* 35 (March–April 1957): 73–81.

Drucker, Peter F. "The Care and Feeding of Small Business." *Harper's Magazine*, August 1950, 74–79.

———. "How Big Is Too Big?" *Harper's Magazine*, July 1950, 23.

——. *Innovation and Entrepreneurship: Practice and Principles*. New York: Perennial Library, 1985.

——. "This War Is Different." *Harper's Magazine*, November 1950, 19–27.

Edelman, Murray. *The Symbolic Uses of Politics*. Urbana: University of Illinois Press, 1964.

Edwards, Corwin D. *The Price Discrimination Law: A Review of Experience*. Washington: Brookings Institution, 1959.

Einhorn, Henry A. "Competition in American Industry, 1939–58." *Journal of Political Economy* 74 (1966): 506–11.

Eisenhower, Dwight D. *The Eisenhower Diaries*. Ed. Robert H. Ferrell. New York: Norton, 1981.

——. *Public Papers of the Presidents of the United States: Dwight D. Eisenhower*. Washington: GPO, 1953–59.

Elder, Charles D., and Roger W. Cobb. *The Political Uses of Symbols*. New York: Longman, 1983.

Elzinga, Kenneth G. "The Robinson-Patman Act: A New Deal for Small Business." In *Regulatory Change in an Atmosphere of Crisis: Current Implications of the Roosevelt Years*, chap. 4. London: Academic Press, 1979.

Emmet, Boris, and John E. Jeuck. *Catalogues and Counters: A History of Sears, Roebuck, and Company*. Chicago: University of Chicago Press, 1950.

Esch, Harriette H., comp. *Statutes and Court Decisions Pertaining to the Federal Trade Commission, 1949–1955*. Vol. 5. Washington: GPO, 1957.

——. *Statutes and Court Decisions Pertaining to the Federal Trade Commission, 1956–1960*. Vol. 6. Washington: GPO, 1961.

Fabricant, Soloman. "Is Monopoly Increasing?" *Journal of Economic History* 13 (1953): 89–94.

Faith, Robert L., Donald R. Leavens, and Robert D. Tollison. "Antitrust Pork Barrel." In *Public Choice and Regulation: A View from Inside the Federal Trade Commission*, ed. Robert J. MacKay, James Miller III, and Bruce Yandle, chap. 2. Stanford, Calif.: Hoover Institution Press, 1987.

"The Fall of Big Business." *The Economist*, 17 April 1993: 13–14.

Fisher, Burton R., and Stephen B. Whithey. *Big Business as the People See It: A Study of a Socio-Economic Institution*. Ann Arbor: University of Michigan Institute for Social Research, 1951.

Fligstein, Neil. *The Transformation of Corporate Control*. Cambridge: Harvard University Press, 1990.

Foner, Eric. *Free Soil, Free Labor, Free Men: The Ideology of the Republican Party Before the Civil War*. New York: Oxford University Press, 1970.

Fontenay, Charles L. *Estes Kefauver: A Biography*. Knoxville: University of Tennessee Press, 1980.

Fraser, Steve, and Gary Gerstle, eds. *The Rise and Fall of the New Deal Order, 1930–1980*. Princeton: Princeton University Press, 1989.

French, Michael J. "Manufacturing and Marketing: Vertical Integration in the U.S. Tire Manufacturing Industry, 1890–1980s." *Business and Economic History*, 2d ser., vol. 18 (1989): 178–87.

——. *The U.S. Tire Industry: A History*. Boston: Twayne Publishers, 1991.

Freyer, Tony A. "The Federal Courts, Localism, and the National Economy, 1865–1900." *Business History Review* 53 (Autumn 1979): 343–65.

——. *Regulating Big Business: Antitrust in Great Britain and America, 1880–1980*. Cambridge: Cambridge University Press, 1992.

Friedman, Lawrence M. "Law and Small Business in the United States: One Hundred Years of Struggle and Accommodation." In *Small Business in American Life*, ed. Stuart W. Bruchey. New York: Columbia University Press, 1980.

Galambos, Louis. *The Public Image of Big Business in America, 1880–1940: A Quantitative Study in Social Change*. Baltimore: Johns Hopkins University Press, 1975.

——. "Technology, Political Economy, and Professionalization: Central Themes of the Organizational Synthesis." *Business History Review* 57 (1983): 471–93.

Galambos, Louis, and Joseph Pratt. *The Rise of the Corporate Commonwealth: U.S. Business and Public Policy in the Twentieth Century*. New York: Basic Books, 1988.

Galbraith, John Kenneth. *American Capitalism and the Concept of Countervailing Power*. Boston: Houghton Mifflin, 1952.

——. *The New Industrial State*. 2d ed. Boston: Houghton- Mifflin, 1971.

Gardner, James B. "Political Leadership in a Period of Transition: Frank G. Clement, Albert Gore, Estes Kefauver, and Tennessee Politics, 1948–1956." 2 vols. Ph.D. diss., Vanderbilt University, 1978.

Garson, G. David. *Group Theories of Politics*. Sage Library of Social Research, vol. 61. Beverly Hills, Calif.: Sage Publications, 1978.

Gault, Edgar H. *Fair Trade with Especial Reference to Cut-Rate Drug Prices in Michigan*. Michigan Business Studies, vol. 9, no. 2. Ann Arbor: University of Michigan Bureau of Business Research, 1939.

George, Edwin B. "Business and the Robinson-Patman Act: The First Year." In *Business and the Robinson Patman Law: A Symposium*, ed. Benjamin Werne. New York: Oxford University Press, 1938.

Glover, David A. *The Attack on Big Business*. New York: Columbia University Press, 1954.

Goodwin, Craufurd D. "Attitudes toward Industry in the Truman Administration: The Macroeconomic Origins of Microeconomic Policy." In *The Truman Presidency*, ed. Michael J. Lacey, chap. 3. Cambridge: Cambridge University Press, 1989.

Gordon, Thurlow M. "The Robinson-Patman Anti-Discrimination Act." In *Business and the Robinson Patman Law: A Symposium*, ed. Benjamin Werne. New York: Oxford University Press, 1938.

Gorman, Joseph Bruce. *Kefauver: A Political Biography*. New York: Oxford University Press, 1971.

Graham, Otis L., Jr. *Losing Time: The Industrial Policy Debate*. Cambridge: Harvard University Press, 1992.

Grandy, Christopher. "Original Intent and the Sherman Antitrust Act: A Reexamination of the Consumer-Welfare Hypothesis." *Journal of Economic History* 53 (June 1993): 359–73.

Grattan, C. Hartley. "Small Business, I Love You." *Harper's Magazine*, February 1946, 145–50.

Gray, Virginia. "State Legislatures and Policy Innovators." In *Encyclopedia of the American Legislative System*, 3 vols., ed. Joel H. Silbey. New York: Charles Scribner's Sons, 1994.

Green, George Earl. "The Small Business Administration: A Study in Public Policy and Organization." Ph.D. dissertation, University of Colorado, 1965.

Greenstein, Fred I. *The Hidden-Hand Presidency: Eisenhower as Leader*. New York: Basic Books, 1982.

Gressley, Gene M. "Thurman Arnold, Antitrust, and the New Deal." *Business History Review* 38 (Summer 1964): 214–31.

Griffith, Robert. "Dwight D. Eisenhower and the Corporate Commonwealth." *American Historical Review* 87 (February 1982): 87–122.

——. "Forging America's Postwar Order: Domestic Politics and Political Economy in the Age of Truman." In *The Truman Presidency*, ed. Michael J. Lacey, chap. 2. Cambridge: Cambridge University Press, 1989.

Grunberg, Emile. "The Mobilization of Capacity and Resources of Small-Scale Enterprises in Germany." *Journal of Business* 14 (October 1941): 319–44; 15 (1942): 56–89.

Gwartney, James D., and Richard L. Stroup. *Economics: Private and Public Choice*. 5th ed. New York: Harcourt, 1990.

Hamilton, Richard. "The Politics of Independent Business." In *Restraining Myths: Critical Studies of U.S. Social Structure and Politics*, chap. 2. New York: Sage Publications, 1975.

Harper, F. J. "'A New Battle on Evolution': The Anti-Chain Store Trade-at-Home Agitation of 1929–1930." *Journal of American Studies* (Great Britain) 16 (1982): 407–26.

Harrison, Bennett. *Lean and Mean: The Changing Landscape of Corporate Power in the Age of Flexibility*. New York: Basic Books, 1994.

Hawley, Ellis. "The Corporate Ideal as Liberal Philosophy in the New Deal." In *The Roosevelt New Deal: A Program Reassessment Fifty Years Later*, ed. Wilbur J. Cohen, 85–105. Austin, Tex.: Lyndon B. Johnson School of Public Affairs, 1986.

——. "Herbert Hoover, The Commerce Secretariat, and the Vision of an 'Associative State.'" *Journal of American History* 61 (June 1974): 116–40.

——. *The New Deal and the Problem of Monopoly: A Study in Economic Ambivalence*. Princeton: Princeton University Press, 1966.

——. "Remarks Concerning Martin J. Sklar's *The Corporate Reconstruction of American Capitalism, 1890–1916*." *Business and Economic History*, 2d ser., 21 (1992): 40–42.

Hayek, Friedrich A. von. *The Essence of Hayek*. Ed. Chiaki Nishiyama and Kurt R. Leube. Stanford, Calif.: Hoover Institution Press, 1984.

Hayes, Samuel L., and Donald H. Woods. "Are SBICs Doing Their Job?" *Harvard Business Review* 41 (March–April 1963): 7–19, 178–98.

Hays, Samuel P. "Political Choice in Regulatory Administration." In *Regulation in Perspective: Historical Essays*, ed. Thomas K. McCraw. Cambridge: Harvard University Press, 1981.

Hazlett, Thomas W. "The Legislative History of the Sherman Act Re-examined." *Economic Inquiry* 30 (April 1992): 263–76.

Heath, Jim. "American War Mobilization and the Use of Small Manufacturers, 1939–43." *Business History Review* 46 (Autumn 1972): 295–319.

Henderson, Richard B. *Maury Maverick: A Political Biography*. Austin: University of Texas Press, 1970.

Hickman, Bert G. *The Korean War and United States Economic Activity, 1950–1952*. New York: National Bureau of Economic Research, 1955.

Higgs, Robert. *Crisis and Leviathan: Critical Episodes in the Growth of American Government*. New York: Oxford University Press, 1987.

———. "Origins of the Corporate Liberal State." *Critical Review* 5 (Fall 1991): 475–95.

———. "Wartime Prosperity?: A Reassessment of the U.S. Economy in the 1940s." *Journal of Economic History* 52 (March 1992): 41–60.

Hirsch, Julius. "Facts and Fantasies Concerning Full Employment." *American Economic Review* 34, no. 1, supplement, pt. 2 (March 1944): 118–27.

Hofstadter, Richard. "What Happened to the Antitrust Movement?: Notes on the Evolution of an American Creed." In *The Business Establishment*, ed. Earl F. Cheit, chap. 4. New York: John Wiley & Sons, 1964.

Hollander, Stanley C. "The Effects of Industrialization on Small Retailing in the United States in the Twentieth Century." In *Small Business in American Life*, ed. Stuart W. Bruchey, chap. 9. New York: Columbia University Press, 1980.

———. "United States of America." In *Resale Price Maintenance*, ed. B. S. Yamey, chap. 3. Chicago: Aldine Publishing, 1966.

Hooper, Carolyn Nell. "Public Policy toward Small Business: Implications for Efficient Utilization of Resources." Ph.D. diss., University of Texas at Austin, 1968.

Horowitz, David. "The Crusade against Chain Stores: Portland's Independent Merchants, 1928–1935." *Oregon Historical Quarterly* 89 (Winter 1988): 341–68.

Hosmer, W. Arnold. "Small Manufacturing Enterprises." *Harvard Business Review* 35 (November–December 1957): 111–22.

Hovenkamp, Herbert. *Enterprise and American Law, 1836–1937*. Cambridge: Harvard University Press, 1991.

Hower, Ralph M. *History of Macy's of New York: 1858–1919*. Cambridge: Harvard University Press, 1943.

"How the Air Force Aids Small Business." *Aviation Week*, August 1952, 21–25.

Hughes, Jonathan R. T. *The Governmental Habit Redux: Economic Controls from Colonial Times to the Present*. Princeton: Princeton University Press, 1991.

Humphrey, Hubert H. *The Education of a Public Man: My Life and Politics*. Ed. Norman Shorman. Garden City, N.Y.: Doubleday, 1976.

Hunter, Graham. "The Truth about the 'Squeeze' on Small Business." *Forbes*, 15 December 1948, 22.

Ingham, John. *Making Iron and Steel: Independent Mills in Pittsburgh, 1820–1920*. Columbus: Ohio State University Press, 1991.

Institute of Distribution. *The Chain Store Is an American Asset: True or False?* New York: Institute of Distribution, n.d.

Ippolito, Pauline M. "Resale Price Maintenance: Empirical Evidence from Litigation." *Journal of Law and Economics* 34 (October 1991): 263–94.

Jewkes, John, David Sawers, and Richard Stillerman. *Sources of Invention*. New York: Macmillan, 1958.

Johnson, Chalmers, ed. *The Industrial Policy Debate*. San Francisco: ICS Press, 1984.

Johnson, Richard Eric. "The McGuire Act and Its Effect on Resale Price Maintenance." M.S. thesis, University of Pittsburgh, 1961.

Johnson, Robert Wood. *"But, General Johnson": Episodes in a War Effort*. Princeton:
Princeton University Press, 1944.

———. *Spreading the Work: The Salvation of American Industry*. Washington: GPO, 1943.

Jones, Rudolph. "The Relative Position of Small Business in the American Economy
since 1930." In *The Survival of Small Business*, ed. Vincent P. Carosso and Stuart
Bruchey, chap. 2. New York: Arno Press, 1979.

Judd, Richard J., and Barbra K. Sanders. "Regulation, Small Business, and Economic
Development: A Historical Perspective on Regulation of Business." In *Small Business in a Regulated Economy: Issues and Policy Implications*, ed. Richard J. Judd,
William T. Greenwood, and Fred W. Becker, chap. 15. New York: Quorum Books,
1988.

Judkins, C. J. "Do Associations Represent the Small Business Firm?" *Domestic Commerce*, July 1946, 15–20.

Kaplan, A. D. H. *Big Enterprise in a Competitive System*. Washington: Brookings Institution, 1954.

———. *Small Business: Its Place and Problems*. New York: McGraw, 1948.

Katzmann, Robert A. "Federal Trade Commission." In *The Politics of Regulation*, ed.
James Q. Wilson, chap. 5. New York: Basic Books, 1980.

———. *Regulatory Bureaucracy: The Federal Trade Commission and Antitrust Policy*.
Cambridge: MIT Press, 1980.

Keehn, Richard H., and Gene Smiley. "Small Business Reactions to World War II Government Controls." *Essays in Economic and Business History* 8 (1990): 303–16.

Kefauver, Estes. *In a Few Hands: Monopoly Power in America*. New York: Pantheon
Books, 1960.

Kennedy, Letty. "Estes Kefauver: A Profile." M.A. thesis, Boston University, 1975.

Kerr, K. Austin. "Small Business in the United States during the Twentieth Century."
Paper presented at a conference titled "Comparative Enterprise Management: The
Lessons of Business History," Budapest, Hungary, 13–15 June 1989.

Key, V. O., Jr. *Politics, Parties, and Pressure Groups*. New York: Thomas Y. Crowell,
1942.

Kintner, Earl W., ed. *The Legislative History of the Federal Antitrust Laws and Related
Statutes*. Part 1 (The Antitrust Laws). Vol. 1. New York: Chelsea House Publishers,
1978.

Kirk, Russell, and James McClellan. *The Political Principles of Robert A. Taft*. A Project
of the Robert A. Taft Institute of Government. New York: Fleet Press, 1967.

Kirkland, Edward. *Dream and Thought in the Business Community, 1860–1900*. Ithaca:
Cornell University Press, 1956.

Klein, Richard. "SBA's Business Loan Program." *Atlanta Economic Review* 28
(September–October 1978): 28–37.

Kleit, Andrew N. *Efficiencies without Economists: The Early Years of Resale Price Maintenance*. Washington: Bureau of Economics (Federal Trade Commission), 1992.

Knox, Robert Lee. "Workable Competition in the Rubber Tire Industry." Ph.D. diss.,
University of North Carolina at Chapel Hill, 1962.

Kolko, Gabriel. *The Roots of American Foreign Policy: An Analysis of Power and Purpose*. Boston: Beacon Press, 1969.

——. *The Triumph of Conservatism: A Reinterpretation of American History, 1900–1916*. Chicago: Quadrangle, 1963.

Kovaleff, Theodore Philip. *Business and Government during the Eisenhower Administration: A Study of the Antitrust Policy of the Antitrust Division of the Justice Department*. Athens, Ohio: Ohio University Press, 1980.

Kuratko, Donald F. "Small Business Challenging Contemporary Public Policy: A Coalition for Action." In *Small Business in a Regulated Economy: Issues and Policy Implications*, ed. Richard J. Judd, William T. Greenwood, and Fred W. Becker, chap. 8. New York: Quorum Books, 1988.

Laffer, Arthur B. "Vertical Integration by Corporations, 1929–1965." *Review of Economics and Statistics* 51 (1969): 91–93.

Lebergott, Stanley. *The Americans: An Economic Record*. New York: Norton, 1984.

Lebhar, Godfrey M. *The Chain Store: Boon or Bane?* New York: Harper and Brothers, 1932.

——. *Chain Stores in America, 1859–1962*. 3d ed. New York: Chain Store Publishing Corporation, 1963.

Lee, Stewart M. *Consumers Look at Discount Houses*. Greeley, Colo.: Council on Consumer Information, 1958.

——. "Problems of Resale Price Maintenance." *Journal of Marketing* 23 (January 1959): 274–81.

Leigh, Warren W. *Gross Margins and Net Profits of Tire Dealers, 1923–1948*. Akron: Privately printed, 1949.

——. "The Quantity-Limit Rule and the Rubber Tire Industry." *Journal of Marketing* 17 (October 1952): 136–55.

LeLoup, Lance T., and Steven A. Shull. *Congress and the President: The Policy Connection*. Belmont, Calif.: Wadsworth Publishing Company, 1993.

Letwin, William. *Law and Economic Policy in America: The Evolution of the Sherman Antitrust Act*. New York: Random House, 1965.

Leuchtenberg, William. "The New Deal and the Analogue of War." In *Change and Continuity in Twentieth Century America*. Columbus: Ohio State University Press, 1964.

Leyerzapf, James W. "The Public Life of Lou E. Holland." Ph.D. diss., University of Missouri at Columbia, 1972.

Libecap, Gary D. "The Rise of the Chicago Packers and the Origins of Meat Inspection and Antitrust." *Economic Inquiry* 30 (April 1992): 242–62.

Lichtenstein, Nelson, ed. *Political Profiles: The Kennedy Years*. New York: Facts on File, 1976.

Lief, Alfred, ed. *The Brandeis Guide to the Modern World*. Boston: Little, Brown and Company, 1941.

Lilienthal, David Eli. *Big Business: A New Era*. 1st ed. New York: Harper, 1953.

Lindstrom, Talbot S., and Kevin P. Tighe, comp. *Antitrust Consent Decrees: Voluntary Antitrust Compliance Analysis and History of Justice Department Consent Decrees*. New York: Lawyers Co-operative Publishing Company, 1974.

Livesay, Harold. "Lilliputians in Brobdingnag: Small Business in Late-Nineteenth-Century America." In *Small Business in American Life*, ed. Stuart W. Bruchey, chap. 5. New York: Columbia University Press, 1980.

Livingston, James. *Origins of the Federal Reserve System: Money, Class, and Corporate Capitalism, 1890–1913*. Ithaca: Cornell University Press, 1986.

———. "A Reply to Gerald Berk." *Journal of Policy History* 3 (1991): 85–89.

Loveman, Gary, and Werner Sengenberger. "Introduction: Economic and Social Reorganization in the Small and Medium-Sized Enterprise Sector." In *The Re-Emergence of the Small Enterprises: Industrial Restructuring in Industrialized Countries*, ed. Werner Sengenberger, Gary Loveman, and Michael J. Piore. Geneva: International Institute for Labour Studies, 1990.

Lowery, David, and William D. Berry. "The Growth of Government in the United States: An Empirical Assessment of Competing Explanations." *American Journal of Political Science* 27 (November 1983): 665–94.

Lowi, Theodore J. *The End of Liberalism: The Second Republic of the United States*. 2d ed. New York: Norton, 1979.

Lumer, Wilfred. *Small Business at the Crossroads: A Study of the Small Business Retreat of 1953–1955*. Washington: Public Affairs Institute, 1956.

Lunde, Berlie Loren. "The Role of Small Business in Defense Production with Special Reference to Air Force Contracts." M.B.A. thesis, University of Pittsburgh, 1956.

Lustgarten, Steven A. "Firm Size and Productivity Growth in Manufacturing Industries." In *Small Business in a Regulated Economy: Issues and Policy Implications*. ed. Richard J. Judd, William T. Greenwood, and Fred W. Becker, chap. 9. New York: Quorum Books, 1988, 141–54.

Lustig, R. Jeffrey. "Pluralism." In *Encyclopedia of American Political History: Studies of the Principal Movements and Ideas*, 3 vols., ed. Jack P. Greene, 2:910–21. New York: Charles Scribner's Sons, 1984.

McConnell, Grant. "Lobbies and Pressure Groups." In *Encyclopedia of American Political History: Studies of the Principal Movements and Ideas*, 3 vols., ed. Jack P. Greene, 2:764–76. New York: Charles Scribner's Sons, 1984.

McCoy, Drew R. "Political Economy." In *Thomas Jefferson: A Reference Biography*, ed. Merrill D. Peterson. New York: Charles Scribner's Sons, 1986.

McCraw, Thomas K. *Prophets of Regulation: Charles Francis Adams, Louis D. Brandeis, James M. Landis, Alfred E. Kahn*. Cambridge: Belknap Press of Harvard University Press, 1984.

McCullough, David. *Truman*. New York: Simon & Schuster, 1992.

McGee, John S. "The Decline and Fall of Quantity Discounts: The Quantity Limit Rule in Rubber Tires and Tubes." *Journal of Business* 27 (July 1954): 225–44.

———. "The Robinson-Patman Act and Effective Competition." Ph.D. diss., Vanderbilt University, 1952.

MacGowan, T. G. [Firestone Tire & Rubber]. "Trends in Tire Distribution." *Journal of Marketing* 10 (January 1946): 265–69.

MacKay, Robert J., James Miller III, and Bruce Yandle. *Public Choice and Regulation: A View from Inside the Federal Trade Commission*. Stanford, Calif.: Hoover Institution Press, 1987.

McKean, Eugene C. *The Persistence of Small Business: A Study of Unincorporated Enterprise.* Kalamazoo, Mich.: W. E. Upjohn Institute for Community Research, 1958.

MacLean, Joan Coyne, ed. *President and Congress: The Conflict of Powers.* Reference Shelf. Vol. 27, no. 1. New York: H. W. Wilson, 1955.

McQuaid, Kim. *Big Business and Presidential Power: From FDR to Reagan.* New York: William Morrow, 1982.

——. "Corporate Liberalism in the American Business Community, 1920–1940." *Business History Review* 52 (Autumn 1978): 342–68.

Mansfield, Harvey C. "The Congress and Economic Policy." In *The Congress and America's Future,* ed. David B. Truman, 2d ed., chap. 6. Englewood Cliffs, N.J.: Prentice-Hall, 1973.

Marcus, Sumner. "The Small Business Act of 1953: A Case Study of the Development of Public Policy Affecting Business." D.B.A. diss., University of Washington, 1958.

Mason, Edward S. "A Review of Recent Literature." In *Economic Concentration and the Monopoly Problem.* Cambridge: Harvard University Press, 1957.

Mayer, Kurt. "Small Business as a Social Institution." *Social Research* 14 (1947): 332–49.

Mayfield, Frank M. *The Department Store Story.* New York: Fairchild, 1949.

Meltzer, Allan H., and Scott F. Richard. "Why Government Grows (and Grows) in a Democracy." *The Public Interest* 52 (Summer 1978): 111–18.

Meyers, Jerome Gilbert. "Reactions of the Independent Retailer to the Evolution and Development of the Department Store, the Mail Order House, and Discount Operations." M.B.A. thesis, Ohio State University, 1962.

Milburn, George. *Catalog.* New York: Harcourt, Brace, and Company, 1936.

Millett, Allan R., and Peter Maslowski. *For the Common Defense: A Military History of the United States of America.* New York: Free Press, 1984.

Mills, C. Wright. *White Collar: The American Middle Classes.* New York: Oxford University Press, 1965.

Miscamble, Wilson D. "Thurman Arnold Goes to Washington: A Look at Antitrust Policy in the Later New Deal." *Business History Review* 56 (Spring 1982): 1–15.

"Mobilization Plans for Industry." *Army Information Digest* 6 (1951): 11–21.

Mokry, Benjamin W. "Encouraging Small Business Startups: An Alternative to Smokestack Chasing?" In *Small Business in a Regulated Economy: Issues and Policy Implications,* ed. Richard J. Judd, William T. Greenwood, and Fred W. Becker, chap. 10. New York: Quorum Books, 1988.

Moody's Investors Service. "The Outlook for Chain Stores." *Business and Industries Guide* 58 (26 September 1930): I-421–35.

Morris, Charles R. "It's *Not* the Economy, Stupid." *The Atlantic Monthly,* July 1993, 49–62.

Mowery, David C. "Industrial Research and Firm Size, Survival and Growth in American Manufacturing, 1921–1946: An Assessment." *Journal of Economic History* 43 (December 1983): 953–80.

Mrozek, Donald J. "Organizing Small Business during World War II: The Experience of the Kansas City Region." *Missouri Historical Review* 71 (1977): 174–92.

Murphy, Ralph William. "Small Business Ideology: An In-Depth Study." Ph.D. diss., University of Washington, 1978.

Nasar, Sylvia. "Myth: Small Businesses as Job Engine." *New York Times*, 25 March 1994, C1–C2.

National Conference of State University Schools of Business, comp. *Report on Problems and Attitudes of Small Business Executives: Result of a National Survey in February 1945*. N.p.

National Federation of Independent Business. *Attitudes of Independent Business Proprietors toward Antitrust Laws, 1943 to 1963*. San Mateo, Calif.: n.p.

Neal, Nevin Emil. "A Biography of Joseph T. Robinson." Ph.D. diss., University of Oklahoma, 1958.

Nelson, Donald M. *Arsenal of Democracy: The Story of American War Production*. New York: Harcourt, Brace and Company, 1946.

Nichols, John P. *The Chain Store Tells Its Story*. New York: Institute of Distribution, 1940.

Nisbet, Robert. *Twilight of Authority*. New York: Oxford University Press, 1975.

Niskanen, William A., Jr. *Bureaucracy and Representative Government*. Chicago: Aldine Atherton, 1971.

Noble, George L., Jr., and Hugh G. Francis [army ordnance officials]. "The Role of Small Business in Defense Mobilization Planning." *Federal Bar Journal* 13 (April–June 1953): 227–32.

Noone, Charles M., and Stanley M. Rubel. *SBICs: Pioneers in Organized Venture Capital*. Chicago: Capital Publishing Company, 1970.

Nordlinger, Eric A. *On the Autonomy of the Democratic State*. Cambridge: Harvard University Press, 1981.

Novak, Michael. *The Spirit of Democratic Capitalism*. Lanham, Md.: Madison Books, 1982, 1991.

Nutter, G. Warren. *The Extent of Enterprise Monopoly in the United States, 1899–1939: A Quantitative Study of Some Aspects of Monopoly*. Chicago: University of Chicago, 1951.

Nutter, G. Warren, and Henry Adler Einhorn. *Enterprise Monopoly in the United States: 1899–1958*. New York: Columbia University Press, 1969.

Opinion Research Corporation. *Dealers in Hot Competition: A Report of the Public Opinion Index for Industry*. Princeton, N.J.: Opinion Research Corporation, 1957.

Oppenheim, S. Chesterfield, and Glen E. Weston. *Unfair Trade Practices and Consumer Protection: Cases and Comments*. 3d ed. St. Paul, Minn.: West Publishing, 1974.

Overstreet, Thomas R., Jr., and Alan A. Fisher. "Resale Price Maintenance and Distributional Efficiency: Some Lessons from the Past." *Contemporary Policy Issues* 3 (Spring 1985): 43–56.

Palamountain, Joseph Cornwall, Jr. *The Politics of Distribution*. Cambridge: Harvard University Press, 1955.

Parkany, John. "Federal Trade Commission Enforcement of the Robinson-Patman Act, 1946–1952." Ph.D. diss., Columbia University, 1955.

Parris, Addison W. *The Small Business Administration*. New York: Frederick A. Praeger, 1968.

Patman, Wright. *Complete Guide to the Robinson-Patman Act*. Englewood Cliffs, N.J.: Prentice-Hall, 1963.

———. *The Robinson-Patman Act: What You Can and Cannot Do under This Law*. New York: Ronald Press, 1938.

Patterson, James T. *Mr. Republican: A Biography of Robert A. Taft*. Boston: Houghton Mifflin, 1972.

Peacock, Alan T., and Jack Wiseman, *The Growth of Public Expenditure in the United Kingdom*. Princeton: Princeton University Press, 1961.

Peltason, Jack W. "The Reconversion Controversy." In *Public Administration and Policy Development: A Case Book*, ed. Harold Stein. New York: Harcourt, 1952.

Peltzman, Sam. "The Growth of Government." *Journal of Law and Economics* 23 (October 1980): 209–87.

Pepper, Roger S. *Pressure Groups among "Small Business Men."* M.A. thesis, 1940. Rpt., New York: Arno Press, 1979.

Phillips, Joseph D. *Little Business in the American Economy*. Illinois Studies in the Social Sciences, vol. 42. Urbana: University of Illinois Press, 1958.

Pickett, William B. *Homer E. Capehart: A Senator's Life, 1897–1979*. Indianapolis: Indiana Historical Society, 1990.

Piore, Michael J., and Charles F. Sabel. *The Second Industrial Divide: Possibilities for Prosperity*. New York: Basic Books, 1984.

Polsby, Nelson. *Community Power and Political Theory*. New Haven: Yale University Press, 1963.

Posner, Richard A. *The Robinson-Patman Act: Federal Regulation of Price Differences*. Washington: American Enterprise Institute for Public Policy Research, 1976.

Postrel, Virginia. "Populist Industrial Policy." *Reason*, January 1994, 4, 6.

Proxmire, William. *Can Small Business Survive?* Chicago: Henry Regnery, 1964.

Raucher, Alan R. "Dime Store Chains: The Making of Organization Men, 1880–1940." *Business History Review* 65 (Spring 1991): 130–63.

Reday, Joseph Z. [lieutenant commander, U.S. Naval Reserve]. "Industrial Mobilization in the U.S." *U.S. Naval Institute Proceedings* (October 1953): 1065–75.

Reich, Robert B. *The Next American Frontier*. New York: New York Times Books, 1983.

Rhyne, Elisabeth Holmes. *Small Business, Banks, and SBA Loan Guarantees: Subsidizing the Weak or Bridging a Credit Gap?* New York: Quorum Books, 1988.

Robertson, Ross M. "The Small Business Ethic in America." In *The Vital Majority: Small Business in the American Economy: Essays Marking the Twentieth Anniversary of the U.S. Small Business Administration*, ed. Deane Carson. Washington: GPO, 1973.

Robinson, Roland I. "The Financing of Small Business in the United States." In *Small Business in American Life*, ed. Stuart W. Bruchey, chap. 12. New York: Columbia, 1980.

Roice, Terry Gene. "The Economic Philosophy of Senator Joseph C. O'Mahoney and the Concept of Federal Incorporation." Ph.D. diss., University of Wyoming, 1971.

Ross, Thomas W. "Store Wars: The Chain Tax Movement." *Journal of Law and Economics* 39 (April 1986): 125–37.

———. "Winners and Losers under the Robinson-Patman Act." *Journal of Law and Economics* 27 (October 1984): 243–71.

Roth, Matthew W. *Platt Brothers and Company: Small Business in American Manufacturing*. Hanover, N.H.: University Press of New England, 1994.

Rowe, Frederick M. *Price Discrimination under the Robinson-Patman Act*. Boston: Little, Brown and Company, 1962.

Ryant, Carl. "The South and the Movement against Chain Stores." *Journal of Southern History* 39 (May 1973): 207–22.

Sabel, Charles, and Jonathan Zeitlin. "Historical Alternatives to Mass Production: Politics, Markets and Technology in Nineteenth-Century Industrialization." *Past and Present* 108 (1985): 134–63.

Sammons, Wheeler. "Legislative History: Half the Verdict Is In on the Patman Act." In *Business and the Robinson Patman Law: A Symposium*, ed. Benjamin Werne. New York: Oxford University Press, 1938.

Sapir, Michael. "Review of Economic Forecasts for the Transition Period." *Studies in Income and Wealth* 11 (1949): 275–351.

Sawyer, Albert E. *Business Aspects of Pricing under the Robinson-Patman Act*. Boston: Little, Brown and Company, 1963.

Sawyer, Charles. *Concerns of a Conservative Democrat*. Carbondale: Southern Illinois University Press, 1968.

Schalk, A. F., Jr. "Significant Merchandising Trends of the Independent Tire Dealer." *Journal of Marketing* 12 (April 1948): 462–69.

Scheele, Henry Z. *Charlie Halleck: A Political Biography*. Foreword by Dwight D. Eisenhower. Introduction by Everett M. Dirksen. New York: Exposition Press, 1966.

Schlesinger, Arthur M., Jr. *The Age of Jackson*. Boston: Little, Brown and Company, 1945.

Schmelzer, Janet Louis. "The Early Life and Early Congressional Career of Wright Patman, 1894–1941." Ph.D. diss., Texas Christian University, 1978.

Schmidt, Emerson P. "The Role and Problems of Small Business." *Law and Contemporary Problems* 11, no. 1 (Summer–Autumn 1945): 205–19.

Schoenebaum, Eleanora W., ed. *Political Profiles: The Eisenhower Years*. New York: Facts on File, 1980.

———. *Political Profiles: The Truman Years*. New York: Facts on File, 1978.

Schrieber, Albert N., Sumner Marcus, Robert A. Suterrmeister, and Edward G. Brown. *Defense Procurement and Small Business: A Survey of Practices and Opinions of Small Business Firms Selling to Defense Programs*. Seattle: University of Washington Press, 1961.

Schultze, Charles L. *The Public Use of Private Interest*. Washington: Brookings Institution, 1977.

Schwarz, Jordan A. "Wright Patman: The Last Brandeisian." In *The New Dealers: Power Politics in the Age of Roosevelt*, chap. 13. New York: Knopf, 1993.

Schweiger, Irving. "Adequacy of Financing for Small Business since World War II." *The Journal of Finance* 13 (September 1958): 323–47.

Scoville, John Watson, comp. *Fact and Fancy in the T.N.E.C. Monographs: Reviews of the 43 Monographs Issued by the Temporary National Economic Committee*. Series "The Right Wing Individualist Tradition in America," sponsored by the National Association of Manufacturers. 1942. Rpt., New York: Arno Press, 1972.

Scranton, Philip. *Figured Tapestry: Production, Markets, and Power in Philadelphia Textiles, 1885–1941*. Cambridge: Cambridge University Press, 1989.

——. *Proprietary Capitalism: The Textile Manufacture at Philadelphia, 1800–1885.* Cambridge: Cambridge University Press, 1983.

Seltzer, Alan L. "Woodrow Wilson as 'Corporate Liberal': Toward a Reconsideration of Left Revisionist Historiography." *The Monopoly Issue and Antitrust, 1900–1917,* vol. 2 of *Business and Government in America since 1870: A Twelve-Volume Anthology of Scholarly Articles,* ed. Robert F. Himmelberg, 249–78. New York: Garland, 1994.

Sengenberger, Werner, and Gary Loveman. *Smaller Units of Employment: A Synthesis Report on Industrial Reorganization in Industrialized Countries.* Rev. ed. Geneva: International Institute for Labour Studies, 1988.

Shapiro, Edward S. "Walter Prescott Webb and the Crisis of a Frontierless Democracy." *Continuity* 8 (1984): 43–61.

Shapiro, Irving S., with Carl B. Kaufmann. *America's Third Revolution: Public Interest and the Private Role.* New York: Harper and Row, 1984.

Shughart, William F., II, and Robert D. Tollison. "Antitrust Recidivism in Federal Trade Commission Data, 1914–1982." In *Public Choice and Regulation: A View from Inside the Federal Trade Commission,* ed. Robert J. MacKay, James Miller III, and Bruce Yandle, chap. 12. Stanford, Calif.: Hoover Institution Press, 1987.

Sklar, Martin J. *The Corporate Reconstruction of American Capitalism, 1890–1916: The Market, the Law and Politics.* Cambridge: Cambridge University Press, 1988.

——. *The United States as a Developing Country: Studies in U.S. History in the Progressive Era and the 1920s.* Cambridge: Cambridge University Press, 1992.

Sloan, John W. *Eisenhower and the Management of Prosperity.* Lawrence: University Press of Kansas, 1991.

——. "The Management and Decision-Making Style of President Eisenhower." *Presidential Studies Quarterly* 20 (Spring 1990): 295–313.

Smith, Hilda Chiarulli. "Resale Price Maintenance, 1940–1950." Ph.D. diss., Syracuse University, 1955.

Smith, R. Elberton. "The Army and Small Business." In *United States Army in World War II: The War Department: The Army and Economic Mobilization,* chap. 18. Washington: Office of the Chief of Military History, Department of the Army, 1959.

Smith, Theodore H. "Small Retail Credit Sources." *Law and Contemporary Problems* 11, no. 1 (Summer–Autumn 1945): 274–80.

Sniegoski, Stephen J. "The Darrow Board and the Downfall of the NRA." *Continuity* 14 (Spring/Fall 1990): 63–83.

Solomon, Steven. *Small Business USA: The Role of Small Companies in Sparking America's Economic Transformation.* New York: Crown Publishers, 1986.

Soltow, James. "Origins of Small Business: Metal Fabricators and Machinery Makers in New England, 1890–1957." *Transactions of the American Philosophical Society* 55 (December 1965): 1–58.

Sowell, Thomas. *A Conflict of Visions: Ideological Origins of Political Struggles.* New York: Quill, 1987.

Sparkman, John. " 'Let's Put More Plants to Work on Defense!' " *Sales Management,* 1 June 1951, 88.

——. *Ten-Year Record of the Select Committee on Small Business, United States Senate, 1950–1960: Statement by Senator John Sparkman.* Washington: GPO, 1959.

Spritzer, Donald E. "New Dealer from Montana: The Senate Career of James E. Murray." Ph.D. diss., University of Montana, 1980.

——. *Senator James E. Murray and the Limits of Post-War Liberalism*. New York: Garland, 1985.

Stein, Herbert, and Murray Foss. *An Illustrated Guide to the American Economy: A Hundred Key Issues*. Washington: AEI Press, 1992.

Steindle, Joseph. "Small and Big Business: Economic Problems of the Size of Firms." In *The Survival of Small Business*, ed. Vincent P. Carosso and Stuart Bruchey, chap. 1. New York: Arno Press, 1979.

Stern, Louis W., and Thomas L. Eovaldi. *Legal Aspects of Marketing Strategy: Antitrust and Consumer Protection Issues*. Englewood Cliffs, N.J.: Prentice-Hall, 1984.

Stigler, George J. *Capital and Rates of Return in Manufacturing Industries*. Princeton: Princeton University Press, 1963.

——. "Competition in the United States." In *Five Lectures on Economic Problems*. 1949. Rpt., Freeport, N.Y.: Books for Libraries, 1969.

——. "The Economic Effects of Antitrust Legislation." In *Essence of Stigler*, ed. Kurt R. Leube and Thomas Gale Moore. Stanford, Calif.: Hoover Institution Press, 1986.

Stone, Alan. *Economic Regulation and the Public Interest: The Federal Trade Commission in Theory and Practice*. Ithaca: Cornell University Press, 1977.

Strasser, Susan. *Satisfaction Guaranteed: The Making of the Mass Market*. New York: Pantheon Books, 1989.

Sutton, Francis X., Seymour E. Harris, Carl Kaysen, and James Tobin. *The American Business Creed*. Cambridge: Harvard University Press, 1956.

Sylla, Richard. "The Progressive Era and the Political Economy of Big Government." *Critical Review* 5 (Fall 1991): 531–57.

Taylor, Telford. "All Business Needs Small Business." *Purchasing*, March 1952, 70–72.

Tedlow, Richard S. *New and Improved: The Story of Mass Marketing in America*. New York: Basic Books, 1990.

Thorelli, Hans B. *The Federal Antitrust Policy: Origination of an American Tradition*. Baltimore: Johns Hopkins University Press, 1955.

Thurow, Lester C. *Head to Head: The Coming Economic Battle among Japan, Europe, and America*. New York: William Morrow, 1992.

——. *The Zero-Sum Solution: Building a World-Class American Economy*. New York: Simon & Schuster, 1985.

Timberg, Sigmund, ed. *Symposium: Twenty Years of Robinson-Patman—The Record and Issues*. New York: Federal Legal Publications, 1956.

Truman, Harry S. "I am Advocate of Small Business—Truman" [address before Washington College]. *Commercial and Financial Chronicle*, 6 June 1946, 3091.

——. *Memoirs*. Vol. 1. Garden City, N.Y.: Doubleday, 1955.

Urofsky, Melvin I. *A Mind of One Piece: Brandeis and American Reform*. New York: Charles Scribner's Sons, 1971.

Van Auken, Philip M., and R. Duane Ireland. "Divergent Perspectives on Social Responsibility: Big Business versus Small." In *Small Business in a Regulated Economy: Issues and Policy Implications*, ed. Richard J. Judd, William T. Greenwood, and Fred W. Becker, chap. 12. New York: Quorum Books, 1988.

Vatter, Harold G. "The Position of Small Business in the Structure of American Manufacturing, 1870–1970." In *Small Business in American Life*, ed. Stuart W. Bruchey. New York: Columbia University Press, 1980.

——. *The U.S. Economy in World War II*. New York: Columbia University Press, 1985.

Vaughn, Donald Earl. "Development of the Small Business Investment Company Program." Ph.D. diss., University of Texas at Austin, 1961.

Vawter, Roderick L. *Industrial Mobilization: The Relevant History*. Washington: National Defense University Press, 1983.

Vinyard, C. Dale. "Congressional Committees on Small Business." Ph.D. diss., University of Wisconsin, 1964.

Voelker, William H. "Rise and Fall of 'Fair-Trade' Laws." M.P.A. thesis, University of New Orleans, 1985.

Vogel, David. "A Reply to Gerald Berk." *Journal of Policy History* 3 (1991): 90–93.

Vozikis, George S., and Timothy S. Mescon. "Stages of Development and Stages of the Exporting Process in a Small Business Context." In *Small Business in a Regulated Economy: Issues and Policy Implications*, ed. Richard J. Judds, William T. Greenwood, and Fred W. Becker, chap. 6. New York: Quorum Books, 1988.

Walker, Henry James, Jr. "A Political History of a Public Man: John Sparkman of Alabama." M.A. thesis, University of Alabama, 1990.

Waugh, William L., Jr., and Deborah McCorkle Waugh. "Economic Development Programs of State and Local Governments and the Site Selection Decisions of Smaller Firms." In *Small Business in a Regulated Economy: Issues and Policy Implications*, ed. Richard J. Judd, William T. Greenwood, Fred W. Becker, chap. 7. New York: Quorum Books, 1988.

Weinstein, James. *The Corporate Ideal in the Liberal State, 1900–1918*. Boston: Beacon Press, 1968.

Weissman, Rudolph L. *Small Business and Venture Capital: An Economic Program*. Introduction by Ernest G. Draper. New York: Harper, 1945.

Weller, Cecil Edward, Jr. "Joseph Taylor Robinson and the Robinson-Patman Act." *Arkansas Historical Quarterly* 47 (1988): 29–36.

Welsh, Charles A. "The Murray Report on Small Business." *Industrial and Labor Relations Review* 1 (October 1947): 96.

Willing, Pearl Rushfield. "A History of the Management Assistance and Educational Programs of the Small Business Administration from 1953 to 1978." Ph.D. diss., New York University, 1982.

Wilson, James Q. *Bureaucracy: What Government Agencies Do and Why They Do It*. New York: Basic Books, 1989.

——. "The Politics of Regulation." In *The Politics of Regulation*, ed. James Q. Wilson, chap. 10. New York: Basic Books, 1980.

"Would Industrial Policy Help Small Business?" *Business Week*, 6 February 1984, 72–74.

Yamey, B. S., ed. *Resale Price Maintenance*. Chicago: Aldine Publishing, 1966.

Zeigler, Harmon. *The Politics of Small Business*. Washington: Public Affairs Press, 1961.

——. "Small Business in the Political Process." Ph.D. diss., University of Illinois at Urbana-Champaign, 1960.